GEORGE WASHINGTON'S SOUTH

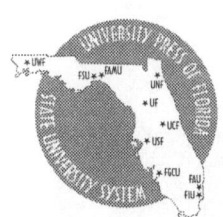

Florida A&M University, Tallahassee
Florida Atlantic University, Boca Raton
Florida Gulf Coast University, Ft. Myers
Florida International University, Miami
Florida State University, Tallahassee
University of Central Florida, Orlando
University of Florida, Gainesville
University of North Florida, Jacksonville
University of South Florida, Tampa
University of West Florida, Pensacola

UNIVERSITY PRESS OF FLORIDA

Gainesville · Tallahassee · Tampa · Boca Raton · Pensacola · Orlando · Miami · Jacksonville · Ft. Myers

George Washington's South

EDITED BY
TAMARA HARVEY AND GREG O'BRIEN

Copyright 2004 by Tamara Harvey and Greg O'Brien
Printed in the United States of America
All rights reserved
First cloth printing, 2004
First paperback printing, 2005

Library of Congress Cataloging-in-Publication Data
George Washington's South / edited by Tamara Harvey and Greg O'Brien.
p. cm.
Includes bibliographical references.
ISBN 0-8130-2689-x; ISBN 0-8130-2917-1 (pbk.)
1. Southern States—Civilization—18th century. 2. Regionalism—Southern States—History. 3. Southern States—Social conditions—18th century. 4. Southern States—Ethnic relations. 5. Washington, George, 1732-1799—Influence. 6. Presidents—United States—Biography.
I. Harvey, Tamara, 1966- II. O'Brien, Greg, 1966-
F213.G48 2004
975'.03—dc21   2003054081

The University Press of Florida is the scholarly publishing agency for the State University System of Florida, comprising Florida A&M University, Florida Atlantic University, Florida Gulf Coast University, Florida International University, Florida State University, University of Central Florida, University of Florida, University of North Florida, University of South Florida, and University of West Florida.

University Press of Florida
15 Northwest 15th Street
Gainesville, FL 32611-2079
http://www.upf.com

George Washington's South

EDITED BY
TAMARA HARVEY AND GREG O'BRIEN

Copyright 2004 by Tamara Harvey and Greg O'Brien
Printed in the United States of America
All rights reserved
First cloth printing, 2004
First paperback printing, 2005

Library of Congress Cataloging-in-Publication Data
George Washington's South / edited by Tamara Harvey and Greg O'Brien.
p. cm.
Includes bibliographical references.
ISBN 0-8130-2689-x; ISBN 0-8130-2917-1 (pbk.)
1. Southern States—Civilization—18th century. 2. Regionalism—
Southern States—History. 3. Southern States—Social conditions—18th century.
4. Southern States—Ethnic relations. 5. Washington, George, 1732-1799
—Influence. 6. Presidents—United States—Biography.
I. Harvey, Tamara, 1966- II. O'Brien, Greg, 1966-
F213.G48 2004
975'.03—dc21   2003054081

The University Press of Florida is the scholarly publishing agency for the State University System of Florida, comprising Florida A&M University, Florida Atlantic University, Florida Gulf Coast University, Florida International University, Florida State University, University of Central Florida, University of Florida, University of North Florida, University of South Florida, and University of West Florida.

University Press of Florida
15 Northwest 15th Street
Gainesville, FL 32611-2079
http://www.upf.com

CONTENTS

List of Illustrations   vii

Acknowledgments   ix

Introduction   1

PART I.
ON THE MAP AND OFF: THE SOUTH AS A DIVERSE REGION

1. Remapping Boundaries in the Old Southwest, 1783–1795   23
Daniel H. Usner Jr.

2. Mapping the "American South": Image, Archive, and the Textual Construction of Regional Identity in the Age of Washington   42
Martin Brückner

3. "And Die by Inches": George Washington and the Encounter of Cultures on the Southern Colonial Frontier   69
Warren R. Hofstra

4. "This Gown . . . Was Much Admired and Made Many Ladies Jealous": Fashion and the Forging of Elite Identities in French Colonial New Orleans   86
Sophie White

PART II.
GEORGE WASHINGTON AS PERSON, SYMBOL, AND SOUTHERNER

5. George Washington and Three Women   121
Don Higginbotham

6. George Washington: Publicity, Probity, and Power   143
David S. Shields

7. George Washington, the South, and the Poetics of National Memory   155
Carla Mulford

PART III.
FREE AND ENSLAVED BLACK AMERICANS IN GEORGE WASHINGTON'S SOUTH

8. Slave Flight: Mount Vernon, Virginia, and the Wider Atlantic World   197
    Philip D. Morgan and Michael L. Nicholls

9. "Under the Color of Law": The Ordeal of Thomas Jeremiah, a Free Black Man, and the Struggle for Power in Revolutionary South Carolina   223
    William R. Ryan

PART IV.
GEORGE WASHINGTON AND SOUTHERN INDIANS

10. George Washington, Dragging Canoe, and Southeastern Indian Resistance   259
    Peter H. Wood

11. Creeks and Americans in the Age of Washington   278
    Robbie Ethridge

12. George Washington and the "Civilization" of the Southern Indians   313
    Theda Perdue

List of Contributors   327

Index   331

ILLUSTRATIONS

1. "A New and Exact Map of the Dominions of the King of Great Britain on the Continent of North America" (1715) 47
2. "A General Map of the Southern British Colonies in America" (1776) 53
3. Cartouche of "A Map of the most Inhabited part of Virginia containing the whole Province of Maryland with Part of Pensilvania, New Jersey, and North Carolina" (1777) 57
4. Map of South Carolina (1796) 61
5. "A Map of the Southern Section of the United States" (1815) 63
6. Account of John Crowson with Thomas Chester, 1744 78
7. Account of Edward Rogers with Richard Rogers, 1746 80

ACKNOWLEDGMENTS

George Washington's South emerges from a conference held at the University of Southern Mississippi in October 1999 designed to use the bicentennial of George Washington's death as an opportunity to examine current research into the late-eighteenth-century South. Twelve historians, literary specialists, art historians, and anthropologists journeyed to Hattiesburg to present their work. We wish to thank those participants, ten of whom contributed essays to this volume, as well as everyone who served as panel chairs and took part in the discussions.

Many people helped coordinate the conference. Charles Bolton and Noel Polk joined us as organizers, with important early help from Jon Sensbach. Lynn Gammill, Mississippi vice regent of the Mount Vernon Ladies' Association, supplied the original idea for the conference, provided important organizational encouragement throughout the planning and implementation stages, and sponsored a wonderful dinner one evening for all participants. Noel Polk also treated all of us to an old-fashioned catfish fry another evening. The University of Southern Mississippi's Department of Continuing Education, especially Mary Ann Iverson, made the bulk of the local arrangements. Kathy Bailey of that department arranged media publicity. The Department of History provided logistical support, including graduate students to help shuttle participants to various venues. The Hattiesburg–Forrest County Library, especially Pamela Pridgen and Sean Farrell, sponsored a luncheon for participants and the general public. The Historic Natchez Foundation, headed by Ron Miller and Mimi Miller, welcomed conference attendees for tours of Natchez. Then University of Southern Mississippi president Horace Fleming welcomed participants and guests at the start of the conference. Lastly, George Washington himself, in the form of historical interpreter William A. Sommerfield, opened our conference. Mr. Sommerfield entertained the public and schoolchildren with his vast knowledge of our first president.

Generous financial assistance was provided by the L. O. Crosby Lecture Fund, the USM Department of History, and the Mississippi Humanities Council.

As we considered publishing papers from this conference, Meredith Morris-Babb, editor at the University Press of Florida, expressed an interest from the beginning, and we are grateful to her and the press for displaying confidence in us and to all those readers, anonymous and otherwise, whose suggestions helped make this a stronger work.

GREG O'BRIEN
TAMARA HARVEY

INTRODUCTION

TAMARA HARVEY AND GREG O'BRIEN

From March to July of 1791, President George Washington toured the southern states, encountering wild adulation at many of his stops. In Charleston, South Carolina, young men greeted the war hero and leader of the new federal government with a song of patriotic fervor:

> He comes! He comes! The hero comes.
> Sound, sound your trumpets, beat your drums,
> From port to port let cannons roar
> His welcome to our friendly shore.[1]

From Virginia to Georgia and back again, the public response to Washington from southerners during his southern tour was overwhelmingly positive and grateful. Here was the man already being touted as the "father of the country," who had led the poorly organized thirteen colonies to victory over the world's most powerful empire and then relinquished his command at war's end before assuming a leadership role as the first president under the new Constitution. For many Americans, Washington stood as a symbol for a new era: a symbol of perseverance, public virtue, and continuity in a rapidly changing universe. By the 1790s, southerners shared with northerners their hero worship of Washington, but the southern states' Euro-American citizens likely saw him as one of their own. After all, he was a Virginian who owned several farms and hundreds of slaves, as did economically and politically powerful elites throughout the South. He saw the nation's future, and a significant portion of his financial well-being, as intimately tied to western lands between the Blue Ridge Mountains and the Mississippi River. Other white southerners also viewed the

West (present-day Tennessee, west Georgia, Alabama, and Mississippi) with longing, attested to by the numerous land companies and land sale schemes of the time. For white southerners, Washington was a man who could be trusted to protect their general interests within the new government.

If white southerners of his day saw a bit of themselves in Washington, scholars have also seen the South as a key to "Washington the man rather than Washington the statesman," as Archibald Henderson puts it in *Washington's Southern Tour, 1791*.[2] The topic of Washington and the South promises insight into the elusive personal attributes of our most iconic president. But, as much as traveling in the South may have appealed to this Virginian, in letters describing his southern tour he seems to view the region primarily as a statesman and an outsider. In these letters, Washington comments on economic potential and possible political unrest that linked the South more to the western frontier in his mind than to the Virginia low country he called home.[3] He writes little about the grand estates and gracious hospitality that would have marked his southern tour as a return to the familiar, though he experienced both.

Washington's southern tour in 1791 was the last of three regional visits he made during the early years of his presidency. Intended to promote the new government, these presidential tours were of a piece with the Federalist insistence on overcoming divisive regionalism through a strong federal government. Five years later, Washington made this nationalistic argument again in his "Farewell Address" of 1796. In this address, he famously asks his readers to move beyond regional perspectives: "The name of AMERICAN, which belongs to you, in your national capacity, must always exalt the just pride of Patriotism, more than any appellation derived from local discriminations. With slight shades of difference, you have the same Religion, Manners, Habits and political Principles. You have in a common cause fought and triumphed together. The independence and liberty you possess are the work of joint councils, and joint efforts; of common dangers, sufferings and successes."[4]

Washington develops this plea to common roots and common cause by emphasizing the economic interdependence of the nation's regions, explaining, "The *North*, in an unrestrained intercourse with the *South*, protected by the equal Laws of a common government, finds in the productions of the latter, great additional resources. . . . The *South* in the same Intercourse, benefitting by the Agency of the *North*, sees its agriculture grow and its commerce expand." He concludes by defining the entire nation's economic activity as "an indissoluble community of Interest."[5]

Reinforcing this point, the dissemination of the address in newspapers allowed the entire reading public of the United States to see themselves as Washington's intended audience, rather than those few in a single locality who might have been privileged to hear him deliver such an address. But despite his concern "that any ground should have been furnished for characterizing parties by *Geographical* discriminations: *Northern* and *Southern; Atlantic* and *Western;* whence designing men may endeavour to excite a belief that there is a real difference of local interests and views," such differences did exist, just as the father of his country feared.[6] Washington promoted nationalism and unification of the young country's states in his capacity as military commander and president, yet he also recognized the persistent regionalism present in the early republic.

The contributors to this collection of essays make "geographical discriminations" and take up the serious concern of exploring the multiple identities that contributed to the constitution of the "American South" emerging in the late eighteenth and early nineteenth centuries. They do so in conjunction with an exploration of the identities of Washington himself, both as icon and as historical individual. Such an undertaking faces several challenges, not least of which is the resistance of Washington as man, politician, and symbolic figure to analysis on such terms. For one thing, as the passages above indicate, Washington took pains, once he gained prominence and influence beyond Virginia, to avoid regional partisanship as he endeavored to strengthen the uniting states. For another, current scholarship confronts the difficulty of distinguishing a "regional Washington" from the myth of the man so foundational to our national imagination. The identity of the United States and the identity of George Washington are so inextricably linked that, as almost every scholar of Washington has observed, there is something remarkably impenetrable about this man. Any single "identity" asserts an essential sameness or unity, a merging of actions and interpretation that transcends, excludes, and merges divisions, complexities, and multiplicities. Identities are in some ways always simplifications, but they are also usually "true" as well—true like a well-hung door because they fit the space and become defined by their function. No American identity is so strong and true as that of George Washington. Regardless of the perpetual examinations, co-options, and demystifications that keep him in play as a symbol, his identity remains startlingly unchanged. Consequently, our strategy has been to highlight productive tensions among the essays in this collection. Regarding approaches to the late-eighteenth-century South, we combine broad mapping projects with local studies that in many ways disrupt those maps. And with Washington himself our contributors explore his position as icon as well as personal attributes and actions neglected in his iconology.

George Washington and his contemporaries understood that the South was distinctive in its agricultural economy and overwhelming reliance upon slavery, but the South was unique as a region in other respects as well. Southerners, by and large, did not openly rebel against their national government during Washington's lifetime, but a variety of emerging regional identities developed in tension with that being promoted by the federal government. Placing Washington in the context of the early-republic South provides an opportunity to see both the first president and this contentious zone in a new light. The essays in this collection address four primary issues: the composition of the geographic and cultural boundaries of the late-eighteenth-century South, the ways that George Washington interacted with the early-republic South and was shaped by those interactions, the position of both free and enslaved black Americans with respect to Washington personally and within the region, and the manner in which Washington associated with the South's largest landholders, the southern Indians. Including the South's Indian people in this discussion enables us to view the South in its geographic entirety, and Indian land was one of the chief concerns of the national and state governments after the American Revolution. As president, Washington crafted the direction of American Indian policy and thus shaped the futures of generations of red, white, and black southerners.

In this introduction we focus on two questions: How was the South constituted and understood in the late eighteenth century? And, how does studying George Washington in relation to the South add to our understanding of him? While introducing the essays included in this volume, we discuss the South as a region and Washington as a southerner. We also suggest connections among these essays, for instance with respect to gender and to local studies, that may be seen as alternatives to those issues highlighted by the sections of this collection. In emphasizing a variety of intersections among these interdisciplinary essays, we are always looking to our third and most significant question: How do explorations of Washington and the South, a man and a region, shed light on each other?

THE SOUTH DURING THE EARLY REPUBLIC

In *My Tears Spoiled My Aim, and Other Reflections on Southern Culture*, John Shelton Reed discusses the problem of defining the South today. Does Texas count? Does Missouri? Or Florida? Reed suggests that the presence of kudzu or a higher proportion of "Dixie" to "American" in the phone book are just a couple of the many socioeconomic, cultural, and institutional measures that can be used to limn out what we know to be "the South." The South, Reed argues, is a shared concept—what a geographer would call a "vernacular" region.[7] It exists in a coherent but imperfectly defined way in our collective imagination, shaped significantly by the Civil War but also by economic relations and cultural differences that were already emerging in the late eighteenth century.

Examining Washington's southern tour from March to July 1791 provides some insight into the boundaries of the "vernacular" South of his time. His itinerary traced the borders of what was then considered the southern United States. He traveled through Maryland, Virginia, North Carolina, South Carolina, and Georgia, with his southward journey following the eastern seaboard to just south of Savannah, Georgia, while the most western points on his inland northward trek were Augusta, Georgia, and Charlotte, North Carolina. The "Address from the Citizens of Augusta" delivered when he stopped there begins, "Sir, Your journey to the Southward being extended to the Frontier of the Union, affords a fresh proof of your indefatigable zeal in the service of your Country, and an equal attention and regard to all the people of the United States," suggesting that his travels took him to both the southern and western extremes of the new nation. This was the southern United States in 1791.[8]

Washington witnessed the "official" South double in size during his presidency. Rapid Euro-American movement and settlement westward produced the southern states of Kentucky in 1792 and Tennessee in 1796 and the Mississippi Territory (including most of present-day Alabama and Mississippi) stretching to the Mississippi River in 1798.[9] Part 1 of this collection, "On the Map and Off: The South as a Diverse Region," explores the construction of cultural boundaries in the late-eighteenth-century South and sheds light on two regions not usually considered in discussions of the emerging American South, the backcountry Appalachian frontier and French Louisiana.

Daniel Usner's "Remapping Boundaries in the Old Southwest, 1783–1795" and Martin Brückner's "Mapping the South: Image, Archive, and the Construction of Regional Identity in the Age of Washington" help to delimit further the "American South" as understood and contested in the late eighteenth century. Both explore how ideological investments and, as Usner puts it, the "ambitions and fears of late-eighteenth-century officials" did not reflect or presage distinct regional boundaries but rather worked fundamentally to constitute those boundaries. While both insist on the dynamic construction of boundaries that shape the South as a region, their approaches are very different. Usner focuses on the ways in which international boundaries, boundaries between societies on the borderlands, and relations among ethnic groups often marked by border crossings contributed to the remapping of the area that would become the Mississippi Territory of the United States in 1798. Brückner, on the other hand, reads maps for what they say about definitions of the "American South" as imagined region rather than for literal representations of political and social relations.

Together they sketch out the general area of the South in this period. Brückner analyzes eighteenth-century maps of the American South, most of which were produced in London for middle- and upper-class audiences and focus primarily on the European settlements that would become the first southern states, i.e., those on the eastern seaboard. Usner, on the other hand, looks to the western territories—the emerging American South. Their work brings home a simple but important point hinted at by the citizens of Augusta in their address to President Washington: in the late eighteenth century the region we know as the American South was both south and west—south as opposed to the northern United States, west as seen from the perspective of United States expansion. On the London maps studied by Brückner, the western areas are often blurry and undermapped, while those areas visited by Washington on his southern tour are more fully delineated. What is now considered the American South was then, as Brückner and Usner demonstrate, actively being constructed as a region by a range of formal and informal mapping activities through which political and social boundaries were repeatedly redrawn.

Besides showing us the boundaries of what was considered the southern United States during his presidency, Washington's southern tour also serves to highlight the significance of regionalism in the political rhetoric of the time. His stated purpose for undertaking his tours of the northern, eastern, and southern states was "to acquire knowledge of the face of the Country, the growth and Agriculture thereof and the temper and disposition of the Inhabitants towards the new government."[10] This last point betrays a fear of insurrection, especially among those in the South and West most distant from the seats of power and understood to be the most independent and rebellious. In Midway, Georgia, the southernmost point of Washington's travels, he was "impress[ed] . . . with the most sensible satisfaction" by the address delivered by the Congregational Church and Society of Midway, one of numerous such addresses delivered at every stage of his regional tours. In this address the people of Midway insisted:

"Distant as our situation is from the seat of Government, permit us to assure you that our influence, however inconsiderable in the national scale, shall not be wanting in encouraging submission to the laws of the United States, and thus, under GOD, perpetuating the blessings of an efficient, federal government, now so happily established."[11]

This address, significantly delivered at the point most distant from the center of the new federal government, could not have fit better with Washington's agenda, for the rhetoric of region in the United States at this time was heavily charged by debates over the balance of power between states and the federal government. Indeed, Washington's regional tours were literally directed by these debates: in his earlier northern tour he bypassed Rhode Island because it had not yet ratified the constitution; his southern tour was postponed until North Carolina ratified. His "Farewell Address" exemplified the Federalists' repeated insistence on overcoming regional interests in the name of national unity. In appealing to the gains to be had through commerce among the states, Washington and other Federalists emphasized interdependence in the name of national interest. According to Peter Onuf, the tensions between center and periphery built into the checks and balances of the new government created a "dynamic political geography [that] reinforced the American tendency to think spatially about national identity and about their own place in the nation."[12] Transcending distance and differences was from the beginning essential to the ideology of the United States. But as Onuf goes on to argue, this rhetoric ironically heightened sectional consciousness: sectional identity was no more real than national identity but rather was shaped by the political rhetoric that placed them in opposition. Both Federalists and their opponents, the Jeffersonian Republicans, participated in creating this rhetorical opposition, and in both cases negative sectional interests were opposed to the greater interests of the union. For Federalists, this dangerous sectionalism was best checked by a strong central government and economic interdependence; for Jeffersonian Republicans the possibility that particular sectional interests would have undue influence in this central government posed the main threat. Washington's comments on his southern tour are just one piece of evidence indicating that the frontier elements of the South posed a significant threat to the Union and flavored his understanding of the region as a whole.

Washington's summation of what he learned of the situation and disposition of people in the southern states during his presidential tour consisted of two main points: that southerners were becoming more industrious in their manufactures but were not yet on a par with industries in the

North, and that there was a general acceptance of the federal government by southerners. Many southerners, led famously by Patrick Henry, George Mason, and Richard Henry Lee in Virginia, Thomas Person in North Carolina, and Rawlins Lowndes, Aedanus Burke, and Thomas Sumter in South Carolina, had opposed the new constitution as "anti-Federalists" until it was formally adopted by the requisite nine states. Federalist supporters of the Constitution like Washington had feared that Henry might try to form a separate "Southern Confederacy," and Person called Washington "a damned rascal and traitor to his country for putting his name to such an infamous paper as the new Constitution."[13]

Though southern approval of the new national government was not a given, Person's beliefs remained a minority sentiment. Southern support for the stronger, more centralized national government became exemplified specifically by southern acquiescence to the federal taxation of "home made spirits," or corn whiskey, despite Washington's belief that "such a law could never be executed in the southern States, particularly in Virginia and North Carolina."[14] Farmers living in the western parts of the southern states bitterly opposed a tax on the one product they could produce in abundance. Nevertheless, it was left to Pennsylvania farmers to actually revolt against the federal tax, before being humbled by a national army with President Washington at its head.[15]

One of the most divisive factors contributing to sectionalism and the one that most significantly marks the South as region in our historical imagination is slavery. Though a proponent of gradual abolition such as was adopted by many northern states after the American Revolution, Washington backed measures that would secure the support of southern slaveholders for the new constitution and national government. During his southern tour, for example, Washington arranged to have a letter from Thomas Jefferson, written in his capacity as secretary of state, sent to the Spanish governor of Florida, insisting that fugitive slaves not be admitted into the Spanish territories and that arrangements be made for the return of any apprehended slaves to their owners. This action anticipated Washington's signing into law of the Fugitive Slave Act in 1793.[16] Moreover, during this same trip he sent a letter directing his secretary, Tobias Lear, to return many of his personal slaves to Mount Vernon in order to evade Pennsylvania laws allowing slaves to sue for freedom after six months' residence.[17] Washington's personal interests and public diplomacy in some ways coincided, in others conflicted, reflecting the personal and public tensions surrounding the issue of slavery.[18] Slavery was undoubtedly the most significant southern institution governing numerous compromises struck by politicians in an attempt to secure union. Slavery, and the plantation agriculture it made possible in the South, contributed mightily to American sectionalism, but Washington kept nearly all of his thoughts on slavery private, for he understood the danger of conflict that existed if he, as unifier of a new nation, spoke on the subject.[19] Instead, as Philip D. Morgan and Michael L. Nicholls demonstrate in their essay for this collection (discussed at greater length below), Washington acted quietly to protect his personal interests by pursuing those men and women who attempted flight from enslavement on his estates while publicly supporting the gradual abolition of slavery. On other matters of importance to the South, Washington expressed his views more freely and crafted future trends.

Not all Africans and African-Americans in the South were enslaved. In his essay for this collection, William R. Ryan chronicles the plight of Thomas Jeremiah, a free black man living in Charleston, South Carolina, just prior to the Revolutionary War. Jeremiah, a skilled pilot, a slaveholder, and a man of considerable means, was found guilty of collaborating with the British to encourage rebellion among the region's black majority. The evidence against him was thin at best, leading to a confrontation between the royal governor, William Campbell, who attempted to engineer a pardon for Jeremiah, and patriots who sought his execution. This confrontation was complicated by struggles on the patriot side between radicals who urged a blockade that would impede trade and conservatives whose challenge to British authority stopped short of actions that would hurt their economic interests. Ryan urges us to understand Jeremiah's trial and execution in the context of a three-way struggle among blacks, Whigs, and Tories, providing fascinating insight into the many forces and interests that shaped the Revolutionary War in South Carolina.

As Usner's essay reminds us, although both free and enslaved Africans inhabited the Mississippi Territory throughout the late eighteenth century, the "Old Southwest" was then primarily Indian country. Southern Indians still held large land areas and had a significant impact upon politics, diplomacy, and trade. Yet the tide was rapidly turning, as population numbers show. In the entire South, from Virginia to Florida to east Texas, there existed rough numerical parity as late as 1715, with about 90,000 Indians, 96,000 Europeans, and 31,000 Africans. By 1790 the numbers had shifted dramatically, to only 56,000 Indians, more than a million Euro-Americans, and almost 1.7 million Africans.[20] Those Europeans and Africans were largely confined to the Atlantic Coast, the Gulf Coast, and places on the Mississippi River. In the interior South, the Cherokee, Creek, Seminole, Choctaw, and Chickasaw Indians were still the principal powers. During Washington's southern tour in 1791, Catawba Indians from South Carolina visited him seeking help in their fight to retain their lands, and Washington commented on the ongoing conflicts between Georgians and the Creek Indians, while in their address the people of Midway particularly praised Washington for his part in the recent treaty with the Creek nation, suggesting one reason for their enthusiastic statements of support for the new federal government.

Washington's southern tour helps us understand the boundaries of the southern United States during the late eighteenth century, including the mutability of these boundaries both because of the threats of dissolution posed by those who might resist the new federal government on the frontier and in the statehouses and because of the expansion that was, year by year, changing the shape of the nation. Likewise, the dominance of the frontier in the South and ongoing negotiations and confrontations with American Indians were significant both in influencing national understanding of southern character and in altering the shape of the southern United States on maps. It is hard to escape the perspective described by Onuf in which sectional identity and federal unity are locked in an antithesis by turns productive of and destructive to the stability of the federal government. But we also include essays in this section that do not fit easily into emerging understandings of the American South as either a part of or a challenge to the new republic.

It is no surprise, then, that those essays focusing on local studies that challenge any notion of a unified regional South are all in some way "western" in focus, treating French colonial New Orleans, Creek territories in present-day Alabama, and western Virginia. These areas and communities are often considered peripheral to our understanding of the South in the late eighteenth century. Nonetheless, the essays on Creek Indians in what is now west Georgia and Alabama, on fashionable elites in French New Orleans, and on settlers of the Shenandoah Valley of Virginia provide important insights into some of the diverse groups who populated the South. These essays are also concerned in some way with economics and commercial dynamics that differ from those that were being developed among the newly united states. While battles raged over federal assumption of state debts and Alexander Hamilton's plans for a central bank in the early republic, other economic exchanges continued outside the parameters of these debates.

The region that would become the American South was multinational in the late eighteenth century. In addition to American Indians and frontiersmen from the United States vying for land, France and Spain and England were still important colonizing presences. Indeed, some of those frontiersmen who worried Washington and others with their disregard for federal authority actually carried on negotiations with European nations. In her essay, Sophie White provides insight into the cultural values of French colonial elite society and cultural and economic exchanges between France and its colonies by tracing the history of a single gown ordered from Paris by the chevalier de Pradel for his wife. From this history we gain knowledge of the practices of colonial elites like George Washington who purchased clothing and luxury goods from Europe. But though they bear a certain resemblance to such exchanges between England and the British colonies, White emphasizes the differences that governed commercial relations between France and French colonial Louisiana, where "governmental and geographical impediments hampered the growth there of a viable colonial economy—and, indeed, hindered the development of a homespun tradition." White's exploration of the Pradel gown sheds light on gender relations and changing class formations in French colonial Louisiana as well as the complex commercial and cultural exchanges between France and New Orleans. Juxtaposed with other articles in this collection, her study enriches our understanding of the ongoing role of European cultural and economic forces in the late-eighteenth-century American South and the cultural practices of the elite classes in the Americas, including many of those governing the newly formed United States.

Warren Hofstra, on the other hand, looks at tensions between the world of goods in which Washington lived and the economic life of people for whom he held much personal disdain, the inhabitants of the Shenandoah Valley, as a vehicle for understanding Washington's developing sense of public virtue. Washington was familiar with the valley from an early age as a surveyor and eventually as a landowner. However, his economic world differed dramatically from the exchange economy that organized the Virginia backcountry. As Hofstra explains, the "Newtonian world of debits and credits ordered space," requiring relative proximity among participants. Moreover, it was a world in which balance rather than economic growth was paramount. As a leader, Washington's relations with the people settled in the valley were often fractious, as local concerns such as food production and family often overrode valley citizens' support of Washington's demands for militia service and other public actions. Washington's personal ambitions, and his eventual position as leader of a vast republic that required economic mechanisms operating beyond the local, put him at odds with these western settlers, but his response was to emphasize a type of virtue that surmounted these differences, reinforcing self-sacrifice as a fundamental virtue of the new republic.

Robbie Ethridge also complicates our mapping of the South during this period by examining societal changes among the late-eighteenth- and early-nineteenth-century Creek Indians. In a novel approach, she looks outward on the world from the viewpoint of a local Creek community or village. By so doing, she is able to discern several changes occurring within Creek communities as they tried to adapt to an invasive American presence in the deep South. Here again we see both conflict and compromise between different economic practices and worldviews. Ethridge provides insight into these dynamics without resorting to an elegy of loss.

Detailed examinations such as those found in these essays highlight the need to look for and analyze areas on the community level, exposing local challenges to general and regional identities, and broadening our comprehension of the South as a whole. The "vernacular" South is imprecise, as John Shelton Reed points out, not only because of the large-scale political and social changes that constantly reshape it but also because of the local nature of the vernacular. What Washington saw and thought during his southern tour is important to our understanding of the American South during the late eighteenth century. What he did *not* see also sheds light both on the South and on Washington himself.

GEORGE WASHINGTON AS SOUTHERNER

How is Washington the individual associated with the South? Most obviously as a Virginian who fully embraced the values of his class, not only dancing and riding and sitting in the pew reserved for his illustrious family but also participating in a regional economy both exploitive in its "paternalism" and exploited as a colonial dependent of British interests. His successes in the west as surveyor and officer set the groundwork for his later Revolutionary War achievements and led to his extensive acquisition of western lands. He had gentrified low country social habits and affinities, but personally and presidentially he looked westward for economic growth.

During his southern tour, the only address delivered to Washington that claimed him as a native son was in Fredericksburg. Elsewhere in the South he was greeted as general, president, and father of his country in terms differing little from those used on his tours of other American regions. He was a Virginian, but his ties to the larger region that came to be known as the American South are in many ways tenuous. As "American,"

Washington was abstracted to such a degree that he became broadly representative. His were the virtues of independence, self-sacrifice, and disinterestedness—at once a democratic George to replace George III as father of his people and Cincinnatus, a noble everyman leaving the plow to serve his country in its time of need but eager to return when his service was no longer required. In these symbolic ways he was both above and of the people, an object of reverence and emulation. But seen regionally, the material conditions of Washington's existence come into clearer focus, and we see that the father of his country was part of a hierarchical, paternalistic society in which the plow he returned to was guided by another and his studied appearance of disinterestedness was undergirded by the manners, politics, and economics of his class.

George Washington is the greatest of the "great men" in the history of the United States, and this fact inflects any discussion of his life and character. The regional focus of this collection is in some ways intended to complicate "great man" histories without simply rejecting both the influence and the insights of traditional treatments of Washington as man and symbol. Just as, to understand the American South in the late eighteenth century, we combine examinations of how the region as a whole was mapped at the time with local studies that trouble those maps, to understand Washington himself it is useful to engage his position as American icon as well as more specific aspects of Washington's life and character that do not fit easily into conventional images of the man.

Peter H. Wood sheds light on the historical contingency of Washington's stature by developing parallel biographies of Washington and the Cherokee chief Dragging Canoe, one of Washington's contemporaries and counterparts. Both men led mass resistance movements against colonial oppressors, acted according to their societies' strong sense of probity, and worried constantly about their families' safety, but Dragging Canoe has become a marginal figure in American history while Washington could not be more central. This dual biographical approach to historical narrative offers the chance to view historical contemporaries who made similar choices in life while living in radically different cultures, and it allows us to imagine more vividly a South of many characters and diverse histories. The very preeminence of the figure of Washington gets in the way of understanding him; Wood's approach not only illuminates a relatively neglected Cherokee leader but also helps us see Washington better for the unfamiliar comparison.

If the life of Dragging Canoe reminds us that Washington's preeminence is in many ways an accident of history, David Shields shows us that

Washington did much to secure this status for himself. Shields considers Washington's construction of a public persona in terms of characterology and public virtues, arguing that Washington made himself "an allegorical figure of public probity." Best understood according to the prevailing "stage theory" of the time, he performed public roles that positioned him between the valorous state of nature of Native Americans on the one hand and the decadent British officer corps on the other. Washington's understanding of public character was not simply a matter of personal self-presentation, however. Later in his career, his cultivation of the virtue of civility informed his support of a republican public sphere that included, among other things, room for oft-contested dramatic performances and the informal participation of women in matters of the republic via salons and drawing rooms.

Carla Mulford also looks to Washington's self-construction according to the public values of his class in the late-eighteenth-century South, identifying the virtue of self-mastery in terms of both Whig "country party" politics and emerging Revolutionary ideals as a key element of his public self-presentation. She associates this performative self-creation with a "poetics of national memory" (derived from *poesis*, the process of making) that is a simultaneously personal and public invention of Washington as representative of the United States. She then explores the cultural reach of the values embraced by Washington himself through readings of poetry by Annis Stockton, Phillis Wheatley, and Jonathan Odell. While it is not surprising that Stockton, a Federalist and close friend of Washington, would echo these values in her encomiums, it is instructive to learn that Wheatley, an enslaved African, and Odell, a British loyalist, engage the image of Washington on similar grounds, though their uses of his image vary greatly.

While Wood, Shields, and Mulford help us understand better the construction of Washington as American icon through self-fashioning and public mythmaking, Don Higginbotham, Theda Perdue, Philip D. Morgan, and Michael L. Nicholls look more carefully at his interactions with others in ways that bring out less familiar aspects of his personal and public history. In contrast to an emphasis on Washington's reputation and his status as icon, Higginbotham helps give flesh to the biographical man by looking at his relationship to three women: his mother, Mary Ball Washington, his friend and neighbor Sally Cary Fairfax, and his wife, Martha Dandridge Custis Washington. This "founding father's" relationship to women is no small matter, and tellingly myriad assumptions have been made that tend on the whole to remove him from the realm of female influence. Through careful examination of the evidence that has been used to stereotype these women (and the evidence that has been ignored to do the same), Higginbotham shows the influence of Washington's close relationships with women on his personal and public life. These relationships informed a lifelong comfort around women that, Higginbotham argues, made "Washington a sound man to lead a revolution" and shaped his presidency in positive ways.

While his reputation may have been enhanced in often unacknowledged ways by his relationships with some women, Washington's concern for his reputation was challenged by his actions with respect to at least forty-seven slaves who ran away from his estates between 1760 and 1799. In their thorough study of Washington's experience with the men and women who attempted to flee slavery, understood in the broader context of slave flight in late-eighteenth-century Virginia, Philip D. Morgan and Michael L. Nicholls cite several instances, including Washington's pursuit of Oney Judge, a personal servant to Martha Washington who would decades later recount her experiences, in which he acted aggressively to retrieve those who attempted escape, while insisting that his actions be kept confidential to protect his reputation. Based on their study of Washington's experiences of slave flight and those of other Virginia slaveholders, Morgan and Nicholls find that fewer slaves in Virginia attempted escape than in other British-American colonies, but those who did were especially successful, particularly if they were men and skilled in trades. Washington's frustrations over slave flight seem to have increased over the course of the eighteenth century even though the number of slave escapes decreased markedly by the 1790s, leading Morgan and Nicholls to suggest that those experiences had as much bearing on Washington's support of the gradual abolition of slavery as any more noble motives.

Few issues faced by the new government drew more attention than relations with Indian nations. As the United States fought a protracted war against the Ohio Valley Indian Confederacy in the early 1790s, the country was also trying to define its relationship with Indians. Policy makers debated whether it was best to wage war on Indian peoples (a nearly impossible undertaking, given the poor financial condition of the young government), or pay Indians to vacate their lands, or follow some other avenue. Theda Perdue tackles this issue by focusing on Washington's significant role in formulating an Indian policy in the South based upon "civilizing" Native people. If Indians could be turned into literate, Christian, individual-landholding farmers, Washington and other officials argued, then maybe they could join the wider American body politic while also relinquishing much of their lands. Such goals flew in the face of Indian realities, however, and the result for Indians was calamitous.

Many of our contributors point us toward the values of Virginia gentry and particularly toward self-manufactured "transparency" of character arising from civility and self-mastery. "Transparency" connotes an approach to both self and society that differs in significant ways from post-Romantic notions of individualism. It also points us toward the peculiar iconicity of Washington—the sculptural silence that he and his contemporaries fostered and that has been sustained by succeeding generations. These essays address both Washington's efforts to construct transparent character and the iconicity that grew around him and carried its own invisible impenetrability. In contrast, both Higginbotham and Perdue focus particularly on gender in ways that uncover some of the specific biases of this transparency. While Higginbotham redresses the biases of past historical narratives that inscribe notions of male dominance into the iconology of Washington by denigrating the power and influence of the women closest to him, Perdue explores the ways in which Washington himself attempted to impose Western, male-centered gender roles onto Indian communities in an attempt to "civilize" them. The "self-mastery" fostered by Washington but also idealized and even exaggerated by others masks a range of dependencies and hierarchies. On the one hand, Shields, Mulford, and Higginbotham all discuss relationships between Washington and women that belie attempts to isolate him from the female world of the drawing room. On the other hand, in his Indian policy Washington attempted to impose on Native peoples models of self-sufficiency that depended on male self-mastery and female subservience.

INTERSECTIONS BETWEEN WASHINGTON AND THE REGION

The conference that provided the impetus for this volume was organized to commemorate the bicentennial of Washington's death. Both well-established and emerging scholars of this period were invited to present papers based on new research that would be accessible and interesting to academics and nonacademics alike. With an eye to the regional interests of our community (the conference was held at the University of Southern Mississippi in Hattiesburg in October 1999), we asked that papers focus on George Washington and the South in this period. We allowed our contributors much latitude with respect to the "and." In some essays Washington is quite central; in others he is a more tangential figure. Many of the essays that focus on Washington are concerned with his cultural role as icon; he served and continues to serve a significant symbolic function in the American imagination.

There is a danger in reading the history of the South at this time as simply the history of men like Washington, however. Women, free and enslaved Africans and African-Americans, American Indians, non-elite whites, and non-English whites offered competing notions of what the late-eighteenth-century South was all about. Moreover, if we extend our concept of the South beyond the states bordering the Atlantic Ocean to include areas that Spain claimed in the 1790s, namely the lands to the south and west of Georgia all the way to New Orleans, and if we push the period back to the pre–Revolutionary War era as well as forward into the early nineteenth century, we can gain new insights into both the continuity and the transformations occurring in the early-republic South. This essay collection is not the final word on either Washington or the early-republic South, but it is an enlightening survey of new interdisciplinary work that exposes the fruitful possibilities of combining regional and biographical history.[21] This compilation teaches us more about Washington and more about the South of his lifetime than we knew before, and it suggests possible avenues for future research into both.

The essays that follow undertake an interdisciplinary investigation of intersections between an emerging regional identity, "the American South," and the identity of its most significant son, George Washington. By linking him with this region, a region that has always been heterogeneous both within itself and with respect to the "United States" as a single entity, we hope to analyze both the region and the man. Washington has come to symbolize America; he transcends region and interest, representing in turn a transcendent America. Indeed, Washington better represents America as a whole than he does the South, for as the essays in this book illustrate, this was a far more multifaceted and heterogeneous region than any member of the Virginia gentry could possibly represent. By exploring simultaneously Washington and the South, the essays in this collection provide dynamic, multivalent ways of understanding both a man and a region that are too often endowed with a monolithic, falsely unified identity.

NOTES

1. *The Diaries of George Washington*, ed. Donald Jackson and Dorothy Twohig, 6 vols. (Charlottesville: University Press of Virginia, 1976–79), 6:128.

2. Archibald Henderson, *Washington's Southern Tour, 1791* (Boston: Houghton Mifflin, 1923), xxv.

3. See Washington's letters to David Humphreys (July 20, 1791), the marquis de Lafayette (July 28, 1791), and Gouverneur Morris (July 28, 1791) in *The Papers of George Washington: Presidential Series*, ed. Dorothy Twohig, 9 vols. to date (Charlottesville: University Press of Virginia, 1987–), 8:358–61, 377–84.

4. George Washington, *Writings* (New York: Library of America, 1997), 965. On Washington's "Farewell Address," see also Joseph J. Ellis, "The Farewell: Washington's Wisdom at the End," in *George Washington Reconsidered*, ed. Don Higginbotham (Charlottesville: University Press of Virginia, 2001), 212–49.

5. Washington, *Writings*, 965–66.

6. Ibid., 967.

7. John Shelton Reed, *My Tears Spoiled My Aim, and Other Reflections on Southern Culture* (New York: Harcourt Brace, 1993), 5.

8. *Papers of George Washington: Presidential Series*, 8:194.

9. On Washington and western lands, see W. W. Abbot, "George Washington, the West, and the Union," in Higginbotham, *George Washington Reconsidered*, 198–211.

10. *Diaries of George Washington*, 5:452–53.

11. *Papers of George Washington: Presidential Series*, 8:177–78.

12. Peter S. Onuf, "Federalism, Republicanism, and the Origins of American Sectionalism," in *All Over the Map: Rethinking American Regions*, ed. Edward L. Ayers et al. (Baltimore: The Johns Hopkins University Press, 1996), 14.

13. See note 3. For Person quote, see John Richard Alden, *The South in the Revolution, 1763–1789* (Baton Rouge: Louisiana State University Press, 1957), 398; see also Herbert J. Storing, ed., *The Anti-Federalist: Writings by the Opponents of the Constitution* (Chicago: University of Chicago Press, 1985), 273–74.

14. Washington's letter to David Humphreys (July 20, 1791) in *The Papers of George Washington: Presidential Series*, 8:359.

15. See Thomas P. Abernethy, *The South in the New Nation, 1789–1819* (Baton Rouge: Louisiana State University Press, 1961), 35, and Thomas P. Slaughter, *The Whiskey Rebellion: Frontier Epilogue to the American Revolution* (New York: Oxford University Press, 1986).

16. See Fritz Hirschfeld, *George Washington and Slavery: A Documentary Portrayal* (Columbia: University of Missouri Press, 1997), esp. 189–91.

17. See the letter from Tobias Lear of April 5, 1791, and Washington's reply from Richmond, April 12, 1791, in *Papers of George Washington: Presidential Series*, 8:67–68, 84–86.

18. See Hirschfeld, *George Washington and Slavery*. Also, Joseph J. Ellis includes a chapter on the general silence arising around the issue of slavery during the early years of the republic in *Founding Brothers: The Revolutionary Generation* (New York: Alfred A. Knopf, 2000), 81–119.

19. Dorothy Twohig, "'That Species of Property': Washington's Role in the Controversy over Slavery," in Higginbotham, *George Washington Reconsidered*, 116.

20. Peter H. Wood, "The Changing Population of the Colonial South: An Over-

view by Race and Region, 1685–1790," in *Powhatan's Mantle: Indians in the Colonial Southeast*, ed. Peter H. Wood, Gregory A. Waselkov, and M. Thomas Hatley (Lincoln: University of Nebraska Press, 1989), 38–39.

21. *George Washington Reconsidered*, edited by Don Higginbotham, is an important recent essay collection on Washington, albeit one in which all the essays but two have been previously published.

Part 1

On the Map and Off:

The South as a Diverse Region

Chapter 1

REMAPPING BOUNDARIES IN THE OLD SOUTHWEST, 1783–1795

DANIEL H. USNER JR.

In a circular letter to state governors upon resigning his command of the Continental Army, General George Washington wrote on June 8, 1783, "The citizens of America, placed in the most enviable condition, as the lords and proprietors of a vast tract of continent, comprehending all the various soils and climates of the world, and abounding with all the necessaries and conveniences of life, are now, by the late satisfactory pacification, acknowledged to be possessed of absolute freedom and independency. They are, from this period, to be considered as actors on a most conspicuous theatre, which seems to be peculiarly designated by Providence for the display of human greatness and felicity."[1] That same year Carlos III of Spain received a secret memorandum from his ambassador to France, warning just what a belief like Washington's might mean for those parts of the North American continent still claimed by European powers. "This federal republic is born a pigmy," wrote Pedro Pablo de Abarca y Bolea, conde de Aranda, since it needed assistance from both France and Spain to obtain its independence. "The day will come," however, "when she will be a giant, a colossus formidable even to these countries. She will forget the services she has received from the two powers, and will think only of her own aggrandizement." As the conde de Aranda foresaw this process, "The first step of this nation, after it has become powerful, will be to take possession of the Floridas in order to have the command of the Gulf of Mexico, and, after having rendered difficult our commerce with New Spain, she will aspire to the conquest of that vast empire."[2]

The early vision and apprehension expressed respectively by these two men, especially when mixed with the advantage of historical hindsight, make it all too easy to view what happened in the Gulf Coastal South between the American Revolution and the end of George Washington's presidency as an inexorable and natural process—what later generations of Americans would call the "manifest destiny" of the United States. That the United States acquired Louisiana in 1803, possessed all of Florida by 1820, and invaded Mexico in 1846 might serve as convincing evidence for the inevitability of what both Washington and the conde de Aranda predicted. Yet we historians are supposed to know better. The ambitions and fears of late-eighteenth-century officials were not merely prophecies. They actually contributed to the ideological forces and political decisions that went into the shaping of events. In this particular case, nothing less than a remapping of boundaries in the Gulf Coastal region of North America was actively under way.

There is a serious problem with viewing the 1780s and 1790s as a prelude to later periods of United States territorial expansion. Occupation of a region formerly claimed by other nations—whether Native American or European—and then its incorporation into the early republic are portrayed as predetermined and desirable stages in an almost mechanical movement. The means of expansion are consequently taken for granted, seeming to require little scrutiny or explanation. The transformation of social relations actually experienced by inhabitants of the region is effaced and voices of resistance and protest are silenced. The powerful grip of inevitability also makes alternative paths seem implausible and unworthy of consideration. If we are going to understand disputed and contested territories in a specific historical context, the narratives produced in the process of American territorial expansion must be recognized as a vital part of the process.[3]

The rhetoric of expansionism, in association with diplomacy and policy, was one means of remapping the continent through language. Defining or redefining cultural spaces contributed deeply to the mastery of American institutions over newly acquired places, translating a desire for territory into a destiny of possession. Contests over territory—between indigenous and invading peoples, between the United States and European empires—are reduced to interesting but fruitless examples of interference with the inexorable success of American continental expansion. But demystifying the role of mastery in the definition of cultural spaces, as Jack Greene explains, "enables us to comprehend that the forms, behaviors, and representations by which almost any given space is defined are usually the products not of simple imposition by those groups who would eventually succeed in asserting their control over that space but of a process of negotiation between those groups and other contesting groups whom they were trying to bring—and to keep—under their domination."[4]

In order to rescue what actually happened inside contested regions, it is useful to examine boundaries and borders under the new light of comparative and theoretical analysis.[5] The region that became the Mississippi Territory of the United States in 1798 invites us to explore three types of boundaries whose interconnectedness is becoming better understood: the international boundary between nation-states or empires, boundaries between and around societies situated on the borderlands, and boundaries between ethnic groups within both indigenous and colonial territories. Between 1783 and 1795, these boundaries underwent a complex process of remapping on the ground as well as on paper. The United States and Spain engaged in a diplomatic struggle over borderlines and commerce along the Mississippi River, seeking dominance over a promising territory. But such master mapping is seldom that simple. The process of remapping the lower Mississippi Valley was also contested and influenced by groups of people actually living in the region. American Indians, European settlers and traders, and African-American slaves presented rival identities and interests. Local and intercultural relations were therefore intertwined with international negotiations. And as distant authorities attempted to redraw the map, people on the ground negotiated over rights and resources. Crossing borders, in order to protect old practices or to grab new opportunities, was also an important part of the story.

Mississippi during the Age of Washington is fertile ground for this line of analysis. Several different American Indian nations still comprised altogether the largest population living in the region, but a diverse colonial society had also taken root during the eighteenth century. And now, in the aftermath of the Revolution, American settlement and trade were threatening to encroach rapidly. An analytical approach to the convergence and clash of these societies that focuses on the remapping of boundaries might provide a useful new framework for rescuing the "Old Southwest" in the early republic from the deadening details that clutter most narratives. It also directs greater attention to the people actually living inside the contested zone, most of whom were American Indians throughout the period under investigation.[6]

The first boundary to be examined here, the international boundary between Spanish provinces and the United States, calls for the broadest framework of analysis. Treaties signed in 1783 were inconsistent in their references to this region, contributing to the existence of a "disputed territory" between the end of the American Revolution and the late months of George Washington's presidency. The treaty between England and the United States, recognizing the latter nation's independence, granted Americans free navigation of the Mississippi River and located the southern boundary of the new nation at the thirty-first northern parallel. But the treaty signed by England and Spain never mentioned navigation of the Mississippi, while ceding East Florida to Spain and recognizing Spain's conquest of West Florida during the American Revolution. As delineated in 1764, British West Florida had included the Natchez settlement and all territory as far north as 32°26'. So was the Mississippi River open or closed to American navigation? Was the boundary between the United States and the Spanish provinces of Florida and Louisiana 31° or 32°26' northern latitude? Negotiations over the boundary and commerce dragged on in both the United States and Spain until finally a treaty was signed on October 27, 1795, at San Lorenzo, the village below the southern slopes of the Guadarramas where the royal court resided in autumn. The southwestern boundary of the United States was fixed at the thirty-first parallel east of the Mississippi River, and free navigation of the Mississippi River was secured.[7]

Familiar interpretations of the Treaty of San Lorenzo, signed by United States special envoy Thomas Pinckney, assert that Spain was either threatening U.S. possession or destabilizing the American frontier. "Intrigue" and "conspiracy" are words commonly used to characterize dangers putatively posed by the Spanish in the lower Mississippi Valley during these years. This is largely due to historians' concentration on an infamous cast of public figures that includes Alexander McGillivray, James Wilkinson, and Aaron Burr. But a nationalist theme in the literature also plays a resonating role. According to the prevailing narrative, Pinckney's treaty gained for the United States its rightful claim to territory and cleared the path of future expansion. In the words of Arthur Whitaker, the Treaty of San Lorenzo "marks the beginnings of the disintegration of the Spanish empire as well as the first stage in the territorial expansion of the United States."[8]

But the nationalist view fails to address some significant complications, beginning with President Washington's own position on issues concerning Spain's boundary with the United States. "However singular the opinion may be," Washington wrote to Henry Lee in August 1785, "I cannot divest myself of it, that the navigation of the Mississippi, *at this time,* ought to be no object with us." Even before receiving the gift of a breeding jackass from Carlos III, the president of the new American nation actually preferred temporary obstruction by Spanish officials "until we have a little time allowed to open and make easy the ways between the Atlantic States and the western territory." Without laying the "cement" of commercial ties, through roads and canals, the United States could not expect loyalty from western inhabitants. "There is nothing which binds one county or one State to another," Washington argued, "but interest." Washington publicly promoted the improvement of east-west transportation and personally invested in canal building that would link the Potomac River with Ohio River headwaters.[9]

Washington's position, at odds with the ambitions of many citizens, reflected the existence of conflicting interests that widely divided national opinion. Federal officials of the United States actually discouraged aggressive and rapid encroachment on Indian lands in order to minimize conflict with Native Americans and to control westward movement of citizens. "Although the disposition of the people of the States, to emigrate into the Indian country, cannot be effectually prevented," argued Secretary of War Henry Knox, "it may be restrained and regulated." Territorial officials and military authorities were expected to prevent citizens from trespassing while the national government postponed the purchase of Indian land. It is important to note that this policy was considered appropriate partly because its advocates believed that American Indians would inevitably relinquish their territories. "As population shall increase, and approach the Indian boundaries," according to Knox's forecast, "game will be diminished, and new purchase may be made for small considerations." This assumption was, however, based on the unrealistic assessment that Indians lived in some kind of endangered hunter state—a condition that did not accurately characterize Choctaw, Chickasaw, and Creek peoples in the Gulf South. It nonetheless influenced the United States government's attempt to restrain and regulate westward movement.[10]

Caution in the Washington administration toward the disputed territory was also motivated by fears of independence and separatism on the western frontier. Prominent citizens of the new nation were busily scheming for their personal aggrandizement. People like James Wilkinson and William Blount, supposedly representing United States interests in the West, demonstrated a willingness to conspire with foreign agents in plots to carve out their own dominions on the borderlands. Speculation in western lands also caused great concern. In 1789 the state of Georgia sold to several speculating companies some fifteen million acres of land in the region still being disputed by Spain and the United States and still possessed by American Indians. Company agents were busily pursuing the formation of their own colonies on the east bank of the Mississippi River.[11] In September 1790 James O'Fallon, representing the South Carolina Yazoo Company, requested from George Washington "sufficient authority" to regulate trade with Indians and negotiate land purchases with them. In return, he would provide the president with vital intelligence that "I may occasionally have from the Spanish and Indian borders."[12] But this kind of independent activity jeopardized the government's own objectives and, moreover, violated the Indian Trade and Intercourse Act of 1790. "If the Yazous purchasers, should persist, in forcing a settlement upon the lands of the Choctaws and Chickasaws," Henry Knox reported to Washington in February 1791, "it will be proper to dispossess them by sending a body of troops against them, and to explain the measure, fully, to the Indian nations."[13]

Closer scrutiny of the Spanish side also exposes a shortcoming in the dominant narrative of how the Old Southwest was remapped. Spain's negotiators were more cautious and flexible than we are usually led to believe. By 1787 they reached a compromise position, agreeing to a boundary at the thirty-first parallel except for the Natchez District and to a commission that would inquire into the validity of United States claims. Spain also implemented a generous immigration policy for its province of Louisiana through a proclamation issued by Governor Esteban Miró inviting citizens of the United States to settle on either side of the Mississippi River. Although the Roman Catholic Church was the only public worship that could be permitted, immigrants "will not be molested on religious matters." They were promised grants of free land in proportion to the size of their families and labor forces. This policy was partly motivated by the need to undermine schemes being orchestrated by James Wilkinson, James White, and other adventurers, but it also represented Spain's desire to increase the colonial population and commercial development of Louisiana.[14]

Spain's American Indian policy in Louisiana and Florida was likewise less aggressive toward the United States than references to "Spanish intrigue" suggest. The priority of colonial officials was to secure a stable trade relationship with interior Indian nations, recognizing that political alliance depended mostly on steady and orderly commerce. As Alexander McGillivray reminded the commandant at Pensacola in 1784, "Indians will attach themselves to & Serve them best who Supply their Necessities."[15] Hoping that trade would satisfy southeastern Indians enough to preserve their allegiance, Spain advised its Indian allies to maintain a guarded peace with Americans. For Louisiana's governor, Hector, baron de Carondelet, whose stance was somewhat more bellicose than his predecessor's, this meant discouraging interaction with United States officials and citizens but also relying mainly on Indian allegiance to protect Spanish interests. "The sustaining of our allied tribes in the possession of their lands," he wrote in June 1795, "is an indispensable object both for the conservation of Louisiana under the power of Spain, and to prevent the Americans from securing the navigation of the Mississippi."[16]

So what now seems certain about the "disputed territory" at the international level must be more narrowly stated: the United States government desired control as far south as the thirty-first parallel, and Spain desired a buffer against the United States. But to understand what this meant to people actually living in the region, we must turn to the second type of boundary operating in the Gulf South—that between Indian country and the neighboring provinces of both Spain and the United States. The region over which Spain and the United States disputed their claims was occupied mostly by Choctaws, Chickasaws, and Creeks whose total population numbered approximately thirty thousand people in 1785. To the south and west of these Indian nations was a colonial population of thirty thousand, which Spain was trying to increase in West Florida and Louisiana. To the east and north, citizens of the United States were living in Georgia, Tennessee, and Kentucky. They comprised a rapidly growing population of some seventy thousand people.[17]

After 1783 American Indians faced the probability of mounting pressures from non-Indian nations. Their overall strategy was to secure beneficial trade relations with outsiders and to protect their own territory and sovereignty against erosion. In 1784 Choctaw, Chickasaw, and Creek delegations met with Spanish officials at Pensacola and Mobile, establishing rates of exchange for the deerskin trade and recognizing the Indian nations' territorial boundaries. Indians agreed to ward off American traders and trespassers, but were urged to avoid conflict with the United States. Indian nations in the disputed zone, however, could not afford to dismiss American overtures for trade and alliance, needing as they did to keep as many options open as possible during these uncertain times. So emissaries were sent to Hopewell on the Keowee River to negotiate separate agreements with the United States. In January 1786 Choctaw representatives signed a treaty at Hopewell, formally opening relations with the United States. Although decades of trade with merchants on the Gulf Coast made most Choctaws, Chickasaws, and Creeks prefer familiar connections in

Spanish West Florida and Louisiana, the opportunity to trade with Americans served as leverage when Indians sought better terms from or reported grievances to Spanish officials.[18]

Interaction across the boundary between Indian and non-Indian nations was complicated by social and economic conditions specific to this region, circumstances repeatedly overlooked in the general literature but more familiar to regional specialists. Spain depended upon British merchants to operate the deerskin trade with Choctaws, Chickasaws, and Creeks. The participation of Englishmen and Scotsmen in Gulf Coastal Indian trade began in the 1760s, when England took possession of the Florida provinces. After Spain's repossession of Florida in 1783, British companies continued to dominate. To secure peaceful relations with the Indian population, Spanish officials depended upon the steady flow of trade goods made possible by English and Scottish merchants. Control over their practices and prices, however, proved difficult to achieve, and there was always some degree of mistrust between Spanish officials and British entrepreneurs. By 1788, Panton, Leslie & Company nearly monopolized trade with Indians throughout the region, but other companies competed vigorously at times. With Indians being pulled by rival merchants like James Mather and John Turnbull, colonial authorities found it even harder to regulate and stabilize trade relations with Indians. During the summer of 1787, Choctaws and Chickasaws, unhappy with prices charged by Mather's firm in Mobile, worried Spanish authorities by threatening to trade with Americans.[19]

Spain's encouragement of immigration to Louisiana and West Florida—even by American settlers—further complicated relations with American Indians by imposing local pressures on Indian land and sovereignty. The Natchez District's population of two thousand in 1785 more than doubled within a decade and began to encroach on Choctaw territory. Colonial settlements also grew along the Mobile and Tombigbee rivers, causing unrest among the Alibamons as well as the Choctaws.[20] Like the United States, Spain was trying to pursue incongruent goals on its borderlands. The Spanish needed to maintain peaceful trade and alliance with Native Americans, but also desired to occupy Louisiana and Florida with more colonial subjects. In response to Indian threats against colonists settling upriver from Mobile, Governor Miró decided in May 1789 to station troops in their midst. "It would be a disgraceful subjection," he argued to Alexander McGillivray, "that because the Indians do not approve the settlement of some lands that do not belong to them, we should have to refrain from developing and populating them, and it would also be a dishonor to the nation were we to permit the destruction of these settlements, when all these persons have taken an oath of fidelity to his Catholic Majesty and made themselves his subjects."[21]

The complexity of Indian interests and purposes likewise shaped relationships with bordering Spanish and United States territories. Indians traded with competing merchants in West Florida and Louisiana in order to minimize their dependence on a single company and to disperse their trade debts. American traders simply offered an additional channel for future pursuit of this strategy. Both the Choctaws and the Chickasaws, however, were reluctant to permit the United States to situate trade houses on or within the borders of their territories. Close personal ties with traders working for companies in the Spanish colonies, in addition to apprehension over the motives of many Americans, contributed significantly to this policy of caution. In December 1789 George Washington sent a message to the chiefs of the Choctaw nation, asking them to "guard and protect" his emissary, Major Doughty, and to "show him the places at which trading posts shall be established in order to furnish you with goods."[22] Washington had some reason to expect support for such posts from the Choctaws, given their interest in expanding their own trade opportunities. What he did not understand, though, was how careful and selective Indian people could be in forging trade relations.

In August 1792 a group of Chickasaw and Choctaw delegates met with United States commissioners at Nashville to renew the relationship initiated several years earlier at Hopewell. The main purpose of this conference for the Americans was to solicit these Indian nations' allegiance in the midst of Cherokee and Northwest Indian wars, but the development of trade connections was also on the agenda. Andrew Pickens proposed to the Chickasaw delegates in attendance that a post be located at the mouth of Bear Creek, flowing northward into the Tennessee River near present-day Florence, Alabama. "Trade at that place will be most advantageous to you, where, beside clothing and other necessaries, arms and ammunition shall be kept in plenty…. The people living south of you," he argued, "supply you very sparingly; the President wishes you to have all things in plenty, and be in a situation to defend yourselves against your enemies." Piamingo of Long Town, however, rejected Pickens's proposal. He feared that such a post "would occasion blood to be spilled," referring to the strong likelihood of Indian visitors facing hostility from Tennessee settlers. "If all things were on a right footing," Piamingo would not object. "But it seems as though I had reached over the heads of enemies, to take hold of you. Could I once see the day that whites and reds were all friends, it would be like getting new eye-sight."[23]

The years 1792–93 were an especially trying time for residents and diplomats in the Gulf South. The United States fueled Chickasaw animosity against the Creeks and even considered drawing the Choctaws into the war. Merchants were tugging at Indians from different directions, larger quantities of alcohol were pouring into the trade, and a series of droughts was drastically reducing the amount of food that Indians could produce.[24] But the most serious single threat to peace between Spain and its Indian allies was a fort established in 1791 by Manuel Gayoso de Lemos, governor of the Natchez District. The fort of Nogales was built on the Mississippi River at the site of present-day Vicksburg, just below the mouth of the Yazoo River, and drew heavy opposition from Choctaws led by Franchimastabè and Taboca. Spain claimed this site on the basis that Great Britain had purchased it from the Choctaws during its governance of West Florida. The fort was intended to ward off agents of American land companies, which had received grants from the Georgia legislature, but Gayoso also argued that it would assist Choctaws who crossed the Mississippi to hunt and would provide a place for them to sell their pelts.[25] John Turnbull quickly established a trading post outside the fort. By the spring of 1792, Choctaw protest against trade at Nogales was escalating. Turnbull's Nogales store hurt white traders who were, in the words of Gayoso, "married to the daughters of that nation."[26] Many of the traders with Choctaw family ties, it just so happened, also worked for William Panton's company. Stephen Minor, the Spanish government's emissary to the Choctaws, was warned by Benjamin James that the ruin of these traders "might cause the Indians to move and do us harm, stealing our horses, negroes, and other things" in the Natchez area in order to make up for the loss suffered by their relatives.[27]

The dispute between the Spanish and the Choctaws over Nogales was finally resolved in a conference at Natchez, where Chickasaw as well as Choctaw delegates signed a treaty on May 14, 1792. Choctaw leaders were paid for recognizing Spain's possession of the land around Nogales and the boundary between Spanish and Indian territories east of the Mississippi was clearly delineated.[28] Meanwhile, Spain assigned Jean de la Villebeuvre to serve as a special commissary to the Choctaws and Chickasaws. The French-born military officer was charged with persuading Indians to drive away American traders and with arranging for the construction of a new fort on the Tombigbee River, where an important French fort had once stood. In October 1793 the Spanish negotiated a treaty at Nogales, attempting to pull the Choctaws, Chickasaws, and Creeks into a confederation for more effective vigilance against American encroachment.[29]

The final factor complicating relations across the boundary between Indian and non-Indian territories in the Gulf South was the United States government's own attempt to expand Indian trade while limiting white settlement. In order to secure an alliance with Indian nations in the region claimed by Spain, the Washington administration had to demonstrate a capacity to provide them with presents and trade goods as well as to protect their land against intrusion by its own citizens. In the early years of the republic, this was easier said than done. On August 26, 1790, Washington issued a proclamation that was published in various southern newspapers. It warned citizens of the United States not to violate the treaties made at Hopewell four years earlier with the Choctaw and Chickasaw nations and notified them of his intention to enforce a new congressional law regulating trade and intercourse with Indian nations. Civil and military officers and all other citizens of the United States were required "to govern themselves according to the treaties and act aforesaid; as they will answer the contrary at their peril."[30]

To a great extent, this policy was designed to enhance the United States' position in its ongoing negotiations with Spain over the lower Mississippi Valley. But it also reflected the early republic's dependence upon trade for maintaining peaceful borders with sovereign Indian nations. In October 1792 Secretary of State Thomas Jefferson wrote to the American commissioners in Madrid:

> You know that the frontiers of her Provinces, as well as of our States, are inhabited by Indians holding justly the right of occupation, and leaving to Spain and to us only the claim of excluding other nations from among them, and of becoming ourselves the purchasers of such portions of land from time to time as they chuse to sell. We have the thought that the dictates of *interest*, as well as *humanity* enjoined mutual endeavors with those Indians to live in peace with both nations, and we have scrupulously observed that conduct. Our Agent with the Indians bordering on the territories of Spain, has a standing instruction to use his best endeavors to prevent them from committing acts of hostility against the Spanish settlements.[31]

Although Jefferson still denied that Spain had any valid claim to the territory, he understood that "Indians on our frontier have treaties with Spain and us." And of course he dismissed a Spanish charge that the United States was meddling with allies of Spain:

> We have endeavored to cultivate their friendship, to merit it by presents, charities, and exhortations to peace with their neighbors,

and particularly with the subjects of Spain. We have carried on some little commerce with them, merely to supply their wants. Spain too has made them presents, traded with them, kept agents among them, though their country is within the limits established as ours at the general peace. However, Spain has chosen to have it understood that she has some claim to some parts of that country, and that it must be one of the subjects of our present negotiations. Out of respect for her then, we have considered her pretensions to the country, though it was impossible to believe them serious, as coloring pretensions to a concern with those Indians on the same ground with our own, and we were willing to let them go on till a treaty should set things to right between us."[32]

Spanish officials stationed in Louisiana were keenly aware of the United States' overtures to Indian nations in the disputed zone. While Jefferson was explaining policy to commissioners in Madrid, Jean de la Villebeuvre reported to Louisiana governor Carondelet from the Choctaw nation that an American officer brought gifts to the Choctaws "as a sign of friendship" and urged them to "maintain the peace with all the nations."[33] Carondelet then wrote to the conde de Aranda, "The purpose of the United States is clear; persuaded by the misfortunes which their arms have experienced, that the republic has not arrived at a position of sufficient power to conquer or destroy the Indian nations, not to injure this colony as long as they are our allies, they have changed their plans, adopting the policy of attracting our nations away from us by trade and presents."[34] Spanish colonial officials responded to American trade initiatives by bolstering support for the Panton Company, which benefited already from the strong personal ties between its traders and Indian families. When Americans attempted to operate a warehouse at Chickasaw Bluffs (present-day Memphis) on the Mississippi River in the summer of 1792, Governor Carondelet worried that the Panton Company would be reduced to trading only with the lower Choctaws. "As the upper Choctaws are the best hunters and warriors of the nation and as they are closer to that warehouse than to Panton's, all of them will go there." But by the summer of 1795, this company was operating its own trade store at Chickasaw Bluffs—under the protection of the newly constructed fort of San Fernando de las Barrancas.[35]

The United States continued to pursue an aggressive trade policy in the Gulf South, clearly trying to avoid the kind of military confrontation with Indians that proved so costly north of the Ohio River. The federal government opened its first public trade house on the eastern border of Creek territory in 1795 and, after the Treaty of San Lorenzo was signed, would establish other posts among the Choctaws and Chickasaws. Carondelet had worried that American trade would ruin the Panton Company's commerce with southern Indians. But the company easily turned to the United States government for support as soon as the disputed zone became American territory.[36]

Inside the Indian nations of the Gulf South and the rival empires that bordered them, a third type of boundary also underwent remapping during the 1780s and 1790s. What are called the Spanish provinces of Louisiana and Florida for convenience at one level of analysis constituted a diverse society of different ethnic groups at the end of the eighteenth century. The most significant boundary within colonial society was that between slaves and settlers, but each of these social statuses included people with various origins and positions. Within the slave population were descendants of Africans who had been shipped to Louisiana a half-century earlier and newcomers arriving from West Africa, Caribbean islands, and other parts of North America. The free population contained descendants of French and German settlers, more recent Acadian and Canary Island immigrants, and English and Anglo-American settlers. This multiethnic and multilingual colonial society proved difficult to govern, but represented Spain's commitment to expanding population, plantation agriculture, and commerce in its Gulf South possessions. The outbreak of revolution first inside France and then in Saint Domingue, its most important slave colony, intensified Spanish officials' fears of rebellion among Louisiana's Francophone population. Their efforts to secure peaceful borders with Indian nations as well as with the United States were significantly sharpened by anxiety over internal insurrection.[37]

Indian societies still occupying and governing the land contested by Spain and the United States were also diverse and complex. The Choctaw, Chickasaw, and Creek nations interacted with each other across territorial boundaries and often conflicted over shifting borderlands that lay between them. Within each Indian nation, towns maintained a great deal of political autonomy, and kinship networks operated as distinct social groups. Further complicating intertribal and intratribal boundaries was the growing number of non-Indian traders who married into Indian families. Not only did these individuals wield influence upon particular village and tribal leaders, but their children began to grow into a distinct ethnic group inside Indian society.[38]

The multiplicity of boundaries inside both Indian and colonial societies in the Gulf South had a major effect on life in the disputed imperial borderland between Spain and the United States. The space contested by international groups proved to be inviting ground for border crossings of various kinds, just when colonial rulers were escalating efforts to raise the legal barriers between them. A wide variety of individuals tried to remap social boundaries and ethnic identities in order to escape bondage or seek opportunity. Some people crossed international boundaries for trade, some for employment and mobility, and others in attempts to find freedom. As Spain and the United States tried to solidify social and political boundaries, the borderland became even more volatile as a means of resistance or flight. While some individuals worked to support the empires' goals in the disputed zone, others intentionally or inadvertently acted to subvert them.[39]

Many men who were serving the interests of companies and empires crossed boundaries in their daily life. Traders and officials from various geographical backgrounds moved effectively between different ethnic groups, even contributing to the emergence of people with newly mixed identities. In this contested territory of the Old Southwest during the Age of Washington, Anglo-Americans demonstrated a willingness to take Indian wives equal to that of Franco-Americans who had traded in the region much longer. The versatile and improvisational behavior of these men, like evidence from other colonial regions, belies a still prevailing notion that the English and their American descendants spurned trade and intermarriage with American Indians.[40] Benjamin James arrived as an agent of Georgia land interests in 1785, but became a resident trader at the Choctaw town of West Yazoo and fathered three Choctaw children before his departure in 1797. Ebenezer Folsom, from North Carolina, served as a Choctaw interpreter for the Spanish government. Like his brothers Nathaniel and Elmore, he married a Choctaw woman. Turner Brashears left Maryland during the American Revolution, became a trader in Choctaw country for the Panton Company, and married a daughter of Taboca, the Choctaw chief. John Turnbull, the aggressive rival of Panton, relied heavily upon the trading activity of two sons born to an Indian woman. Other non-Indian guests among Mississippi Indians included Louis Catin, a free mulatto trader living in a Choctaw village, and Jean de la Villebeuvre, the French-born soldier serving as Spain's special emissary to the Choctaws. Stephen Minor, an Anglo-American from Pennsylvania, was also employed in the Spanish military.[41]

Slaves frequently crossed borders in this disputed territory for a different, but no less important, set of reasons. Many attempted to free themselves by fleeing either to Indian country or to another colonial province. Others were sold to Indians or Indian traders within the larger process of slavery's territorial expansion. The accelerating movement of black men and women across the region aggravated official attempts to maintain rigid social boundaries, allowing some slaves to take advantage of uncertainty while subjecting others to the schemes of slave dealers. In 1784 two young African-Americans, Bob and Nance, were being taken into the Choctaw nation by John Cole from North Carolina, whose brother was a trader. Two white men, with their faces and hands blackened, attacked Cole and captured Bob and Nance. The slaves were probably sold by these bandits in Pensacola.[42] Two years later in the Natchez District, London and Kate were helped by Margaret Woods in an escape from Stephen Minor.[43] In 1788 a Negro owned by Alexander McGillivray's sister and sometimes hired out in Pensacola was passing as a free man in New Orleans with a document provided by the commandant of Mobile.[44]

In 1780–90 a slave named James escaped from his owner David Hodge in Pensacola, was captured by Alibamon Indians, and was brought to Mobile. The commandant gave him to Choctaw trader Simon Favre's mother, who had lost a slave killed by Indians in 1783.[45] That same winter, twenty to thirty slaves were moving from Choctaw territory to the Big Black River, where Hardy Perry ended his twenty or so years of trading.[46] In May 1790 "a Negro fellow named Tom or Peter" was being taken from Nashville to Natchez by Andrew Jackson. He had run away from his owner in New Orleans and was passing as a free man on the Nashville-to-Natchez road. The United States decided to return this slave "to Keep us a good Understanding."[47]

Remapping Mississippi during the Age of Washington was a far more complicated process than Spanish and American diplomats could have imagined. Their dispute over a territorial boundary overlay various forms of negotiation among competing groups and rival interests. By examining the interconnectedness among different types of boundaries—between empires, between Indian nations and colonial provinces, and between people inhabiting native and colonial societies—we can realize how the cultural space that eventually became the state of Mississippi was shaped by intercultural as well as international relations. Proposing a new comparative framework for North American history, Jeremy Adelman and Stephen Aron write that "as colonial borderlands gave way to national borders, fluid and 'inclusive' intercultural frontiers yielded to hardened and more 'exclusive' hierarchies." The expansion of United States interests into the lower Mississippi Valley would indeed jeopardize previously formed alliances and exchanges in this particular borderland. But as the region was being redefined on political maps at the end of the eighteenth century, social boundaries and personal identities continued to be contested among people interacting with each other on the ground.[48]

NOTES

1. *The Writings of George Washington*, ed. Worthington Chauncy Ford, 14 vols. (New York: G. P. Putnam's Sons, 1889–93), 10:255.

2. Charles Gayarré, *History of Louisiana: The Spanish Domination* (New Orleans: Redfield, 1854), 393–94.

3. Michel-Rolph Trouillot, *Silencing the Past: Power and the Production of History* (Boston: Beacon Press, 1995).

4. Jack P. Greene, *Imperatives, Behaviors, and Identities: Essays in Early American Cultural History* (Charlottesville: University Press of Virginia, 1992), 2.

5. Peter Sahlins, *Boundaries: The Making of France and Spain in the Pyrenees* (Berkeley and Los Angeles: University of California Press, 1989); Renato Rosaldo, *Culture and Truth: The Remaking of Social Analysis* (Boston: Beacon Press, 1989); Thomas M. Wilson and Hastings Donnan, eds., *Border Identities: Nation and State at International Frontiers* (Cambridge: Cambridge University Press, 1998).

6. Important works that have recently focused on the population inhabiting present-day Mississippi and Alabama at the end of the eighteenth century are Mary Ann Wells, *Native Land: Mississippi, 1540–1798* (Jackson: University Press of Mississippi, 1994); Claudio Saunt, *A New Order of Things: Property, Power, and the Transformation of the Creek Indians, 1733–1816* (Cambridge: Cambridge University Press, 1999); James Taylor Carson, *Searching for the Bright Path: The Mississippi Choctaws from Contact to Removal* (Lincoln: University of Nebraska Press, 1999); and Greg O'Brien, *Choctaws in a Revolutionary Age: 1750–1830* (Lincoln: University of Nebraska Press, 2002).

7. *American State Papers: Foreign Relations*, 3 vols. (Washington, D.C.: Gales and Seaton, 1832), 1:546–49; Samuel Flagg Bemis, *Pinckney's Treaty: America's Advantage from Europe's Distress, 1783–1800* (1926; rev. ed., New Haven: Yale University Press, 1960); Arthur Preston Whitaker, *The Spanish-American Frontier, 1783–1795: The Westward Movement and the Spanish Retreat in the Mississippi Valley* (1927; Lincoln: University of Nebraska Press, 1969).

8. Whitaker, *Spanish-American Frontier*, 201. For a new approach to the United States' response to the dissolution of Spain's American empire, but one that still focuses on policy makers instead of people living in the contested regions, see James E. Lewis Jr., *The American Union and the Problem of Neighborhood: The United States and the Collapse of the Spanish Empire, 1783–1829* (Chapel Hill: University of North Carolina Press, 1998).

9. *Writings of George Washington*, 10:488; Bemis, *Pinckney's Treaty*, 95–98; Charles Royster, *The Fabulous History of the Dismal Swamp Company* (New York: Alfred A. Knopf, 1999), 294–98.

10. *American State Papers: Indian Affairs*, 2 vols. (Washington, D.C.: Gales and Seaton, 1832), 1:53.

11. Thomas P. Abernethy, *The South in the New Nation, 1789–1819* (Baton Rouge: Louisiana State University Press, 1961), 74–191; C. Peter Magrath, *Yazoo: Law and Politics in the New Republic: The Case of Fletcher v. Peck* (Providence: Brown University Press, 1966).

12. *American State Papers: Indian Affairs*, 1:115.

13. *The Papers of George Washington: Presidential Series*, ed. Dorothy Twohig et al., 9 vols. to date (Charlottesville: University Press of Virginia, 1987–), 7:411–12; Whitaker, *Spanish-American Frontier*, 126–33.

14. Jack D. L. Holmes, *Gayoso: The Life of a Spanish Governor in the Mississippi Valley, 1789–1799* (Baton Rouge: Louisiana State University Press, 1965), 33–38, 139–45.

15. John Walton Caughey, *McGillivray of the Creeks* (Norman: University of Oklahoma Press, 1938), 65.

16. Whitaker, *Spanish-American Frontier*, 139, 153–70; Holmes, *Gayoso*, 146–57; Jack D. L. Holmes, "Juan de la Villebeuvre and Spanish Indian Policy in West Florida, 1784–1797," *Florida Historical Quarterly* 58 (April 1980): 387–99.

17. Daniel H. Usner Jr., *American Indians in the Lower Mississippi Valley: Social and Economic Histories* (Lincoln: University of Nebraska Press, 1998), 43, 74.

18. Holmes, "Villebeuvre and Spanish Indian Policy," 392; Wells, *Native Land*, 185–208. For an insightful look at the Treaty of Hopewell that advances our understanding of the Choctaws' diplomatic protocol, see Greg O'Brien, "The Conqueror Meets the Unconquered: Negotiating Cultural Boundaries on the Post-Revolutionary Southern Frontier," *Journal of Southern History* 67 (February 2001): 39–72.

19. Miró to Sonora, June 1, 1787, and O'Neil to Miró, June 8, 1787, Papeles Procedentes de la Isla Cuba, legajo 37, Archivo General de Indias, Seville. William S. Coker and Thomas D. Watson, *Indian Traders of the Southeastern Spanish Borderlands: Panton, Leslie & Company and John Forbes & Company, 1783–1847* (Gainesville: University Presses of Florida, 1986) is a comprehensive treatment of these companies and their role in Indian commerce and policy.

20. Coker and Watson, *Indian Traders*, 121–24.

21. Caughey, *McGillivray of the Creeks*, 228–29.

22. *Papers of George Washington: Presidential Series*, 4:416.

23. *American State Papers: Indian Affairs*, 1:284–88.

24. Cabinet Opinion on Secret Indian Agent, June 1, 1793, *The Writings of Thomas Jefferson*, ed. Paul Leicester Ford, 10 vols. (New York: G. P. Putnam's Sons, 1892–99), 6:275–77; de la Villebeuvre to Carondelet, September 5, 1792, *Spain in the Mississippi Valley, 1765–1794*, ed. and trans. Lawrence Kinnaird, 3 vols. (Washington, D.C.: American Historical Association, 1946–49), 3:75–77; de la Villebeuvre to Gayoso, August 30, 1793, Dispatches of the Spanish Governors of Louisiana (hereafter DSGL), WPA transcripts, Louisiana Historical Center, New Orleans.

25. Gayoso to Carondelet, January 17, 1792, DSGL.

26. Gayoso to Carondelet, April 14, 1792, DSGL.

27. Diary of Lieutenant don Esteban Minor, March 25, 1792, DSGL. Also see Christopher J. Malloy and Charles A. Weeks, "Shuttle Diplomacy, Eighteenth-Century Style: Stephen Minor's First Mission to the Choctaws and Journal, May-June 1791," *Journal of Mississippi History* 55 (February 1993): 31–51.

28. Holmes, "Villebeuvre and Spanish Indian Policy," 394–95; Coker and Watson, *Indian Traders*, 157–81; Wells, *Native Land*, 194–200.

29. Gayoso to Carondelet, July 21, 1792, *East Tennessee Historical Society Publications* 27 (1955): 90.

30. *Papers of George Washington: Presidential Series*, 6:342.

31. *Writings of Thomas Jefferson*, 6:118–19.

32. *Writings of Thomas Jefferson*, 6:336–37.

33. De la Villebeuvre to Carondelet, September 5, 1792, *Spain in the Mississippi Valley*, 3:75.

34. Carondelet to conde de Aranda, October 1, 1792, *East Tennessee Historical Society Publications* 28 (1956), 129–30.

35. Carondelet to conde de Aranda, July 31, 1792, Papers of Panton, Leslie & Company, University of West Florida Library, Pensacola; Abernethy, *South in the New Nation*, 148–49; Coker and Watson, *Indian Traders*, 198–99; David J. Weber, *The Spanish Frontier in North America* (New Haven: Yale University Press, 1992), 283–85.

36. Coker and Watson, *Indian Traders*, 192–201; Usner, *American Indians in the Lower Mississippi Valley*, 75–78; Reginald Horsman, "The Indian Policy of an 'Empire for Liberty,'" in *Native Americans and the Early Republic*, ed. Frederick E. Hoxie, Ronald Hoffman, and Peter J. Albert (Charlottesville: University Press of Virginia, 1999), 46–49.

37. Morris S. Arnold, *Colonial Arkansas, 1686–1804: A Social and Cultural History* (Fayetteville: University of Arkansas Press, 1991); Carl A. Brasseaux, *The Founding of New Acadia: The Beginnings of Acadian Life in Louisiana, 1765–1803* (Baton Rouge: Louisiana State University Press, 1987); Gwendolyn Midlo Hall, *Africans in Colonial Louisiana: The Development of Afro-Creole Culture in the Eighteenth Century* (Baton Rouge: Louisiana State University Press, 1992); Kimberly S. Hanger, *Bounded Lives, Bounded Places: Free Black Society in Colonial New Orleans, 1769–1803* (Durham: Duke University Press, 1997); Thomas N. Ingersoll, *Mammon and Manon: The First Slave Society in the Deep South, 1718–1819* (Knoxville: University of Tennessee Press, 1998); Daniel H. Usner Jr., *Indians, Settlers, and Slaves in a Frontier Exchange Economy: The Lower Mississippi Valley Before 1783* (Chapel Hill: University of North Carolina Press, 1992).

38. See note 6.

39. Wilson and Donnan, *Border Identities*, 10–25.

40. For an insightful critique of the simplistic dichotomy between British and non-British types of colonization, see Philip D. Morgan, "Encounters between British and 'Indigenous' Peoples, c. 1500–c. 1800," in *Empire and Others: British Encounters with Indigenous Peoples, 1600–1850*, ed. Martin Daunton and Rick Halpern (Philadelphia: University of Pennsylvania Press, 1999), 42–78.

41. *East Tennessee Historical Society Publications* 22 (1950): 146–47; 24 (1952): 111–12; 27 (1955): 90, 95; 28 (1956): 127–28; 29 (1957): 146; Kinnaird, *Spain in the Mississippi Valley,* 2:148–49, 154–55, 158; Gayoso to Carondelet, January 17, 1792, DSGL; Diary of Minor, March 13–April 3, 1792, DSGL.

42. Testimony against Lawrence by John Cole, Mobile, July 29, 1785, Papeles Procedentes de la Isla Cuba, transcripts, North Carolina State Archives, Raleigh.

43. Minor Family Papers, 1783–1852, Natchez Trace Collection, University of Texas, Austin.

44. Caughey, *McGillivray of the Creeks.*

45. Suit for return of runaway slave belonging to David Hodge of Pensacola, September 17, 1789–January 11, 1790, Spanish Judicial Records, Louisiana Historical Center, New Orleans.

46. Grand-Pré to Miró, January 4, 1790, *Spain in the Mississippi Valley,* 2:291.

47. Robertson to Gayoso, May 17, 1790, *East Tennessee Historical Society Publications* 23 (1951): 86.

48. Jeremy Adelman and Stephen Aron, "From Borderlands to Borders: Empires, Nation-States, and the Peoples in Between in North American History," *American Historical Review* 104 (June 1999): 814–41.

Chapter 2

MAPPING THE "AMERICAN SOUTH"

Image, Archive, and the Textual Construction of Regional
Identity in the Age of Washington

MARTIN BRÜCKNER

In the 1796 "Farewell Address," taking stock of his political fight against sectionalism and local violence, President Washington delivers a blunt and for many a disturbing critique of the conception of regional identity. "In contemplating the causes which may disturb our Union," Washington warns Congress and the general public, "it occurs as matter of serious concern that any ground should have been furnished for characterizing parties by Geographical discriminations: Northern and Southern, Atlantic and Western; whence designing men may endeavour to excite a belief that there is a real difference of local interests and views."[1] Washington here deliberately challenges the perceived notion that regions are a geographic, physical reality by addressing their "real difference" as being the result of man-made artifice and underhanded scheming. More precisely, Washington reminds his audience that just as "local interests and views" are used by "designing men" to assert regional identities, they are in fact fundamentally rhetorical constructions, and as such contingent on literary conventions rather than on a particular region's geographic space.

It is significant to note that Washington's antiregionalistic remarks, pitting his constructionist view against an implied sectional essentialism, call attention to the directional signifiers of cartography, the "Geographical discriminations: Northern and Southern, Atlantic and Western." In a speech that is ostensibly devoted to bridging the growing gulf between some of the then 16 U.S. states, the outgoing president concedes that during his watch the geopolitical figure of the nation has become redrawn into a dangerously simplistic quadrangle. Where throughout the 1780s federalists and anti-federalists envisioned the code of law as the primary agent conferring a distinct formal identity upon particular regions, Washington now diagnoses a nation that has grown accustomed to using the signs of the cartographic grid for describing regions and local identities. By drawing this simplistic and polarized overview map of the United States, Washington accepts as a political reality that cartographic writings are powerful agents that inform and even structure the emotional construction of American identities. As much as Washington is lamenting the fact that the mere suggestion of cartographic terms like "the North" and "the South" have become a polemical means to "excite" the passions of a local people, he ultimately acknowledges it is in large part the design of maps that has enabled "designing men" to present regionalism as a matter of both local sentiment and personal affect, and thus as a salient belief structure.

Writing this essay on George Washington and conceptions of the late-eighteenth-century South, I wish to follow Washington's cautionary remarks and explore the cartographic representation of the "Southern" region in selected examples of eighteenth-century British and American maps. Maps have long served as the textual backdrop through which scholars have traced political events and socioeconomic factors in an effort to define the beginnings of the southern region. We can quickly point to regional studies on settlement patterns, economic systems, climate and topography, and political boundaries, all of which deploy more or less faithfully the images of eighteenth-century maps showing southern provinces and states.[2] The map historian William Cumming in his magisterial study *The Southeast in Early Maps* defines the critical role maps have played in the field of Southern culture studies. "Through these cartographic records," he writes, "one can trace the origin and development of the fascinating misconceptions of the continent in the minds of the early explorers; they show vividly the expansion of the frontier and the shifting location of Indian tribes; they throw light on the complex history of the imperialistic struggles of France, Spain, and England during the period; and they delineate—often erroneously—shifting political divisions and boundary surveys."[3]

Cumming describes the cartographic archive pertaining to the American South according to an older perception that views maps as mirrors of the real world, a perception that is still prevalent in cartographic dictionaries and handbooks.[4] Regional studies tended to follow suit, and have over time unquestioningly assumed that maps were the ideal factual records for proving the reality of regions and regionalist ideologies.[5] But while this understanding of maps has provided historians and geographers with a valuable tool for illustrating the results of empirical and comparative studies of local places, in practice when discussing maps showing southern regions it has primarily served to reify rather than explain the rationale for partitioning American identities along cartographic lines. In the specific context of the late-eighteenth-century comments by Washington, I find that neither detailed histories of geopolitical borderlines nor statistical charts on demography, productivity, and literacy are particularly helpful for explaining exactly why a sparsely populated region should be called the "American South," and why a geographically diverse people should subordinate their local identities to the explicitly cartographic labels of "South," "southern," and "southernness."[6]

For the purposes of this essay, I want to make the relationship of eighteenth-century cartography to regional studies the object of critical analysis. I am taking my cues from Edward Ayers and Peter Onuf, who have reminded us that, just as "American identities are rooted in places on the national map, . . . the national compass that gives us our bearings, the map that defines where we stand, is itself an imaginative construction, an icon of nationhood."[7] As I wish to consider maps as icons of the American South and ultimately southern identity, I will be discussing maps as a text rather than as a mirror of history or geographic reality. In this I follow the recent development in the field of historical cartography initiated by J. B. Harley, who contends that maps are first and foremost textual artifacts which, like all formal systems of modern communication, operate through signs, symbols, and rhetorical conventions.[8] Moreover, I follow his assertion that, like all other texts, maps are always collaborative products. They abide by technological rules as well as those of the marketplace; the concrete map image and text are shaped as much by the interaction between individual cartographers, publishers, and map readers as by patronage, censorship, and the state.[9]

In what follows, then, I will argue eighteenth-century maps invented "the South" as a region, and examine the ways in which cartographic texts depicted and informed popular notions of "southern" identity.[10] Bearing Washington's antiregionalist warning in mind, I have to ask: When in the course of Washington's life did the label "American South" first start to appear on maps? What were the popular frames of reference and organizational categories used for naming and placing the South? And, more important, how did these maps represent British American colonists and later American citizens in terms of a southern regional identity? With these questions in mind, I will present three phases in the course of which eighteenth-century maps represented the American South as a distinct region. At the same time, I will discuss several representative maps as popular texts, as artifacts that can be read with the same kind of attention and analytical tools with which we usually examine printed words and images. Thus, I will examine the literary properties of maps in order to better understand the ways in which cartography shapes our understanding of regions in America. But ultimately, I wish to explore some of the historical cognitive processes by which maps performed a certain kind of identity work that allowed (or forced) Washington and his contemporaries to debate the reality of a southern regional identity inside the compass of an emerging national consciousness.

PHASE ONE: THE SOUTH AND THE CARTOGRAPHIC
MARGINS OF EMPIRE

The cartographic history of the region Washington addressed as "Southern" begins in Restoration England, between the 1670s and 1690s and on the desks and drawing boards of the Plantations Office, better known as the Board of Trade. In these decades the British Empire introduced for the first time in its history a modern centralized bureaucracy that, equipped with office buildings and civil servants and its own letterhead, was given the explicit charge to collect information on the Crown's colonial possessions.[11] Both the king and the Parliament demanded that the office provide new analytical and archival schemes through which to define, classify, and record the colonial lands in America to better evaluate their real and future economic value. In response, the officers William Petty (focusing on Ireland) and John Locke (focusing on the Caribbean) proposed land management plans that formed the basis of modern statistical surveys and, more famously, modern theories of property, personal autonomy, and the role of government. Working with these men was the lesser-known professional civil servant William Blathwayt, who during the 1680s compiled the comprehensive cartographic archive that is today known as the *Blathwayt Atlas* (1683). Consisting of print and manuscript maps, the atlas represented the English colonies in America in great topographic detail and, for our purposes more interestingly, made official use of the cartographic rationale for sectioning off the area that today constitutes the southern region.[12]

Until Blathwayt's atlas, the few maps made by English cartographers that actually made it into the popular sphere of scribal or printed artifacts were providing a highly abstract, metaphorical, and above all fragmentary image of the American South. The most prominent atlas and textbook maps of John Ogilby, James Moxon, John Sellers, and Richard Morden focused primarily on the geodetic boundaries as defined by the various land charters that established the provinces of Virginia and greater Carolina. Using cartographic symbols and drawings to embellish rather than describe the land, the majority of late-seventeenth-century maps sketched the southern provinces separately as discrete and unconnected territories.[13] Only a handful of regional overview maps, in particular those of the Dutch cartographer Willem Blaeu, showed the southern region collectively and established, at least visually, the cartographic framework of a yet untitled southern region somewhere between 29° and 39° latitude.[14] The cartographic image of this region, however, changed dramatically when at the beginning of the eighteenth century the growing competition among the European empires suddenly demanded regional representations rather than local ones. Beginning with Guillaume Delisle's "Carte du Mexique et de la Floride" (1703) and "Carte de la Louisiane" (1718), French, Dutch, and German mapmakers expanded or contracted the southern region, depending on the imperial sponsor. The boundaries of the region moved up and down the Atlantic coastline, at times reaching New York, and in and out of the western hinterland: French maps considered the Appalachian Mountains the western border, while British maps aimed for the Mississippi River.

In his function of secretary of the Plantations Office, William Blathwayt constantly scoured the European markets for "American" maps, while sharing freely his cartographic archive with London-based mapmakers. Among the foremost cartographers at the turn of the eighteenth century was Herman Moll, who, as William Cumming observes, "was as open and effective a protagonist of British territorial claims in North America as was Delisle for the French."[15] Moll produced one of England's first popular general atlases, called *The World Described* (1709–20). The centerpiece of Moll's atlas was the 1715 "Map of the Dominions of Great Britain in North America" (fig. 1). And it is with this map that I want to begin my discussion of the first phase in which maps and the conventions of cartographic composition created the image of the American South as a distinct region.[16]

On first sight, the reader realizes that the map was a representational map, designed for public display, artistic appreciation, and above all for showcasing diverse mapping strategies. The map reader is torn between different frames of reference: our eyes wander between the topographical map in the upper half, the picture inset on the middle right, and the set of

Fig. 1. "A New and Exact Map of the Dominions of the King of Great Britain on the Continent of North America." Herman Moll, *The World Described* (London, 1715). Courtesy of the American Antiquarian Society.

smaller maps lining the bottom margin. In its total appearance, written words compete with symbolic and pictorial images for the reader's attention. One way of examining the map, then, is to start at the top, the designated "North" of the British American domain.

At the top, the textual space of the map carefully balances the agendas of political power and the mapmakers' patronage. Moll displays the king's title at the top of the map; at the same time, he includes a dedication to his patron Walter Douglass at the map's center, showing the latter's coat of arms. Moll uses both of these signatures to submit North America (as the Crown's property) and his map (as a subsidized artifact) to the proper authorities without upsetting the balance of power, courtly censors, or social etiquette. Having thus sorted out the issue of authority, Moll presents the image of British America in the form of a topographic map that is supplemented by notes on the margins describing the population, the fishing industry, and the postal roads.

Going to the center of the map, we see a large picture inset of Niagara Falls showing beavers building a dam. This vignette is a classic example of how imperial mapmakers depicted the popular fantasy of America being an industrious colony. For the metropolitan map reader in London, America here appears as a colony in which the inhabitants raise revenue by working the natural environment and by forming a natural society in which labor is performed without supervision and by natural instinct. For the American colonists, of course, this vignette suggested a different picture: by presenting the American population exclusively in the animal form of the beaver, Moll's map conveyed the idea that the Empire viewed both the Native American and the British American population in terms that dehumanized the individual on the one hand, while on the other (wittingly or not) reducing the American society to the model of a labor camp rather than a self-sufficient and self-governing community.

Parallel to the allegorical story displayed in the vignette, Moll's topographical map reinforces the cartographic story of British colonization. The topographical map ostensibly records the British possessions of landed territories by following standard mapmaking conventions: it traces the lines of coasts, rivers, and mountains; it uses the Mercator projection, the compass, and the geographic grid. In its cartographic sweep of the British dominion, Moll's overview map covers everything from Newfoundland to Virginia—but not the South. When it reaches the Carolinas, the map abruptly ends as if the mapmaker made a mistake or simply ran out of space. Instead, having omitted the Carolinas from the continental mainland, Moll transposes the image of greater Carolina to the bottom of the map sheet, creating a separate frame that holds a smaller-scale, more detailed map of the Crown's southern possessions.

This representation (or rather misrepresentation) of the British southern colonies is as symptomatic of the ways in which cartographers invented the American South as it suggests far-reaching implications for the cartographic definition of southernness. Moll's cartographic representation suggests that the South literally did not fit and therefore did not belong on the map of imperial British America. This reading can be supported by considering that, although the southern region appears in a magnified and thus privileged scale, it is nonetheless presented unequally in relation to the other British provinces: the Carolinas appear not beside but below, indeed at the lower end of, the comparatively larger collective body of British mainland colonies. Considering the schematic layout of Moll's geodetic signs, we discover that the majority of colonies are distinguished by their immediate boundaries and marked by their territorial contiguity. By contrast, the southernmost region is marked by its visible separation from the imperial domain. Unlike any other geographic region on this map, only the Carolinas are set within a separate frame and thus become visually detached from the North American continent, and implicitly from the regional cultures of the mid-Atlantic area.

Moll's map here symbolically presents the enclosure of the southern region as a distinct and separate territorial entity. Historically speaking, Moll's map illustrates what the British media were already reporting to their audience—namely that, as Jack Greene has shown on several occasions, the southern province of Carolina was historically and culturally different from the other mainland colonies.[17] But when assuming the cartographer's point of view, Moll's map also reenacts, in addition to economic, social, or political differences, an ancient symbolic tradition by which cartographers and geographers defined southern regions in culturally negative terms. Ever since Ptolemy and Strabo in classical Greece, and more recently Mercator and Varenius in Renaissance Europe, for a cartographer to name a place "South" was to define a place outside of existing normative political and social borders: the South is where you find exotic humanoid creatures like the Sciopod, Doghead, and Cyclops; the South is where the natural order is overturned, natural laws become corrupted, and civilization as Europeans know it ceases to exist. Thus, by locating the Carolinas outside the contiguous body of the colonial domain, Moll's map inscribes an antisouthern bias, a bias that eighteenth-century naturalists and geographers from Count Buffon to Jedidiah Morse would continually develop into a mythopolitical code of classificatory thinking according to which places located in the geographic North outperform and outvalue the South.[18]

Moll's map exacerbated this bias along textual and economic lines. Having implicitly established the American southern region as culturally alien and unstable according to the European standard of regional identity, the map further destabilizes the southern regional image in that its large-scale close-ups present the southern provinces in the culturally negative textual terms of illicit commerce. The inset maps resemble in form and function the so-called Geographical Cards that British merchants and their investors used at gambling tables in public coffeehouses and salons in late-seventeenth- and early-eighteenth-century England.[19] These playing cards tended to show the American continents as well as the British possessions in North America. Though they were crudely made small-scale overview maps, the engravers inscribed a north-south division that rendered the South's relationship to the northern continental territories ambiguous at best. Without immediate cartographic ties to the continent (as established by compass, grid, and borders), Moll's inset maps appear textually mobile, as if they can be cut away from the larger map, shuffled like geographic playing cards, to be deposited either on the table's margins or, given their position on the map, at the bottom end of the empire's deck of political cards—in the vicinity of the West Indies rather than northern continental possessions. In this context, the American South becomes more than an exotic and alienable commodity. If we consider the century's emerging debates over the virtue and vice of commerce, the southern regions' separate representation places the South inside a cultural narrative of fiscal and moral irresponsibility and dubious economic activities.[20]

Here I would like to step back for a moment and reconsider the first phase of mapping the South. I chose Moll's map as a starting point for my discussion because it helped me to understand the degree to which, textually as well as historically, maps formed a southern regional conception. Moll's cartographic example helped me to demonstrate how a map functions like a literary text, how its images and symbols constitute a language that has its own grammar and story. Before proceeding, I think it absolutely important for us to understand that, like a poem or a novel or a legal document, maps provided a creative space that offered not only cartographers but those affiliated with the process of mapmaking and map reading—from sponsors, censors, and printers to students, readers, and consumers—a complex playing field upon which ideological battles were inscribed, new rhetorical strategies were tested, and ultimately the meaning of a place was created. In the context of the late-seventeenth- and early-eighteenth-century British mapping industry, Moll's popular overview map of the British dominions is crucial in that it brackets the southern region and defines it as a separate, exotic, and above all a marginal entity. As the South emerges on the textual margins of the map, it attracts the reader's attention by asserting, if not a physical sense of reality, at least a virtual sense of regional presence. Thus, on the one hand, the map's overdetermined representation of the American South emphasizes regional autonomy and the distinct separation of cultures along geodetic borderlines. On the other hand, by publishing the idea of a southern region within the world of cartographic texts, Moll's map affiliates the South with the popular genre of semifictional maps. In the context of early-eighteenth-century cartography, the representation of the American South as a region was structurally indistinguishable from the maps illustrating Swift's novel *Gulliver's Travels* or travel reports submitted to the Plantations Office.

PHASE TWO: WRITING THE "AMERICAN SOUTH"

It was not until the mid-eighteenth century that British mapmakers began to offer regional overviews of the American South to the general public. With the onset of the British-French conflict in North America, London cartographers were called on by magazine editors and publishers to prepare general but simple maps that explained the territorial claims of France and England and, as the conflict turned into war, showed the location of the British military positions and soldiers.[21] Between 1747 and 1764, periodicals like the *Gentleman's Magazine,* the *London Magazine,* and the *Universal Magazine* published overview maps by Herman Moll, Emmanuel Bowen, and Thomas Kitchin, showing, for example, "the North Parts of America claimed by France under the Name of Louisiana" (Moll) or "the British Plantations extending from Boston in New England to Georgia; including all the back Settlements in the respective Provinces, as far as the Mississipi" (Bowen). During this time the magazine map reader encountered regional maps, dividing British America into northern, middle, and southern colonies. In 1755, as the King's Geographer, Bowen prepared a set of foldout maps dividing the British possessions into three sections. In "A Map of the British and French Settlements in North America [Part Second] containing . . . New York, Pensilvania, New Jersey, Mary Land, North Carolina, South Carolina, Georgia, Louisiana . . . exhibiting the just Boundaries of the French Encroachment," as explained by the title, the southern region that so far had fallen out of the cartographic frame of reference was now reattached to the continent. Defined against a larger continental backdrop ranging from Labrador to Venezuela, the "American South" was defined by this mapmaker in relation to British imperial ambitions; showing only geodetic lines (here between 29° and 41° latitude) and a bare minimum of topographic symbols, the map pulled together the southern parts of British America into an abstract region more representative of geopolitical desires than of actual political realities.[22]

Within a decade Bowen's maps found many imitators. As a result, a new cartographic genre emerged in which mapmakers increasingly depicted the individual colonies as larger regional entities rather than autonomous provinces. Following this generic shift, government maps and commercial atlases presented North America in increasingly directional terms, drawing maps showing just the northern or the southern possessions. The perfect example illustrating this development is the *American Military Pocket Atlas* (1776). Compiled from various sources during the decade before the Revolution by the London mapmakers Robert Sayer and John Bennett, it promised British officers easy access to colonial roads and topographic features by splitting the cartographic image of British America into three sections: the "Northern British Colonies," the "Middle British Colonies," and the "Southern British Colonies."[23]

The third map, called "A General Map of the Southern British Colonies in America" (fig. 2), shows that as a region the American South's dimensions are defined by the map's physical limits to the north, the southern territorial boundaries, and the blank space west of the Mississippi. This kind of image suggests that at least three discursive codes influenced the southern cartographic design. First, speaking from the perspective of the map industry, the southern region emerges as a textual construct that is limited by the physical boundaries established by the size of the atlas. The regional presentation of the South follows a strict cost-profit ratio, which tends to reduce rather than expand the number of maps. Though there is no concrete evidence, I could imagine that a call for three rather than, say, five regional maps representing North America was a practical measure among mapmakers to control the price of the final product. Second, the South emerges rather haphazardly from the rigid code of international property laws. On the one hand, citing diplomatic negotiations and treaties in their preface, the mapmakers not only defined the territorial boundaries between provinces but faithfully enclosed the southern terrain with unbending cartographic lines. On the other hand, they also separated the Middle from the Southern British Colonies with a line drawn between Virginia and North Carolina, ignoring among other things the widely

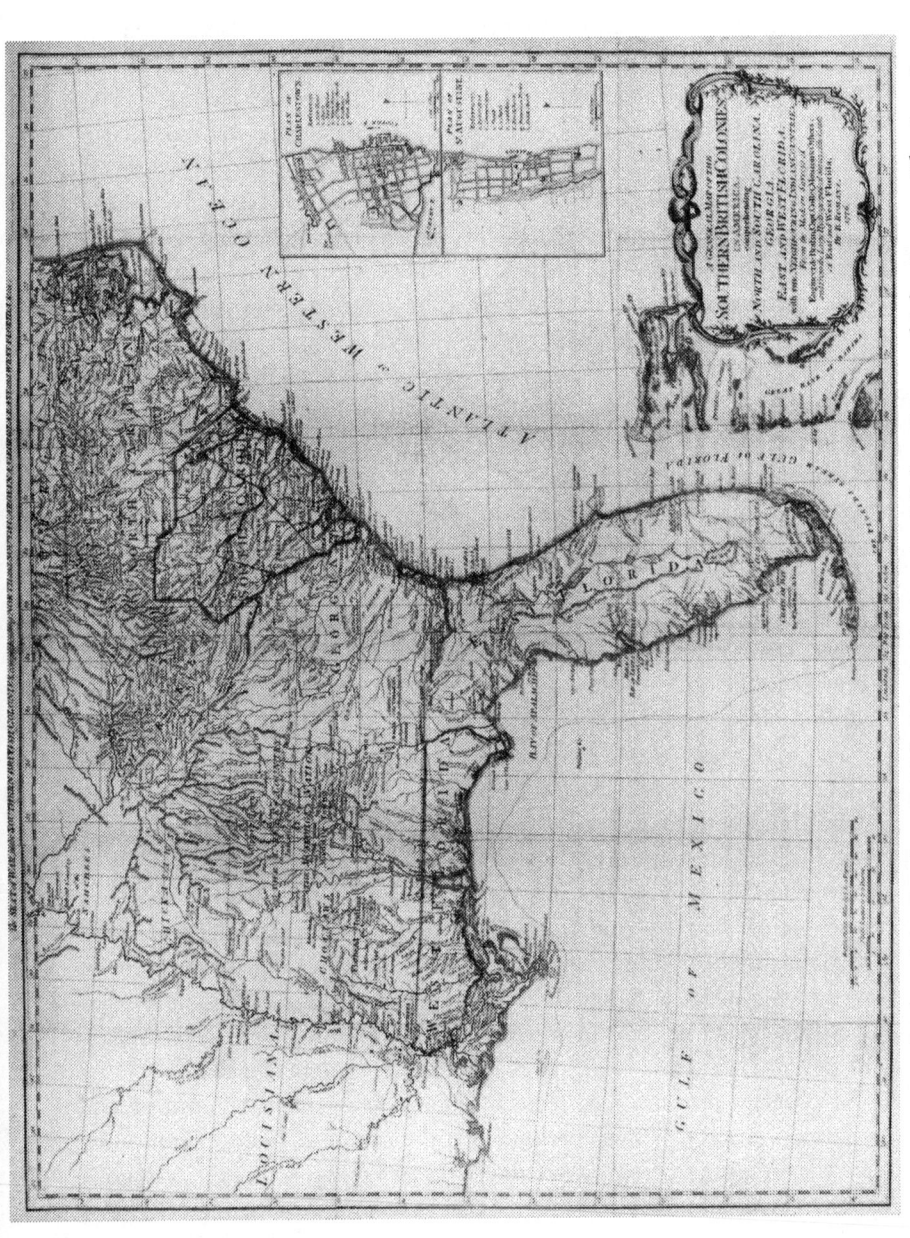

Fig. 2. "A General Map of the Southern British Colonies in America." Robert Sayer and John Bennett, *The American Military Pocket Atlas* (London, 1776). Courtesy of the University of Delaware.

published results of the Mason-Dixon survey. Finally, this arbitrary construction of the South as a regional entity is complicated by the cartographer's lack of information about the western territories. Using an empty, negative textual space for the western territories, the *Military Atlas* creates the Southern Colonies out of a cartographic contrast. By juxtaposing the richly inscribed area of the southern colonies against the uninscribed territories further west, the atlas invokes a popular discursive logic. By the same token that places, like regions, become real precisely because the thick display of map symbols, the same places can be made unreal by the omission of cartographic signs. Considering the popular map reader's expectation that it is the maps's primary objective to show real places, for this atlas to show in great cartographic detail the southern colonies thus serves a dual function: it invents as well as guarantees the South as a certain quantifiable reality, as a distinct place of its own.

In the context of the *Military Atlas* it is here crucial to note that the cartographic definition of the South—however inconclusive at the time—receives its official imprimatur from within the British institution of the military. According to the *Oxford English Dictionary*, in 1777 British intelligence officers describing the Clinton campaign in South Carolina used for the first time the name "American South" in their official correspondence. The popular press quickly followed suit, as newspapers, gazetteers, and magazines co-opted the label to describe the vicissitudes of war in a more limited territorial context. Looking at the "Southern" maps published by magazines and atlases, it becomes obvious that the representation of the American South is the product of imperial institutional convenience, and not the expression of a locally formulated idea of region and regional self-identification. The cartographic code used in large-scale overview maps—the grid lines, topographic signs, settlement symbols, and place-names—rarely contained visual signposts for conveying regional differences. The symbolic codes showing mountain ranges and rivers, as well as the letters and their font size indicating places, represented a homogenized environment in which the local or regional was subordinated to an imperial agenda based on geopolitics rather than identity.

Eighteenth-century mapmakers, being fully aware of the uniform and culturally uninformative appearance of the northern, middle, and southern map images, turned once again to the map margins in order to specify the cartographic narrative of regions. In the margins of the regional maps published during the second phase, cartographers tended to display next to the topographical map image of the region the ornamental device called a "cartouche." The mapmaker's handbook defines a cartouche as "a feature of a map or chart, often a decorative inset, containing the title, legend, or scale."[24] As G.N.G. Clarke has recently contended, this definition "ignores the subtle relationship between the scientific and decorative; it fails to see them . . . as a series of interrelated indexes which bind the map within a series of ideological assumptions as to the way the land is viewed."[25] Always an echo of the larger cultural consensus of how eighteenth-century Englishmen and women were imagining American regions, the cartouches displayed on American maps offered more than decorative elements; rather, they provided a visual index by which British imperial cartographers wittingly created the story of regional significance and of fixed regional identity.

The most spectacular set of cartouches used to describe the British colonies in North America appeared in William Faden's *The North American Atlas* (1777).[26] Published in folio size, this atlas was immensely popular among the upper and middle classes on both sides of the Atlantic; designed to instruct and entertain a growing audience of armchair geographers, *The North American Atlas* became a gift book for the young and a status symbol for the old. Throughout the atlas, Faden decorated the topographic maps with new and old cartouches made by a new generation of map engravers, which besides Faden included Thomas Jefferys, Joshua Fry, and Peter Jefferson. While the actual map images were recording the political narrative of British territorial possession, the cartouches shown along with the maps developed a more subtle narrative that celebrated next to imperial power also regional cultures. It is significant for us to note that Faden's decorative cartouches provided a visual commentary on almost all the maps, moving from the general continent to the local provinces. In order to show the level of narrative complexity as well as the key symbolic elements that were used in fixing regional narratives, I will discuss three cartouches—one describing the North American continent and two representing the cartographic region of the American South.

The cartouche that accompanies Faden's opening atlas map, "The British Colonies in North America," is placed in direct opposition to the topographical image of the eastern half of the North American continent. It tells the story of the American provinces being part of a world defined by commerce and trade. At its base, the cartouche depicts the Atlantic Ocean, a harbor, and ships of the merchant marine; on land, it portrays a selection of the British inhabitants of North America, ranging from merchants to clerks and workers, these last being depicted as Africans. The top of the cartouche shows on either side the buildings of a plantation and of a rural farmstead; further down, images of vegetation imply at once bountiful produce and a profitable enterprise. A fishing net stretched between oaks and palmetto trees signifies from north to south the geographic extension of British power (as does the juxtaposition of the farm buildings). The icon of the fishing net furthermore functions as a visual trope suggesting cultural cohesion and uniformity. Aside from representing a shared economy, it implies the larger network of the cartographic grid and thus affiliates the cartouche with the cartographic discourse as the common grounds facilitating both the transatlantic and the interregional traffic of goods and ideas.

This cartouche functions as an introduction to the atlas as a whole; it establishes a visual index of the key elements that will define the regions, including place-names, colors, and allegorical tableaux. In its introductory function, however, the cartouche also contains a strong optical bias that privileges the northern over the southern parts. By placing the Atlantic to the left of the sketch, the engraver occupies a northern position looking southward along the Atlantic coastline. At the same time that the cartouche presents the shore as being the representative stage of British American material culture, it also presents it as a directionally "southern" defined object of the viewer's gaze. Thus, the opening atlas map steers the map reader's response toward the ideologically motivated terms that European narratives traditionally reserved for representations of southern places and southernness; viewing British America from a cartographically northern viewpoint, the continent is cast according to a North/South hierarchy in which the southern parts, being cartographically south of Europe on the world map, become determined as culturally objectifiable lands, reducing northern and southern sections to the position of alienable property.

Faden's atlas develops the notion of a particularly southern form of objectification explicitly in "A Map of the most Inhabited part of Virginia containing the whole Province of Maryland with part of Pensilvania, New Jersey, and North Carolina," originally drawn by Joshua Fry and Peter Jefferson in 1751. Faden recycles the map's cartouche (fig. 3), offering the Anglo-American audience one of the first symbolically coded glimpses showing a southern region in distinct and concrete terms. The cartouche presents the southern Atlantic world of commerce, its vehicles of traffic, and its staple merchandise, tobacco. It exudes a sense of material physicality: the scene teems with everyday objects that range from a clay pipe and a hammer to a storage house and a fully-rigged ship. At the same time, the cartouche also stages the business of everyday life: it shows the haggling between idle merchants, just as it presents as the real workers African slaves lifting goods and serving white men. Indeed, in contrast to Faden's other atlas cartouches, such as those showing New England and the greater

Fig. 3. Cartouche of "A Map of the most Inhabited part of Virginia containing the whole Province of Maryland with Part of Pensilvania, New Jersey, and North Carolina." William Faden, *The North American Atlas* (London, 1777). Courtesy of the University of Delaware.

New Jersey region, the Fry-Jefferson cartouche is densely populated with real people. Whereas the northern scenes depict allegorical scenes of historical events (the New England cartouche shows the Puritans landing at Plymouth Rock) or dominant economies (the New Jersey cartouche shows a bucolic farm scene), the southern cartouche is driven by a theatrical realism reminiscent of eighteenth-century paintings and literature. Like the drawings of Hogarth and the novels of Henry Fielding, the cartouche fulfills a narrative function that is intended to tell realistic stories of human characters and their activities. Decorating Faden's map showing central Virginia and North Carolina (the map image uses 38° latitude as its northern border), the Fry-Jefferson cartouche tells a regionally specific story about local character types that are classified not only by economic but also by racial differences. Expanding from already existing popular accounts describing the British American southern culture, the cartouche's pictorial narrative is the only one in the atlas that calls attention to this difference and thus to the southern culture's regional identity by detailing in great realistic detail the physiognomic and performative differences between a white leisured and a black laboring class.[27]

On the eve of the American Revolution, decorated atlas maps like those collected by William Faden had become popular to the point of being perceived as objective truth, with the image of the South as a region and regional identity emerging from economic identification rather than from a process of discursive alienation. Indeed, my very reading of Faden's atlas as being a commentary on the way in which regions and regional identities are cartographically constructed on first sight serves to underline what empirical historical analysis has demonstrated many times, namely that the American South and southern regional identities emerged solely from economic activities in conjunction with the realities of a southern geography, its climate, natural resources, and corresponding cash crop industries. At the same time, however, the Fry-Jefferson cartouche also supports my thesis regarding the South's cartographic invention in that its figural constellation insists that any discussion of regional identity must always be viewed in the light of its textual creators and the discursive means of creation. A closer look reveals that the only white figure working in the harbor scene is a clerk writing or checking a list or document. With his head near the perspectival center of the cartouche and his back turned to us, this figure surveys the harbor scene for the general map reader. As the implied self-portrait of the cartographer, this figure serves to remind the reader of the authorial and textual origins that define the map image, its allegorical scenes, and the idea of southern regionalism.

William Faden's *North American Atlas* demonstrates the extent to which the textual nature of a southern regional identity must be viewed as a reification of a literary culture rather than natural geography in a different cartouche introducing "A Map of South Carolina and part of Georgia" (1780). There the cartouche is dominated by the image of a monumental stone inscribed with the map's title, the list of the region's royal officers, and the engraver's as well as the cartographer's name. With the monument being the focal point, the cartouche shows the stone to be part of a southern natural setting (emblematized by palm trees, vines, and gourds) in which a native population (cast as black figures) performs manual labor without the immediate supervision of a British white landowner or merchant. Viewed against this scene, the monumental presentation of the map title becomes, as G.N.G. Clarke argues, "a title *to* the land: an inference given added credence by the way the 'stone' slab is drawn with a three-dimensional appearance (with the attendant effect of weight and depth) and, finally . . . how its presence (as arbiter of ownership) is stressed by the way in which the natives work on or around it."[28] To this I would add that the monument's inscription implies not so much proprietary claims as the written word for asserting authority and proprietorship over the combined region of South Carolina and Georgia. The title's actual image resembles a book's frontispiece in which the names of the map's patron, the publisher, and the author-cartographer claim possession of the printed artifact and its written contents rather than the actual southern lands. While naturalizing the display of a self-supervised slave culture as the token idea of southern identity, the cartouche in fact acknowledges its manifold textual origins, the greater canon of printed documents of travel reports, royal edicts, local geography books, and other maps, as the true "natural" environment of the "American South."

As we have seen so far, during the second phase the southern map image underwent significant changes between 1715 and 1780. Comparing Herman Moll's map of the British Empire and William Faden's atlas maps, we discover how during this time topographic information provided by such surveyors as William De Brahm, John Collet, and Henry Mouzon gradually ossified the regional outline of the South, making its regional image comparable to that displayed by our modern historical maps.[29] At the same time, these large-scale atlas maps demonstrate how cartographic (rather than political) editorial decisions built up the southern territory as a specific regional entity. In view of the allegorical commentaries of the map's decorative cartouches, we can see how, in the process of cartographic writing, mapmakers gradually inscribed a regional sense of cultural identity.

What is striking in the history of eighteenth-century maps, however, is not so much how palm trees, gourds, and African figures came to identify the South as a specific material slave-based economy, but rather how over the century cartographers gradually reassigned America's colonial identity to the southern region. Whereas in 1715 Moll considered it fitting to define North America as the ideal colony by describing the native population as beavers working without human supervision, in 1780 mapmakers such as Jefferys and Faden applied the expectation of colonial servitude only to the southern environment and the working figures of African slaves. This cartographic revaluation of colonialism suggests that throughout the century mapmakers developed the dominant European narrative in which the negative preconceptions of colonial identities became gradually paired with the northern European prejudice against any geographic locale called "southern," a narrative bias that can be found in the writings of surveyors and mapmakers-turned-authors like Jonathan Carver's *Trav-*

els *Through the Interior Parts of North-America* (1778), Hector St. John de Crèvecoeur's *Letters From an American Farmer* (1782), and Thomas Jefferson's *Notes on the State of Virginia* (1784). Using a generally antisouthern narrative, cartographic commentaries from cartouches to map advertisements effectively marketed southern regional identities in the historically received terms of colonial identity, and constructed the "American South" as the last real colony in North America.

PHASE THREE: NATIONALISM AND THE UNWRITING
OF SOUTHERN REGIONALISM

I would like to end my discussion of the mapping of the American South by turning briefly to the early national decades. During the first three decades of the nation, the image of the southern region all but vanishes from the cartographic archive. In the wake of the constitutional debate, the federalist and geographer most notorious for his anti-South attitude, the New England minister Jedidiah Morse, published on two occasions Joseph Purcell's map of the southern region called "A Map of the States of Virginia, North Carolina, South Carolina, and Georgia." The Purcell map illustrated Morse's magisterial textbook *American Geography* (1789) and its subsequent edition published under the title *The American Universal Geography* (1793). This textbook propagated regional characteristics in order to differentiate New Englanders from southern types. One of its more infamous examples appears in the 1793 edition where Morse describes the people of New England as "a hardy race of free, independent republicans" known for their industry, who live without any "temptations to luxury" in a state of "happy mediocrity." Further to the south, the people of Maryland, on the other hand, are identified by "a disconsolate wildness in their countenances, and an indolence and inactivity in their whole behaviors, which are evidently the effects of solitude and slavery."[30]

Morse's sectionalist representation of the nation's geography, however, was counterbalanced by a cartographic horizon consisting primarily of national maps. After the Revolution cartographers concentrated on the production of national overview maps, some of the more prominent being John Wallis's map "The United States of America" (1783) and Abel Buell's first American-made map, "A New and Correct Map of the United States of North America" (1784).[31] American politicians and citizens flocked to these maps because they confirmed recent historical events in a tangible form. By offering a first glimpse of the new nation-state, national maps became the ideal vehicle for visualizing the material form and contents of what

Fig. 4. South Carolina. Mathew Carey, *Carey's American Pocket Atlas* (Philadelphia, 1796). Courtesy of the American Antiquarian Society.

many people perceived to be an abstract or even an untenable fiction, namely that there could be a national union between disjointed regions and politically disparate people.

Coinciding with the publication of national maps, the first U.S. American atlases eschewed regional maps of the country's northern, mid-Atlantic, southern, or western sections. Mathew Carey's *American Pocket Atlas* (1796) and Joseph Scott's *Atlas of the United States* (1796) instead included maps showing the unity of the nation and its constitutive members, the individual states. In the case of Carey's atlas, the prefatory national map is structurally similar to the local map of South Carolina (fig. 4); both maps display a territory that through its cartographic design appears physically self-contained. Both the national and the state maps emphasize geopolitical boundaries and, in contrast to previous British maps, deemphasize other topographic and thus regionally specific cultural information about the state itself. In fact, state maps prevent the reader from looking for symbolic tokens of similarity or difference; they leave the reader metaphorically swimming in a high sea of cartographically undetermined surroundings. Thus marked as distinct and separate forms, state maps suggest the political autonomy of states while at the same time erasing regional continuities.

It is tempting to invoke the historical debate between federalist and anti-federalist factions as the cause for the general absence of sectional overview maps in early national atlases. After all, the lack of regional representation corresponds directly with the federalist desire for national unity. The absence of regional maps could be explained as a result of governmental intervention and censorship when we consider that Congress took nominal control over the production of maps with the Copyright Law of 1790. Advertised on the inside of every book printed in the United States as "an Act . . . securing the copies of Maps, Charts, and Books," the law conferred upon maps the status of a regulated commodity. At the same time, by assuming the role of political guardian and patron, the government made the work of map engravers and publishers subject to political approval rather than to the economic laws of supply and demand. Washington's 1796 "Farewell Address" was only one example in a series of federalist appeals in which national maps dictated political discourse and vice versa. "Citizens by birth or choice, of a common country, that country has a right to concentrate your affections. The name of American, which belongs to you, in your national capacity, must always exalt the just pride of Patriotism, more than any appellation derived from local discriminations."[32] Exhorting his audience to be national patriots rather than local ones, Washington, who already demanded the affection of the people, used his rhetorical clout to realign local pride with the cartographic "name of American" and thus the mapped entity called the "United States."

The image of the national map determined the work of American cartographers until the Anglo-American conflict of 1812. Until then atlases and geography textbooks alike showed first the nation and then the states, thus inadvertently enacting the federalist philosophy of "divide and rule." As if conceptualizing states as miniature copies of the larger nation-state, the map images prevented readers from looking too closely at the immediately neighboring areas, not to mention greater regions. It was not until the second-generation cartographer John Melish introduced "A Map of the Southern Section of the United States" (fig. 5) into his popular *Military and Topographical Atlas of the United States* (1813) that the cartographic image of the southern region was again included in a national American atlas.[33]

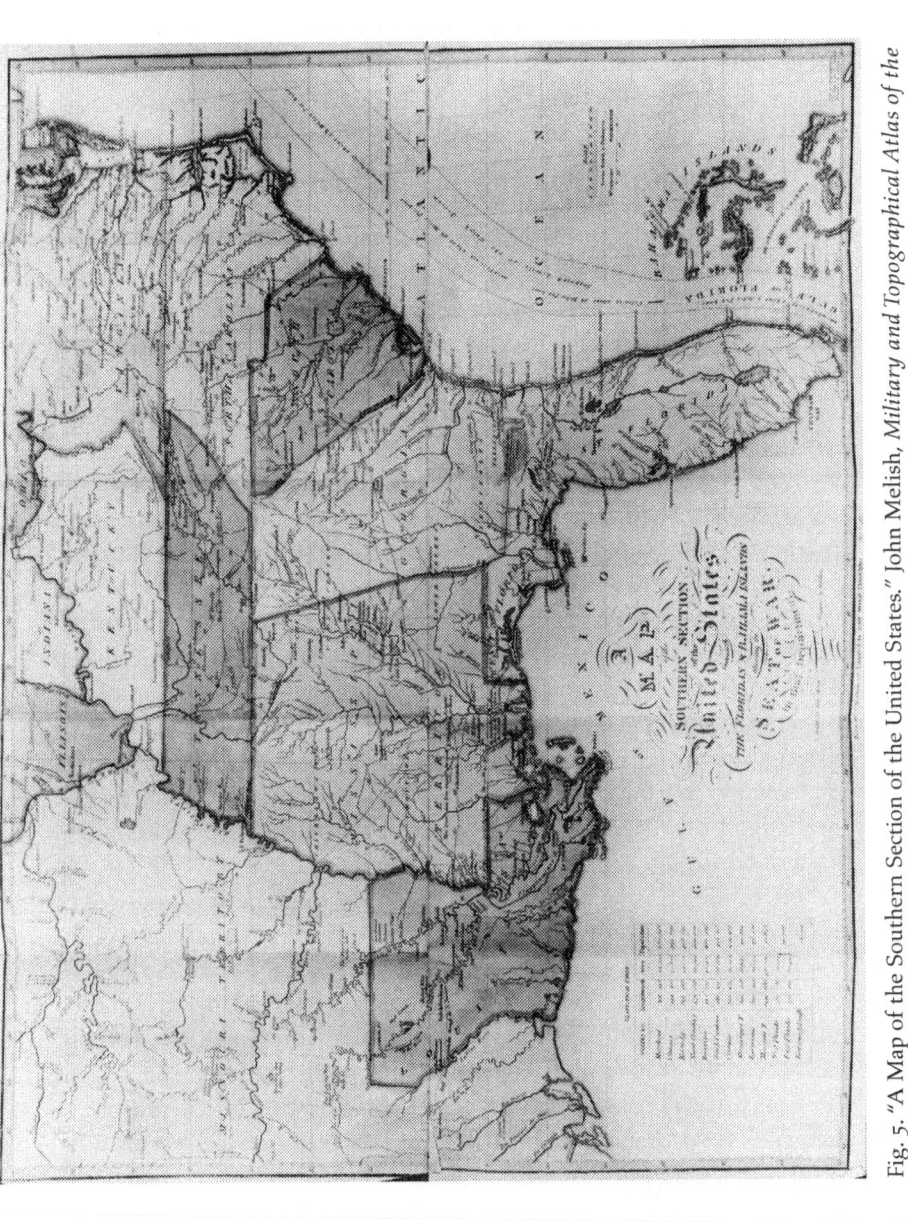

Fig. 5. "A Map of the Southern Section of the United States." John Melish, *Military and Topographical Atlas of the United States* (Philadelphia, 1815). Courtesy of the American Antiquarian Society.

Melish's regional image of the American South is now predicated on the Mason-Dixon line, splitting the South at roughly 39° latitude from the nation's northern sections. Unlike previous maps, which tended to imply outside narratives and cultural metaphors when commenting on regional aspects, this map is undecorated, and thus turns the reader's attention directly to the map, to the conventional map signs and symbols used in the production of modern topographic maps. On first sight, the greater map image emphasizes geophysical and political boundaries. This generalized overview seemingly withholds crucial topographical or symbolic signs necessary for distinguishing the region from its neighbors. The map's initial identity work thus consists of keeping the regional image as general as possible. It prevents the local readers from clearly identifying particular places and inhibits them from identifying themselves directly with their hometowns and immediate surroundings. In short, individual readers cannot easily locate themselves on the map. On second sight, however, the map's collective representing of "the Southern Section of the United States" begins to open its cartosemantic umbrella to gather under its label the otherwise insufficiently defined local map reader. If we apply the terms of identity work as defined by Anthony Wallace, on the one hand Melish's generalized overview map of the South minimizes the often deeply entrenched distances of distrust, rivalry, and fear that exist between local people. On the other hand, the map's vague representation of the region's territorial neighbors also serves to maximize the feeling of trust between local map readers, projecting the map's proposed collective "Southern" identity as protection against the undetermined, alien identities that lurk behind the blankness of the map margins, across the northern and western borders.[34]

Yet in the end, although Melish's map shows the American South to be no longer a haphazardly assembled construct, it still acknowledges cartographic writing as the primary site from which mapmakers and readers derived their definition of southern regions and regional identity. Substituting bold letters and varied print fonts for the ornamental aspects of heraldics and cartouches, the map title's elaborate presentation once again illustrates that the authority of regional identity rests on the practice of cartographic writing and its related discourses. Nearly twenty years after Washington's "Farewell Address," the construction of the American South had finally become a cartoliterary reality, as the Melish atlas reinvented the "Southern" region in explicitly sectional terms. As close reading of both the map title and the cartographic image reveals, Washington's warning about the cartographic nature of regionalism was now more valid than ever before. Melish's map of the "Southern Section" shows the subtlety with which the textual habits of mapmaking and map reading created a unified entity, weaving seamlessly local centers and peripheries into one cartographic territory, the South. It furthermore illustrates the way in which selective cartographic signs and symbols steered our local affection and how maps like this one could become substitute sources of regional self-identification.

Finally, it is precisely the cartographic practice of selection and generalization that reminds the reader of the artificial nature of regional conceptions, southern, northern, or otherwise. Having compared a century's worth of maps from 1715 to 1815, I conclude that the American South has consistently been represented as an "imagined community." In line with Benedict Anderson's argument that "the convergence of capitalism and print technology . . . created the possibility of a new form of imagined community, which in its basic morphology set the stage for the modern nation," eighteenth-century mapmakers underwrote the construction of a geopolitical South through cartographic inscription and the mass circulation of maps and atlases.[35] The "American South" appeared literally first as a printed outline map and place-name on military maps before entering into the material text of transregional newspapers, gazettes, and novels. Yet in this context it is helpful to remember that, even as a cartographic print product, the South entered both the map and the Anglo-American popular consciousness from the margins. As mapmakers added or subtracted topographic text to socioeconomic signs, the South emerged as a metaphoric source of separate identities as much as a distinct and inherently different geographic regional reality. That this geographic difference is called by the name "South" or "southern" must be understood as a conventional sign of the mapping trade; at least throughout the eighteenth century, mapmakers and authors of cartographic writings are accountable for why we address American identities in terms of the geographic compass, and why we divide and categorize the American nation-state according to the cardinal points North and South.

NOTES

1. *The Writings of George Washington from the Original Manuscript Sources, 1745–1799*, ed. John C. Fitzpatrick, 39 vols. (Washington, D.C.: U.S. Government Printing Office, 1931–44), 35:223.

2. The following sources present a cross-section of geographic and cartographic studies detailing aspects of the southern mapping project. For a general survey, see D. W. Meinig, *The Shaping of America: A Geographical Perspective on 500 Years of*

History, (New Haven: Yale University Press, 1986), and Seymour I. Schwartz and Ralph E. Ehrenberg, *The Mapping of America* (New York: Abrams, 1980). For specific discussions of southern land-use patterns, land surveying, and local mapping practices, see Edward T. Price, *Dividing the Land* (Chicago: University of Chicago Press, 1995) and Sarah S. Hughes, *Surveyors and Statesmen: Land Measuring in Colonial Virginia* (Richmond: Virginia Surveyors Foundation, 1979).

3. William P. Cumming, *The Southeast in Early Maps,* 3d ed. (Chapel Hill: University of North Carolina Press, 1998), xiii.

4. See, for example, Helen M. Wallis and Arthur H. Robinson, eds., *Cartographical Innovations: An International Handbook of Mapping Terms to 1900* (Tring, Herts.: Map Collector Publications, 1987).

5. This positivist attitude toward maps informs many of the classic texts on regionalism. See, for example, the essays in Merrill Jensen, ed., *Regionalism in America* (Madison: University of Wisconsin Press, 1951); Raymond D. Gastil, *Cultural Regions of the United States* (Seattle: University of Washington Press, 1975); and to a degree also Michael Bradshaw, *Regions and Regionalism in the United States* (Jackson: University Press of Mississippi, 1988).

6. A most recent example illustrating the tension between cartography and the explanation of the "American South" can be found in Andrew Frank's *The Routledge Historical Atlas of the American South* (New York: Routledge, 1999). The author grapples with the cartographic label "American South," invoking "the adage applied to obscenity—I can't exactly define it, but I know it when I see it. It seems that everyone recognizes the region's existence, but few can coherently define it" (10).

7. Edward L. Ayers et al., *All Over the Map: Rethinking American Regions* (Baltimore: The Johns Hopkins University Press, 1996), vii.

8. See his introduction, "Text and Contexts in the Interpretation of Early Maps," to *From Sea Charts to Satellite Images: Interpreting North American History Through Maps,* ed. David Buisseret (Chicago: University of Chicago Press, 1990), 4.

9. I will cite only a few titles by way of introducing an increasingly prolific field of inquiry. Among the pathbreaking essays by J. B. Harley are "Maps, Knowledge, Power," in *The Iconography of Landscape,* ed. Denis Cosgrove and Stephen Daniels (Cambridge: Cambridge University Press, 1988), 277–311, and "Deconstructing the Map," *Cartographica* 26, no. 2 (1989): 1–20. For critical applications of historical cartography, see Denis Wood and John Fels, "Designs on Signs: Myth and Meaning in Maps," *Cartographica* 23, no. 3 (1986): 54–103, and Matthew H. Edney, "Reconsidering Enlightenment Geography and Map Making," in *Geography and Enlightenment,* ed. David N. Livingstone and Charles W. J. Withers (Chicago: University of Chicago Press, 1999), 165–98. For a general history of eighteenth-century American mapmaking, see Buisseret, *From Sea Charts to Satellite Images,* and Schwartz and Ehrenberg, *The Mapping of America.* For the contexts of southern mapmaking, see William P. Cumming's *The Southeast in Early Maps* and *British Maps of Colonial America* (Chicago: University of Chicago Press, 1974).

10. My thinking on the artificiality of regional identity has been influenced by Benedict Anderson, *Imagined Communities: Reflections on the Origin and Spread*

of Nationalism, rev. ed. (London: Verso, 1991); Edward W. Soja, *Postmodern Geographies: The Reassertion of Space in Critical Social Theory* (London: Verso, 1989); and Henri Lefebvre, *The Production of Space*, trans. Donald Nicholson-Smith (Oxford: Blackwell, 1991).

11. For a brilliant discussion of the power of Restoration bureaucracy in England and greater Europe, see James C. Scott, *Seeing like a State* (New Haven: Yale University Press, 1998); also see David Buisseret, ed., *Monarchs, Ministers, and Maps* (Chicago: University of Chicago Press, 1992). For an account of the more specialized context of the American colonies, see Buisseret's essay, "The Estate Map in the New World," in his collection *Rural Images: Estate Maps in the Old and New Worlds* (Chicago: University of Chicago Press, 1996), 91–112.

12. See Jeanette D. Black, *The Blathwayt Atlas*, vol. 2, *Commentary* (Providence: Brown University Press, 1975), 5–13 passim. For a more general description of the use of late-seventeenth-century cartography in imperial politics, see her essay "Mapping the English Colonies in North America: The Beginnings" in *The Compleat Plattmaker*, ed. Norman J. W. Thrower (Berkeley and Los Angeles: University of California Press, 1978), 101–26.

13. See the maps collected in Cumming, *Southeast*, plates 25–40.

14. See the Willem Blaeu map "Virginia partis australis, et Floridae (1640)" in Cumming, *Southeast*, plate 26. Meinig explains the history behind this cartographic frame in more detail; see *The Shaping of America*, 145, 173.

15. Cumming, *Southeast*, 23.

16. My reading of Moll's "Map of the Dominions" applies Harley's hermeneutic key to critical map reading spelled out in Buisseret, *From Sea Charts*, 5–12, and the analysis of the map margins by G.N.G. Clarke, "Taking Possession: The Cartouche as Cultural Text in Eighteenth-Century American Maps," *Word & Image* 4, no. 2 (1988): 455–74.

17. Having been settled from the British West Indies, its cultural composition and outlook pointed to the Caribbean, not to Virginia or Florida. See Jack P. Greene's various essays on this topic collected in his *Interpreting Early America* (Charlottesville: University Press of Virginia, 1996).

18. Here I apply different works on ancient and early modern mapping projects, such as J. B. Harley and David Woodward, eds., *The History of Cartography*, vol. 1 (Chicago: University of Chicago Press, 1987); Mary Campbell, *The Witness and the Other World* (Ithaca: Cornell University Press, 1988); Margarita Bowen, *Empiricism and Geographical Thought: From Francis Bacon to Alexander von Humboldt* (Cambridge: Cambridge University Press, 1981); and David N. Livingstone, *The Geographical Tradition* (Oxford: Blackwell, 1993).

19. Geoffrey L. King, *Miniature Antique Maps* (London: Map Collector Publications, 1996), 125, 134–35.

20. Here I invoke the classic study on colonial American economic debates by J.G.A. Pocock, *The Machiavellian Moment: Florentine Political Thought and the Atlantic Republican Tradition* (Princeton: Princeton University Press, 1975).

21. On the rise of magazine maps, see Louis De Vorsey, "Eighteenth-Century

Large Scale Maps," in Buisseret, *From Sea Charts*, 67–71. For maps in British periodicals, see Christopher M. Klein, *Maps in Eighteenth-Century British Magazines* (Chicago: University of Chicago Press, 1989).

22. In the course of the eighteenth century, as William Cumming and Louis De Vorsey have pointed out, maps showing the southern provinces tended to show a mix of European and Native American borderlines. This mix undermines many of our modern-day attempts at locating and "fixing" the exact region of the American South. See Cumming, "Mapping the Southern British Colonies," in his *British Maps*, 18–20, and De Vorsey, *The Indian Boundary in the Southern Colonies, 1763–1775* (Chapel Hill: University of North Carolina Press, 1966).

23. See Robert Sayer and John Bennett, *The American Military Pocket Atlas* (London, 1776). Folded to the size of a quarto edition, the atlas maps also contained, next to large-scale overview maps, several smaller-scale topographical maps showing river mouths and towns "which now are, or probably may be the theatre of war."

24. Norman J. W. Thrower, *Maps and Man* (Englewood Cliffs, N.J.: Prentice-Hall, 1972), 168.

25. Clarke, "Taking Possession," 455.

26. Faden's atlas maps are also reproduced in part by Thomas Jefferys's posthumously published *American Atlas* (London: Robert Sayer and John Bennett, 1775).

27. A similar narrative is produced by a cartouche introducing James Cook's *A Map of the Province of South Carolina* (London, 1773).

28. Clarke, "Taking Possession," 462.

29. For biographical and bibliographical information on individual mapmakers, see R. V. Tooley, *A Dictionary of Mapmakers* (London: Map Collectors Circle, 1974); Schwartz and Ehrenberg, *The Mapping of America*; and Cumming, *Southeast*, passim.

30. Jedidiah Morse, *The American Universal Geography; or, A View of the Present State of all the Empires, Kingdoms, States, and Republics in the known World, and of the United States of America in Particular* (Boston, 1793): 140–49, 352.

31. Schwartz and Ehrenberg, *The Mapping of America*, 205–15. On the nationalizing function of these maps, see my essay "Lessons in Geography: Maps, Spellers, and Other Grammars of Nationalism in the Early Republic," *American Quarterly* 51, no. 2 (1999): 311–43.

32. *Writings of George Washington*, 35:219.

33. See Walter W. Ristow, *American Maps and Mapmakers: Commercial Cartography in the Nineteenth Century* (Detroit: Wayne State University Press, 1985), 182.

34. See Anthony F. C. Wallace, "Identity Processes in Personality and in Culture," in *Cognition, Personality, and Clinical Psychology*, ed. Richard Jessor and Seymour Feshbach (San Francisco: Jossey-Bass, 1967), 67–68.

35. Anderson, *Imagined Communities*, 46.

Chapter 8

"AND DIE BY INCHES"

George Washington and the Encounter of Cultures on the Southern Colonial Frontier

WARREN R. HOFSTRA

By the spring of 1789 George Washington's place in the pantheon of Revolutionary leaders was secure. Some Americans might have feared for his reputation in the face of the storms of political faction intensified by recent conflicts over the ratification of the Constitution. But most expected Washington to stand head and shoulders above all controversy precisely because he was, in their minds, the perfect embodiment of republican virtue.

Throughout the first summer of Washington's presidency, there appeared numerous testimonials to the man who more than any other American placed the public's interest above his own. The press was filled with effusions of praise such as the poem "A Hero Great and Good," composed by a student at the Richmond Academy and delivered in the great man's presence. As its author, master Edmund Bacon, envisioned,

> Each future babe shall learn to lisp thy name;
> To love thy worth and emulate thy fame.
> When'er the powers of infant reason dawn,
> Full in his view thy portrait shall be drawn.
> Hence on his mind these truths will be impress'd;
> That virtue only can be truly blest.[1]

Or consider the acrostic "Our Saviour and Our Guide" penned by "A bard, beyond the mountains, with firm toil, / Who near *Ohio* cultivates his soil":

> *G*eneral! immortaliz'd by virtuous fame!
> *E*ngland's brave foe! to *France* how dear thy name!
> . . . .
>
> Wise, valiant! may thy name still brighter grow;
> And make mankind to worth and virtue bow.²

George Washington was the indispensable man in the new republic because republican-minded men and women regarded virtue as essential to the survival and vitality of the government and the way of life they had created. Virtue was not just doing good, but doing good for all the people all the time. Where power, excessive power or abusive power, could destroy life, liberty, and property, virtue would check power and render it incorruptible. Perfection, all knew, lay beyond the capacity of mankind, but the checks of balanced government were designed to restrain the unprincipled pursuit of self-interest. Washington, more than any other person of his age, came closest in the eyes of contemporaries to the man who could exercise power within the limits of office and remain unswayed by corrupting influences. Cognizant of his own image and its power to instill virtue in others, Washington advocated that "virtue or morality is a necessary spring of popular government.—The rule indeed extends with more or less force to every species of free Government.—Who that is a sincere friend to it, can look with indifference upon attempts to shake the foundation of the fabric."³ To Washington, virtue was public morality: the words "civic" and "virtue" often went hand in hand, and the virtuous person was a public person.

The identification of Washington with virtue was nothing new in 1789. Surely, the act that fixed the image of Washington as the virtuous leader in the public mind was his resignation from command of the Continental Army in 1783. His return to private life at that critical moment when a corruptible man might have looked to monarchy to perpetuate his power cast all his actions during the Revolution, and indeed long before, in the glowing light of virtue. This latter-day Cincinnatus, however, had projected himself as a model of republican virtue thirty years earlier in his career as a public man when he strove to master circumstances he found personally trying and politically almost overwhelming. In command of Virginia forces during the Seven Years' War and charged with the responsibility of defending the Old Dominion's frontiers, Washington was probably the most visible Virginian in colonial affairs. The debacle of the attack on Jumonville in 1754 and the subsequent retreat from Fort Necessity under questionable circumstances catapulted Washington into the arena of public men. According to his biographer Douglas Southall Freeman, the young commander found "that his expedition was the theme of every man's talk in Williamsburg. He was himself conspicuous, not to say already famous."[4] News of Washington's exploits soon reached England, and an account published in the *Gentleman's Magazine* prompted comment by King George himself. These events helped give occasion for the first of Washington's famous resignations, but the genuine heroism he displayed in the infamous defeat of the British general Edward Braddock in 1755 restored Washington's military fortunes. In command of the Virginia Regiment, Washington assumed responsibility for securing the lives and property of a rapidly growing population of largely non-English subjects of the British crown living west of Virginia's Blue Ridge.

Ironically, the germ of Washington's virtue began to sprout in his intense dislike for the people under his charge. He had nothing kind to say about them in his journals. German settlers "really ... seem[ed] to be as Ignorant a Set of People as the Indians." That a local justice of the peace would serve him dinner with "neither a Cloth upon the Table nor a Knife to eat with" left him aghast. "A parcel of Barbarian's and an uncouth set of People" was the best he could say about these men and women, and they handed the future president his first political defeat in 1755, denying him a seat in the Virginia House of Burgesses.[5] Nonetheless, Washington had sworn to defend them. The success of his first command depended on their security. The simple fact of the matter was that Washington had to assume responsibility for people he neither understood nor liked. But in this confrontation with the alien "other," Washington came face to face with the essence of republican politics—with the necessity of promoting the welfare of people whose support was necessary in public life even if sympathy with their way of life was impossible. In accepting responsibility for strange people who frustrated and angered him, George Washington assumed the mantle of virtue—he began to craft an image of himself as a virtuous man. At the same time that he condemned the people of the backcountry as "obstinate, self-willed, [and] perverse," for instance, he could also write to Robert Dinwiddie, lieutenant governor of Virginia, that he was "too little acquainted, Sir, with pathetic language, to attempt a description of the peoples distresses; though I have a generous soul, sensible of wrongs, and swelling for redress—But what can I do? If bleeding, dying! would glut their insatiate revenge—I would be a willing offering to Savage Fury: and die by inches, to save a people! I *see* their situation, *know* their danger, and participate [in] their *Sufferings*; without having it in my power to give them further relief, than uncertain promises."[6] Pathetic, in fact, Washington's words were. But what strikes the modern ear—and maybe Dinwiddie's—as disingenuous was Washington's authentic attempt to place public good above personal feelings. He was quite literally inventing himself in the image of virtue by acting publicly in ways transcending his personal situation.

Washington's situation was deeply invested in what can be described as the encounter of cultures that defined the southern backcountry frontier. The notion that the North American frontier in the eighteenth century is a case study of Anglo-American expansion and Indian victimization, as older historical models suggest, has been supplanted by a broad scholarly consensus about North American frontiers as those places where many women and men with varied cultural, racial, and national backgrounds encountered one another and engaged in complex cultural exchanges lacking any foreordained outcome. Most recent historical writing has focused on the frontiers of Native American encounters with French, Spanish, English, or Dutch colonists. But little new work has been done on the cultural composition of English frontiers populated by non-English peoples from the north of Ireland or central Germany. And redefining the frontier among scholars has, as yet, had little impact on public perceptions of the pioneer experience widely recognized as fundamental to American history, except where revisionism provokes political controversy. Situating George Washington in this conflicted field serves little purpose, but as a representative of the Anglo-American world of the Chesapeake tobacco planter, the young Washington came face to face with the very different world of the southern backcountry. This encounter is the key to understanding the self-invention of George Washington as the model of republican virtue.

I

Washington came into the world of the Chesapeake planter in family circumstances neither rich nor poor but holding great promise for wealth and preferment. Despite the early death of his father, which circumscribed the opportunities available to him, Washington sought eagerly to fulfill that promise. Evident to the young man, however, was that if he was to rise in the world, he must do so by dint of his own effort. His brother Lawrence's marriage to Ann Fairfax, daughter of William Fairfax, master of Belvoir and agent for Thomas, Lord Fairfax, proprietor of Virginia's Northern Neck, no doubt fired his ambitions. At Belvoir the aspiring young man saw what money could buy. The Anglo-American, Atlantic world was then on the leading edge of what historians have come to call the consumer revolution. New developments and rapid growth in English industry, manufacturing, distribution, and finance were rapidly transforming the British empire into an empire of goods. Fine and utilitarian textiles, ceramics, furnishings, and clothing were more available than ever before. With this empire of goods also came fresh notions of refinement, gentility, civility, and education defining a new culture of manners for the class to which George Washington aspired. But the world of the tobacco planter was also the rough world of slavery and tobacco—a competitive and sometimes corrosive world in which wealth meant power and power meant dominion over the lives of others. Great inequalities between rich and poor, powerful and powerless, free and slave, white and black were manifest in the values of social hierarchy, class deference, and household patriarchy. As the English traveler Isaac Weld saw it, "In the lower parts of Virginia, there is a disparity unknown elsewhere in America, excepting in the large towns. Instead of the lands being equally divided, immense estates are held by a few individuals, who derive large incomes from them, whilst the generality of the people are but in a state of mediocrity. Most of the men also, who possess these large estates, having received liberal educations, which the others have not, the distinction between them is still more observable."[7] At Belvoir, however, George Washington would have heard, as well, of a different world, a new world, the world of the West. Lord Fairfax had recently arrived in Virginia fully intent on developing his proprietary lands beyond the Blue Ridge.

In the Shenandoah and smaller valleys of the Appalachians, new communities were forming on lands recently taken up. Settlers were farmers, not planters—a distinction recognized in the common speech of Washington's day. A few eventually came to grow some tobacco, but grains and livestock were the mainstays of their lives. Mixed farming assured survival, if not abundance, in an exchange economy. The culture of wheat, rye, barley, and oats and the herding of cattle, horses, sheep, and swine reflected agricultural traditions deeply rooted in Irish, Scottish, and Germanic homelands. Ethnic diversity was complemented by religious pluralism. Dissenters clearly outnumbered Anglicans. Because family members and indentured servants could meet most of the varied labor needs of the farm, African-American slaves were few. Slavery, although rarely protested on moral grounds, nonetheless begot dependence, and escaping dependent social or economic relations had driven most backcountry men and women from the Old World to the New. In a cultural environment where disparities of wealth and power were less than they were in the Chesapeake, achieving economic competence for the family was the reason why most men and women worked the land, produced, traded, and accumulated patrimonies for their children. "Perhaps the most powerful drive in the British-American colonizing process from the seventeenth century through much of the nineteenth century, and from the eastern to the western coasts of North America, was the drive for personal *independence*," historian Jack P. Greene has written. "Quite simply, *independence* meant freedom from the will of others. It was the opposite of *dependence*, which was subordination or subjection to the discretion of others. Independence implied a sovereignty of self in all private and public relations, while dependence connoted the very opposite."[8]

It was this world, later called New Virginia, that George Washington entered for the first time in March 1748. Attached to a surveying party for Fairfax, Washington learned three important lessons during his first foray into the backcountry. First, his route to wealth and reputation in Chesapeake society lay in the West with its abundance of good land. Second, surveying was the means to acquire good land. Surveyors knew the land intimately, and, besides, they earned a considerable income. "A good Reward and Dubbleloon" Washington bragged, was "my constant gain every Day that the Weather will permit my going out."[9] And finally, Washington came to understand the people he would be among—and ultimately depend upon for the realization of his ambitions—would be very different from those of the tidewater world in which he sought to rise.

Washington's alienation from the world of the backcountry would grow into antipathy and revulsion during his command of the Virginia Regiment. He knew that the promise of his life—his aspirations to wealth and preferment—depended upon a successful defense of the Virginia frontier. But the people of the backcountry refused to supply the provisions he requisitioned for his army. Worse still, they simply rejected militia duties. As Washington advised the speaker of the House of Burgesses, John Robinson, "The timidity of the Inhabitants of this Country is to be equaled by nothing but their perverseness."[10] To his brother John Augustine Washington, the young commander wrote, "You may, with almost equal success, raise the Dead to Life again, as the force of this Country."[11] He condemned his headquarters town, Winchester, as a "vile hole" and proclaimed that he was "tired of the place, the inhabitants, and the life I lead here."[12]

Another incident brought into sharp focus the conflict of cultures and values betrayed by Washington's criticisms. Writing to Governor Dinwiddie in October 1755, the colonel of the Virginia Regiment described "Circumstances" that he "related only to shew, what a panick prevails among the People, how much they are alarmd at the most usual, and customary Cry's—and yet how impossible it is to get them to act in any respect for their common safety's; an Instance of this then appeard," Washington continued, when "Colo. Fairfax, who arrivd in Town while we were upon the Scout, immediately sent to a Noble Captain (not far off) to repair with his Company forthwith to Winchester: with coolness and moderation this great Captn answerd, that his Wife, Family, and Corn was at stake, so were those of his Soldrs therefore it was not possible for him to come, such is the Example of the Officer's! Such the Behaviour of the Men! And such the unhappy Circumstances on which our Country depends!"[13] To the Noble Captain, the protecting of his household and its sustenance—the competence and the independence it brought—unquestionably came before any duty to defend the colony or the king's interest. But for Washington, the resistance of ordinary people to his command created a dilemma: the culture or world in which the ambitious young man sought to rise contrasted sharply with the one in which and through which he sought to realize his aspirations. It was this dilemma that made Washington's experience in the backcountry so powerful and so influential in the development of both his character and his career. Mastering his revulsion for the people for the sake of the success he coveted would ultimately compel him to see himself as the virtuous leader who could place the public welfare before self-interest. But this dilemma also broadens the study of Washington's character and career into an examination of the backcountry and the distinctive world that so immeasurably influenced him and the nation he helped to found. To study the young Washington, therefore, is to study the southern backcountry.

II

There are many approaches to describing the distinctive world that emerged west of Virginia's Blue Ridge in the Shenandoah Valley and its southern extensions during the eighteenth century. The region's mixed farm economy, ethnic diversity, religious pluralism, and its landscape of dispersed farms and market towns are all defining aspects. But the values of this world that best explain why the Noble Captain placed his family and farm before king and country are revealed in sharpest relief through the exchange economy in which these values were embedded. The competence of each farm family depended upon trade with neighbors and acquaintances dispersed over sometimes large areas. Self-sufficiency was not a formula for independence. It was only through exchanging labor, the surpluses of farm production, or other goods of local extraction and manufacture such as skins, furs, or textiles that any family could provide for its sustenance from year to year and its continuity on the land from generation to generation.

Simply put, an exchange economy is one in which goods and services flow among producers and consumers through the medium of debits and credits. It is not a barter economy based on the direct exchange of one good for another or the payment of wages in commodities. Such economies are limited in their application across time because they frustrate the accumulation of capital, and they work poorly across extended space because exchange depends on face-to-face transfers. Barter economies are plainly ill adapted to rapidly developing and expanding cultural frontiers. Exchange and barter economies, however, both allow for economic activity in the absence of secondary and tertiary contributions by merchants, manufacturers, and other middlemen. An exchange economy also bears certain similarities to a cash economy; indeed, many exchanges involve cash. Money, in essence, functions as an anonymous means of exchange enabling trade among many people separated by distance and time. In other words, the benefit of what is produced in one place can be realized anywhere, and the value of production accrues from year to year—obvious advantages to anyone struggling to establish a frontier farm. Exchange economies require the valuation of goods and services in currency equivalents—a bushel of wheat for three shillings ten pence, a day's work at harvest for two shillings, and so forth. But money need not change hands in an exchange economy. Currency and bullion, in fact, are traded much as any other commodity, although they are often scarcer than wheat or corn, and an exchange economy can work perfectly well on little or no money.

What makes an exchange economy function, then, is neither barter nor money but book accounts. Methods for keeping accounts were well developed by the eighteenth century, having emerged from the merchant exchanges of Renaissance Italy and spread to northern Europe with the expansion of early modern commerce. Merchants often kept account books in a double-entry system. Every debit entry required a credit, just as any exchange entails a giver, or creditor, and a receiver, or debtor. If a customer purchased a bolt of cloth worth one pound five shillings, then he or she would be reckoned as debtor for that amount, and the merchant would enter it in the customer's debit column of an account book. The merchant would also enter the same amount as credit in a dry goods account. The reverse took place when the customer brought in a bushel of wheat or a pound of wool—credits in the customer's account and debits in the wheat or wool account.

Merchants, however, were scarce in frontier exchange economies, and most trade went on among farm families or with the blacksmith down the road or the shoemaker a few miles away. Here the economic world appeared most commonly in the single-entry accounts people kept with each other—a calf, so many bushels of barley, a day's work received as credit here and there over the course of a month or a year, and similar goods or services given as debit over a comparable period. Where they survive, accounts appear sometimes in the same daybooks and ledgers that merchants kept, but more often on slips of paper torn from a large sheet because paper was scarce. Accounts also survive because when sworn before a justice of the peace, they became legal evidence in a suit for recovery of debt. From time to time accounts required balancing—rendering debits equal to credits—and debt was simply the sum by necessity added to the credit column to achieve balance. Balances due could be carried over from year to year—literally from page to page—in account books. But death or departure, often to further frontiers, or the accumulated frustration of a creditor could trigger a debt suit. County courts and common law procedures were therefore as essential to the function of the economy as was keeping accounts. Where county court records have survived as ended causes or judgments, they represent a rich trove of information about the economic and social life of households in developing societies like those George Washington encountered during his days in the southern backcountry.

This is not to say that the workings of this economy would have been foreign to Washington. Indeed an exchange economy functioned in much the same way throughout the Chesapeake world of his day. But here the large-scale production of tobacco could for a few generate great quantities of credit for exchange on London, not local, markets. Credit offset the import of goods fueling the consumer revolution and sustaining the cultures of refinement and gentility. In the mixed-farm, agriculturally diverse economy that families from Ireland or Germany brought with them through Pennsylvania or that a smaller number of lesser planters carried west from the Chesapeake, the exchange economy worked well to support the economic competence of households and the independence of the Noble Captain who could stand up to the likes of Lord Fairfax or George Washington and flatly refuse service to king and country because his "Wife, Family, and Corn" were at stake.

III

Surviving accounts, often drafted in the uncertain handwriting of farmers or artisans, do indeed frequently reference corn because of its wide use in daily subsistence. In 1745, for instance, Thomas Chester sued John

Crowson for £6 4s. 7½d., a sum that included four barrels and two pecks of "indian Corn" (fig. 6). That a bushel of wheat, 19¼ bushels of rye, 34 pounds of beef, and 198 pounds of pork also appeared in the account indicates the extent to which corn was deeply embedded in a variety of persistence pursuits. Partially offsetting Crowson's debt was credit for "work done to the mill trunk" at Chester's sawmill.[14] Corn also appeared regularly in exchanges among neighboring farmers. When a settler named Beckett sued John Davidson in 1751 on accounts dated several years ear-

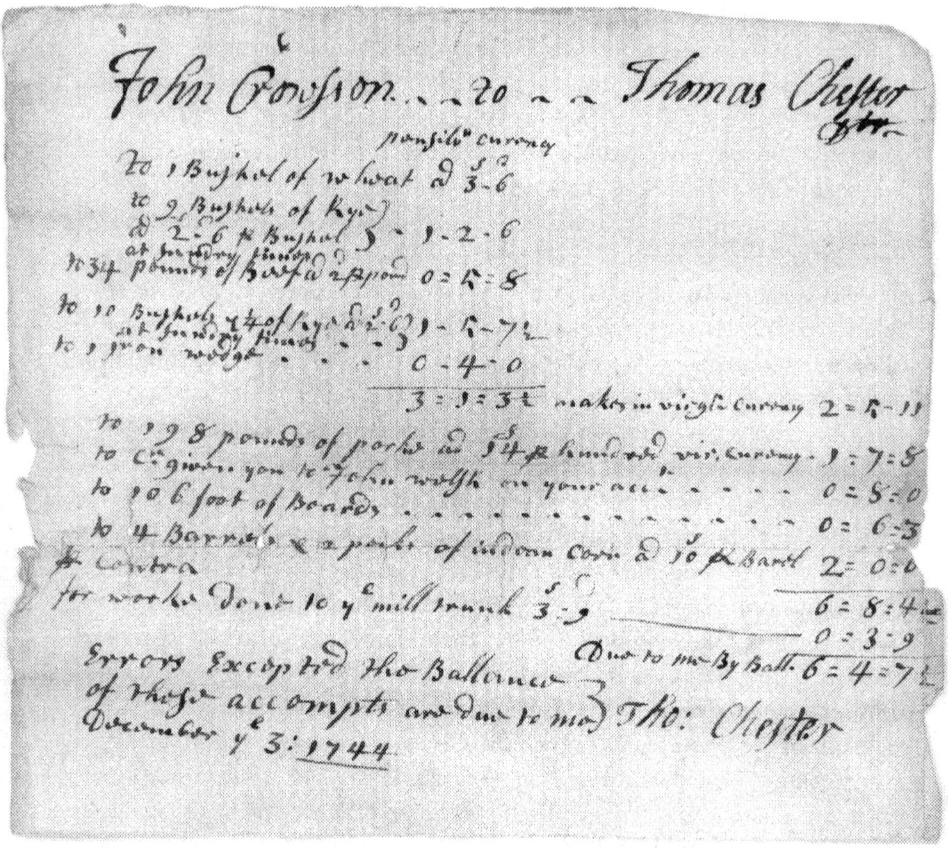

Fig. 6. The exchange of goods and services carefully recorded in book accounts as debits and credits supported the economic competence of settler households in the Shenandoah Valley, as the trade documented here between John Crowson and Thomas Chester suggests. *Source:* Account of John Crowson with Thomas Chester, December 3, 1744, *Chester v Crowson,* May 1745, Ended Causes, 1743–1909, Frederick County Court Papers, Library of Virginia, Richmond. Courtesy of the Library of Virginia.

lier, the defendant had already received thirty-three pounds of cheese, three quarts of liquor, hog's fat, and back meat. In return Davidson had given Beckett "Indian Corn," wheat, some steel, and weaving spools, and had made two bushels of rye into malt, probably for brewing.[15] In all of these accounts, neither corn nor any other commodity appeared in quantities or contexts suggesting commercial transactions. Corn, wheat, rye, oats, barley, malt, cheese, butter, and very commonly labor for a day or a job were exchanged back and forth in patterns that sustained the economic competence, not the economic advancement, of households.

The subsistence orientation of most transactions in the 1740s and 1750s, the decades of George Washington's involvement in the backcountry, was most evident in exchanges involving wheat. Within twenty years wheat would become the commercial mainstay of the Shenandoah Valley economy as farmers grew more wheat than any other grain, ground it at local mills, and shipped flour by wagon across the Blue Ridge to markets in Alexandria and Fredericksburg. Often trading on the accounts of Philadelphia firms, merchants in Virginia ports transferred credits for flour into debits for imported goods brought from or through the Pennsylvania entrepôt. All this, however, lay in the future, and in Washington's frontier days wheat appeared more typically in exchanges such as James Davis and blacksmith John Shearer conducted. In return for "Sharpening Plow Irons and Mending a Pitch fork & 2 Rings Made," "Mending 2 Clevieses," placing a "Clapper in a bell," and nailing "4 Shoes to the Gray Colt," Davis gave Shearer one and one-half bushels of wheat, a pair of shoes, and a quart of whiskey. But mixed in with Shearer's smithy accounts were various quantities of wheat and corn that he also supplied to Davis. Wheat was simply shuttled back and forth as part of a more complex pattern of exchange.[16] Sometime knitter and occasional lawyer Richard Rogers demonstrated the protean quality of wheat in the exchange economy by accepting "Indian Corn" and wheat in return for drafting mortgages, bills of sale, and deeds or providing other legal services for Edward Rogers and in the meantime knitting several pairs of hose for him (fig. 7). Significantly Richard Rogers accepted wheat on Edward Rogers's account from the latter's debtors. The system of book accounts, in other words, could accommodate exchanges separated in both time and place from the keeper of accounts.[17]

Despite wheat's future economic primacy, tobacco appeared in Shenandoah Valley accounts and was sent east to warehouses in Falmouth, Fredericksburg, and elsewhere. Some tidewater planters such as Carter Burwell operated quarters in the Shenandoah Valley as early as the 1740s and might have cultivated tobacco with slaves, but Burwell's presence suggests,

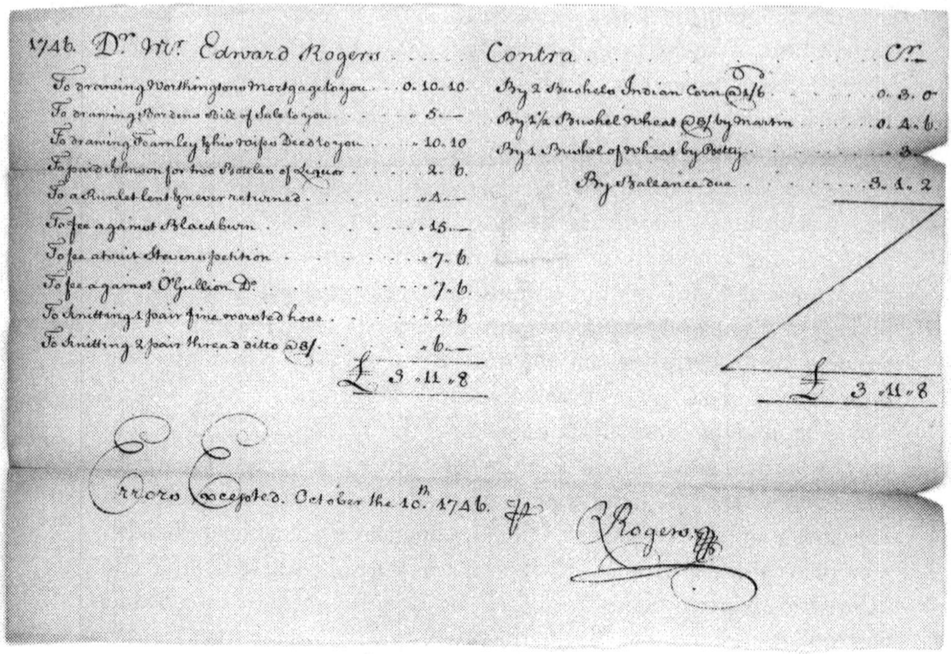
1746. Dr. Mr. Edward Rogers		Contra	Cr.
To drawing Worthingtons Mortgage to you	0.10.10	By 2 Bushels Indian Corn @1/6	0.3.0
To drawing Bordens Bill of Sale to you	5.—	By 1½ Bushel wheat @3/ by martin	0.4.6
To drawing Fearnley & his wifes Deed to you	10.10	By 1 Bushel of wheat by Betty	3.
To paid Johnson for two Bottles of Liquor	2.6	By Balance due	3.1.2
To a Runlet lent & never returned	4.—		
To fee against Blackburn	15.—		
To fee at suit Stevens petition	7.6		
To fee against O'Gullion Do.	7.6		
To knitting 1 pair fine worsted hose	2.6		
To knitting 2 pair thread ditto @3/	6.—		
	£ 3.11.8		£ 3.11.8

Errors Excepted. October the 10th 1746. ₰ R Rogers

Fig. 7. Keeping accounts allowed settlers such as Edward Rogers and Richard Rogers to track exchanges over substantial distances and across considerable periods of time. *Source*: Account of Edward Rogers with Richard Rogers, October 10, 1746, *Rogers v Rogers*, August 1747, Ended Causes, 1743–1909, Frederick County Court Papers, Library of Virginia, Richmond. Courtesy of the Library of Virginia.

at the very least, that economic connections between eastern and western Virginia existed during Washington's early days and that tobacco production was a signifier of Chesapeake culture in the backcountry. Some tobacco was traded among farmers with other items of household exchange, and tobacco was also used to pay rents or appeared in notes of hand to settle debts. An occasional debt suit entailed numbered hogsheads in eastern warehouses.[18]

Trade in linens, however, was more characteristic of the economic cultures recent immigrants brought from Germany and Ireland to the Virginia backcountry. The capacity to produce flax, yarn, and linen textiles was evident in more than two-thirds of the probate inventories taken among Scots-Irish households in one open-country neighborhood, and as early as 1739 the governor of Virginia, William Gooch, commented that "our new Inhabitants on the other side of the Mountains, make very good Linnen which they sell up and down the country."[19] Like tobacco, linen was used to pay debts, and in one instance Abraham Hollingsworth sued Richard Mercer on a note of hand promising to pay an obligation in "rie at two shillings pr bushell till it Coms to that to be deliverd at Isack Perkens mill . . . and the Quantity of twenty five yeards of sufiecnt nine hunder Lining Cloth yeard wide."[20] Tobacco for some, linen for others—the point is that both commodities entered the exchange economy that allowed for the conversion of one item into another, facilitating trade in the absence of money.

What, then, is the worldview encompassed by these accounts—by the passing back and forth of goods and services in an exchange economy with debits and credits carefully equated to monetary values but little money changing hands? This was a world that a modern system of consumer exchange based on credit and debit cards, cash, and checking accounts poorly prepares twenty-first-century Americans to understand. This was also a world that George Washington's experience and his expectations prevented him from accepting.

The world of the exchange economy was a kind of Newtonian world operating according to natural law and comprehensible to the human mind through the exercise of observation and reason. Double-entry bookkeeping had indeed developed as part of the same complex intellectual changes that produced a vision of a universe composed of heavenly bodies moving according to mathematical principles that Newton described. Where Newton's world exhibited order and harmony, the world of the exchange economy typified the Newtonian concept of balance. The metaphor of a clockwork mechanism applied to both the natural and economic worlds of the eighteenth century. Just as an escapement device measured out the impulsive force of a spring or falling weights, so the periodic reckoning and forwarding of accounts checked the seemingly random character of economic activity. Differences in the values of debits and credits were expressed not as debt (a flaw in the system that could destroy it) but as the sum necessary to place debits and credits in equilibrium—in other words, the balance due. The balance wheel of the exchange economy functioned in the settling of accounts. Every debit had to be compensated by an equal and opposite credit. What Edward Rogers owed Richard Rogers and Richard owed Edward must equal, because for the goods by which Edward was a debtor to Richard, Richard was at the same time creditor to Edward.

The Newtonian world of debits and credits ordered space. Farmers could deliver wheat to a mill for credit at a store miles away. The crops or work that two farm households exchanged could appear in the books of a local blacksmith. A merchant could acquire cloth or ceramics from an importer in a coastal city on credit for flour delivered by a miller to a commission merchant at another port in a different colony. Similarly, keeping book organized time. Accounts could be balanced once a year, and an imbalance, instead of breaking the system, only deferred the final reckoning of accounts, often to the final reckoning of one of the trading partners. This was a rational world. Its proper functioning depended upon the universal knowledge of numbers. What literacy was to the world of books, numeracy was to the world of account books. Because economic competence depended upon the ability to cast numbers in accounts, a knowledge of mathematics and the principles of keeping book might have been viewed by many men and women as more essential to their way of life than was the ability to read. If the exchange economy rested upon a widespread capacity to think numerically, then it also depended on the universal efficacy of reason—the faith that people would behave rationally, that is, predictably. Exchange economies functioned well in face-to-face communities where people knew one another and could assess with considerable confidence the likelihood that others would meet their obligations or that their assets were sufficient to cover their debts if a case went to law.

Like the Newtonian world, an exchange economy was essentially static. What the double entry of debits and credits and the periodic rendering of accounts allowed individuals was the perception that the complex fabric of their obligations—literally their community—was in balance. What it did not permit was the ready calculation of profit, because it did not sort out income and expenditures. A tally of all balances due would yield an individual's total excess of debits over credits, but none of the accounts surviving from the Virginia backcountry of Washington's day give any evidence of such calculations. That individuals did not reckon all their accounts at the same time and rarely even once a year would have complicated the process in any case. If economic growth is, in some measure, the aggregate of profits over time, then the system of book accounts fostered a worldview in which economic activity did not create new wealth. For one person or household to amass wealth through excessive profits would therefore mean less available wealth for the community. Entrepreneurial activity threatened others with incompetence and dependence, and ambitious people were often viewed with deep suspicion. This is not to say that exchange economies lacked distinctions of wealth but that wealth was measured less in money than in the depth of one's credit and the extent to which obligations could be drawn upon for political authority or for conspicuous display in, for example, election to office or the construction of a new house.

Was George Washington, as an ambitious man, the subject of the mistrust inherent in the conceptual world of an exchange economy? The demands he placed on men for militia service and upon their households for provisions clearly threatened the security of families in the backcountry. But connections among Washington, the exchange economy, and the populace he often despised are more subtle and significant than a simple answer to that question would allow. Understanding the Newtonian world of economic exchange in the eighteenth century helps explain why family and farm came before king and country. The mechanism of these economies worked well to provide for the competence and independence of households without the intervention of superior authority apart from the common law. Like a clock, once wound they ran according to internal principle, not external force. What the Noble Captain saw as a matter of priorities that could be met best without encumbrance by men such as Washington, the aspiring young commander viewed as perfidy and treachery.

In acknowledging that duty obligated him to assume responsibility for people he judged in this light, however, Washington recognized that he must assume the persona of a virtuous man. "The supplicating tears of the women; and moving petitions from the men," Washington plaintively wrote Governor Dinwiddie, "melt me into such deadly sorrow, that I solemnly declare, if I know my own mind—I could offer myself a willing Sacrifice to the butchering Enemy, provided that would contribute to the peoples ease."[21] Washington could justify this disingenuous message to the governor precisely because he was so genuinely struggling with the problem of protecting people he did not like. Virtue for Washington was born in this encounter.

Washington could never write as Thomas Jefferson did that "those who labor in the earth are the chosen people of God, if ever He had a chosen people, whose breasts He has made His peculiar deposit for substantial and genuine virtue."[22] In his life Washington came to acquire vast western lands, which he never conceived in Jeffersonian terms as an "empire of liberty." Instead he chose to keep these lands under his control as landlord and maintain a tenant class subservient to him. As president he worked to link western regions to the nation through transportation improvements and economic development that would enhance the value of his holdings. About the rebellious followers of Daniel Shays, Washington would ask, are the "people getting mad? Are we to have the goodly fabrick we were nine years raising, pulled over our heads?" Later in 1794 he condemned western Pennsylvania farmers protesting the excise or whiskey tax as a "daring and factious spirit" who unless subdued would erect "Mob and Club

Govt."[23] But to draw attention to Washington's failure to put himself in the place of settler households and farm families objecting to taxes and economic insecurity after the American Revolution is, in another sense, to underscore his great ability to cast himself so thoroughly in a republican image that the high standards he set for the sacrifice of self in public life rendered the success of the national experiment dependent, in the minds of many, upon this very virtue.

NOTES

1. *South Carolina Independent Gazette,* June 25, 1791. Reprinted in *A Great and Good Man: George Washington in the Eyes of His Contemporaries,* ed. John P. Kaminski and Jill Adair McCaughan (Madison, Wisc.: Madison House, 1989), 184–87.

2. "Our Saviour and Our Guide," in Kaminski and McCaughan, *A Great and Good Man,* 137.

3. George Washington, "The Farewell," in Kaminski and McCaughan, *A Great and Good Man,* 227–28.

4. Douglas Southall Freeman, *George Washington: A Biography,* 7 vols. (New York: Charles Scribner's Sons, 1948–57), 1:422.

5. George Washington, April 4 and March 26, 1748, *The Diaries of George Washington,* ed. Donald Jackson and Dorothy Twohig, 6 vols. (Charlottesville: University Press of Virginia, 1976–79), 1:18, 15; George Washington to Richard, 1749–50, *The Papers of George Washington: Colonial Series,* ed. W. W. Abbot et al., 10 vols. (Charlottesville: University Press of Virginia, 1983–95), 1:43–44.

6. Washington to Robert Dinwiddie, November 9 and April 22, 1756, ibid., 4:1–10, 3:33–35.

7. Isaac Weld Jr., *Travels through the States of North America . . . During the Years 1795, 1796, and 1797,* 2 vols. (London: John Stockdale, 1807; New York: Johnson Reprint, 1970), 1:146–47.

8. Jack P. Greene, "Independence, Improvement, and Authority: Toward a Framework for Understanding the Histories of the Southern Backcountry during the Era of the American Revolution," in *An Uncivil War: The Southern Backcountry during the American Revolution,* ed. Ronald Hoffman, Thad W. Tate, and Peter J. Albert (Charlottesville: University Press of Virginia, 1985), 12.

9. Washington to Richard, *Papers of George Washington: Colonial Series,* 1:44.

10. Washington to John Robinson, April 16, 1756, ibid., 3:6–8.

11. Washington to John Augustine Washington, May 28, 1755, ibid., 1:289–93.

12. Ibid.; Washington to Dinwiddie, December 2, 1756, ibid., 4:34, 37.

13. Washington to Dinwiddie, October 11, 1755, ibid., 2:101–8.

14. *Chester v Crowson,* May 1745, Ended Causes, 1743–1904, Frederick County Court Papers, Library of Virginia, Richmond.

15. *Bucket v Davidson,* May 1751, ibid.

16. *Warth v Davis*, February 1752, ibid.

17. *Rogers v Rogers*, August 1747, ibid.

18. Lorena S. Walsh, *From Calabar to Carter's Grove: The History of a Virginia Slave Community* (Charlottesville: University Press of Virginia, 1997), 205, 209–10; in Ended Causes, Frederick County Court Papers: *Heath v Babb*, December 1752; *Chester v Hanks*, February 1750; *Hardin v Self*, April 1745; *Hardin v Edge*, August 1748.

19. Warren R. Hofstra, "The Opequon Inventories, Frederick County, Virginia, 1749–1796," *Ulster Folklife* 35 (1989): 59–61; William Gooch to Board of Trade, July 7, 1739, Original Correspondence, Board of Trade, 1736–1740, C.O. 5/1324, Colonial Office Papers, Public Record Office, London.

20. *Hollingsworth v Mercer*, August 1746, Ended Causes, Frederick County Court Papers.

21. Washington to Dinwiddie, April 22, 1756, *Papers of George Washington: Colonial Series*, 3:33–34.

22. Thomas Jefferson, *Notes on the State of Virginia* (London: John Stockdale, 1787; New York: Harper and Row, 1964), 157.

23. Washington to Benjamin Lincoln, November 7, 1789, and Washington to Daniel Morgan, October 8, 1794, Washington Papers, Library of Congress, Washington, D.C., as quoted in Dorothy Twohig, "The Making of George Washington," in *George Washington and the Virginia Backcountry*, ed. Warren R. Hofstra (Madison, Wisc.: Madison House, 1998), 25.

Chapter 4

"THIS GOWN ... WAS MUCH ADMIRED AND MADE MANY LADIES JEALOUS"

Fashion and the Forging of Elite Identities
in French Colonial New Orleans

SOPHIE WHITE

At his presidential inauguration in April 1789, George Washington wore a "complete suit of home spun clothes."¹ This renewed nod to the resources and potential of the nation can been seen as a conscious political statement, a nonverbal rallying cry addressed this time to the new republic.² Washington's championing of the homespun lobby in post-Revolutionary America was all the more notable because the republic remained still overwhelmingly dependent on manufactured goods imported from Britain. It was to remain so despite continuing attempts to bolster the popularity of homespuns, and indeed, at his second inauguration in 1793, Washington wore a black velvet suit of European manufacture.³ Washington's short-lived adoption of homespun after the Revolution was the more significant given his habits in the pre-Revolutionary period. It is to these established sartorial practices that we need to look for the significance of Washington's very public and politically motivated break with precedent. Washington, like his fellow colonists, had not only shopped for textiles and clothing in America from the goods imported from Europe, he had also commissioned garments and textiles directly from merchants in England, engaging in detailed, animated dialogues about the width of a shirt ruffle, the grade of a cloth, and the fashionability and gentility of wearing a certain color in America.⁴ Washington's political gesture toward American homespun—in the context of the seemingly straightforward act of dressing—must be measured against this international background of supply and consumption.

Washington's commercial relationship with England marked him as being at the pinnacle of society and as a man who had the resources and the contacts to interact with merchants and associates in England in the construction of his visual persona. In French colonial Louisiana, we can draw the same distinction between those colonists who were dependent for their choice of dress on the selection of goods available in the colony and those elite colonists who, like Washington, had the means, and the contacts, to procure clothing through kin relations and business contacts in France. But this was not Washington's South. In Louisiana under the French regime (1699–1769), a wide range of governmental and geographical impediments hampered the growth of a viable colonial economy—and, indeed, hindered the development of a homespun tradition.[5] The colony's severe economic problems can be measured in the critical and ongoing shortages of imported commodities into the colony, and in the increased reliance on alternative economic systems that these shortages encouraged.[6] These conditions of consumption framed the role that dress could play in New Orleans.[7] This essay looks outside Washington's domain to colonial Louisiana, an environment marked by fluid social relations and permeable socioeconomic boundaries through much of the colonial period. Here we shall see how in response to these conditions the local elite sought, collectively, to reinforce and extend European hegemony by granting specific values to the promotion of those European fashions common to their peers and kin in France and current in New Orleans. This gave rise to a sartorial language that conveyed position within a culture that was modeled after rigid European paradigms, but that also adapted these models to the particular situation of an economically unstable, sparsely settled, and racially diverse colonial society situated in the American South.[8] It is to this use of dress by the upper reaches of New Orleans society, beyond Washington's world and yet paralleling his elite colonial experience, that my investigation is addressed. Jean-Charles, chevalier de Pradel, and his wife, Alexandrine, will be used to introduce this world.[9] Their experiences will be juxtaposed with those of two members of the administrative ranks, the notary Chantalou and his wife.[10] These case studies reveal the gendered character of the elite consumer experience in French colonial New Orleans, illustrating in the process the extent to which these colonial identities were calibrated on, and targeted to, both metropolitan and local peer relations.

In 1751, not long before a young Major George Washington prepared to engage in the first of many battles against the French, a silk gown was ordered from Paris for the wife of the chevalier de Pradel. This gown was ordered from a fashionable Parisian silk merchant, and to its recipient it bore all the hallmarks of the best French taste. Pradel's order of such a gown (at the behest of his wife) can be read as the particular expression of one colonial family's taste, a finite moment in that family's personal treatment of material culture.[11] This will provide, first, the basis for my discussion of the function of dress in the construction of elite colonial identities in French New Orleans. Second, this analysis will reveal the complex gender divisions and delineations of elite colonial consumerism. Furthermore, this event occurred at a key moment in the transformation of Louisiana from an outpost of the French Crown into a colonial American (and arguably southern) society. Thus this single episode—a proxy commission meant for one female colonist—illustrates the approach of the colony's elite with regard to dress and fashion in the context of material and cultural exchange with Europe. I suggest that it can also serve as a paradigm for the broader context of Louisiana's long-term evolution from a frontier society with fluid social boundaries into a plantation society that promoted stricter delineations.[12] This shift was marked by the increasing promotion of rigid class, race, and economic demarcations, as expressed nonverbally through dress.

In its formative early period as a colony, Louisiana was a fluid frontier society, with large segments of the colonial population involved in the local supply system.[13] Though derived from a hierarchical Old World model, this society was in thrall to an ongoing contest for status and position facilitated by the conditions of consumption in the colony.[14] The potential in early French Louisiana for a break with the past meant, for example, that St. Ange, a baker's son from Burgundy, could rise in the ranks of the military in Louisiana and build up a modest fortune through the fur trade.[15] He could modify his name so that it now sounded like a noble title, and buy what represented the most expensive woman's gown ever sold in Louisiana under the French regime, a striped silk satin gown lined in pink taffeta with matching stockings, shoes, and mittens, at a price of eight hundred livres.[16] This transaction took place in 1725 in Upper Louisiana, the purchase of such finery taking on added significance given the buyer's shifting social and economic status. In this early colonial environment, fashion could be and was used to help effect the transition from a modest social standing to a vastly improved one. This did not fail to create friction with the elite, and in several instances high-ranking colonists complained bitterly of being sartorially snubbed by social inferiors. The transgression of rituals of hat etiquette, to cite one example, generated a number of protests. Thus in 1740 a dispute erupted between the commanding officer of the Pointe Coupée post and a merchant, a quarrel that resulted in the commander physically assaulting the merchant with his cane and sword. The commander asserted that his actions had been set off by the brazenness of the merchant, who had dared to speak to him, an officer, without removing his hat as a sign of respect.[17] By 1751 one of the last complaints about a breach of etiquette between whites was recorded. In that year the *ordonnateur*–the top functionary in the colony, second in command only to the governor—made known to officials in France his grievance upon being snubbed by an inferior, a military officer who had flatly refused to remove his hat in Ordonnateur Michel's presence.[18] Given this evidence of the strained relations between white colonists of varying rank, it is perhaps not surprising that those who made up the highest echelons of society in New Orleans looked to France for affirmation of their perceived superior standing, and closed rank. In this light, the precise terms that frame the gown ordered from Paris by the chevalier de Pradel for his wife may be read as an assertion of a distinctly and pointedly aristocratic gesture within a broader colonial culture of luxurious consumption abetted by malleable identities. Yet this fluidity of colonists' identities was evidenced even in the person of Pradel. For Pradel actively constructed a place for himself at the pinnacle of Louisiana's society by virtue of his name and pedigree, aided by his economic success.

The chevalier de Pradel was the youngest son of an impoverished noble French family from the Limousin region. French-born, he went to Louisiana in 1715 with a minor military commission.[19] He spent more or less the remainder of his life in New Orleans until his death in 1764. Pradel married in Louisiana in 1730. His wife, Alexandrine de la Chaise, was of somewhat less exalted origins, although her father had wielded considerable political influence in the colony as the representative of the Compagnie des Indes and as *ordonnateur*.[20] Pradel built up his modest family inheritance, initially through small-scale commercial (retail) activities and then through agricultural ventures (using slave labor) that vastly increased his material prosperity.[21] By midcentury Pradel was securely positioned as a key figure, if an idiosyncratic one, in the colony's elite circles. The composition of this elite at midcentury is revealed by Governor Kerlerec. Shortly after his arrival in the colony in 1753 to take up his new post, this governor oversaw the arrangements for the celebration of a *Te Deum* dedicated to the health of France's dauphin. The *Te Deum* festivity was a state-sponsored affair, and Governor Kerlerec arranged for the provision of two wine fountains in the town, one for the troops, the other for the populace. Kerlerec himself personally hosted a more exclusive reception, a supper for 113 ladies and their 200 or so escorts.[22] These colonists, the privileged guests of the governor, were a motley group of settlers of varying rank, mixing minor nobles, official functionaries, and military officers, joined by plantation owners and merchants. Yet this was no sartorial "democracy." Indeed, among the colonial elite, social distinctions did not vanish altogether, and the governor and his wife customarily surrounded themselves with an even more exclusive inner circle of intimates. Thus, in contrast to the public realm of the *Te Deum* festivity, we find that when it was the turn of the chevalier de Pradel to entertain the governor at his plantation, only twenty-five "of the choicest ladies and gentlemen" were invited.[23] This inner circle, I will show, shared the same aesthetic, shopped for clothing together, and sought to outdo one another in the fashions that they wore. Into this closed society, sometime in 1751, Madame de Pradel's gown was introduced.

The chevalier de Pradel gave details of the gown's commission in a personal letter of May 24, 1751, to his older brothers in France. He specified that he had ordered a summer gown of brocaded taffeta, the selection of the silk design having been left to the taste of M. Corvoisier, silk merchant on the rue des Bourdonnais. Pradel added that it was his wife who had directed him to apply to that particular mercer for the order, and we will return to this point.[24] It is clear from Pradel's letter that this was his first contact with the firm of Corvoisier et Richer. When the outfit arrived in New Orleans, Pradel reported that it was much admired and, pertinently, "made many ladies jealous."[25] Madame de Pradel's gown, commissioned from a fashionable mercer in Paris, created a stir in New Orleans, no doubt as much by virtue of its provenance as of its actual appearance. The shop of Corvoisier et Richer, called Le Lyon d'Argent (the Silver Lion), was located on the rue des Bourdonnais, a street that housed the establishments of the most luxurious silk merchants in Paris.[26] Mercers were one of the most important of the Parisian trade guilds; those who specialized in the sale of silks and cloth of gold or silver, as did Corvoisier et Richer, were among the most prestigious of all shopkeepers.[27] Their recommendations carried weight with the silk designers and weavers of Lyons—the preeminent European manufacturers of figured silks—and their advice in matters of taste was eagerly sought by those wishing to appear fashionable.[28] Madame de Pradel, by virtue of her patronage of a firm of fashionable Parisian mercers, allied herself to their prestige and promoted herself successfully as an arbiter of taste in New Orleans. Pradel and his wife may have had an unspoken aim to underline the contrasts between their elevated station and that of the numerous middling settlers who were freely laying claim to fashionable dress and an enhanced social status. But their words betray a greater concern with impressing the members of their own group. Not only did the chevalier de Pradel comment that the ladies in the colony were magnificently attired, but he added that "in order not to appear ridiculous, one must do as others do."[29] By his reference to "others" he meant the other members of his own immediate circle. This was not a concern with impressing onlookers of lesser rank—though that may have happened as well. It was a desire for peer approval and expressed a quest for social cohesion among these peers, and this has implications for our reading of the role of (high) fashion in French colonial Louisiana. It is to this closed circle that we must look for clues about the role of fashion in the forging of colonial identities, namely that of elite female consumers.[30]

In his letters, Pradel offered numerous insights into the workings of this nuclear group of privileged settlers. Pradel was informally separated from his wife. Though she lived in New Orleans and he lived on his plantation, Monplaisir, on the outskirts of the city, he kept abreast of her expenditures and was familiar with her lifestyle. In one letter, responding to his elder brother's concern about the profligate spending of his wife in New Orleans, Pradel wholeheartedly if somewhat disingenuously agreed. The expense, he added,

> is caused by the acquisitions my wife makes from merchants; a beautiful silk in the latest fashion; beautiful embroidered sleeve ruffles; and all the accessories of ladies who wish to shine and be in step with the governor's wife. These are things which my wife cannot resist. But . . . I never refuse her anything.[31]

A key feature of Pradel's description here, as in other correspondence, was the pleasure he took in recounting his family's success with the local elite, specifically the circle of the sitting governors.[32] They socialized together at formal and informal events, and his account of the immediate entourage of the governor's wife suggests that shopping for this group was a social pastime, rather than merely a way to acquire necessary apparel. Indeed, there was an edge to this pastime, since at stake was not only the possession of the latest fashions but the prestige of sharing these with the governor's wife and, indeed, being on a par with her. Like the entourage of Madame de Pradel and Governor Kerlerec's wife, brought together by the pastime of shopping and dressing, other women in the colony formed such ties by virtue of their kin relations. This was brought out in the dispute that arose between members of the Superior Council and the *ordonnateur* concerning some contraband English galloon brought from one of the posts into the company store in New Orleans for measuring and accounting. Three councilors, Fazende, Fleuriau, and Péry, had taken some of this gold and silver lace from the store, ostensibly on credit (this was the source of the dispute).[33] Fazende and Fleuriau were married to two sisters, and another councilor, Bruslé, was married to the women's cousin, three alliances that were described in an official communication as giving "to our society a new charm, these three ladies each being amiable and well born."[34] Councilor Bruslé alone had not taken any of the galloon, but had expressed his fear that once one of the women learned of the existence of this lace, the others—meaning his wife—would follow in wanting some.[35] It is notable in this context that, following her death, most of the fine clothing sold at Dame Bruslé's postmortem auction in 1769 was bought by her granddaughter, suggesting that it was in good enough condition to be worn by her following any necessary alterations or remodeling.[36] Also inventoried with Dame Bruslé's effects were items left in her care by her daughter, Dame Favrot, who was on a visit to France. The latter owned many suits of clothes made from fabrics whose description bears a striking resemblance to those of her mother.[37] The willingness of three generations of women from the same family to wear the same clothes, as implied here, was by no means exceptional. Yet I suggest that this should be seen as a further sign of the binding ties of shared fashion and appearance among a select group. Clothing, then, acted as a social glue, bringing together the members of the same circle, but also pitting them against one another in a contest for preeminence.

In this peer-judged contest fought among whites of French heritage living in a colonial society, laying claim to knowledge of new fashions from Europe took on particular significance. The description of Madame de Pradel's gown will serve as a focal point for evaluating the nuanced character of the cultural relationship with France. Indeed, the details volunteered by Pradel about the stylistic appearance of his wife's gown are not simply relevant to a purely formalist analysis of fashion in the colony. Rather, these provide a means of evaluating the transfer of Parisian fashions to New Orleans, while setting the framework for an analysis of the relationship between colonists and their originary culture. In seeking to locate the meaning of things for Louisiana's elite consumers, this essay will contextualize that article of dress, drawing particular attention to the wealth of detail that conditions our knowledge of consumption. The interpretation of the physical features of the gown is a crucial step in understanding the wider meaning of the role of fashion in forging identities. Close examination of the stylistic evidence therefore is key. According to his letter, Pradel had instructed Corvoisier to have the gown made up for his wife and designated the kind of textile: brocaded taffeta. He may additionally have indicated a color preference and price range, but there is no information on these aspects. The bill rendered by Corvoisier et Richer read:[38]

26½ ells of brocaded taffeta with a white ground at 10 livres the ell	265 £
⅔ ell of white florence taffeta to line the sleeves at 5 livres the ell	37
Paid to the seamstress for the making and trimming of the gown	17
For one large-size packing case	3
Total:	288 £ 7

The gown is not known to have survived, nor are there additional references to its appearance in the documentary record.[39] Fortunately, a number of clues are present in the reference to provide an image of this gown. For example, the price of the silk for the gown, ten livres per ell, indicates that the taffeta with its white ground was brocaded not in gold or silver but in colored silks.[40] Further, taffeta silks were often of mediocre quality. However, these very characteristics translated into the lustrous, lightweight, paper-thin fabrics ideal for use in the floating, hooped dresses popular in this period.[41] An extant Lyons silk fragment dating from circa 1745–50 gives a good indication of the general appearance of Madame de Pradel's taffeta. Tabby-woven of off-white silk with a monochrome liseré pattern, it is brocaded with a floral design in tones of pearl, pink, orange, red, violet, green, yellow, blue, and turquoise.[42]

In New Orleans, the popularity of taffetas may have hinged on another quality, one that highlights the impact on dress of the environment in one "southern" climatic region. Taffeta was a plain (tabby) weave. As such, it was claimed as particularly suitable for summer wear by fashion commentators in eighteenth-century France, with denser satin and twill weaves advocated for the cooler seasons.[43] Taffeta's suitability to hotter weather was of no little consequence in New Orleans, which remained clement year-round though especially hot and humid in the summer. The question of how far these seasonal variations were observed in Louisiana was partly answered in Madame de Pradel's request for a *summer* gown made of taffeta, suggesting that, in her circle at least, such seasonal differences were observed. This is supported by her desire to order from Corvoisier et

Richer for each of her daughters (in France) a *taffeta* gown in their choice of color, to wear the following summer.[44] Madame de Pradel's own taffeta gown arrived from France sometime before June or July, and we may speculate whether she did wear it only for summer, switching to twilled and satin silks (or woolens) by the end of the season. And yet, there is some evidence to suggest that climatic considerations subjugated fashion considerations when it came to the selection of temperature-appropriate textiles in New Orleans: of the silks listed in surviving inventories, taffetas are identified far more frequently than other, denser silk weaves.[45]

The prevalence of cotton and linen clothing in the wardrobes of a majority of New Orleans inhabitants may be another sign of concession to the climate, a preference confirmed in merchants' records.[46] Cotton and linen-based textiles featured prominently in the probate inventories of both modest and wealthy settlers in the Lower Mississippi Valley, with *indiennes* (calicoes) found in the richer households through much of the French period, and coarser checked or striped cottons prevalent in modest wardrobes.[47] The records of Dame Bruslé's 1769 postmortem inventory and auction sale have survived and are a case in point.[48] Dame Bruslé—one of the three cousins whose husbands appropriated the contraband gold lace—had a wardrobe characterized by the richness of its materials and patterning. Along with many silk garments, she owned petticoats and jackets of printed calico, a cotton skirt, a cotton mantle, and one of striped muslin. Yet, whatever the impact of the climate on the dress worn by even the wealthier classes in the colony, the popularity of cottons there paralleled their growing popularity in England and France through the eighteenth century for fashionable dress and furnishings, some of high quality.[49] Similarly, the fashion for lightweight silks—taffetas of the kind ordered by Madame de Pradel for her summer gown—offered another means of reconciling the demands of an extreme and unfamiliar climate with the needs of high fashion. While this factor complicates the process of evaluating the fashionability (according to dominant French standards) of New Orleans's elite settlers, it does suggest an altered attitude toward imported goods on the part of colonists living in a unique physical environment.

The stylistic features of Madame de Pradel's gown thus offer us an opportunity to consider the question of how taste was mediated between colonial client and Parisian merchant. This has implications for the reciprocal perceptions by colonists and French apparel professionals of each other's presumed taste and fashionability. As Pradel and his wife were not in Paris for its purchase, the selection of the actual fabric for the gown was left to the silk merchant Corvoisier or his partner, and probably was from regular stock rather than a special order. Surviving correspondence between Parisian silk merchants and their clients brings out the utter need for trust in the merchants' good taste and knowledge of fashion.[50] Not only the selection of a fabric but the choice of cut for Madame de Pradel's gown was left to the "taste" of the merchant Corvoisier.[51] This was doubtless a collaborative effort between Corvoisier and the seamstress. The latter would have been responsible for selecting the trimmings, since in the sales memo these are listed together with her services rather than itemized with the materials charged by Corvoisier.[52] The styles of gowns remained relatively static in this period, and it is in the fabrics and the surface decorations that a wearer could best denote his or her adherence to fashion. Madame de Pradel may therefore have desired to have her gown made up for this reason alone, as an acknowledgment of the growing role of seamstresses in devising fashionable trimmings.[53] The trimmings on Madame de Pradel's gown are not described; they may have consisted of robings, fly braid, or other surface decoration, as seen in surviving gowns from the period.[54] Certainly from the quantity of fabric (26½ French ells of taffeta) needed for Madame de Pradel's gown, it is clear that this was a voluminous garment, probably an open sack, a *robe à la française*, with matching petticoat and stomacher.[55] It would be worn with boned stays and a pair of hoops, which provided the basic shape for the gown.[56] The description of Madame de Pradel's gown from the invoice, while suggestive, is not detailed enough to indicate whether Corvoisier had selected remaindered stock or the latest patterns in silks for his colonial client. There was variety enough in colors and patterns of taffetas to engender a thriving—though admittedly choice—market in seasonal silk patterns. The mode in patterned silks was ephemeral. The written sources indicate that names, and therefore designs, changed with each season, if only in minor details. The material evidence is insufficient to allow us to date surviving silk designs so precisely, although vertical meandering designs with naturalistic flowers and foliage were popular at midcentury.[57] The flip side of this world of fast-changing fashion was that old stock could be left unsold on the shelf, discarded in favor of the newest patterns and colors, and therefore devalued. For this reason, and following established practice, remaindered goods were sent to the provinces or to the colonies, where the clientele was not expected to be so knowledgeable about or desirous of the very latest in fashion.[58] Indeed, Governor Perier complained that Louisiana was treated as the dumping ground for merchandise that couldn't sell in France for a good price.[59] Furthermore, stocks of textiles and ready-made clothing left unsold in the

French West Indies were sometimes shipped to Louisiana for sale there, meaning a double delay in the transmission of new French fashions to New Orleans.[60] Given colonists' dependency on French exports of manufactured goods, such time lags would have had a marked impact on the materials available to settlers for the elaboration of their appearance. However, because of the absence of surviving garments and the lack of visual sources, it is difficult to document this.

A notable exception to this shortage is found in the portraits of one family from the French colonial period in Louisiana. Though they are now dispersed, on the basis of biographical information and details of dress I have dated these portraits of the d'Auberville family members to circa 1760–64 and concluded that they were painted in France. Two of the portraits are of sisters, Marie Louise Le Seneschal d'Auberville and her younger sister Céleste.[61] In contrast to the Pradel daughters, who were to have their choice of color for their taffeta gowns, the d'Auberville sisters wear gowns cut from the same piece of silk, further evidence that the two portraits were painted contemporaneously. The cut of their gowns is almost identical and is of the same striped watered taffeta in the same pinkish-red color. Most of the rendition of the taffeta is unfinished except for the ground color, but the stripes are seen clearly on the two sitters' left sleeves: one inch apart, deeper pink on paler pink ground. This is significant because stripes were making their renewed appearance in high fashion in the first half of the 1760s.[62] The sisters' striped taffetas can be compared to surviving gowns and extant textile samples dating to this period.[63]

From 1748 to 1757 the father of the two girls was acting *ordonnateur*, the position held earlier by Madame de Pradel's father. The d'Auberville family was a fairly typical one among Louisiana's elite, one that combined ancestors from Canada and France, of both high and lowly birth, coupled with a rise in economic and social standing accomplished in America.[64] D'Auberville's widow and her two daughters had spent the years 1759 to 1764 in France, at Versailles, where in all probability their portraits were painted before the family's permanent return to Louisiana in 1764. The d'Auberville sisters doubtless planned to bring their gowns, bought in France, back with them to wear in Louisiana. There they would have joined Madame de Pradel and the other well-to-do ladies of fashion in the colony who had selected taffeta as the weave of choice for their silk gowns. By their choice of a *striped* fabric, they marked themselves as knowledgeable about this recent Parisian fashion. The fact that the two sisters planned to bring back to the colony portraits of themselves in this new emerging fashion would have served to underline the continuity in their appearance with the fashions worn at Versailles. I suggest that we should draw a parallel between this family's deployment of material culture and that of the chevalier de Pradel. Pradel's son had married well in France. A portrait of Pradel's daughter-in-law hung in the elder Pradel's house, witness both to her importance within his family and to the continuity of his connections with France.[65] Similarly, when Pradel planned for the return to New Orleans of his daughters after their education at an Ursuline convent in Brittany, foremost among his concerns was that they not arrive looking like "former nuns."[66] Rather than have them buy their new clothes in the more convenient port of La Rochelle, Pradel made plans for them to acquire their Louisiana wardrobes in Paris, namely from the same prestigious firm of Corvoisier et Richer, a clear endorsement of the ascendancy, among elite colonists, of personally commissioned metropolitan high fashion.

Pradel's correspondence hints at the difficulties inherent in commissioning clothes by proxy from afar, for long-distance shopping was not without its challenges. For instance, George Washington complained repeatedly about the bad fit of the garments shipped to him from Britain.[67] Though Washington attributed these shortcomings to his unusual height and problems of measurement, some of the blame can be ascribed to the new fashion for ever tighter clothes, which he was not accustomed to. Transactions by correspondence, such as those between Washington and his factors, or between Corvoisier and his Louisiana client, were based on the tradition of provincial clients commissioning goods from metropolitan merchants. Theirs was a relationship based on trust, and was not always successful. Pradel, for instance, not satisfied with the goods sent by his regular agent in Paris, considered switching allegiances and using Corvoisier for all his future commissions.[68] The relationship was made more complicated by the distance between France and Louisiana, by the bias of the metropolitan French against colonists, and by the notions of fashion peculiar to the settlers of a sparse, isolated, and marginalized colony.[69]

This general point can be illustrated by drawing on the evidence of other proxy commissions from New Orleans. We find a useful counterpoint to Pradel's relationship with his Paris agents in the relationship between another French-born colonist, Augustin Chantalou, and his contact in France. Chantalou was the chief clerk of the Superior Council, Royal Notary, and Attorney of Vacant Estates in New Orleans: in other words, while not on a par socially with Pradel, he was a key bureaucrat. Chantalou had an ongoing partnership between 1752 and 1754 with a merchant named Testar at the major Atlantic port of La Rochelle for the sale in the colony of French manufactured goods, mostly textiles and clothing, in return for furs and other raw materials.[70] Their wives also engaged together and for their personal profit in the petty retail trade of fashionable goods, such as pompons, which Madame Testar selected for Madame Chantalou to sell in New Orleans.[71] But Chantalou also commissioned clothing for himself and his family from his business partner in France, and there is some indication that the two men were related by marriage. This suggests that Chantalou and his wife looked to their peers, in this case their kin relations in France, for the provision of clothing deemed appropriate to their particular social standing.

Among the more personal transactions between Chantalou and Testar was the former's request in 1752 for two wigs from France for his own use. Testar had the wigs made at once according to Chantalou's instructions, and with what he claimed to be great care.[72] In contrast to the experience of Pradel, a member of the fashionable elite, in ordering a gown from the mercers Corvoisier et Richer of the rue des Bourdonnais in Paris, Chantalou was not so happy with the result of his commission, made through the provincial port of La Rochelle. His criticism of the wigs is instructive:

> I have received ... the two wigs which you sent me. They are rather well made, for any other but myself. I am distressed at not being able to make use of them. They are too short at the front by at least an inch, though the gray is quite beautiful. If you would care to have another two wigs made for me, I should be much obliged, and please request that the wig-maker not use any [animal] hair as he has in the ones I have received. Given all this, I set you no price limit.[73]

What is notable about Chantalou's complaints is that these concern the style of the wigs. The quality was acceptable, and the gray hair (*grisaille*) was well rendered. But he found his wigs to be too short by at least one inch. Chantalou was writing in 1752. The styles established in the previous decade called for wigs that curled or rolled down to the nape, where the hair was either left loose in a long bob or tied in a low knot. By the early 1750s in France, it was fashionable for wigs to be shorter around the face, sometimes with only one roll at the sides. In other words, it seems that the wig-maker had produced wigs in the fashionable style for Chantalou, reflecting the new shorter sides popular in France. This shift was dramatic enough for Chantalou to reject the wigs altogether and request new ones. Whether Chantalou had rejected the wigs because of his old-fashioned notions of style, or because he was unaccustomed to seeing the new styles and judged the shortness to be a mistake rather than intentional, is unclear.

The second seems more likely, for in his request for a second set of wigs, Chantalou made clear that price was to be no object (the more—and longer—the hair, the higher the price). It seems in this instance that there was a time lag in the acceptance of new fashions. Such a time lag can be read as a positive reinforcement of the familiar, an endorsement of the customs and fashions *already* in place in the colony. The question of the dissemination of French fashion to Louisiana thus becomes an issue for consideration in the context of colonists' self-fashioning.

Information about the latest French fashions was transmitted to colonists in a number of different ways. Recent arrivals in the colony brought with them news of the latest styles, and indeed Pradel himself traveled back to France on a number of occasions, sometimes accompanied by his wife. Periodicals filled in some of the gaps in information, as might the fully attired dolls that were circulated in the provinces and abroad by merchants as a way to advertise their goods and services.[74] Such sources of information, or advertising, familiarized the colonial clientele with some of the latest French styles and fashions, although the nuances of how they received this information and the precise ways in which they acted upon it remain unclear. For in spite of the presence in the colony of these types of information, disadvantages remained because of the distance from Europe, disadvantages that might have been exploited by merchants in France. Given this, we need to revisit Pradel's description of his wife's shopping expeditions in New Orleans with Governor Kerlerec's wife, where he referred to the purchase of articles "à nouvelle mode," in the newest fashion. Without accompanying visual and material evidence, it is unclear just how fashionable and novel these silks and accessories really were, compared to those in France. Articles described as in the latest taste were occasionally listed in lading bills of merchandise imported from France, such as the "stockings in the new taste" and the "modish fine cotton lining material" sent for the account of Chantalou by his partner Testar.[75] Furthermore, while lading bills did not always spell out that a particular article was representative of the latest fashion, this was usually understood to be the case. A listing for four caps "electricity style" shipped by Testar to Chantalou in August 1753 hints at the seasonal terminology typical of fashion marketing in Paris—in this instance referring to the vogue for all things relating to electricity.[76] Lading bills were written up by the merchants in France, describing the merchandise sent on ships bound for Louisiana, and it was they who identified these goods as fashionable, no doubt using the term as a marketing ploy. Merchants in New Orleans were expected to keep their French partners informed, and their letters offer useful insights into the state of fashion in the colony. Chantalou commented on the goods that were selling well, but also gave feedback on those that had failed to find a market. While women's stockings were in demand, he wrote in 1752, blue, red, and green-hued ones were not selling.[77] This may have been because they were deemed to be old-fashioned overstocks, or because they were not recognized as being in the latest taste. In France, fashions in colors fluctuated with the seasons.[78] Stockings reflected these changes, since it was fashionable for stockings to match or complement the suit.[79]

In a colonial setting such as Louisiana, the reception of different styles, colors, and patterns inevitably raises questions about the colonists' willingness to accept the unfamiliar. It seems that in the case of the stockings left unsold, it was indeed the novelty of their color and style that had prejudiced customers. The following year Testar again made an important purchase of "good quality novelty stockings" which he sent to Chantalou in New Orleans.[80] However, the latter was mostly annoyed with Testar for sending this new consignment of stockings in the latest colors and styles. "There are large quantities of them [in the colony]," he wrote, exasperated, "and few people are wearing them."[81] This clash between Chantalou's and Testar's perspectives on the same fashions serves to bring out the contrasts between the perception of fashion in New Orleans and in France, including provincial France.

Some of the crucial issues brought up in this discussion are: the question of how fully those colonists with pretensions to fashion were aware of the latest changes in textiles and fashions in France, and how preoccupied they were with these changes; how far behind they lagged in their wholehearted adoption of the new fashions that did make their way to Louisiana; and how much they may have been (or felt they were) misled by agents in France. All of these nuance our view of the material relationship between colony and founding country; however, these questions remain, because of the shortcomings of the material and visual evidence, open to speculation. For instance, Madame de Pradel's reliance on the taste of the silk merchant Corvoisier for her gown obscures the dynamic between colonists' active and passive assimilation of French taste. The construction of her appearance was contrived with the help of a fashionable merchant in France. Yet this was not achieved without a degree of input from Madame de Pradel—her choice of supplier and her preference for a patterned silk taffeta—through the intermediary of her husband. In this way she could attempt to communicate her own sartorial priorities, whether informed by the climate or by her own aesthetic taste, while leaving the actual choice of cloth, color, and cut to her agent in France. Similarly, George Washington left the final choice of cloth, color, and cut to his agents in England, but he made repeated attempts to communicate his own sartorial priorities.[82] Thus Madame de Pradel, like members of the elite in other American colonies, did not simply accept indiscriminately the fashion imported from Europe but found ways to convey her own notions of what was suitable for wearing in the colony, a clear illustration of the ascendancy of a fresh colonial aesthetic.

We find a parallel in the wardrobe items that Chantalou commissioned Testar to buy for his wife. In 1752 Chantalou requested his French partner's assistance in obtaining new boned stays, two stomachers, tippets of blond lace, a winter mantle trimmed with lace, a lace headdress, two pairs of mules, and two more pairs of shoes made from either gold or silver cloth.[83] Testar gave details about this commission in a letter the following year.[84] For example, a short winter mantle with trimmings for Madame Chantalou was sent from Paris along with other goods ordered for his own wife's use. But Testar also offered some evidence of the difficulty of buying personal clothing for others, even those within his own socioeconomic class. He complained repeatedly about Chantalou's lack of precision, while explaining how he dealt with this by using his own initiative to decide on styles and other details.[85] Thus, despite the fact that Chantalou did not give detailed enough instructions, such as his wife's size or preferred color, Testar went ahead and had his wife's shoemaker make four pairs of shoes.[86] Madame Chantalou declared her shoes perfect and ordered another four pairs of mules and four pairs of shoes in the same size, in a fabric of Madame Testar's taste. This suggests that Madame Testar may well have known Madame Chantalou's size (and taste) from past experience, and known that there would be a good fit, suggesting once again the likelihood of a kin relationship between the two women.[87] Even jewelry was purchased from France through intermediaries. Chantalou having dropped hints since 1753 about wanting some garnet earrings for his wife, Testar eventually sent some.[88] It seems, however, that neither Chantalou nor his wife was entirely happy with the results, even though Testar had elicited the help of "one of my friends with taste" in selecting the garnet earrings.[89] Chantalou's response was to give an unusually detailed description of Madame Chantalou's desired style: "She desired earrings made of fine garnets mounted in gold, with a single pendant rather than a girandole, but since I anticipate that this would be expensive, she will do without."[90] Garnets recur more than any other stone, semiprecious or precious, in records from throughout the French colonial period. Rarely these were for earrings, but more commonly we find listings for strands of garnets at a more modest price.⁹¹ Madame Chantalou's request for the earrings can be read as an expression of her rank, for hers were more impressive pieces of garnet jewelry than those commonly found in the colony. Her preference for garnets meant that her choice remained firmly planted within the aesthetics of the community.

In the contacts of Pradel and Chantalou with their respective agents, strikingly, it was the men of the household who oversaw the commissioning of apparel from France. The issue of gender as it relates to the process of clothing consumption is one therefore that warrants special consideration in this instance. It has been argued of this period that women played a greater role in the selection of dress than men, the latter being viewed by society as unsuited to the task. Based on evidence from the diaries of a Lancashire gentlewoman, Amanda Vickery contends that "while female consumption was repetitive and predominantly mundane, male consumption was, by contrast, occasional and impulsive, or expensive and dynastic."⁹² This statement is borne out in the respective relationships of the chevalier de Pradel and his wife to shopping. Pradel's correspondence shows that he was responsible for all orders placed in France, while his wife is mentioned only as shopping in New Orleans. It was Pradel who placed the actual order for his wife's taffeta summer gown, which was an expensive and substantial purchase. But it was she who was responsible for the more mundane clothing matters, as witnessed by her return to the plantation to see to her grown son's clothes.⁹³

There was a further distinction. While Pradel commissioned his important purchases, whether of clothing or furnishings, from men in France, he addressed his mundane requests for household linens and underwear to women there. What's more, the men charged with his important commissions were all professionals—agents or merchants—while the women tended to be his female relatives. Thus, the luxurious furniture and furnishings for his plantation were ordered via his correspondents in Lorient and Paris.⁹⁴ In contrast, he wrote his brother to ask that his niece negotiate the purchase of the fabric for napkins, tablecloths, and sheets, which he expected his daughters to hem on their arrival in New Orleans from France.⁹⁵ Not surprisingly, this expectation that women engage together in household and clothing matters bore on their relationships with one another. Not only did they engage together in the same social and household activities, but their dress reflected this closeness. We find this connectedness in the shared pastimes of Madame Kerlerec's entourage, who went shopping together for leisure, or in the fashions shared by Mesdames Fazende, Fleuriau, and Bruslé, who had been expected to pounce on the same contraband galloon. We also find it in the sartorial relationship, both personal and financial, between the female relatives of merchants in France and in the colony. In a letter to Chantalou, Testar included a note on behalf of his wife that embodied the interconnectedness of business and pleasure in kin relationships:

> Please receive, your dear wife and yourself, a thousand compliments from my wife, who counts on your kindness to dispose of her little consignment of merchandise. She would be charmed if Madame Chantaloup [sic] found among this consignment some item that might please her. She asks her not to make any fuss about this and just to help herself to it.[96]

As with Pradel and his wife, the fact that husbands interjected themselves into these long-distance relations between women raises questions about the parameters of men's influence over their wives. The extraordinary character of the contact between Louisiana and France enabled the involvement of husbands in the dealings of their wives, as the unrestricted everyday interactions between women living and socializing in the colony did not.

While touching on many different aspects of the provision of dress to the colony, the correspondence between Testar and Chantalou provides a glimpse into the fashion consciousness, wardrobe, and appearance of one New Orleans woman, the wife of Augustin Chantalou, Attorney of Vacant Estates, chief clerk of the Superior Council, and entrepreneur. It also indicates that Chantalou sought an appropriate French provincial yardstick—that of their Testar relations at La Rochelle—against which to judge the dress of his wife. The documents make clear which items were sent for Madame Chantalou's personal use and which were for trade. She wore respectable mantles that were trimmed with fine lace, her feet were clad in silver-brocaded shoes and mules, her head was adorned with pompons, and she yearned for fine gold-mounted garnet earrings. The construction of her appearance was contrived with the help of her connections in France. The reliance of Chantalou and his wife on the taste of others, much like Pradel's reliance on the taste of the mercer Corvoisier for his wife's dress, problematizes the question of colonists' agency in fashioning their identities. Nevertheless, the evidence suggests that their acceptance of this imported taste, irrespective of its pedigree, was tempered by a discriminating reaction to some of the goods chosen for them. Those colonists who, like Pradel or Chantalou, had direct links to France were responsible with their wives for introducing new French fashions and, in so doing, made these respectable. Differences between the elite and the functionary class were expressed in their preferred source of clothing and textiles—and, by implication, in the quality and exclusivity of those goods. For example, Pradel disparaged the merchandise assembled by merchants at Rochefort and La Rochelle, while Chantalou supplemented his livelihood and stocked his family's wardrobe through contacts with these.[97] The standards of dressing adhered to by the Pradel and Chantalou households–the one representative of the nobility, the other standing for the professional, officeholder class—were affirmations of the stratification that still dominated France's social order. Yet, while superimposing these derivative sartorial practices onto New Orleans's fledgling society, Pradel and Chantalou and their wives adapted these modes of dressing to their new circumstances. They stamped their own notions of acceptable or desirable elements onto the goods sent them for their personal use. In this way, they served as intermediaries in the transfer of new fashions from France to the colony and moderated these according to prevailing local outlooks and standards of demeanor.[98] This collective responsibility for the introduction, revision, and spread of European fashion in New Orleans had as its ultimate consequence the emergence of a negotiated sartorial identity in the colony, one that we can tentatively begin to identify as localized, even regional.

The chevalier de Pradel's later life in Louisiana was marked by an increasing material prosperity. His lifestyle reconciled wants and desires that were both French-derived and steeped in the colonial experience. This duality was expressed by Pradel in a letter to his brother in which he enclosed a plan of his new house: "You will see by this plan ... that, although we are here in another world, we like to have our pleasures, and we see to our creature comforts as much as possible."[99] Pradel encouraged his wife, son, and daughters to show themselves to advantage, and he devoted himself to updating and furnishing his plantation, acquired from Governor Perier in 1750, according to the latest trends popular in France.[100] The plantation under Pradel's ownership consisted of a principal house with galleries, a brick staircase, and glazed windows, and, in a carryover of the Anglomania fashion in France, grounds that included a fan-shaped pleasure garden in the English taste. The house was furnished with nine-foot-tall gilded mirrors, marble-top tables, oil paintings, and wall hangings, all ordered from Paris.[101] Local influences were not eliminated altogether, as seen in the style of architecture and in Pradel's order of some lacquer for application by his own workmen.[102] Pradel exhibited increasing pride in his achievements, yet his boasts were aimed not only at his peers in the colony but also at another audience, his direct family members back in France. This was brought out in his choice of language: not only was his the most beautiful and the best furnished *plantation* in the colony, it was akin to a *château*.[103] The chevalier de Pradel and his wife were unquestionably of the highest social rank in Louisiana's unexceptional elite circles. But it was Pradel's improving economic status that had enabled him to raise his standing in the colony a notch or two, as he progressed from a minor member of the French provincial nobility and a retired captain into a respected, wealthy planter and important slave owner, in much the same way that Washington could deploy his wife's wealth to his social advantage. In 1751, one year after negotiating the purchase of Governor Perier's plantation, Pradel sealed his newfound position of affluence with the purchase of a gown from France. This gown, through the intermediary of his wife, advertised the continuity between Pradel's French origins and his position in Louisiana. It was the ultimate irony that Pradel, who used material goods and his ties to France to assert his preeminence in New Orleans society, was in the end betrayed by his very consumerism. Not enough money was left after his lavish expenditure to provide adequate dowries for his daughters to marry well in France. He had had them educated in France and had furnished them with rich wardrobes. But ultimately, instead of finding suitors in France, he resigned himself to bringing them back to Louisiana to find husbands there, their wardrobes to be deployed in the service of that operation.[104]

It must be reiterated that this essay has focused on the elite and their approach to fashion. It concerns the responses of a tiny minority of colonists to dress, and analyzes the image they projected. Nonetheless, from the narrowly focused analysis of elite dress presented here we can make further inferences about the emergence of a new colonial order and the construction of a class system that was peculiar to New Orleans. Through his careful manipulation of material culture, the chevalier de Pradel, an impoverished minor nobleman, established his place at the highest echelons of this colonial town. For the functionary Chantalou, it was through links with his peers at La Rochelle, who provided him with apparel and trade goods, that he underlined his role as an important officeholder of the French Crown. The framework for these developments was etched on a template of class relations originating in France, but was made more pliable by the unique conditions—for instance the particularly harsh economic climate—that characterized the colony.

The period from midcentury to the end of the French regime in Louisiana marked a first transition in the shift from a fluid emerging society—indeed, a "frontier exchange economy," to draw on Daniel H. Usner Jr.—to one of a more fixed character, in a process that was to converge with the rise of the plantation economy.[105] The seeds of this evolution were sown during the latter part of the French regime.[106] It was a transition that was marked by the repression of those social and economic activities that were perceived as a direct threat to local authority. Henceforth, rather than new laws being dispatched from Europe for application in Louisiana, it was increasingly the elite merchant and slave-owning colonists who formulated local policy. This is seen in the proliferation of edicts written and enacted in New Orleans under both the French and the Spanish regimes. The merchant-led New Orleans Rebellion of 1768 was a further sign of the ascendancy of this local elite.[107]

Already by midcentury the colonial elite was enthusiastically expressing its power by means of sartorial display. By this date, following a period of economic stability in the colony, men like Pradel had achieved a certain affluence. Their energies could now be devoted to the consolidation and expression of their power through nonverbal means such as the display of their persons and their property. They did not strive to assert their sartorial supremacy over white social inferiors. Instead, their resources were increasingly devoted to competing with one another, with their peers, in a genteel contest for social preeminence. Thus in 1751 Pradel placed an extraordinary order with a Parisian silk merchant for a taffeta gown for his wife, a symbol of his prestige.

Concomitant with the new confidence of the slave-owning class, from midcentury and over the next two decades prior to the cession to Spain, New Orleans was to witness a drop in complaints about the behavior and dress of white colonists of lesser standing. In 1751, the year that Pradel placed his order for the gown, a new police code was formulated in the colony. Primarily aimed at blacks, this regulation sought not only to control the movements of the wider population but also to limit the social and mercantile interactions between members of different groups, classes, or races.[108] At the same time, there was a sharp rise in the number of prosecutions of blacks, in the face of increasing resistance by respectable white colonists protective of their private property. These prosecutions were for crimes that revealed the increasing consumerism of slaves and free blacks, specifically their consumption of clothing and textiles.[109] In spite of these restraints, evidence for slaves' resistance to the local elite may be found in the court cases of the period. In particular, these texts reveal the perceived threat offered by blacks' manipulation of dress. By 1765 in New Orleans, it was no longer the disrespectful white colonist of lower standing who was singled out for not cocking his hat to a superior. Instead we find a free black, a sailor recently arrived from Paris, who complained to the court that he had been assaulted by a group of white men and imprisoned, not because he was armed—carrying a sword, his aggressors claimed—but because he was wearing a hat trimmed with braid and a gold button.[110] For the dominant slave-owning classes, there was a new focus of attention as a different segment of the population, also using dress, showed itself to pose a more acute risk to social order.

It is against this backdrop that we should consider the first sumptuary law in Louisiana.[111] This was a clause in the 1786 "Proclamation of Good Government" of Governor Miró, under the Spanish colonial regime. It was not concerned with the dress or behavior of whites. Rather, it was aimed exclusively at free black and mulatto women, and prohibited them from wearing feathers and curls in their hair, as had been fashionable in European dress in that period, mandating instead the use of handkerchiefs to cover the head.[112] New Orleans was entering a new phase. But the colony could not escape the imprint left from its formative years, where dress had been used to negotiate the boundaries between distinct peoples in a contested environment, and also, ultimately, to cement the inexorable expansion of the power and position of the emerging white elite. This white minority looked to Europe for concrete affirmation of its status, but was firmly planted within the experience of life in one burgeoning plantation colony situated in the American South.

NOTES

1. *Pennsylvania Gazette,* May 13, 1789. My thanks to Catherine Haulman for this reference. Washington's determined efforts to procure this homespun cloth are documented in *The Writings of George Washington from the Original Manuscript Sources 1745–1799,* ed. John C. Fitzpatrick, 39 vols. (Washington, D.C.: U.S. Government Printing Office, 1931–44), 30:182, 183–84, 280, 280n.

2. Washington's views on the potential of homespuns as alternatives to imported textiles are most clearly expounded in a letter of 29 January 1789 to the Marquis de Lafayette (*Writings,* 30:186–87).

3. Chicago Historical Society, Accession # 1920.304 abc.

4. Examples of Washington's keen sense of dress are scattered throughout his writings. Anne Wood Murray provides a straightforward account of the most pertinent examples in her article "George Washington's Apparel," *Antiques* 117, no. 1 (1980): 120–25. See also James L. Kochan, "'As Plain as Blue and Buff Could Make It': George Washington's Uniforms as Commander-in-Chief and President, 1775–1799," in *Dressing 'Em Up: 18th Century Costume and Custom* (Washington, D.C.: 44th Washington Antiques Show, 1999), 94–101.

5. Standard works on the economy of the colony include John G. Clark, *New*

Orleans, 1718–1812: An Economic History (Baton Rouge: Louisiana State University Press, 1970), N. M. Miller Surrey, *The Commerce of Louisiana During the French Regime, 1699–1763* (New York: Columbia University Press, 1916), Daniel H. Usner Jr., *Indians, Settlers, and Slaves in a Frontier Exchange Economy: The Lower Mississippi Valley Before 1783* (Chapel Hill: University of North Carolina Press, 1992).

6. The frontier exchange economy described by Usner (ibid.) brought together whites, Native Americans, and blacks, and provided an important measure of material relief to colonists. Small-scale and alternative systems of supply familiar from Europe (probate auctions, the used- or stolen-clothes market) further increased the opportunities for the exchange of goods and services within the colony. Key works on European supply models include Daniel Roche, *La Culture des apparences: Une histoire du vêtement (XVIIe–XVIIIe siècle)* (Paris: Fayard, 1989), and Beverly Lemire, *Dress, Culture, and Commerce: The English Clothing Trade before the Factory, 1660–1800* (New York: St. Martin's Press, 1997).

7. This is the premise of my dissertation, "Trading Identities: Cultures of Consumption in French Colonial Louisiana, 1699–1769" (University of London, 2000), which examines the role of dress and consumption in managing gender, race, class, and ethnic encounters in a colonial context.

8. The settler population of Louisiana around 1731 numbered some five thousand, with twice as many blacks as whites; see Charles R. Maduell Jr., comp. and trans., *The Census Tables for the French Colony of Louisiana from 1699 through 1732* (Baltimore: Genealogical Publishing, 1972), 113–41, 150. Even though the colonial population of Lower Louisiana had more than doubled by 1763, it remained insignificant when judged against the vastness of the territory; see Usner, *Frontier Exchange Economy*, 108.

9. The extant letters of the chevalier de Pradel have been published in A. Baillardel and A. Prioult, *Le Chevalier de Pradel: Vie d'un colon français en Louisiane au XVIIIe siècle d'après sa correspondance et celle de sa famille* (Paris: Maisonneuve Frères, 1928); this key work is hereafter cited as Pradel. Further references to Pradel are scattered throughout the New Orleans Notarial Archives, Parish of Orleans (hereafter NONA), and the Records of the Superior Council of Louisiana, Louisiana State Museum (hereafter RSCL).

10. Chantalou's personal correspondence is in the RSCL.

11. Though the gown has not survived, it is treated here as an artifact, the interpretation of its significance drawing on some of the methodologies common to material culture studies; on the range of such methodologies, see Cary Carson's essay "Material Culture History: The Scholarship Nobody Knows" in *American Material Culture: The Shape of the Field*, ed. Ann Smart Martin and J. Ritchie Garrison (Winterthur, Del.: Henry Francis du Pont Winterthur Museum, 1997).

12. See Usner, *Frontier Exchange Economy*, who argues that, in Lower Louisiana, the earlier frontier exchange economy gradually gave way to a plantation-based slaveholding society with a more rigid hierarchy and a regulated economy akin to

that of its North American neighbors. In Upper Louisiana, with the exception of St. Louis, a similar process took place, with agriculture rather than the fur trade dominating the economy there by the close of the French regime, resulting in the decrease in importance of daily contact with Native Americans; see Carl J. Ekberg, *French Roots in the Illinois Country: The Mississippi Frontier in Colonial Times* (Urbana: University of Illinois Press, 1998).

13. Pradel himself engaged in trade (*Pradel*, 55, 83, 108), usually deploying front persons to retail his goods (56, 95–96, 119, 121).

14. That this was cause for social tension can be seen in the lawsuit brought in 1730 by one Demoiselle Millon against her prospective mother-in-law, Françoise Jalot Delasource Carrière. Dame Carrière had dishonored the young woman by publicly proclaiming that she had had a child out of wedlock in France. Demoiselle Millon argued that new immigrants to the colony were entitled to their privacy, and the Council ruled in her favor (RSCL 1730091601). It is notable that Dame Carrière was one of the founding members of a laywomen's confraternity formed in New Orleans to promote high moral standards and social order in the colony. See Emily Clark, "'By All the Conduct of Their Lives': A Laywomen's Confraternity in New Orleans, 1730–1744," *William and Mary Quarterly*, 3d ser., 54, no. 4 (1997), 780.

15. St. Ange was an officer who was twice named commander of Fort de Chartres in the Illinois Country; see Glenn R. Conrad, *First Families of Louisiana* (Baton Rouge: Claitor's Publishing Division, 1970), 1:188, 185. St. Ange was only a half-pay officer, and in 1722 was recorded as receiving a monthly salary of forty livres, according to France's Archives Nationales Colonies (hereafter ANC), ser. B, vol. 43, fols. 265–267). It is likely that he, like other officers in outlying posts, made use of the advantages of his position to engage in trade for his own profit. For an in-depth study of the involvement of New France officers in the fur trade, see Joseph L. Peyser, *Jacques Legardeur de Saint Pierre: Officier, Gentleman, Entrepreneur* (East Lansing: Michigan State University Press, 1996).

16. Kaskaskia Manuscripts, Randolph County Courthouse, Chester, Illinois (hereafter KM) 25:10:13:1; the sum was payable in pelts. St. Ange generally went under the name Sieur Robert Groston de St. Ange, which implied an elevated status, though his original name was simply Robert Grotton *dit* (known as or nicknamed) St. Ange. In the fluid society of the Illinois Country, aided by his military promotions, he quickly took on a new status by converting his moniker into the attribute of a title. On this shift, see Winstanley Briggs, "Le Pays des Illinois," *William and Mary Quarterly*, 3d ser., 47, no. 1 (1990): 47–48. Most modern references to St. Ange have failed to make the distinction between his original and acquired status; see, for example, Glenn R. Conrad, ed., *A Dictionary of Louisiana Biography*, 2 vols. (New Orleans: Louisiana Historical Association, 1988), or W. B. Douglas, "The Sieurs de St.-Ange," *Illinois Historical Society Transactions* (1909): 36–38. For further examples of name transformations, see Fontaine Martin, *A History of the Bouligny Family and Allied Families* (Lafayette: Center for Louisiana Studies, 1990), 9, and Marcel Giraud, *A History of Louisiana*, vol. 2, trans. Brian Pearce (Baton Rouge:

Louisiana State University Press, 1991), 125n. 33. It is notable that most of these instances took place in the colony's early settlement period.

17. RSCL 1740123001.

18. ANC, ser. C13A, vol. 35, fol. 283, 15 July 1751. Contrast this complaint with the submissive behavior of witnesses called before the Superior Council, described as removing their hats before taking the stand, in a case from the same year (RSCL 1751062403). Further instances of social tension are described in Carl A. Brasseaux, "The Moral Climate of French Colonial Louisiana, 1699–1763," *Louisiana History* 27 (1986), 27–42.

19. Pradel, 15, gives as 1713 his date of arrival in the colony, but see Marcel Giraud, *A History of Louisiana*, vol. 1, trans. Joseph C. Lambert (Baton Rouge: Louisiana State University Press, 1974), 275–76nn. 83, 85, 87.

20. Pradel, 79–80.

21. See note 13; *Pradel*, 272; RSCL 1764032701.

22. ANC, ser. C13A, vol. 37, fol. 52, no. 10, 5 May 1753. For other accounts of this event, see *Pradel*, 211, and Gustave Devron, ed., "Dernières Pages du Manuscrit d'un Anglais ayant Habité la Louisiane de 1719 à 1753," *Comptes-Rendus de l'Athénée Louisianais*, 7th ser., 1 (January 1900): 27–30, reprinted in Marc de Villiers du Terrage, *Les Dernières Années de la Louisiane française* (Paris: E. Guilmoto, 1904), 6. That original account is now lost; see "A Chapter of Colonial History," *Louisiana Historical Quarterly* 6, no. 4 (1923): 543–67.

23. *Pradel*, 252 (all translations are my own). Compare this figure to the number of prominent ("first") families in Virginia, Connecticut, and New Hampshire, as summarized by Kevin M. Sweeney, "High-style Vernacular: Lifestyles of the Colonial Elite," in *Of Consuming Interests: The Style of Life in the Eighteenth Century*, ed. Cary Carson, Ronald Hoffman, and Peter J. Albert (Charlottesville: University Press of Virginia, 1994), 3.

24. *Pradel*, 184, 189.

25. From a letter written prior to 25 September 1752 (probably in June or July, according to the editors), ibid., 190. The original French reads: "a fait beaucoup de *jalouses*" (my emphasis). As will become apparent, my translation of this class-neutral gendered noun into "jealous ladies" reflects my reading of Pradel as preoccupied exclusively with his own social circle.

26. The shop of Jean-François Barbier, among whose clients was the king of France, was located here. The rich records relating to this firm are discussed by Mary Schoeser-Boyce in "The Barbier Manuscripts," *Textile History* 12 (1981): 37–58.

27. The partnership of Corvoisier et Richer had substantial assets, and the volume and assortment of their stock would have reflected this; see Carolyn Sargentson, *Merchants and Luxury Markets: The Marchands Merciers of Eighteenth-Century Paris* (Malibu: J. Paul Getty Museum, 1996), 27n. 62.

28. Ibid., chap. 5, 97–112; see also Aileen Ribeiro, *The Art of Dress: Fashion in England and France, 1750–1820* (New Haven: Yale University Press, 1995), 42–43.

29. Letter of 10 April 1755, *Pradel*, 265.

30. The growing interest in considering the lives of women in New Orleans

should pave the way for more nuanced readings of female identity in French colonial Louisiana. In an important article on the experience of women in colonial New Orleans, Emily Clark has proposed the model of a fluid, democratic (and somewhat activist) space for women of varying rank and race in New Orleans in the 1730s and 1740s, centered around the activities of a laywomen's confraternity tied to the Ursulines ("Conduct of Their Lives," 785–87). By presenting evidence of sartorial elitism, the body of material introduced in the present study leads to questions about the extent of social cohesion among the confréresses, but does not contradict Clark's broad thesis. It can be argued that the existence in New Orleans of a popular women's association with permeable social boundaries did not necessarily preclude the creation of smaller, more intimate coteries within the confines of that organization. It should, however, be noted that although Madame de Pradel's two sisters were members of the confraternity, she herself was nowhere identified as a confréresse (ibid, 781, and personal communication with the author). Madame de Pradel, who lived apart from her husband and who sent her daughters to an Ursuline convent in France rather than have them educated by the New Orleans Ursulines (*Pradel*, 145–73)—a choice not unprecedented among high-standing colonists (see RSCL 1763083005)—may have had reason to abstain from close association with the confraternity.

31. Letter of 10 April 1755, *Pradel*, 252. One should observe that such profligacy was not the domain of his wife alone, as revealed by Pradel's increasing expenditure for his plantation house; see note 101.

32. See letters of 25 January and 8 March 1733 and 10 April 1755, *Pradel*, 119, 127–28, 252.

33. ANC, ser. C13A, vol. 9, fol. 287, 1 December 1725.

34. ANC, ser. C13A, vol. 9, fol. 13, 20 January 1725.

35. ANC, ser. C13A, vol. 9, fol. 287, 1 December 1725.

36. Historical Records Survey, WPA, *The Favrot Papers, 1695–1769*, vol. 1 of *Transcriptions of Manuscript Collections of Louisiana* (New Orleans: Louisiana State Museum, 1940), 110–15.

37. Ibid., 45.

38. *Pradel*, 189.

39. Madame de Pradel's postmortem records are not known to have survived, nor was her wardrobe itemized or described in her husband's postmortem inventories, RSCL 1764032701 and NONA FM&K-9 [72913–956] 1764–03/20.

40. According to a memo written in 1751 by France's Intendant of Commerce, de Gournay, gold- or silver-brocaded silks cost from 13 to 400 livres per ell, whereas silk-embroidered silks cost from 4 to 30 livres per ell. This memo is discussed in Lesley Miller, "French Silks (1650–1800)," in *Textiles: 5,000 Years*, ed. Jennifer Harris (New York: Harry N. Abrams, 1993), 181. De Gournay's information is supported by evidence from the 1753 inventory of another silk merchant on the rue St.-Honoré, Antoine Porlier; see Sargentson, *Merchants and Luxury Markets*, appendix 9, 164.

41. Miller, "French Silks," 181, states that this shift in fashion was reflected in the proportion of looms in Lyons working on plain versus brocaded silks.

42. My thanks to Lesley Miller for pointing me to this fragment, which is published in Chiara Buss, ed., *The Meandering Pattern in Brocaded Silks, 1745–1775,* trans. Neil Harvey (Milan: Ermenegildo Zegna, 1990), 44–47.

43. Jacques Savary des Brûlons in his five-volume *Dictionnaire universel de commerce* (Geneva: Frères Cramer and C. Philibert, 1723–30) and Jean Paulet (see Miller, "French Silks," 180) were among those who advocated this distinction.

44. Letter of 1 March 1753, *Pradel,* 206.

45. For example, in papers relating to the retail store kept by the widow Gervais in New Orleans, out of seventeen references to pure silks, only two were not taffetas (RSCL 1747122003).

46. In the RSCL, *indiennes,* dimities, *cottonades,* and *siamoises* (most of which were washable) figured prominently in the lading bills of merchandise sent to the colony, as confirmed in the quantitative analysis being conducted by Robert S. DuPlessis of the prevalence of cottons and linens in merchants' inventories in Louisiana as compared to Montreal, Philadelphia, and Charleston; see his "Cloth and the Emergence of the Atlantic Economy" in *The Atlantic Economy during the Seventeenth and Eighteenth Century: New Perspectives on Organization, Operation, Practices, and Personnel,* ed. Peter A. Coclanis (Columbia: University of South Carolina Press, 2003). In this subtle essay, DuPlessis notes the popularity of linens and cottons among the urban dwellers of the climatically matched towns of New Orleans and Charleston, a trend New Orleans seems to have led.

47. See RSCL 1735072501, 1738052702, 1764061701 for some key examples of the use of cottons and cotton mixes by men and women. The use of such textiles extended increasingly to furnishings, for example coverlets, wall hangings, and curtains (RSCL 1730012301, 1758060201, 1758111601, 1759012401).

48. Historical Records Survey, *Favrot Papers,* 58–69 (inventory of effects) and 110–115 (sale at auction of effects). Some of the items listed in the inventory were those left by Madame Bruslé's daughter on her departure for France. Since they are not always identified as such, I use the records of the auction sale of Madame Bruslé's effects on 9 and 10 February 1769 as the basis for my discussion of her wardrobe.

49. A woman's petticoat of calico of the highest quality, painted and printed in India for the European market and dating from 1750–55, is illustrated on Harris, *Textiles,* 4. The fashion for cotton fabrics as the main driving force behind the Industrial Revolution is reexamined by Beverly Lemire in *Fashion's Favourite: The Cotton Trade and the Consumer in Britain, 1660–1800* (Oxford: Oxford University Press, 1991).

50. Mercers were acknowledged arbiters of fashion, and they were flattered as such: "I bow to your honesty in telling me which are the most modish patterns and fabrics," wrote one member of the nobility to a silk merchant whose services she was soliciting (Barbier letters, 28 October 1785, Victoria and Albert Museum, quoted in Sargentson, *Merchants and Luxury Markets,* 102).

51. In acknowledgment of the same reverence due to British purveyors of dress, George Washington constantly deferred to their judgment, leaving up to them the

actual selection of a fashionable cloth, or a fashionable color, to be made "according to the present taste" (*Writings*, 2:339).

52. Although Pradel may have asked for the gown to be made up purely to avoid paying duty on the textile, I do not believe that the avoidance of duty was Pradel's primary motive here. Silk merchants sometimes worked in tandem with tailors and dressmakers (who may have operated within the same premises) in the whole conception of an outfit; see Schoeser-Boyce, "The Barbier Manuscripts," and Gilberte Vrignaud, *Vêture et parure en France au dix-huitième siècle* (Paris: Messene, 1995), esp. 31–54.

53. Pamela A. Parmal, "Fashion and the Growing Importance of the *Marchande des Modes* in Mid-Eighteenth-Century France," *Costume* 31 (1997): 68–77.

54. A gown of yellow silk taffeta brocaded in white silk trimmed with white fly braid and self-fabric ruffles sewn in serpentines down the front of the bodice and the skirt, now at the Victoria and Albert Museum (T.426–1990), is a typical example; see Avril Hart and Susan North, *Fashion in Detail: From the 17th and 18th Centuries* (New York: Rizzoli, 1998), 34, 50.

55. For examples of the amount of fabric needed for different kinds of gowns, see Aileen Ribeiro, *Dress in Eighteenth-Century Europe, 1715–1789* (London: Batsford, 1984), 48–49. Though most silks were woven in half-ell widths, taffetas were often produced in full widths, meaning a reduction in the yardage required. It is worth bearing in mind that brocaded silk for a gown of this kind might take seven to ten days to weave, an estimate extrapolated from figures given in Natalie Rothstein, ed., *Barbara Johnson's Album of Fashions and Fabrics* (London: Thames and Hudson, 1987), 30.

56. We may speculate as to whether a pair of hoops to wear with the gown was included with the "garniture," since by the early 1750s the squarer, shelflike hoops of the previous decade (*paniers à coudes*) had given way to smaller side hoops (*paniers doubles*), necessarily affecting the silhouette of the outfit and the cut of the gown. References to hoops and stays in Louisiana are rare, most dating to the second quarter of the eighteenth century (RSCL 1739093001, 1739081103, 1746031001; KM 44:1:3:1). No stay-makers are known to have operated in the colony, although there was at least one tailor/dressmaker in the colony adept at repairing hoops (RSCL 1729100801). Custom-made stays and hoops were ordered from France, and the difficulties inherent in such an enterprise are brought out in the correspondence, discussed below, between the New Orleans functionary Augustin Chantalou and his business partner, the merchant Testar at La Rochelle (RSCL 1752100102, 1753083005).

57. These stylistic features are found in the extant silk discussed in note 42. Peter Thornton, *Baroque and Rococo Silks* (London: Faber and Faber, 1965), points to the relative lack of precisely dated French figured silk samples from the period (19n. 3), while noting that designs were subject to seasonal change (18–22). Miller ("French Silks," 180) suggests that the fashionable elite in Paris could identify textile patterns by the year, although this was not the case in the provinces; indeed, the Warner archives demonstrate that textile manufacturers introduced new seasonal designs at

least twice a year. However, Miller and Sargentson's collaborative work on the designing and marketing of Lyons silks has served to moderate the prevailing view that silk designs changed at a rapid pace, by noting that most changes were subtle, with earlier patterns retaining some of their original features. This makes it all the more remarkable that contemporaries could distinguish the older from the newer patterns. See Lesley E. Miller and Carolyn Sargentson, "Paris-Lyon: Patterns of Distribution of Luxury Silk Fabrics in the 18th Century," in *Echanges et cultures textiles dans l'Europe pré-industrielle*, ed. Jacques Bottin and Nicole Pellegrin, *Revue du Nord*, special issue no. 12 (1996), 247–57.

58. Sargentson, *Merchants and Luxury Markets*, 105–7, states that often these goods were valued at between one-quarter and one-half of their Paris market price by the time they were finally disposed of, as little as one year after their introduction. Michael Sonenscher argues that it was precisely "by, firstly, reiterating cycles of new products, secondly by dumping outdated goods at knockdown prices and thirdly by switching goods between different markets at various stages of the product cycle" that France succeeded in maintaining its competitiveness in the international market; see "Fashion's Empire: Trade and Power in Early 18th-Century France" in *Luxury Trades and Consumerism in Ancien Régime Paris: Studies in the History of the Skilled Workforce*, ed. Robert Fox and Anthony Turner (Aldershot, U.K.: Ashgate, 1998), 234.

59. ANC, ser. C13A, vol. 10, fols. 192–192v, 2 November 1727.

60. For example, RSCL 1737041001, 1743041001, 1749061801.

61. This would make them the earliest known surviving portraits of white colonists from the French regime in New Orleans. See "Visual Sources in Louisiana," appendix A of White, "Trading Identities." The paintings of Marie Louise and Céleste are respectively in the Historic New Orleans Collection (Mrs. Bouligny Baldwin provenance) and privately owned by Mrs. Villeré Drackett. They are all reproduced in Martin, *Bouligny Family*.

62. Thornton, *Baroque and Rococo Silks*, 130, and Madeleine Delpierre, *Dress in France in the Eighteenth Century*, trans. Caroline Beamish (New Haven: Yale University Press, 1997), 54.

63. Although not as richly trimmed, their striped taffeta gowns bear a resemblance to a surviving sack gown from ca. 1760 in the collections of the Kyoto Costume Institute, made of a checked taffeta; see The Kyoto Costume Institute, *Revolution in Fashion: European Clothing, 1715–1815* (New York: Abbeville Press, 1990), 38, 40 (detail). A pink striped gown in the Victoria and Albert Museum, London (760–1899) is even closer in appearance to the gowns of the d'Auberville sisters. See also the taffeta samples reproduced in Vrignaud, *Vêture*, 113–15.

64. Martin, *Bouligny Family*, 1–78.

65. RSCL 1764032701; NONA FM&K-9 [72913–956] 1764–03/20.

66. Letter of 10 April 1755, *Pradel*, 265.

67. Washington, *Writings*, 2:372, 395, and esp. 492.

68. *Pradel*, 190, 206.

69. Louisiana never recovered from its negative early reputation; see Carl A. Brasseaux, "The Image of Louisiana and the Failure of Voluntary French Emigration, 1683–1731," in *Proceedings of the Fourth Meeting of the French Colonial Historical Society* (Washington, D.C.: University Press of America, 1979), 47–56.

70. Their correspondence survives in large part, shedding light on trading practices between merchants in the colony and in France. The broader commercial aspects of this partnership are discussed in J. Clark, *New Orleans, 1718–1812*, 99–102. The majority of ships to Louisiana originated at La Rochelle, though this remained but a minor destination for French outfitters; see ibid., 37, 83, and John G. Clark, *La Rochelle and the Atlantic Economy During the Eighteenth Century* (Baltimore: The Johns Hopkins University Press, 1981), 29.

71. RSCL 1752100101, 1753083004; see also RSCL 1753083005.

72. RSCL 1752061601.

73. RSCL 1752100101.

74. A copy of the *Mercure de France*, the main periodical source for information on fashion in this period, was itemized in a Louisiana inventory from 1769, and it is likely that this, like other reading materials, would have been widely circulated among interested parties; see *Louisiana Historical Quarterly* 9, no. 3 (1926): 433. Pradel himself published a letter in the August 1722 edition of the *Mercure* (fols. 95–96) about his impressions of the colony. A 1770s doll with its linen shift, boned stays, cotton petticoats, pocket, silk petticoat, and *polonaise* gown, in the Colonial Williamsburg collection, is photographed in Linda Baumgarten, *Eighteenth-Century Clothing at Williamsburg* (Williamsburg: Colonial Williamsburg Foundation, 1986), 14. Roche, *La Culture des apparences*, 451–52, specifies that the merchants of the rue St.-Honorén were involved in their production and, although he does not cite any sources, that such dolls did indeed make their way to the New World. Only one reference to a doll is found in the records pertaining to Louisiana, this in the records of the succession of Louise Pellerin, the widow of Philippe Lefebvre, chief surgeon in the Swiss troops (RSCL 1740060604, 1740060607). Although there is an allusion in the records to her having an infant, the widow was also responsible for importing a large quantity of fine apparel into the colony, most of it unused and likely intended for sale (RSCL 1739093001).

75. RSCL 1752082401. See also RSCL 1737020105, 1737060104, 1741021801.

76. RSCL 1753083004. For other instances of fashions being named after current events or popular whims, see Ribeiro, *Eighteenth-Century*, 111.

77. RSCL 1752100101. Stockings have been identified as one of the luxury or "populuxe" items that heralded France's shift to a consumer society; see Cissie Fairchilds, "The Production and Marketing of Populuxe Goods in Eighteenth-Century Paris," in *Consumption and the World of Goods*, ed. John Brewer and Roy Porter (London: Routledge, 1993), 232–35. Fairchilds defines populuxe items as "cheap copies of aristocratic luxury items" and notes the increasing presence of quantities of stockings in inventories of lower-class Parisians in the eighteenth century, echoing the findings of Daniel Roche (*La Culture des apparences*, 161–67). In Louisiana

the popularity of stockings throughout the colony is reflected in a comment by the officer Terisse de Ternan that stockings of all types were selling well in the Illinois Country (RSCL 1729101301).

78. Sargentson, *Merchants and Luxury Markets*, 106.

79. Jeremy Farrell, *Socks and Stockings* (London: Batsford, 1992), 20. See KM 40:5:10:1 for an example of a settler from the Illinois Country insisting on having his stockings match the color of his suit.

80. RSCL 1753112001. These had been purchased from the Bordeaux fair. The importance of fairs to the textile market is addressed by Vrignaud, *Vêture*, 23–45.

81. RSCL 1754052101.

82. Murray, "George Washington's Apparel."

83. RSCL 1752100102.

84. RSCL 1753083004.

85. RSCL 1753083005.

86. RSCL 1753083005. Testar again took the initiative in his selection of the tortoiseshell snuffbox (whether with or without hinges) and the table service (whether of porcelain or crockery) that Chantalou had requested.

87. RSCL 1754052101.

88. RSCL 1753051001.

89. RSCL 1753112001.

90. RSCL 1754052101. Girandole earrings consisted of three pendants hanging down branchlike from a single top setting; see Diana Scarisbrick, *Jewellery* (London: Batsford, 1984), 16–17. Madame Chantalou was signaling that she wanted a single drop garnet.

91. See RSCL 1764020101 and 1766122901 for references to earrings; the latter also for references to garnet rings; RSCL 1759070902, 1765072201, and 1766122303 for references to garnet "coliers" or "branches." The detailed description of a necklace of fine garnets and seed pearls is found in RSCL 1748040601. In RSCL 1737060105, the wholesale merchant Paul Rasteau is listed as purchasing three dozen necklaces of garnets for six livres the dozen from the estate of a deceased merchant, and his store carried two types of garnet necklaces (RSCL 1737100201).

92. Amanda Vickery, *The Gentleman's Daughter: Women's Lives in Georgian England* (New Haven: Yale University Press, 1998), 164–68. There is, however, one important distinction between the sources drawn on by Vickery and those available from French colonial Louisiana, namely the total lack of any surviving correspondence between women. Only through the intermediary of their menfolk do we find evidence of links between women in the colony and in France, in contrast to the correspondence between Elizabeth Shackleton and her "proxy consumer" in London, Bessy Ramsdon.

93. *Pradel*, 182.

94. Instances of important and exceptional commissions from agents in France are found in *Pradel*, 83, 181, 198, 200, 204.

95. *Pradel*, 263.

96. RSCL 1753083005.

97. Pradel, 265.

98. Amanda Vickery argues for a similar discrimination toward London fashion on the part of provincial gentlewomen in Lancashire (*The Gentleman's Daughter*, 180). Her work thus offers an important critique of the tenacious emulation theory whereby fashion trickled down from the elite to the indiscriminate, imitative masses. See Neil McKendrick, John Brewer, and J. H. Plumb, *The Birth of a Consumer Society: The Commercialization of Eighteenth-Century England* (Bloomington: Indiana University Press, 1982), chap. 2, for an overly influential study of eighteenth-century consumerism premised on the emulation theory; also Grant McCracken, *Culture and Consumption: New Approaches to the Symbolic Character of Consumer Goods and Activities* (Bloomington: Indiana University Press, 1988), chap. 6.

99. Pradel, 283.

100. Pradel, 226–27 on his son's expenditure, 175–76 on the acquisition of Monplaisir.

101. Pradel, 207, 233; NONA FM&K-9 [72913–956] 1764–03/20. See, for comparison purposes, the 1769 description of another important plantation, that of Sieur Jean-Baptiste Prévost, at English Bend, translated in Henry P. Dart and Edith Price, "Inventory of the Estate of . . . Prevost," *Louisiana Historical Quarterly* 9, no. 3 (1926): 411–98.

102. Pradel, 200. The only known image of Monplaisir was executed a century or so later, around 1850. This is reproduced in Samuel Wilson Jr., "Louisiana Drawings by Alexandre De Batz," *Journal of the Society of Architectural Historians* 22, no. 2 (1963). A detailed description of the plantation was given in Pradel's postmortem inventory and appraisal (NONA FM&K-9 [72913–956] 1764–03/20), extracts of which are translated by Wilson in his article. According to Pradel, De Batz, the engineer now better known for his ethnographic depictions (see David Ives Bushnell, *Drawings by A. De Batz in Louisiana, 1732–1735, With Six Plates* [Washington D.C.: Smithsonian Institution, 1927]), had served as Pradel's architect. Pradel himself had made a drawing of the plantation which he sent to his brother in France, and he was expecting a drawing from De Batz, but neither has been traced (*Pradel*, 182–83). Pradel and De Batz probably knew each other as early as 1728, when both were listed as passengers on the ship *Le Dromadaire* (Archives of the Port of Lorient, subseries 2P2, II 12: 1728). De Batz's plan of the Prévost plantation is reproduced in Carl J. Ekberg, "The English Bend: Forgotten Gateway to New Orleans," in *La Salle and His Legacy: Frenchmen and Indians in the Lower Mississippi Valley*, ed. Patricia K. Galloway (Jackson: University Press of Mississippi, 1982), 220–23.

103. Pradel, 235.

104. In fact, Pradel's daughters never did come to Louisiana (*Pradel*, pt. 3, chap. 2).

105. See note 12.

106. But see Thomas N. Ingersoll, *Mammon and Manon in Early New Orleans: The First Slave Society in the Deep South, 1718–1819* (Knoxville: University of Tennessee Press, 1999), 36 and chap. 2, in which he argues that it was much earlier, after 1731, aided by the demise—quite literally, the death—of the poorest and least

respectable of the colonists sent to Louisiana, that New Orleans began to assume a greater social stability, with slaveholding whites bound together by a "compelling common interest."

107. Wilbur E. Meneray, ed., *The Rebellion of 1768: Documents from the Favrot Family Papers and the Rosamonde E. and Emile Kuntz Collection*, trans. Philippe Seiler (New Orleans: Tulane University, 1995), and Carl A. Brasseaux, *Denis-Nicolas Foucault and the New Orleans Rebellion of 1768* (Ruston, La.: McGinty Publications, 1987). The intimate if convoluted relationship between Ordonnateur Foucault and Madame de Pradel is discussed in *Pradel*, 395–409.

108. ANC, ser. C13A, vol. 35, fol. 39, 28 February–1 March 1751. On the formulation of the code of 1751 with a brief summary of the main statutes relating to blacks, both slave and free, see Thomas N. Ingersoll, "Slave Codes and Judicial Practice in New Orleans, 1718–1807," *Law and History Review* 13 (1995): 40–41. Further background information about the events leading up to the formulation of the code, not broached by Ingersoll, is found in Governor Vaudreuil's correspondence, Huntington Library, San Marino, Loudoun Collection (LO 222, 26 September 1750, and O/S LO 257 [ca. 1750]).

109. Fashion was neither the domain of an elite minority nor an exclusively European phenomenon, as poor whites and slaves alike also sought means of using clothing to shape an identity for themselves. Thus we find in Louisiana white indentured laborers negotiating contracts that called for the provision of refined garments in specific colors and fabrics (RSCL [n.d.] 1732012601; KM 40:5:10:1), while slaves of African origin expressed similar regard for the stylistic aspects of the dress they actively sought to acquire (RSCL 1765101001).

110. RSCL 1765101501, 1765101802. These issues are discussed further in White, "Trading Identities," chap. 5, and White, "'Wearing Three or Four Handkerchiefs around his Collar and Elsewhere about him': Sartorial Constructions of Masculinity and Ethnicity in French Colonial New Orleans," *Gender & History* 15, no. 3 (2003).

111. And here I subscribe to Alan Hunt's thesis in *Governance of the Consuming Passions: A History of Sumptuary Law* (New York: St. Martin's Press, 1996) that sumptuary legislation is "rarely, if ever, associated with stable relations of hieratic domination, but is a product of circumstances in which a hieratic social order has come under internal pressure" (105).

112. Miró, Bando de Buen Gobierno, 1 June 1786, Records and Deliberations of the Cabildo, Historic New Orleans Collection, New Orleans, vol. 1, bk. 3, 105–12. Article 6. My thanks to Jennifer Spear for the citation. That it was the elite's perception of and reaction to the diversity of colonial Louisiana's society that led to increasing attempts to "create social order by defining and utilizing racial categories" is argued by Spear in "'Whiteness and the Purity of Blood': Race, Sexuality, and Social Order in Colonial Louisiana" (Ph.D. diss., University of Minnesota, 1999).

Part 11

George Washington as
Person, Symbol, and Southerner

Chapter 5

GEORGE WASHINGTON AND THREE WOMEN

DON HIGGINBOTHAM

For some years now, working on a study of Washington as a Revolutionary leader, I have felt that more could be said about his family relationships to illuminate his later years on the national stage. If his early biographers largely ignored his private life save for extolling his character and physical prowess, his twentieth-century chroniclers zeroed in on his life outside the public arena, with uneven or mixed results.

On deciding to look at Washington's relationship with certain women, it soon became clear that he liked the opposite sex. That is hardly a profound statement, but it might have been said, had the evidence warranted it, that he was uncomfortable in the presence of women or generally displayed a cold or distant attitude toward them. We know that he has often been described, both by contemporaries and by historians, as reserved and aloof, and the statement contains much truth concerning men he did not know well or did not particularly care for. Women, however, usually found Washington polite, attentive, and at ease in their presence. He frequently bantered with them, not averse to using occasional sexual innuendo, and he occasionally engaged them in discussions of public affairs.

In contrast, some historians including Kenneth Lockridge, Joseph Ellis, Winthrop Jordan, and Jack McLaughlin find Thomas Jefferson usually distant and uneasy with the opposite sex, but nonetheless as a widower playful in a romantically suggestive way in Paris with beauties such as Maria Cosway and Angelica Schuyler Church. Lockridge's study of Jefferson's commonplace book, his jottings from literature, contends that Jefferson was a misogynist, at best quite ambivalent toward women as a young man, and generally resentful of his mother. Yet he deeply loved his wife, a passive woman in no way threatening to him. And as president he disbanded Martha Washington's republican court, a regular social gathering designed to get men and women of different parties and from various regions together to foster sociability and defuse national tensions.[1]

This particular undertaking owes a large debt to Douglas L. Wilson's *Honor's Voice*, a study of the young Lincoln's first decade or so in Illinois. Wilson gives special attention to Lincoln's relationship with three women who significantly influenced his life. It seems that three women also stand out in Washington's life before the Revolution: his mother, Mary Ball Washington; his friend and neighbor Sally Cary Fairfax; and his wife, Martha Dandridge Custis Washington.[2]

His relationship with all three needs reassessment. This venture is undoubtedly only a first step in that process. New Washington scholarship should not only set the record straight but also cast aside stereotypical notions of these women. Consciously or not, some historians have pictured them in their relations with Washington in the rigid gender images that prevailed in history and fiction through the 1950s and sometimes later. They have hardly been portrayed as complex individuals whose ties to Washington were multidimensional. Instead we have descriptions of Mary Ball Washington as the shrewish mother, Sally Fairfax as the flirtatious charmer, and Martha Washington as the "plain Jane."[3] After briefly looking at each relationship, this essay will contend that what we might call the family factor throws light on why Washington was a safe man to lead a revolution devoted to freedom and liberty.

Because Mary Ball Washington outlived her husband—he died when George was eleven—and even survived into George's presidency, there have been repeated attempts to measure her influence on Washington. The results have scarcely been fruitful for his formative years. Acolytes of the demigod cult depicted her as "Mary the Mother of Washington," a saintly Roman matron type. If hagiographers pictured her as faultless, as a profoundly positive influence upon a messianic son,[4] Douglas Southall Freeman in the late 1940s set her image that prevails to this day—of a selfish, overbearing, and domineering parent. Freeman's view is that George survived and matured in spite of her, not because of her.[5] Freeman's characterization of Mary Ball received powerful reinforcement from James Thomas Flexner, author of what has long been recognized as the second most influential multivolume biography of Washington, which began appearing in the 1960s. (In fact, a recent poll of historians elevated it above Freeman's tomes, voting it the most valuable of the ten best books on Washington.) Flexner goes so far as to employ the word "termagant" for Mary Ball in the title of a chapter about her.[6] Recent lay publications have joined in the unflattering delineation of Washington's mother. A piece in *American History Illustrated* repeats the standard barbs and adds one other that is said to be the key to Washington's lack of warm feeling for his mother: based on a single source, it is said that she supported Britain, not America, in the Revolution. A French officer, visiting in her hometown of Fredericksburg, reported that he was told that this "lady, who must be over seventy, is one of the most rabid Tories." And on the eve of the bicentennial of Washington's death, an issue of *Mount Vernon: Yesterday, Today, Tomorrow* asked, with reference to the "rocky relationship" between mother and son, "Did His Heart Belong to Mother?"[7]

Although Washington found Mary Ball to be a difficult person many years later, that was not necessarily the case during his youth. Only six of his letters to her are extant, five from the 1750s, then one after a lapse of thirty years, by which time, if not before, she suffered from breast cancer—a condition that may account for her preoccupation with her own welfare.[8] She displayed behavior that mortified her distinguished son when, in 1781, she complained indirectly to the Virginia legislature of impoverishment and seemingly sought a pension or some other form of financial relief. She also, according to Washington, spoke to friends and acquaintances of being neglected by her own family.[9]

And yet she genuinely cared for George. Three and a half years into the war, Mary Ball had asserted that because of his long absence from Mount Vernon, "poor George will be ruined" should anything happen to his overseer. The general had planned to visit his mother in Fredericksburg after the victory at Yorktown, but the illness and death of his stepson Jacky Custis and other matters delayed his arrival. Unaware of his new plans, Mary Ball was away when her son arrived. Her letter to Washington, the only one to survive, hardly exposes the ever-present hard edge invariably attributed to her (although she continued to voice her fear of the future): "I was truly unsy [uneasy] My Not being at ho<me> when you went throu fredirecksburg[.] it was an unlucky thing for me now I am afraid I Never Shall have that pleasure agin[.] I am Soe very unwell & this trip over the Mountins has almost kill'd me[.] I gott the 20 five ginnes you was Soe kind to Send me & am greatly abliged to you for it. . . . pray give my kind Love to Mrs Washington & am My Dear George yo<ur> Loveing and affectinat Mother[.]" On another occasion a planned excursion to her Fredericksburg home suffered a delay because, as Washington wrote, "we have been so fast locked in Snow & Ice since Christmas" (of 1783) that all travel was "suspended." By January 22, 1784, conditions had improved. He expressed eagerness "to discharge that duty" to his mother "on which nature & inclination have a call." On February 14 of that year, while in Fredericksburg visiting "his ancient and amiable parent," Washington was honored by the town fathers with a dinner. He then thanked his hosts for their courteous favors and for their kind words about his "revered Mother." For it was by her "Maternal hand (early deprived of a Father) I was led to Manhood."[10]

Her detractors invariably make the point that Washington did not visit her often, and we have no record of her spending time at Mount Vernon. But Washington also saw infrequently his own brothers and sister, even though there is evidence that shows a good deal of closeness and a sense of responsibility for one another within the family, one example being Washington's positive involvement in the lives of his nieces and nephews. Moreover, Mary Ball lived quite near her daughter, Betty Lewis, who undoubtedly could watch over her and care for her immediate needs.

Washington, although he was once again involved on the national political scene, took time to see his mother three times during her last two years. Just before departing for the Constitutional Convention in Philadelphia, on hearing that Mary Ball was "in the agonies of death," he hurried to Fredericksburg, finding her condition "better than I expected," though she appeared thin and weak, with "little hope of her recovery."[11] The following year, accompanied by his wife, he returned to see her at a time when he was much preoccupied with the fate of the Constitution in the Virginia ratifying convention and in state conventions elsewhere as well. Shortly before he left for New York to assume the presidency in 1789, Washington specifically traveled to Fredericksburg to say farewell to his mother, spending a weekend there. He acknowledged that it would surely be the last time he ever saw her. Since Washington preceded his wife to New York City for the presidential inauguration, Mary Ball offered to lend Martha her coach for the trip, but Martha chose instead to turn to a man who made a practice of renting horses and carriages for private journeys.[12]

According to Mary Ball's critics, she displayed selfish behavior in turning thumbs down on her stepson Lawrence's proposal that George, then fourteen, seek a career in the Royal Navy, because she desired her firstborn to stay at home to look after her and her business affairs. It is said that George subsequently sought to escape her clutches by staying away from Ferry Farm as much as possible, visiting Lawrence's plantation, working as a surveyor, and later serving as a provincial soldier. Some investigators even speculate that Washington's unhappiness with her treatment of him spawned several of his unfavorable characteristics that were so noticeable at the time of the French and Indian War.

The surviving evidence on these counts fails to convict Mary Ball, a woman who hardly had an easy life when widowed in her middle thirties with five children under the age of twelve. It takes no great effort to imagine the devastation she and her children felt. And Augustine's death occurred when George approached the age of establishing his own identity and some measure of personal independence. Evidently Mary Ball held her family together under her own roof, no small accomplishment in itself. She might have done otherwise. "Even when one parent survived," observes Patricia Brady, "children were often parceled out because the financial or emotional burden was too great for one parent alone."[13] Years later George and Martha Washington adopted two of Jacky and Nelly Custis's children after Jacky's death.

As for George's going to sea, Mary Ball took more than a year to make her decision, fluctuating in her attitude and voicing concerns, as a family friend put it, that "mothers naturally suggest."[14] At length, she put the question to her half-brother Joseph Ball in England, who replied that George as a provincial would never have the connections to achieve "any considerable preferment in the Navy." Even a captain of a merchant vessel, he opined, would not live as well as a Virginia planter with "three or four hundred acres of land and three or four slaves."[15]

It is true that Washington as a Virginia military officer in his twenties comes across to us as quarrelsome, sensitive to slights, and extremely ambitious; in short, hardly a completely appealing figure. But the roots of aggressive behavior are not always easy to determine. Domineering mothers—if that is what Mary Ball Washington was—may generate visible aggressions in their sons (or daughters), but they are just as likely to leave their children timid or straitlaced. Conceivably, too, if Washington had been severely damaged by his mother's influence, he might have become effeminate; to the contrary, he was ardently attached to the opposite sex, far more comfortable in the presence of women than Lincoln was.

It is arguable that Mary Ball Washington contributed positively to the aspirations of George and her other sons. If the Washingtons were solidly anchored in the gentry, the same could be said of Mary Ball's father and her guardian, George Eskridge, both highly visible in local affairs, the latter a successful lawyer and a member of the House of Burgesses for nearly thirty years.[16] It is hard to understand why some authorities have contended that George's father, Augustine Washington, married somewhat below his station in selecting Mary Ball as his second wife. The assertion often appears coupled with the statement that Mary Ball was orphaned at age twelve. Yet the Eskridges were at least the social equals of the Balls, and Augustine Washington was well acquainted with the Eskridges; his first wife was a sister-in-law of George Eskridge. A few years ago I serendipitously discovered the burial site of one of Eskridge's daughters in the Yeocomico Church Cemetery, which is in Westmoreland County in the Northern Neck; her casket-length gravestone appeared to be the largest one there. Mary Ball quite likely considered her life with the Eskridges in positive terms. Her own mother spoke of a loving relationship between her daughter and herself and George Eskridge.[17] It seems significant, in terms of Mary Ball's views of her own family experience and her ambitions for her first son, that she named him George, undoubtedly after George Eskridge. Her second and third children, Betty and Samuel, also bore names related to the Eskridges. In so choosing, she had eschewed the name John, which, along with Lawrence and Augustine, had appeared in the Washington family with generational regularity since the 1650s. (Her husband Augustine had already named his sons by his first wife Lawrence and Augustine. He and Mary Ball would later use the name John Augustine for their fourth child.)[18]

Finally, Mary Ball, in addition to holding up her own Ball and Eskridge families as worthy of emulation, may have had another positive influence on George: heredity. A determined, strong-willed woman, she withstood the pressures of three formidable men in deciding against George's embarking on a life before the mast: Lawrence Washington, Colonel William Fairfax, and Robert Jackson, who seems to have been close to both of the other two advocates, as well as something of a friend and unofficial advisor to George's mother. She also showed her independence in 1787 when, despite her advanced age and severe illness, she rejected her son George's urging that she live with one of her children. She must have passed on these firm, unflinching aspects of her nature to her oldest son. Assuredly, they were components of his own makeup, essential ones for any successful revolutionary.[19] But they no doubt at times led to tension and friction between a strong-minded, independent mother and a son who shared her characteristics. Given all that Washington had done for his mother, it was not surprising or improper that she left the lion's share of her estate to him. He seemed deeply touched by certain specific personal items that she bequeathed him. He referred to them as "mementos of parental affection," bestowed "in the last solemn act of life." He valued "them much beyond their intrinsic worth."[20]

Serious historians, popularizers, and novelists have all found more interesting, often downright titillating, Washington's relationship with Sarah ("Sally") Cary Fairfax, the wife of his close friend and nearby neighbor at Belvoir, George William Fairfax. Colonel William Fairfax, George William's father, held a seat on the Royal Council, serving for a time as its president. His relative Thomas, Lord Fairfax, the only British nobleman to make his permanent home in the colonies, held proprietary rights to the vast Northern Neck of Virginia. The Carys, who lived at Cellys, near Hampton in Elizabeth City County, were politically influential and highly cultivated, with deep roots in the Old Dominion. Sally had turned eighteen, two years older than George Washington, when she gave her hand to George William Fairfax and came to live at Belvoir, one of the great houses of the day, where gracious entertainment characterized life within its walls. Young Washington, often a visitor at his brother Lawrence's Mount Vernon, delighted in his many four-mile trips to Belvoir. He enjoyed the banter with other young people, the dancing and card playing, and the other pleasures of mingling with a family noted for its charm, manners, and intellect.[21]

We know that in September 1758, Washington and Sally Fairfax exchanged playful, some authors say flirtatious, letters just a few months before he married Martha Dandridge Custis, a twenty-seven-year-old widow about his own age. The marriage is often described as one of convenience.[22] With his colonial military career nearing an end, he needed a mistress for Mount Vernon, which he had acquired after Lawrence's death, and she sought a manager for her extensive financial resources and a stepfather for her two young children.

The weight of scholarly opinion now holds that Washington had fallen in love with his friend's wife and that he had hardly put his feelings for Sally to rest when he took the widow Custis to Mount Vernon as his wife.[23] Evidently it was a short courtship. And did any lack of instant ardor on his part have something to do with her allegedly being only modestly attractive physically?

Some writers have gone so far as to say that Washington fell in love with Sally the first time he saw her, that she eventually reciprocated his feelings, that they undoubtedly exchanged numerous secret letters, and that they likely met for assignations. Not surprisingly, popularizers and novelists have been particularly bold and provocative. One recent, generally competent study of Colonel Washington in the French and Indian War maintains that from first acquaintance with the new Mrs. George William

Fairfax, he "never afterward would be able to think of her without choking up."[24] Most youths in their late teenage years get over such hormonal surges, especially if directed at the wife of a well-connected friend. But not so Washington. Indeed, when George William and Sally Fairfax moved to England in 1773, never to return to Virginia, Washington bought numerous items from their estate, including an elegant mahogany double chest of drawers that had been in Sally's bedchamber (it must have once held her daintiest garments). This prized piece subsequently resided in the sleeping quarters of George and Martha Washington. It has been suggested that Washington received some sentimental, if not sensual, pleasure from having it there. The "romantics," if that is the proper term for such writers,[25] have seemingly been unaware that another furniture item in the Washington bedchamber, a small bureau, came from Martha's boudoir during her first marriage to Daniel Parke Custis. One hesitates to guess whether there is meaning in their standing on opposite sides of the bedroom![26]

Looking at the record afresh, one finds problems with this portrayal of Washington's attitude toward both Sally Fairfax and Martha Custis on the eve of matrimony. The evidence about Washington and Sally is quantitatively slight if intriguing. They wrote two letters to each other in September of 1758, by which time—if not as early as March of that year—he and Martha Custis were probably engaged.[27] Surely he wrote to Sally admiring statements that could have been interpreted at the time as improper, whatever their exact import. Judging from Washington's end of the correspondence—Sally's missives have not survived—she teased him about the meaning of part of his first letter. His behavior, to some degree possibly reciprocated by her, hardly seems out of character for an age when men and women engaged in such banter replete with suggestive implications.

Examples abound. The intellectual historian Peter Gay writes of "hyperbolic language" in a "hyperbolic century." Certain effusions of the age have to be discounted, he maintains. Writers "peppered their letters with exaggerations that seem cloying today, but were ritual formulas then."[28] The most careful scholars of Benjamin Franklin's years as a diplomat in Paris likewise assert that his interest in French women has been torn from its context: he reveled in their embraces, banter, and confidences, but the evidence stops short of the boudoir. He never credited himself with seductions, nor do the numerous diaries and journals of elite Parisians record such tales. In fact, "there is no shred of evidence" that he had "affairs with French women."[29] The same might be said of Jefferson, who succeeded Franklin as an American diplomat in Paris. He relished metaphors and literary allusions charged with sexual implications in letters to Angelica Church and Maria Cosway, both married women whom Jefferson invited to visit Monticello. But complicating explication of Jefferson's famous Head and Heart Letter to Maria Cosway is that he addressed it to her husband as well. Even his correspondence with Abigail Adams is not without flirtatious metaphors, and when Jefferson visited England in 1786, he and Abigail took several sightseeing jaunts together to some of the kingdom's most celebrated houses and gardens.[30]

Men too could engage each other in correspondence that suggested deep emotional, possibly erotic, ties. The late Richard Showman, editor of *The Papers of General Nathanael Greene*, asked me, as a consultant on the project, to read the eighteen letters that Nathanael Greene wrote Samuel Ward Jr. between 1770 and 1774. At first Showman wondered if this flowery, effusive exchange might reveal more than an emotional link between Greene, still single in his late twenties, and a teenage boy. Eventually we concluded that it did not.[31]

If, for a time at least, Washington's choice of language revealed poor judgment, the best evidence for it appears in his first September letter to Sally, which turned up a century ago, only to disappear again until 1958 when Harvard University acquired it. It reads in part: "You have drawn me my dear Madam, or rather have I drawn myself into an honest confession of a Simple Fact—misconstrue not my meaning—'tis obvious—doubt in [it?] not, nor expose it,—the World has no business to know the object of my Love,—declared in this manner to—you when I want to conceal it." Sally's response, which no longer exists, must have teased the young man with the remark that she found his meaning unclear. For he took up his pen to respond: "I cannot speak plainer without—but I'll say no more, and leave you to guess the rest." It is possible that in this missive he clumsily sought to conceal his intentions regarding Martha Custis, for his own reasons or possibly for reasons of Martha's. But Washington also expressed his frustrations with the military campaign, asserting that he could spend his time more agreeably playing Juba, with Sally taking the part of Marcia in Joseph Addison's *Cato*, a tragedy in which the two romantic characters never address openly their love for each other.

In the letters that historians have found so intriguing, both Washington and Sally make it clear that others knew of their correspondence, and both convey greetings from those members of their circle. Both of Washington's so-called amorous messages to Sally Fairfax—then married for ten years—were written on the same days that he addressed mail to her husband, George William; on each occasion Washington's letters, penned to the Fairfaxes while campaigning with General John Forbes against Fort

Duquesne in Pennsylvania, traveled by the hand of the same dispatch rider. The Fairfaxes received their first letters from Washington at Belvoir and their second missives from him at the home of Sally's parents in Elizabeth City County. To put the matter more bluntly, Washington did not send secret epistles to Sally by some trusted messenger. The letters were carried to their destination over many miles to the Fairfaxes, who were together on their arrival. The ones to George William concerned, among other things, Fairfax's careful, time-consuming efforts to oversee extensive renovations then being undertaken by Washington at Mount Vernon.[32] A probable link between Washington's correspondence with Sally and with George William was his forthcoming marriage to Martha Custis, an event that called for making Mount Vernon larger and more respectable in appearance.

Other surviving evidence about Washington's relationship with Sally Fairfax hardly arouses suspicion, especially in the context of the times. Both of them, several years earlier, at the beginning of Washington's military service on the frontier, had expressed a desire to maintain a correspondence. Sarah Fairfax Carlyle, Sally's sister-in-law, had also requested an epistolary connection with Washington. But few such exchanges appear to have taken place between Washington and either woman. Washington expressed disappointment about not hearing more often from the ladies of Belvoir, who undoubtedly learned a good deal about his activities from Colonel William Fairfax and his son George William, both of whom maintained regular contact with the young colonel and shared their information within the family. There is no evidence of any letters between Washington and his female friends, except for one perfunctory note from Washington to Sally, for more than two years prior to November 1757.[33]

One might think that any serious feelings of the heart might have deepened in the months between November 1757 and early March 1758, a time when Washington left his command and returned to Mount Vernon in an effort to recover from severe diarrhea and a nagging cough. During that same span Mrs. Fairfax's husband visited England on business. The three surviving letters from Washington to Sally during his convalescence contain none of the suggestive or ambiguous language that he employed in his messages of September 1758. All are brief and formal. His first letter, dated November 17, 1757, requested Sally's assistance in procuring and preparing certain medicinal food and drink. He assumed that she had known little if anything about his doings or health for some months. A Washington letter composed February 13, 1758, implied that it had been some time since his neighbor had visited Mount Vernon. It would have been understandable for Sally to travel to see him, in view of their long friendship and his ill health, but there is no evidence that she actually did so.[34]

If Washington ever committed romantic improprieties—or even considered such behavior—with Sally Fairfax, it would have been particularly painful to both families. Highly publicized reports some years earlier of an episode involving accusations of sexual wrongdoing had probably deepened the Washington-Fairfax family ties and made such behavior all the more offensive to both clans. The matter involved Lawrence Washington's charge that their parish rector, Charles Green, had tried to seduce his wife-to-be Ann Fairfax just before their marriage. This sensational episode, which drew press attention even in Pennsylvania, found an out-of-court resolution and still remains murky in fact.[35] Another family sex scandal involving a Fairfax woman and a Washington man would have been unthinkable. Moreover, how might it have jeopardized George's engagement to Martha Custis, a strong, capable woman, of very substantial resources, the wealthiest widow in the Old Dominion, had she been embarrassed by reports of loose talk about unfaithful conduct on the part of her suitor?

Yet the claim has often been made that Washington's loss of Sally, his greatest love, became the emotional crux of his life. Page Smith, a distinguished historian, asserts that in acknowledging that Mrs. Fairfax could not be his, Washington learned a painful lesson about suffering and adversity that would serve him well in the Revolution's trials: "A man who has given up what is for him the dearest thing in life has always thereafter a certain aloofness, a certain detachment; having survived the keenest anguish of all, he knows himself superior to most of the tribulations that the world can place before him. Having denied him what he most wished, the world had lost, to a substantial degree, the power to wound or dismay him further."[36] (Though Douglas Wilson joins those who accept the truth of the Lincoln–Ann Rutledge romance, he scarcely makes Lincoln's loss at her death a defining moment in his life, but rather sees such a contention as "simplistic and hopelessly overdrawn."[37])

How is the Sally Fairfax story relevant to Washington's future public life? Unlike those of his mother and his wife, it is not—except in one respect. He undoubtedly learned a great deal about interacting with the fair sex, including the social graces, from Sally Fairfax and the other women of Belvoir. If there is one constant refrain about Washington and women during his generalship and his presidency, it is, as we have observed, that he was ever comfortable, often charming, in their presence. Even Abigail

Adams, as capable as her husband John of biting assessments of luminaries of the day, admitted to being charmed beyond belief by the polite, affable Virginian.[38]

Belvoir, a majestic home, handsomely furnished, had meant a great deal to Washington. He remembered wonderful times with people he respected and admired. Those who subscribe to views similar to Page Smith's find support in a letter Washington wrote Sally near the end of his life, and some years after the death of George William Fairfax. Washington's lengthy missive, penned May 16, 1798, dealt with various subjects of mutual interest. (In all probability, Washington would not have written except that Sally's in-law Bryan Fairfax, preparing for a trip to England, agreed to deliver personally mail to his relatives there.) He recalled "those happy moments—the happiest in my life—which I have enjoyed in your company." But the statement is in the context of Washington's describing gay times at Belvoir, brought to mind by a recent visit to the ruins there. He passed the letter on to Martha to read and to add a message of her own. Washington had recorded a similar observation about spending the "happiest moments of my life" at Belvoir to Sally's husband George William thirteen years earlier.[39] Few letters were exchanged between the Washington and Fairfax families during the war and afterward. Both George's and Martha's 1798 letters to Sally suggest that there had been no direct communication between them for more than twenty-five years, although Washington and George William had corresponded infrequently until the latter's death in 1787. The Washingtons, at least, had retained their warmth and affection for the other couple. Evidently Sally never replied to her old Mount Vernon neighbors.

Washington's love affair was with the entire Fairfax family—Thomas, Lord Fairfax, who gave Washington his first employment as a surveyor; Colonel William Fairfax, whom Washington described as the key to his advancement in public life; George William and Sally, and the former's siblings, including Washington's sister-in-law Ann and Bryan Fairfax, a man who sat out the Revolution without losing Washington's warm friendship.

Because there is so much more evidence about Washington's relationship with his wife than there is about his lives with the other two women studied in this essay, only a few observations about their forty-year marriage seem in order. Moreover, it is a subject that I write about at some length in a forthcoming book.

The traditional treatment of Martha Washington is of a rather pudgy, plain-looking woman of modest intellect, but certainly kind and pleasant, as well as loyal and dutiful, an ideal wife of a domestic type. Historians usually deploy set descriptions of her—"simple," "stolid," "practical," "bustling," "a good housekeeper." In hindsight, "good Martha's plump hand was the more suitable" than that of "pretty Sally" "for the office of helping" Washington "to fame during life and to immortality after death."[40]

Assuredly her virtues extended far beyond some of these, most of which fall into the "plain Jane" category. First, John Custis IV, father of Daniel Parke Custis, Martha's first husband, considered her "beautifull & sweet temper'd," possessed of the highest "Character." A hard man to please when it came to a bride for his son, he kept Daniel Parke a bachelor until age thirty-seven, when his son married the best "Lady in Virginia."[41] Her portrait, painted by John Wollaston about a year before her engagement to Washington, reveals a remarkably pretty face and an appearance consistent with the eighteenth-century ideal of femininity: "buxom, yet small and delicate," with "sensuality coy and indirect."[42] The British architect Benjamin H. Latrobe wrote that Martha, nearly forty years later, "retains strong remains of physical beauty."[43]

Second, she displayed an independence of mind that has not been appreciated. Her years as a widow and without Washington at Mount Vernon during the Revolutionary War led her to see the benefits of self-reliance. She advised her niece Fanny Bassett Washington, recently widowed, to learn to manage her own affairs. Fanny should be "as independent as your circumstances will admit," Martha wrote, as "dependance is I think a wrached state and you will have enough if you mannage it right."[44]

Third, the Washingtons' few surviving letters show a tenderness and closeness consistent with outside observations about their deep affection for each other.[45] It should not be forgotten that Martha traveled great distances under primitive conditions to be with her husband in the Continental army's winter encampments for eight consecutive years during the Revolutionary War. As she said, she was truly a "perambulator" of the Revolution.[46] Washington, age forty-three when he first beseeched her to come and stay as many months as possible, had reached a stage in life that finds countless men growing restless and feeling a void in their intimate spousal relations—what the French call *le démon de midi*, the devil at high noon. Not so Washington, whose marriage never suffered even a hint of scandal, then or later, from any reputable source, although one encounters occasional reckless stories by British and Loyalist propagandists in the Revolutionary War and by Jeffersonian Republican hacks during his presidency, all of which John C. Fitzpatrick refuted in *The George Washington Scandals*.[47]

All this, of course, does not tell us exactly what Washington thought of his bride-to-be in 1758. No doubt good marriages deepen with the years. If the couple were not passionately in love at the time, that fact tells us little. Because of Washington's military commitments, they had had precious few opportunities for togetherness that year. "It was an age that did not necessarily expect people to marry for love, but trusted that love would come and grow after marriage."[48] Washington, in later years, liked to say that the union of man and woman was the most important step one ever took.[49]

Finally, Washington found Martha to be an asset in his public life. She lent her name and support to the Ladies Association, initiated in 1780 by thirty-three-year-old Esther DeBerdt Reed of Philadelphia, wife of Joseph Reed, who presided over the Pennsylvania state government. The first female war measure in the Revolution, it sought to organize chapters in each of the thirteen states to raise money for enlisted men in Washington's army. All sums collected were to go to Mrs. Washington for distribution. Linda Kerber speculates that Martha Washington played a substantial role in trying to make the undertaking a national enterprise. Certainly she sent a copy of the Philadelphia plan directly to Martha Wayles Jefferson, the wife of Virginia's governor. She, like other females involved in Philadelphia, hoped that each chief executive's spouse would head the fund-raising drive in her state. Martha Washington also recommended to Mrs. Jefferson that she enlist the cooperation of an influential woman in Williamsburg, Sarah Tate Madison, wife of the president of the College of William and Mary. No doubt Mrs. Washington's name lent visibility and significance to the effort. Even so, the Ladies Association achieved only partial success, partly owing to a shortage of currency in the country. Virginia, perhaps because of its link to the Washington name, stood out as one of the few states to raise substantial sums for the soldiers.[50]

Washington, appreciative of his wife's tact and social skills, likely employed her talents in various ways. On one occasion at Valley Forge, he turned to Martha for assistance in dealing with a group of Quaker women from Philadelphia, distraught over the exile of their husbands from home for refusing to sign a loyalty oath to the Pennsylvania Revolutionary government. He asked Martha to entertain them before he met with them, and then, after he expressed sympathy for their concerns (he could do little in a matter for state authorities), he had Martha assuage their feelings as best she could in her private living quarters. Mrs. Elizabeth Drinker, who described Martha as "a sociable pretty kind of woman," and the rest of her party traveled on to Lancaster, carrying a pass from the general, to plead their case to the Supreme Executive Council.[51]

Martha Washington's significant public role as the president's wife—our initial First Lady—has rarely been fully recognized. To critics of the Washington administration's style and legislative endeavors, who depicted them as British and monarchical in tone and content, Martha Washington's "republican court" served as an antidote. On Friday evenings her drawing room filled with congressmen and other officials of the federal government and their spouses from throughout the nation. Martha, dressing modestly, offered her guests lemonade and tea, not wine, hardly reminiscent of London or Paris high society. Sharing the president's passion to strengthen the ties between the various regions of America, partly through these gatherings, she brokered sixteen marriages.

Though hardly one of the most intellectual women of her time, she nonetheless seems to have been conversant with the issues of the day. Often expressing an interest in education, she once read a book, still in manuscript, on the proper schooling for females and gave the author permission to cite her name as an advocate of better education for women.[52] She had the respect and friendship of such bright and well-versed women as Mercy Otis Warren, Elizabeth Willing Powel, Hannah Stockton Boudinot, Elizabeth Schuyler Hamilton, and Abigail Adams. If, to some people at least, the president seemed stiff and formal, his wife must have softened or moderated this side of her husband. Mrs. Adams, wife of the vice president, described her "great ease" and "modest and unassuming" behavior, "not a tincture of ha'ture about her."[53]

Why was Washington a sound man to lead a revolution? To be sure, some of the reasons involve his previous military and political experience. Besides these traditional answers to that question, I would stress that his relationship with three women, which certainly has needed clarification, provides further insight into his revolutionary accomplishments. Never a part of a dysfunctional family, he gained social skills and other forms of sophistication from the Fairfax family at Belvoir. He had an addiction to the whole Fairfax family, and not just to Sally Fairfax, from whom he probably learned how to be comfortable in the presence of charming young women. He prized marriage and family life. He hardly fits the characterization of a modern revolutionary ascetic, of a man alienated from such things as society and family and often displaying unhealthy attitudes about women and sexuality.[54] His emotional and psychological stability enabled him to remain focused on his great tasks of winning a war and uniting a nation.

NOTES

1. Winthrop D. Jordan, *White over Black: American Attitudes Toward the Negro, 1550–1812* (Chapel Hill: University of North Carolina Press, 1968), 461–68; Jack McLaughlin, *Jefferson and Monticello: The Biography of a Builder* (New York: Henry Holt, 1988), passim; Kenneth A. Lockridge, *On the Sources of Patriarchal Rage* (New York: New York University Press, 1992), chap. 3; Joseph J. Ellis, *American Sphinx: The Character of Thomas Jefferson* (New York: Alfred A. Knopf, 1997), esp. 90–97; David S. Shields, *Civil Tongues and Polite Letters in British America* (Chapel Hill: University of North Carolina Press, 1997), 322–24, 326–28, and "George Washington: Publicity, Probity, and Power," in this volume. Sandra Gustafson of Notre Dame University provided helpful insights in commenting on the first version of this essay, which I presented at the Fourth Annual Conference of the Omohundro Institute of Early American History and Culture at Worcester, Massachusetts, June 5, 1998. For reading later drafts I wish to thank for their numerous thoughtful suggestions and corrections Peter R. Henriques of George Mason University, Sylvia Hoffert of the University of North Carolina at Chapel Hill, and the editorial staff of the *Papers of George Washington* project at the University of Virginia: Editor-in-Chief Philander D. Chase, Beverly H. Runge, Frank E. Grizzard Jr., Christine S. Patrick, and Robert F. Haggard.

2. A full examination of Washington and the distaff side would have to include, among other subjects, his relationship with his nieces, with his step-granddaughter Nelly Custis, and with his friend and correspondent Mrs. Eliza Powell of Philadelphia.

3. Some feminist writings that were influential in attacking stereotypical gender roles include Simone de Beauvoir, *The Second Sex*, trans. H. M. Parshley (New York: Alfred A. Knopf, 1953); Germaine Greer, *The Female Eunuch* (New York: McGraw-Hill, 1971); Betty Friedan, *The Feminine Mystique* (New York: W. W. Norton, 1963); Kate Millett, *Sexual Politics* (Garden City, N.Y.: Doubleday, 1970).

4. For Weems's approach to Washington and for Washington mythology in general, see Mason L. Weems, *The Life of Washington*, ed. Marcus Cunliffe (1809; Cambridge: Harvard University Press, 1962), esp. Cunliffe's introduction (ix–lxii), and Bernard Mayo, *Myths and Men* (Athens: University of Georgia Press, 1959), chap. 3.

5. Douglas Southall Freeman, *George Washington: A Biography*, 7 vols. (New York: Charles Scribner's Sons, 1948–57), xix–xx, 1:193, 195, 198, 202, 2:17–18, 49, 107, 199, 246. Freeman, of course, was not the first historian to describe Mary Ball in unflattering terms. The 1920s, a decade of debunking great men, living and dead, saw the beginning of such a trend, but it did not become the dominant view of Washington's mother before Freeman's work. See, for examples, William E. Woodward,

George Washington: The Image and the Man (New York: Boni and Liveright, 1926), 15, 85, 434–35; Rupert Hughes, *George Washington: The Savior of the States, 1777–1781* (New York: William Morrow, 1930), 44–45; Bernard Fay, *George Washington: Republican Aristocrat* (Boston: Houghton Mifflin, 1931), 29; Michael De La Bedoyere, *George Washington* (Philadelphia: J. B. Lippincott, 1935), 40.

6. James Thomas Flexner, *George Washington*, 4 vols. (Boston: Little, Brown, 1965–72), 1:18–25.

7. Frederick Bernays Wiener, "Washington and His Mother," *American History Illustrated* (July/August 1991), 44, 47, 68–72; Howard C. Rice Jr. and Anne S. K. Brown, trans. and eds., *The American Campaigns of Rochambeau's Army, 1780, 1781, 1782, 1783*, 2 vols. (Princeton: Princeton University Press, 1972), 1:73; *Mount Vernon: Yesterday, Today, Tomorrow* 12 (summer 1998), 18. A generally well received novel, William Martin's *Citizen Washington* (New York: Warner, 1999), also limns an unflattering image of Mary Ball Washington. Young George's slave companion calls her Ball-and-Chain.

8. *The Papers of George Washington: Colonial Series* (hereafter cited as *Col. Ser.*), ed. W. W. Abbot et al., 10 vols. (Charlottesville: University Press of Virginia, 1983–95), 1:268–69, 304–5, 336–38, 359–60, 4:430; *The Papers of George Washington: Confederation Series* (hereafter *Conf. Ser.*), ed. W. W. Abbot, Dorothy Twohig, et al., 6 vols. (Charlottesville: University Press of Virginia, 1992–97), 5:33–37. Washington's diary shows that he usually visited his mother when in the vicinity of Fredericksburg; see *The Diaries of George Washington*, ed. Donald Jackson et al., 6 vols. (Charlottesville: University Press of Virginia, 1976–79), passim.

9. Benjamin Harrison to Washington, February 25, 1781, Washington to Benjamin Harrison, March 21, 1781, Washington to John Augustine Washington, January 16, 1783, *The Writings of George Washington from the Original Manuscript Sources, 1745–1799* (hereafter *Writings*), ed. John C. Fitzpatrick, 39 vols. (Washington, D.C.: U.S. Government Printing Office, 1931–44), 21:341 n, 341–42, 26:42–44. Although Washington said that his mother had thus far never complained directly to him of severe economic distress, she had written to his overseer, Lund Washington, with requests a number of times, according to John E. Ferling, *The First of Men: A Life of George Washington* (Knoxville: University of Tennessee Press, 1988), 343–44. And several years later he did have trouble containing his exasperation with her over what seemed to be incessant requests for more financial assistance; see Washington to Mary Ball Washington, February 15, 1787, *Conf. Ser.*, 5:33–37.

10. Mary Ball Washington to Lund Washington, December 19, 1778, quoted in Flexner, *George Washington*, 2:337; Mary Ball Washington to Washington, March 13, 1782, Henry E. Huntington Library (transcription courtesy of Philander D. Chase and Beverly Kirsch); Washington to Charles Thompson, January 22, 1784, *Conf. Ser.*, 1:71; Washington to the Citizens of Fredericksburg, February 14, 1784, *Conf. Ser.*, 1:122–23.

11. *Conf. Ser.*, 5:157, 158–59 n; *Diaries of George Washington*, 5:144. He had only recently "bid an eternal farewell to a much loved Brother [John Augustine]

who was the intimate companion of my youth and the most affectionate friend of my ripened age" (*Conf. Ser.*, 5:157).

12. *Conf. Ser.*, 6:332–33, 334 n; *The Papers of George Washington: Presidential Series* (hereafter *Pres. Ser.*), ed. Dorothy Twohig et al., 10 vols. to date (Charlottesville: University Press of Virginia, 1987–), 1:368, 368 n, 404, 404 n.

13. Patricia Brady, ed., *George Washington's Beautiful Nelly: The Letters of Eleanor Parke Custis Lewis to Elizabeth Bordley Gibson, 1794–1851* (Columbia: University of South Carolina Press, 1991), 2.

14. William Fairfax to Lawrence Washington, September 9–10, 1746, and Robert Jackson to Lawrence Washington, September 16, 1746, in Moncure Daniel Conway, *Barons of the Potomack and Rappahannock* (New York: Grolier Club, 1892), 236–40.

15. Joseph Ball to Mary Ball Washington, May 19, 1747, quoted in Freeman, *George Washington*, 1:198–99.

16. Ibid., 42–45, 530–34.

17. Lucy Brown Beale, "Colonel George Eskridge," *Northern Neck Historical Magazine* 3 (1953): 233–36; *Genealogies of Virginia Families*, 2 vols. (Baltimore: Genealogical Publishing, 1981), 2:732–34.

18. The continued use of certain traditional given names within a family seems to be a clue to family closeness and cohesion, whereas family tensions could lead to dropping such names in subsequent generations. See Martin H. Quitt, "Immigrant Origins of the Virginia Gentry: A Study of Cultural Transmission and Innovation," *William and Mary Quarterly*, 3d ser., 45 (1988): 629–55.

19. Washington to Mary Ball Washington, February 15, 1787, *Conf. Ser.*, 5:33–36; *Pres. Ser.*, 1:368, 368 n. 2. A recent, highly publicized contribution to the nature-versus-nurture literature, one that places genetics and environmental influences outside the family above child-rearing techniques in importance, is Judith Rich Harris, *The Nurture Assumption: Why Children Turn Out the Way They Do* (New York: Free Press, 1998).

20. Will of Mary Ball Washington, May 20, 1788, *The Writings of George Washington*, ed. Worthington Chauncey Ford, 14 vols. (New York: G. P. Putnam's Sons, 1889–93), 14:416–18; Washington to Betty Lewis, September 13, 1789, *Pres. Ser.*, 4:32–35. President Washington, residing in New York, the temporary capital, ordered that his household wear "mourning Cockades & Ribbon." City officials advised that men wear "black crape or ribbon on the arm or hat" and that women display "a black ribbon and necklace."

21. Wilson Miles Cary, *Sally Cary: A Long Hidden Romance of Washington's Life* (New York: De Vinne Press, 1916); Kenton Kilmer and Donald Sweig, *The Fairfax Family in Fairfax County: A Brief History* (Fairfax, Va.: County Office of Comprehensive Planning, 1975).

22. If twentieth-century historians have found Washington's marriage one of mutual convenience, his early biographers all but ignored it, sometimes giving the subject a few lines at best. See John Marshall, *The Life of George Washington*, 5 vols. (Philadelphia: C. P. Wayne, 1804–7), 2:71; Jared Sparks, *The Writings of*

George Washington . . . With a Life of the Author, 12 vols. (Boston, 1834–37), 1:105; Weems, *The Life of Washington,* 53–54.

23. Freeman, as he did in regard to Washington's relationship with his mother, had a substantial impact on subsequent accounts of Washington's interest in Sally Fairfax; see his *George Washington,* 2:335–39. Though the treatment is hardly original with Freeman, his reputation undoubtedly explains why it became the standard one. The first serious account to document the story seems to have been *Sally Cary: A Long Hidden Romance,* written in 1916 by Wilson Miles Cary. Cary seems uncertain or ambivalent about Sally's reaction to Washington's feelings for her.

24. Thomas A. Lewis, *For King and Country: The Maturing of George Washington, 1748–1760* (New York: Harper Collins, 1993), 25. The Washington and Sally romance is unquestioned in numerous sophisticated publications. See, for example, Wayne Barrett, "George and Betsy and Polly and Patsy and Sally . . . and Sally . . . and Sally," *Smithsonian* 4 (1973): 90–99, and John F. Stegeman, "The Lady of Belvoir: This Matter of Sally Fairfax," *Virginia Cavalcade* 34 (1984): 4–11.

25. The term was coined by Nathaniel W. Stephenson, "The Romantics and George Washington," *American Historical Review* 38 (1933): 274–83. Three careful Washington scholars doubted the reputed love affair, although they tended to dismiss it without seriously endeavoring to investigate it. See John C. Fitzpatrick, *George Washington Himself: A Common-Sense Biography* . . . (Indianapolis: Bobbs-Merrill, 1933), 75–80 passim, 110–14 passim, and Nathaniel Wright Stephenson and Waldo Hilary Dunn, *George Washington,* 2 vols. (New York: Oxford University Press, 1940), 1:441–42. The editors of *The Papers of George Washington* also exercise caution in dealing with the relationship; see *Col. Ser.,* 6:13 n.

26. For an analysis of the documents dealing with the presale inventory and accounts of the sales from Belvoir, see William M. S. Rasmussen and Robert S. Tilton, *George Washington: The Man Behind the Myths* (Charlottesville: University Press of Virginia, 1999), 25–28. King Laughlin, a member of the staff of the Mount Vernon Ladies Association, informed me of the location of the two chests of drawers. One cannot be certain that these pieces always remained positioned as described. An early-nineteenth-century painting of the room showed the furniture as described here.

27. Washington to Sarah Cary Fairfax, September 12 and 25, 1758, *Col. Ser.,* 6:10–13, 41.

28. Peter Gay, *Voltaire's Politics: The Poet as Realist* (Princeton: Princeton University Press, 1959), 148.

29. Claude-Anne Lopez and Eugenia W. Herbert, *The Private Franklin: The Man and His Family* (New York: W. W. Norton, 1975), 274–75, quotation on p. 274; Claude-Anne Lopez, *Mon Cher Papa: Franklin and the Ladies of Paris* (New Haven: Yale University Press, 1966), passim.

30. William Howard Adams, *The Paris Years of Thomas Jefferson* (New Haven: Yale University Press, 1997), chap. 7.

31. *The Papers of General Nathanael Greene,* ed. Richard K. Showman, 12 vols. to date (Chapel Hill: University of North Carolina Press, 1976–), 1:14–65 passim.

32. George William Fairfax makes mention of the first letter he received from Washington, the one of September 12, 1758, in a reply of September 15, 1758. Washington's letter to George William of September 25, 1758, survives. See *Col. Ser.*, 6:12 n, 19–20, 38–41. Sometimes overlooked is the fact that George William also knew of the letter that his wife wrote to Washington on September 1, 1758. In fact, he asked his wife to write it. That is the now-missing Sally Fairfax letter that prompted Washington's fascinating missive of September 12, which has stirred so much historical controversy. See George William Fairfax to Washington, September 1, 1758, *Col. Ser.*, 5:436–37.

33. Washington to Sarah Cary Fairfax, April 23, 1756, *Col. Ser.*, 3:418–19.

34. Washington to Sarah Cary Fairfax, November 15, 1757, and February 13 and [March 4], 1758, *Col. Ser.*, 5:56–57, 93–94, 100.

35. Peter R. Henriques, "Major Lawrence Washington Versus the Reverend Charles Green: A Case Study of the Squire and the Parson," *Virginia Magazine of History and Biography* 100 (1992): 233–64.

36. Page Smith, *A New Age Now Begins: A People's History of the American Revolution*, 2 vols. (New York: McGraw-Hill, 1976), 1:549–51, quotation on p. 551.

37. Douglas L. Wilson, *Honor's Voice: The Transformation of Abraham Lincoln* (New York: Alfred A. Knopf, 1998), 114–27, quotation on p. 126.

38. L. H. Butterfield, Mark Friedlaender, and Mary-Jo Kline, eds., *The Book of Abigail and John: Selected Letters of the Adams Family, 1762–1784* (Cambridge: Harvard University Press, 1975), 100. Another woman whom Washington captivated was Lady Henrietta Liston, wife of the British minister, Robert Liston. He became her genuine friend, quite open with her on a variety of subjects. The Listons were guests at Mount Vernon several times after Washington retired from the presidency. See James C. Nicholls, "Lady Henrietta Liston's Journal of Washington's 'Resignation,' Retirement, and Death," *Pennsylvania Magazine of History and Biography* 95 (1971): 511–20.

39. *The Papers of George Washington: Retirement Series*, ed. Dorothy Twohig et al., 4 vols. (Charlottesville: University Press of Virginia, 1998–99), 2:272–75; *Conf. Ser.*, 2:387–88.

40. The final sentence is from De La Bedoyere, *George Washington*, 57.

41. Jo Zuppan, ed., "Father to Son: Letters from John Custis IV to Daniel Parke Custis," *Virginia Magazine of History and Biography* 98 (1990): 86. These quotations are in letters to Daniel Parke Custis from two friends, who declared they were repeating his father's words about Martha Dandridge (86 n). Flexner, *George Washington*, 1:230, departs from numerous other Washington biographers in calling Martha "an extremely pretty woman." This conclusion was shared by Freeman, *George Washington*, 2:285–86.

42. Lois W. Banner, *American Beauty* (New York: Alfred A. Knopf, 1983), 46.

43. *The Virginia Journals of Benjamin Henry Latrobe, 1795–1798*, ed. Edward C. Carter II (New Haven: Yale University Press, 1977), 1:168.

44. Martha Washington to Fanny Bassett Washington, September 15, 1794, in

Joseph E. Fields, ed., *"Worthy Partner": The Papers of Martha Washington* (Westport, Conn.: Greenwood, 1994), 274–75.

45. Both of Martha's messages to her husband are notes written on the bottom or back of letters penned by other family members to Washington. His letters to her escaped her detection since they were stuffed in a small desk drawer apart from other family papers. No doubt for these reasons they avoided destruction when she destroyed her correspondence with her husband before her death in 1802. The two Washington letters to Martha begin with "My Dearest" and so does one of hers to him. Her second letter begins with "my Love." See *Col. Ser.*, 7:495; *The Papers of George Washington: Revolutionary War Series*, ed. Philander D. Chase et al., 12 vols. to date (Charlottesville: University Press of Virginia, 1985–), 1:3, 27, 11:674 n.

46. Fields, *"Worthy Partner,"* 193, 314.

47. John C. Fitzpatrick, *The George Washington Scandals* (Alexandria, Va.: Washington Society of Alexandria, 1929). Another president, the product of a revolution, had a less successful marriage than Washington, and there were rumors about his fidelity to his nuptial vows; see Carol K. Bleser, "The Marriage of Varina Howell and Jefferson Davis: 'I Gave the Best and All My Life to a Girdled Tree,'" *Journal of Southern History* 66 (1999): 3–40.

48. Lopez and Herbert, *The Private Franklin*, 40.

49. "Do not . . . look for perfect felicity before you consent to wed," he advised Elizabeth [Betsy] Custis, Martha's oldest granddaughter. "Love is a mighty pretty thing; but like all other delicious things, it is cloying; and when the first transports of the passion begins to subside . . . and yield, oftentimes too late, to more sober reflections, it serves to evince, that love is too dainty a food to live upon *alone*, and ought not be considered farther than as a necessary ingredient for that matrimonial happiness which results from a combination of causes" (Washington to Elizabeth Parke Custis, September 14, 1794, *Writings*, 33:500–501). Washington informed a French friend that his views on marriage were quite different from those held by many Europeans on "matrimony & domestic felicity" (Washington to Charles Armand-Tuffin, August 10, 1786, *Conf. Ser.*, 4:203–4. Christine S. Patrick has edited a collection of Washington letters on love and marriage on the *Papers of George Washington* project website, http://gwpapers.virginia.edu.

50. Mary Beth Norton, *Liberty's Daughters: The Revolutionary Experience of American Women, 1750–1800* (Boston: Little, Brown, 1980), 177–87; Linda K. Kerber, *Women of the Republic: Intellect and Ideology in Revolutionary America* (New York: W. W. Norton, 1980), 99–105. Martha Washington was in Virginia at the time most of the money arrived. For discussions between General Washington and the women leaders about how to reward the troops, see accounts in Norton and Kerber.

51. Kerber, *Women of the Republic*, 95–98; Elaine Forman Crane et al., eds., *The Diary of Elizabeth Drinker*, 3 vols. (Boston: Northeastern University Press, 1991), 1:297. The Quaker men were released a short time later, although it is unclear what role the Philadelphia women played in that development.

52. Shields, *Civil Tongues,* 322–24, 326–28, and "George Washington: Publicity, Probity, and Power," in this volume.

53. Stewart Mitchell, ed., *New Letters of Abigail Adams, 1788–1801* (Boston: Houghton Mifflin, 1947), 13.

54. Bruce Mazlish, *The Revolutionary Ascetic: Evolution of a Political Type* (New York: Basic Books, 1976). See also, among other relevant literature, Erik H. Erikson, *Dimensions of a New Identity* (New York: W. W. Norton, 1974).

Chapter 6

GEORGE WASHINGTON

Publicity, Probity, and Power

DAVID S. SHIELDS

One of the more provocative of the visual satires by painter Grant Wood was a 1939 canvas entitled *Parson Weems' Fable*. Parson Weems, tricked out like Charles Willson Peale, lifts a fringed drape to reveal the famous episode of the Cherry Tree.[1] The Tree, a topiary pom-pom, is bent low in the proprietary grip of Augustine Washington, George's father. The slender stem is conspicuously hacked. Boy George, gazing up at his father, candidly points at the offending instrument, which looks like a regulation Boy Scout hand axe. His face is free of guile. It is the face on the dollar bill—wigged, fifty, and expressionless—a visage of Olympian dispassion perched atop a six-year-old's body.

Wood's point: George Washington has undergone such a thoroughgoing monumentalization that any representation must lack reality. At that moment when social realism had seized the aesthetic consciences of many American artists, Wood pointed to the founder of the United States as one subject that defied realism. This was an interesting point at a time when Isaak Brodsky, a leading light of socialist realism, was painting homey pictures of V. I. Lenin, the founder of the Soviet Union, taking pains to make him the balding, bearded intellectual uncle of every working Ivan and Ivana in the USSR. We call George Washington the father of our country, but he is no one's dad. Rather he is a national patriarch, a father of the most radical sort, whose sense of the law, the higher powers, the call of duty is so great that, like Abraham drawing Isaac to the rock of sacrifice or Cato surrendering his sons to Rome, Washington could entirely repress domestic sentiment to perform the public work of virtue.

George Washington was decidedly not that new creature of the eighteenth century, "the man of feeling."[2] This is a problem for those in the early twenty-first century who wish to understand Washington. We live in a feeling age. True, our political pundits talk about character, usually about its absence. But we no longer have a characterology. Instead we have psychology that visualizes personality problems in terms of affective disorders and good mental health in terms of emotional equilibrium. Our popular culture has such difficulty picturing individuals actuated by reasoned principles that we tend to view them as aliens or androids: Spock on *Star Trek,* or Data on *Next Generation.* And even in these cases, Data's ambition is to acquire feeling, Spock's to resolve his half-human, half-emotional heritage. Even our qualifications for political leadership tend to elevate empathy over principle. It interests me that popular amusement about President Clinton's mantra "I feel your pain" arose from a doubt that his feeling was genuine. It was not about whether feeling is an inappropriate response to the conditions of the citizenry. Candidates drub one another for a lack of compassion for the people. But lack of compassion is not really a lack of feeling; no, the opposite of compassion in the political discourse is interestedness, that is, a self-serving love of monetary gain, power, or status. Furthermore, disinterestedness is conceived as an altruistic feeling for others. American politics seems incapable of conceiving of the merits of dispassion, or articulating a notion of disinterestedness that is grounded, as it used to be, on the elevation of rational principles over all feeling. Even William J. Bennett, that vocal champion of antique values, offers a sentimentalized view of virtue, with compassion ranked second in his top-ten list, friendship fourth, and loyalty ninth.[3] Rationality does not appear, nor does probity, nor civility. So in a way our common speech lacks the conceptual bridges needed to make George Washington something other than the heartless statue of immaculate marble in the rotunda of the temple of fame.[4]

I am forced to resort to an academic exercise in cultural archaeology to explain why George Washington is the most monumental, least human of the founders. That he is a monument, no scholar has disputed since the 1950s when Marcus Cunliffe published *George Washington: Man and Monument.*[5] I see no benefit in resorting to the academic strategy of demystification, trying to humanize the first president by discovering him to be an embodiment of the reigning vices. How many studies of Washington as slaveholder, crypto-aristocrat, expense-account padder have issued from the press without budging the statue an inch on his pedestal? My presumption is that George Washington is a symbol, indeed an allegorical figure of public probity, troubling an age that has little use for allegory, except in science fiction, and that my task is to say something about how he became abstracted from the fallible flesh, how he turned into stone.

If I were to summarize the process in a sentence, I would say that he turned himself to stone. Somewhere in the process of character formation shared by so many young men of the gentry class in the Anglo-American world, somewhere after he had mastered the rules of civility and was internalizing the military ethic of valor, he began the process of reputation building. Some would argue that his will to public renown was activated by failure, that he began making himself a living complex of ideals after Braddock's defeat and after his failure to secure a regular army commission. Yet the molding of his character in the light of ideals began as early in his boyhood as the "Rules of Civility." There are Freudians who would say that this embrace of the discipline of social convention was his way of replacing the example of his father, Augustine, who died in 1743 when George was eleven. Yet none of the other numerous siblings appears to have composed a like document in the face of the same loss. No, there was some ineluctable urge in the young George, similar to the urge that seized Benjamin Franklin a generation previously, to perfect himself in the light of the *sensus communis*. Both compiled a list of virtues recognized by contemporary society and then tried to enact them. Neither enjoyed the benefit of a classical education. Both followed in the footsteps of older brothers: in George's case, Lawrence. Both sought early on to make a mark in that same society by making themselves conspicuous in public—becoming players in the "theatre of action"—and, interestingly, both would have their reputations secured in print.

The decisive moment in George Washington's life occurred in 1753 when he volunteered to undertake a dangerous communication with the French in the wilds of Ohio for Governor Dinwiddie of Virginia. He was twenty-one, a major in the state militia, and familiar as a surveyor with parts of the western territory. Yet what most recommended him in the governor's eyes was the fact that he was a gentleman. This was crucial, for the negotiator had to represent British imperial authority and appear to the French officer as a representative of a cosmopolitan ideal of civility. As Andrew Cayton has indicated, the ceremonies of civility took on particular importance in wilderness situations when Native Americans were present.[6] They became occasions for projecting the potency of European culture. Despite the foregone failure of the negotiation, Washington did well in his agency, cultivating Native allies and communicating to the French the serious consequences of their fort-building on the frontier. Washington's journal, published by Dinwiddie to agitate the Virginia House of Burgesses into funding a military buildup, conveyed the young major's civility, intelligence, dutifulness, and most vividly his valor.

A word about valor. In 1753 the term had an antique aura. It was the old warrior virtue of European states before they consolidated civility and courtliness. Civility was a quality manifested primarily in the ordinary commerce and conversation of society; valor was that fortitude of spirit and physical courage manifested in times of combat and duress. Some thought to make the ideal irrelevant by making war a matter of commerce. In Britain, Walpole's Robinocracy maintained a fitful peace by cash payment and treaty barter. Walpole's opponents saw this as bribing Britain's enemies and an evidence of the loss of England's ancestral valor. The failure of the expedition upon Cartagena during the War of Jenkins' Ear in 1741 set the public prints in Britain and British America buzzing about the need to restore the "genius of Britain"—meaning the spirit of war. The debacle set into relief two images of military leadership: the bumbling careerist and courtier General Wentworth and the competent old sea dog Admiral Vernon.[7] Wentworth provoked the first of several decades of cartoons suggesting that Britain's officer corps was more concerned with foppish self-display and conquering ladies than fearlessly facing down imperial foes. Admiral Vernon became the first object of the public yearning for an avatar of ancient valor. George Washington's military-minded older brother, Lawrence, was one of the admiral's devotees and named his farm after him: Mount Vernon. Yet the message of Cartagena was that the Vernons of the world were being countermanded by the Wentworths and valor was devalued. So when Washington's journal published his perilous adventures, he acquired in popular eyes that quality deemed most absent in contemporary soldiers. The loss of Fort Necessity may have tarnished that reputation briefly, but it sparked a war between France and Britain on five continents, and Washington's later rescue of the remnants of Braddock's force after its defeat provided the one bright spot in a disaster that set the public oracles fretting over the emasculation of British power.

One intellectual offshoot of the success of the French and Indians was the sense that Native Americans embodied the valor and violence that Britons lacked. The stereotypical characterizations of Natives as barbaric and cruel raised the question whether such a primitive will toward violence was a requisite of valor. Here "stage theory" came into play. Stage theory held that every civilized people developed from a primitive state of nature to civil culture and then decadence. There was much debate in Anglo-America and the metropolis about where symbolically to place Native Americans in this scheme: were they precivil, premoral individuals in the state of nature, or did they embody virtue in its original simplicity and nobility? Wars tended to skew estimates to the former. Nevertheless, the question was, how could Britons receive an infusion of Native martial energy? Answer: by having direct contact with nature as the Natives did, and by enduring the discipline of settler life. It was the Roman poet Virgil in the *Georgics* who first proposed that the morality of Rome would be preserved by those who settled its conquered lands and faced the rigors of life that had once formed the founders of the empire. The Roman colonist learned valor in the agricultural war with nature. Machiavelli elaborated this doctrine and linked it to an image of imperial metropoli suffering inevitable decline as citizens became besotted with luxury and the wealth produced by dominion.[8] As empires sank into ruin, their former dependencies, disciplined by toil, would rise to power.[9]

We can see how these ideas, which floated freely in the republic of letters in countless periodical essays, pamphlets, and poems, served to validate morally the status of American settlers and George Washington. His self-image as a soldier-farmer, his symbolic identification with Republican Rome, and his suspicion of metropolitan degeneracy all derive from an embrace of stage theory. There were those agents of the metropolis, however, who bridled at the thought that British Americans by mere circumstance possessed ancestral values that Britons did not. Officers of the army and navy resented the idea, which first began surfacing in the press at the time of the 1745 conquest of Cape Breton, that "Rough English Virtue" was found more in American arms than English, and that fame "o'er the Old exalts New England's name."[10] Imagine how the following bit of doggerel must have stuck in the craw of the British officer corps:

> Britania strove a Carthegene to gain
> While Numbers perisht on the Wat'ry Main;
> And Wentworth's Forces languish'd ev'ry Day,
> 'Till Rum and Fevers swept whole Hosts away:
> The Spaniards smiling at the ill-laid Scheme,
> Were sure it was concerted in a Dream.
> When Christian Lewis comes to hear what's done
> With his strong Fortress on the Isle Breton,
> He'll sweat the Valour of the British Breed,
> In Western Climes, their Grandsires far exceed;
> And that New England Schemes the Old so pass,
> As much as solid Gold does tinkling Brass.[11]

During the Seven Years' War, Colonel Washington wrangled with English officers over authority. Despite lesser rank, they viewed their commissions as superior to that of the Virginia militia commander. Their condescension determined Washington in the belief that the army had indeed lost its virtue and that the metropolis had become corrupt with pride and the worship of status.

One must keep this in mind when considering Washington's behavior during the Revolution. I think particularly of the most notorious single episode in his command, a scene that would be visualized in plays, novels, and poems for two generations—the execution of John André for his part in Benedict Arnold's treason. André was a paragon of genteel graces: young, handsome, energetic, a talented draughtsman, poet, and conversationalist. He embodied all the qualities of civility that were desired in an "officer and a gentleman." Yet Washington judged him a conspicuous example of someone whose refinement had corrupted his virtue, engaging in secret schemes to traduce another soldier's honor.[12] Then too, André had scripted the event that more than any other had dramatized the dissipation of the English officer corps, the Meschianza. This outdoor extravaganza bidding farewell to General William Howe had included a regatta, a mock medieval tournament, a ball, a corps of Tory girls in Turkish costumes, a fireworks display, and a banquet. André's description of the event, published in London's periodicals, instead of being viewed as a triumph of British gentility, provoked a tempest of complaint that British officers were making love, not war.[13] Washington, having endured the hardships of a winter at Valley Forge, no doubt bridled at news of the British fete. When its author came into his hands, he knew what to do with him, staging a more solemn open-air ceremony of his own with the entire army as witness.

There are many ways to interpret André's execution. In a novel, André, the erring man of feeling, would have been forgiven and gone on, chastened, reformed, grateful, and wise. But war is not fiction, and Benedict Arnold's treason had grave consequences for persons' lives and the cause being contested. Washington in his open-air theater of judgment showed that justice and principle must prevail over sentiment. Washington intentionally chose to appear as unyielding in his adherence to law and justice as Cato condemning his sons. Political sentimentalism, for Washington, was pernicious. Nowadays historians tend to be quite admiring of sentimentalism, citing how the campaigns to make the poor, the imprisoned, the working classes, and slaves appear familiar to the enfranchised led ultimately to the improvement of their conditions. But the modus of sentimentality—to familiarize someone or something, that is, making it part of one's family of care—gave rise to problems. "Familiarity," as Washington well knew, was what enabled the privileges of the privileged classes. General John "Gentleman Johnny" Burgoyne, the most literate of Washington's enemies, drew a telling distinction between familiarity and civility in his play *The Maid of the Woods*.

> Maria: I am afraid I shall never procure any civility in town, upon the terms required.
>
> Lady Bab: Oh, my dear, you have chose a horrid word to express the intercourse of the bon ton; civility may be very proper in a mercer, when one is choosing a silk but familiarity is the life of good company. I believe this is quite new since your time.[14]

Familiarity was the social fluid that permitted favors in political life and favoritism in the administration of justice. At times among the genteel it operated as a class prerogative to operate outside the law. One of the invariable points made by persons describing Washington's character was that he bridled at familiarities. His decorum was so forbidding that only the most audacious dared approach him familiarly. It was an attitude with a strong political grounding. Washington's republicanism denied familiarity and cherished civility.

Civility was, as Lady Bab indicated, a code of behaviors that regulated the interactions of people of different conditions—whether of rank (in the military), of class (in society), of gender (in mixed company), of nationality (in diplomacy), or of politic persuasion (in legislative assemblies). It was a broader language than that of gentility, and less concerned with material display. The performance of civilities displayed that regard for others that was necessary for the integrity of civil society. Here we should recall the first of George's boyhood Rules: "Every action in company ought to be with some sign of respect to those present."

The state of nature lacked civility. The imperial metropolis had allowed civility to degenerate to familiarity and genteel fashionability. Only in the virtuous republic did civility thrive and coexist with the valor of the citizenry. A problem of British America was that it lacked the institutional integrity to constitute a republic. The frontiers and rural districts were too rude, unfinished, and unregulated. (Think of Byrd's portrait of North Carolina, or the Regulator Movement that fought to obtain those institutions that insured civil regulation in the backcountry.) The cities were too crowded with people of different cultural backgrounds. One of the distinctive things about George Washington was his continual effort to overcome the incoherence of civic life in America—his work to construct a public sphere.

Washington supported any initiative that would strengthen the formation of the public world in America. His participation in and tolerance of the foibles of legislatures, his support of the theater, his membership in clubs and associations, his cultivation of military and civic ceremony, his adoption of levees and endorsement of state occasions, his participation in the republic of letters all dramatize this tendency. The urge to enrich the public sphere was something more fundamental than his republican principles. He had little use for republican moralists or evangelicals who criticized the theater. We should remember that Washington's repeated attendance at and visible enjoyment of dramatic performances was what finally legitimized theater in the United States. The public world must have its mirrors where its extravagances are satirized, its achievements celebrated, and its manners consolidated. This the theater provided. Even during the starving time at Valley Forge, Washington had his officers perform Joseph Addison's *Cato* for the troops in the camp cookhouse. For public persons there were risks entailed in promoting an institution where opinion not managed by the government sounded so conspicuously. William Dunlap's play *André* had its moment of Tory defiance when a young officer tears off his cockade and throws it to the ground in protest of the execution of so genteel an officer as André. In the background looms the power of the character designated simply The General.[15] Yet Washington's faith in the good opinion of American audiences was well placed. Dunlap's scene provoked a riot. The play failed. Throughout the 1790s Washington was lauded in prologues and epilogues. The theater burnished his reputation. Yet his decades of theatergoing did more than that: they educated him in a range of public roles, and made him a consummate public actor. This skill proved important, for there was one moment when the fate of the republic hung on his ability to break his stoic Roman mask.

On March 15, 1783, the Continental army, suffering grave privation, threatened rebellion against the control of Congress and proposed to install Washington as king or dictator. In a fateful meeting, the general's praise of their accomplishments and his arguments against usurping power could not assuage the anger of the young officers. He told the assemblage of a letter from a Congressman promising help. He faltered as he opened the paper, stared at it as if uncomprehending its purport, and as the silence expanded to dramatic length, Washington produced a pair of spectacles, objects he had never permitted his subordinates to see before. "Gentlemen, you will permit me to put on my spectacles, for I have not only grown gray but almost blind in the service of my country." This revelation of fallibility and humility instantly transformed the feeling of the room, conveying the depth of Washington's personal feeling for the cause of liberty and the rule of law. For a moment he became the Man of Feeling. We come to understand the truly distinctive quality of Washington when we grasp the paradox that governed his life: that he secured reputation not by seeking power but by declining it. It was a lesson that he sought to instill in the potentially dangerous officer corps by promoting in 1783 the Society of the Cincinnati. The example of the Roman farmer-soldier Lucius Quintus Cincinnatus, who left his plow for the battlefield, succeeded as general and leader, then returned to his farm, provided a form that could rechannel the ambitions of restless young men.

George Washington could play the man of feeling to an all-male audience and redirect its anger to productive ends. When the army was no longer standing, its officers would maintain a place in public with the Society of the Cincinnati. Yet the man of feeling was usually a character in the eighteenth century who played for feminine sympathy. In the list of eighteenth-century *dramatis personae*, the Man of Feeling stood opposite the valorous but crude military man whose braggadocio and hypermasculine behavior set women fleeing. Washington stood at the golden mean between Sir Darby O'Bluster and tearful Tom Likely. Civility trained him to talk to women. After his marriage to Martha Dandridge Custis, he developed a marked taste for the conversation of ladies' tea tables. Perhaps he had developed a peculiar sensitivity to the fact that one's reputation was as much in the hands of the tea madams as of the gazette writers. As Patricia Meyer Spacks has indicated, gossip, the oral news of female private society, was the discursive means by which women disciplined society.[16] One was not the master of one's fate unless one could stand before the tea table's interrogations. Reading through Washington's journal, for instance during the period of the Constitutional Convention, one is struck by how many successive entries are concerned with attendance at someone's tea or salon.

Washington was unlike Jefferson in that he condoned the existence of a women's domain in public.[17] When he became president, he saw that the dignity of the United States depended upon having a civic culture that could communicate the new nation's cultural adequacy to the Old World. When Martha proposed to found a national drawing room where foreign visitors, guests, and persons in government could be received socially, he endorsed it with his presence. Martha's "republican court" was a fascinating institution, protected by a fiction of privacy, yet doing what courts usually do, supplying a standard of manners, permitting the conversation of the ruling classes, and allowing the marriageable persons of ruling families to court. The great experiment of Martha's republican court was to supply a national standard of manners, fashion, and conversation in the absence of any precedent of American culture generally conceived. State and regional parochialism had to be overcome in Congress, and social mixing was the way to do this. The women of the court took the lead in nation building. Martha thought the marriage of intelligent women with representatives from different regions was a powerful way to overcome localism. She brokered a number of marriages—sixteen within the first Congress, including that of James Madison and Dolley Payne. Republicans saw this as the manufacture of a ruling class and screamed aristocracy.[18] The women of the republican court also promoted a cult of personality around President Washington. It was they who set into motion the annual birthday celebrations that reminded radicals so much of monarchical anniversaries. They published poems, with Annis Stockton as the volunteer laureate of the United States publishing paeans to General and President Washington in the *Gazette of the United States*. They commissioned and exchanged paintings. Their subsidiary network of salons throughout the states helped organize his reception during his tours. Modesty forbade the president toot his own horn. But he need not have worried, because the women had taken over the publicity department. The republican court would thrive until 1800, when Jefferson shut it down. During its operation, Jefferson's newspaper flacks attacked it repeatedly as a monarchical entity, a remnant of Old World elitism. Yet they could offer no place for women except the domestic household.

George Washington was not a visionary man in most respects. Yet in one regard his imagination was as strong as any of the founders: that was in visualizing the richness of public life in America and projecting developments in the public sphere. He had little of Jefferson's impulse to minimize the government. He conceived of a strong executive, a robust legislature, a public ceremonial life, a republican court, a civil society composed of a constellation of private associations, a republic of letters, a place for the theater, public sports, and public education (the object of the bulk of his charitable contributions). In such an extensive public world there was a theater of action rich enough to challenge those ambitious of reputation to great works. Washington did not believe that fame would bestow favor on anyone except those who were worthy—that is, who acted with probity, valor, and civility. He believed that celebrity on other grounds would be fleeting.

Indeed, he visualized the government rewarding great persons with honors. But the Congress, fearing the creation of a titled aristocracy, demurred. Nevertheless, Washington set the terms by which repute would be measured for subsequent public leaders. Washington built the rotunda in which his monument is now erected. It is a wholly public building. Parson Weems attempted to domesticate his virtues in the early nineteenth century with his tales of Boy George and the Cherry Tree. But the boy's features were too bland. And in the course of time the boy's body grew the head that George wanted us to see: fifty, dispassionate, and self-possessed with an Olympian dignity.

NOTES

1. Grant Wood, *Parson Weems' Fable*, Amon Carter Museum, Fort Worth, 1970.43; see www.cartermuseum.org/paintings/wood.html.

2. While the designation derived from Henry MacKenzie's popular *The Man of Feeling* (London, 1771), the sentimental novel first appeared in large numbers during the second quarter of the eighteenth century.

3. William J. Bennett, ed. *The Book of Virtues* (New York: Simon and Schuster, 1993). Bennett's chapter titles comprise his list.

4. Alexander Pope's *The Temple of Fame: A Vision* (London: Lintott, 1715) popularized this imaginary edifice in the Anglo-American world during the eighteenth century.

5. Marcus Cunliffe, *George Washington: Man and Monument* (Boston: Little, Brown, 1958).

6. Andrew R. L. Cayton, "'Noble Actors' upon 'The Theatre of Honour': Power and Civility in the Treaty of Greenville," in *Contact Points: American Frontiers from the Mohawk Valley to the Mississippi, 1750–1830*, ed. Andrew R. L. Cayton and Fredrika J. Teute (Chapel Hill: University of North Carolina Press, Omohundro Institute for Early American History and Culture, 1998).

7. David S. Shields, *Oracles of Empire: Poetry, Politics, and Commerce in British America, 1690–1750* (Chicago: University of Chicago Press, 1990), 185–94.

8. In the famous *Discorsi di Niccolò Machiavelli sopra la prima deca di Tito Livio* (Rome: Blado, 1531).

9. Laurence Goldstein, *Ruins and Empire: The Evolution of a Theme in Augustan and Romantic Literature* (Pittsburgh: University of Pittsburgh Press, 1978).

10. "A Poetical Essay on the Reduction of Cape Breton on June 17, 1745," *Gentleman's Magazine* 16 (1745).

11. An Officer that went on the Expedition against Carthagena, "On the Taking of Cape-Breton," *New York Weekly Post-Boy* 131 (July 22, 1745).

12. *The trial of Major John André with an appendix, containing sundry interesting letters interchanged on the occasion* (Palmer, Mass.: Warner, 1810); W. A. Gra-

ham, *Documentary History of the Case of Major John André* (Washington, D.C., 1921).

13. David Shields and Fredrika Teute, "The Crisis of Elite Manners in Revolutionary America: The Meschianza's Message," paper presented at the Organization of American Historians meeting, Chicago, March 1996.

14. John Burgoyne, *The Maid of the Oaks: A New Dramatic Entertainment: As it is performed at the Theatre-Royal, in Drury-Lane* (London: Becket, 1774).

15. William Dunlap, *André; a tragedy, in five acts: as performed by the Old American Company, New-York, March 30, 1798: To which are added, authentic documents respecting Major André; consisting of letters to Miss Seward, The cow chace, proceedings of the court martial, &c.* (New York: Swords, 1798).

16. Patricia Meyer Spacks, *Gossip* (New York: Knopf, 1985).

17. David S. Shields, "George and Martha Washington and the Republican Court," paper presented at the George Washington and the American South Symposium, University of Southern Mississippi, 1999.

18. Rufus Griswold, *The Republican Court, or, American Society in the Days of Washington* (New York: Appleton, 1854).

Chapter 7

GEORGE WASHINGTON, THE SOUTH, AND THE POETICS OF NATIONAL MEMORY

CARLA MULFORD

On April 4, 1790, John Adams wrote from New York to his friend Dr. Benjamin Rush in Philadelphia, expressing his concern about the ways that those he called "tories" were attempting to rewrite the history of the late Revolution against England. Adams believed these men outsiders to the real activities of the Revolution, and he thought they were taking too much credit for "the smallest services." They were employing all "the arts, the trumpetts, the puffs" of political maneuverings, Adams lamented; the effect of their trumpets and puffs would be a rewriting of British American history, but especially the history of the Revolution. "[T]his my friend... is the fate of all ages and nations," Adams wistfully concluded.

John Adams was known as an often insightful, though sometimes anxious and thus sometimes severe, critic. Yet he was listened to carefully by friends and associates. To someone like Rush, Adams's concerns were well worth taking seriously. What were the reasons for Adams's concern? What exactly were these people saying? They were, Adams wrote, telling fables:

> The history of our revolution will be one continued lye from one end to the other. The essence of the whole will be *that Dr. Franklins electrical Rod smote the earth and out sprung General Washington. That Franklin electrised him with his rod—and thenceforward these two conducted all the policy, negotiation, legislation and War.* These underscored lines contain the whole fable, plot and catastrophy. If this letter should be preserved, and read an hundred years hence the reader will say 'The envy of that JA could not bear to think of the

truth.' He ventured to scribble to Rush, as envious as himself, blasphemy that he dared not speak when he lived. But Barkers at the sun and moon are always silly Currs.[1]

Taken in the context of the other letters Adams wrote that week, Adams's concern was not really that Franklin and Washington were receiving praise but that the sheer number of stories being told by people outside traditional status boundaries and his political sphere would stanch the flow of what, for him, were the "true" stories about the war. His concern was about who should be creating the narrative of history, and what that narrative should include.

Adams's comments represent an acute awareness of how events are inextricably intertwined with what people say about those events and how people can manipulate stories to effect certain social and political ends. His was not a peculiarly prescient or special awareness of the rhetorical significance of storytelling. Indeed, it seems that the "tories" Adams spoke of were also well aware of the extent to which storytelling can, in a sense, create history. The era in which the Revolution emerged was marked by what rhetoricians have called an "elocutionary revolution," a heightened sense that the "dynamics of political authority," as Jay Fliegelman has phrased it,[2] were contingent upon the measure of authenticity granted to those who spoke and performed in authoritative ways. Adams was finding that certain men who had, in Adams's view, less centrality in the affairs of the Revolution were entering the theatre of public discourse, center stage, as spokespersons about the Revolution. He found this insulting to the leadership and inaccurate to the actual events he recalled. They were calling into being a history he could not countenance.

George Washington, like Adams, well understood that the construction and production of history was, especially among elite-group persons in positions of power sufficient to take on leadership roles, dependent upon performative aspects as much as on the actual, lived events of everyday people. That is, like Adams and others of his day, Washington saw that the way one presented oneself, as evidenced by elocutionary qualities of poise and self-mastery and by a singular regard for the (paradoxical) relationship between artifice and a "naturalness" of demeanor, functioned as publicity about one's worth. Also like Adams and others, Washington saw that the written record about leaders and their leadership qualities could have a significant effect upon people, almost as much effect as their actual daily, lived experiences or their own memories of the Revolution.

This essay is an exploration of the cultural values of Washington's era and the powerful extent to which such cultural values were instaurated in Washington's day. By speaking of "George Washington and the South," I do not mean to suggest that "the South" was then considered the aggregated and collective entity that it has become in some discussions of the history of, say, the Civil War. Instead, the expression refers here to some of the southern cultural norms that strategically operated to assist the inculcation of elite-group core values on a developing cultural and literate marketplace in this era when the values of the nation were in the process of being inculcated in written discourse. By speaking of a poetics of national memory, I am indicating, first, that the discussion will treat the genre of poetry, then still considered the highest form of writing and the form best suited to the epic events of the American Revolution and its leaders. In discussing this era of nation formation, an era that expressed admiration for classical values and classical writing, a treatment of poetic writings is essential to an understanding of the culture's own sense of the high epic moments that persons then were living out. But by calling this investigation a *poetics*, I mean also to recuperate the root meanings of the word, meanings indicating "invention" and the "process of making,"[3] to articulate a process of the making and marking of cultural attitudes about the formation of the character of "the nation" that occurred in Washington's day and continues to this day to be configured in discussions about what is understood in the expression "the American [U.S.] nation" and in the appellation whereby Washington is the "father of his country." Selections taken from the time Washington had become a military and civil hero through the years when he was called to the presidency, roughly from the 1750s to the 1780s, are signal markers of the effects of the developing performance of American identity that Washington so carefully assisted in constructing.

GEORGE WASHINGTON, THE SOUTH, AND THE VIRTUES OF A NATION

The southern social and cultural world in which George Washington circulated featured several codes of personal and civic behavior associated with a range of elite-group status markers regarding behavior and property. The cultural formation of planter and gentry whites constructed a domain of masculinity based in self-mastery, ability to master the roles and the persons affiliated with the plantation, and the reputation for having these abilities for personal and local social control. As historians have shown, planter and gentry attitudes were, in large part, self-constructions based on what some have considered an anxiety about precisely the qualities just mentioned regarding self-mastery and mastery of others.[4] It would seem that a range of cultural anxieties enhanced—indeed, drove—a critical cultural desire for perfection in the performance of self-mastery, as representative of confidence about oneself and one's place in the world. The performative cultural norms of the planter South were especially marked by a heightened sense of the importance of one's reputation, the stories about oneself that would circulate by word of mouth and in print.

From an early age, Washington concerned himself with learning how to master himself.[5] Like many a younger man of the planter elite, he developed his own guidebook based on a selection of maxims adapted from a European handbook on deportment.[6] Washington's copybook, called "Rules of . . . Civility and Decent Behaviour in Company and Conversation," included such rules of civility and self-discipline as "Every Action done in Company, ought to be with Some Sign of Respect, to those that are Present" (Rule 1); "Strive not with your Superiers in argument but always, Submit your Judgment to others with Modesty" (Rule 40); "Wherein . . . you reprove Another be unblamable yourself; for example is more prevalent than Precept" (Rule 48); and "Associate yourself with men of good Quality if you Esteem your own Reputation; for t's better to be alone than in bad Company" (Rule 56).[7]

The codes of honor and civility were distinctly tied with the performance values of the culture. There were several ways in which a male plantation owner could display his self-mastery, including horseback riding, dancing, oratory, and military achievement. Washington enjoyed a reputation for all of these accomplishments. Yet self-mastery for Washington must not have been easily acquired, given what seems to have been his youthful obsession with his conduct. Indeed, several people in his later life noted that he clearly spent energy restraining his passionate nature. Nonetheless, self-mastery was a quality for which George Washington became well known during his adulthood. As Bertram Wyatt-Brown indicated years ago, the white gentleman's code of honor in the South involved the formation of an inner conviction of self-worth, combined with an assumption that one's sense of worth must be confirmed by the community in which one circulated.[8] The inner conviction of self-worth, it was thought, could be conveyed outwardly and would be interpreted by others as a transparent mark of one's integrity, one's honesty, and one's high quality. If one could behave with a presumption of naturalness, one would be understood transparently as "being oneself" while also conveying the highest degree of civility to the community.[9]

Mastery of one's own actions counted most when it was a matter of note to others. For a southern gentryman of Washington's day, how the plantation household and farms were conducted, including how successful one's plantation was (or one's laborers were) in the production of tobacco, marked one's potential for high reputation.[10] The Washington plantations included the nucleated family and enslaved and indentured laborers, and they were run so as to maximize production, because one's success in getting slaves and indentured servants to produce also seems to have been a mark of honor. The great estates of the plantocracy were self-sustained units, developed around an ideal of independency. If one could display one's independent means, one might secure, first, the attention and trust of one's peers and, second, an insulation from potentially harmful external influences of power, emblematized by changes of influence at court and shifting markets for goods in England. As Paul Longmore has shown, Washington's reputation in Virginia for useful self-control and control over his servants and slaves, when combined with his soldiering successes during the Seven Years' War (also called the French and Indian War) in North America, assisted the invention of George Washington as a figure of wide public importance.[11]

Many of the cultural values associated with the planter elite in Virginia were values affiliated with "country party" Whig politics in England. This cultural system centered as an agricultural ideal the manor life of the English country patriarch who was presumed to live a more virtuous life because he lived in natural surroundings that had been brought to regularity and order. The country party in England declaimed against what it conceived as the corruption of the Crown by entirely self-interested court ministers, against the corruption of the original ideals of liberty traditionally attributed to the English constitution, and against the multiplication of offices and dissensions that kept the political state in disharmony. Country party spokesmen like Henry St. John, Lord Bolingbroke, argued that real patriots were men who were public-spirited without thought of personal gain, men who served their countries rather than themselves. They were independent of influence from the court or the marketplace. Washington fit well into this ideological positioning of the country party, given his upbringing, his plantations, and his inability to secure military commissions from England.[12]

Washington's local renown would become a cultural model in the Revolutionary era. Historians have noted that the Fairfax Resolves of July 1774 rehearsed the Virginia colonists' differences with England in a language associating the Resolves with the ideology of the country party in England. The resolutions held King George III responsible but nonetheless cast blame upon court ministers and not the king himself. Washington chaired the county committee that developed the Resolves, which were radical challenges of England's authority over colonial processes in North America. When the Resolves were published, the only name attached to them in print was Washington's, because he had served as the county chair. The print versions of the Resolves, which appeared in newspapers from Virginia to Massachusetts,[13] would serve to affiliate the successful former military leader with the new endeavor, thus attaching that earlier renown of Washington, along with the cultural model he represented, to the larger endeavor of continental reform.

In 1774, when regional leaders were meeting and beginning to talk about the politics of "the continent,"[14] Washington was emerging as a potential leader whose presence and ability might unite different colonists from dispersed areas. When Congress met in Philadelphia, people were impressed by Washington's tall stature and physical presence, speaking of his "easy Soldierlike Air, & gesture" and his "manly Gait." A Virginian spoke of Washington's self-performance thus: "He is a modest man, but sensible & speaks little—in action cool, like a Bishop at his prayers." A representative from Rhode Island described Washington as "a man noted as well for his good Sense, as his Bravery," and another New Englander noted that Washington was one "who speaks very modestly and in cool but determined style and accent."[15] Washington's name would clearly become known more widely, as it had been locally, as a leader in the attempt to redress the colonists' grievances.

Two kinds of rhetorical appeals were made during these years in an effort to show colonists that war, which was imminent, was also necessary. Both appeals drew upon colonials' self-conceptions of their Britishness, even as they refunctioned colonials' recollection of common British ancestry into a new way of looking at their place in history as on a "new world" continent. Both, too, associated Washington with martial spirit and with the personal qualities required for leadership. Yet the appeals attached significant value to southern cultural norms in their notice of Washington's evident self-mastery as a sign of his ability to master others, including an army.

One of the rhetorical appeals common in the 1770s linked Washington with what was even then a traditional conception of the purposes of the English landing—that it came about as a function of providential design for a chosen people. Back in 1755 Samuel Davies, a reputed Presbyterian minister, had constructed British military leader Edward Braddock's defeat as a providential reminder of English peoples' failings in civil and religious duties. Commenting about Washington's then-recent battle successes in Virginia during the Seven Years' War, Davies gave thanks to the "Lord of Hosts" who had "diffuse[d]" in Washington's direction "some Sparks of his Martial Fire": "As a remarkable instance of this, I may point out to the Public that heroic Youth Col. Washington, who I cannot but hope Providence has hitherto preserved in so signal a Manner for some important Service to his Country."[16] In 1775 Dr. Benjamin Rush retrieved those words and caused them to be printed in *Dunlap's Pennsylvania Packet* on June 26. Washington now was called "Virginia's Hero" from that earlier war, one who was "in the first Action in 1753 & 1754 on the Ohio, & in 1755, was with Braddock, & was the means of saving the remains of that unfortunate Army."[17] The retrieval in 1775 of what had been constructed twenty years earlier as a sign and a prophecy of Washington's future glory focused attention on Washington's presumed virtuous character and his almost antique ethic of interest in his country's welfare—all to the effect that it was their Christian God's design that Washington emerge, a true patriot, at this time.

The second rhetorical appeal incorporated the first appeal and capitalized on a conception of Washington's performance of the personal qualities of altruism and manliness as ideal qualities of a leader, a leader representative of the values of naturalness available only on the American side of the Atlantic. Given the extent to which British people historically held sacred the body of their king, the second appeal worked to attach almost sacred meaning to the body of George Washington. For people used to considering their "nation" as configured in the leadership of a king, it would be difficult to imagine having a nation without one. In terms of the psychology of revolutionary agitation, then, the desacralization of the king was a necessary step to the instauration of a new kind of leader taken from among the people, a better leader for a new commonwealth. The psychology of revolutionary action was such that a transvaluation of kingship—in which a new, better leader would supply the place of another, poorer one—became a useful rhetorical method whereby people could more readily accept leadership without kingship.

Through comments by word of mouth and in print, people became fascinated with the body and deportment of George Washington. "There is something charming to me in the conduct of Washington," wrote John Adams to Elbridge Gerry at the time Washington was appointed military command. Adams continued, "A gentleman of one of the first fortunes upon the continent, leaving his delicious retirement, his family and friends, sacrificing his ease, and hazarding all in the cause of his country! His views are noble and disinterested. He declared when he accepted the mighty trust, that he would lay before us an exact account of his expenses, and not accept a shilling for pay."[18] At nearly the same time, Silas Deane of Connecticut wrote home to Elizabeth Deane that Washington was "his Countrys Freind—who sacrificing private Fortune independent Ease, and every domestic pleasure, sets off at his Countrys call, To exert himself in her defense without so much as returning to bid adieu to a Fond partner & Family. Let Our youth look up to This Man as a pattern to form themselves by, who Unites the bravery of the Soldier, with the most consummate Modesty & Virtue."[19] In printed media circulated widely and in private correspondence (which also would have received wide, though familial and then local, circulation), Washington's figure was employed as a device around which crucial attributes of "the American nation" would be constructed and circulated. It would seem that southern cultural norms, norms that drew upon dissenting English political practice and British American story-making about England's past in North America, were beginning to operate in rhetorically strategic ways to instaurate a core set of values that could serve to define the nation and its publicly acclaimed, virtuous leader, George Washington.

GEORGE WASHINGTON AND THE POETICS OF A NATION

By the time Washington would be ready to enter office, members of the elite were self-consciously aware that they were involved in developing the cultural attitudes that, in their view, could best assist the formation of a national system of intercolonial trade, laws, and customs. The system might best be implemented if people could accept the substitution of George Washington for George III. It would also be assisted if people could learn to accept American goods rather than trade goods from Europe. Such acceptance would require cooperation among differing regions of North America. Washington seems to have understood this very well indeed, if we accept T. H. Breen's assertion that "Washington saw more clearly than did many contemporaries that moral regeneration required cooperation."[20]

In many ways, the national system the elite projected was a system based in attitudes about the transparency of culture like those attitudes held in the South regarding self-mastery, social mastery, and public reputation. The kind of independency formulated as a desideratum for southern planters was the kind of independency sought for the nation. If for

Virginia planters, as Breen has said, the growing sense of a need for independency had a particularly economic basis—that they wished to be free of entanglements with the British merchant system—such an attitude about independency also fell into the ideal of English country Whig rhetoric about the independent life being the most pure because apart from influences of court or marketplace.[21]

While the men in leadership roles made declarations about nonimportation and then about independence, implementation of such goals would require significant changes in the lives of those within their households and on the grounds of their estates. Indeed, the project of fostering a social and economic independency seems to have been where, in many southern and northern gentlemen's minds, elite-group women especially would play a significant role. As the men's comments about George Washington attest, they were very much concerned about their leader's ability to conduct himself well, and they often wrote to one another and to family members about Washington's conduct in all affairs. Yet they clearly understood that only with the interest of the women would the Revolution succeed. As early as 1769, for instance, Christopher Gadsden indicated clear concern that success would hinge on the women's reactions to the boycott then under consideration in South Carolina. Gadsden wrote, "I come now to the last, and what many say and think is the *greatest difficulty* of all we have to encounter, that is, to persuade our wives to give us assistance, without which 'tis impossible to succeed. I allow of the impossibility of our succeeding without their concurrence."[22] Elite men clearly understood the importance of women's activities.

Elite women were thus expected to take up the cultural work of the nation and the inculcation of the nation's presumed values. First among those values was an assumption of independence from the consumer behaviors and expectations of England. As Linda Kerber has pointed out, a key feature of political mobilization in the era of the Revolution among both men and women was the consumer boycott.[23] If boycotts were to be successful, they would have to have the full support of women, especially elite-group women, whose daily lives would, after all, have been the most seriously affected, because they might have to engage in household work untypical of their prior experience and undertake tasks that would create hardship in their households. All women would have to increase their domestic production of goods in order to meet the needs of the family and household in the absence of importations of goods from England. An examination of their papers indicates that, for these elite white women, some degree of pressure was being placed upon them not just to conform to constraints in foreign trade but also to foster, as models for the nation, attitudes of industry and frugality, especially in the use of goods made at home. By the 1770s and 1780s, British American women started writing poems and essays about the relationship between their roles as mothers and their functions as the mothers of the new American republic.

George Washington used his influence to achieve social and political conformity, especially after the Revolution. A signal example resides in Washington's use of his close friendship with Annis Stockton, a poet, to get the word out about what would be expected of women in the new republic. Washington reasoned in a letter to Stockton that a good government would depend upon good morals, and good morals were aligned with certain correct attitudes about trade and local manufacture. His key point was that women had a central role in developing these correct attitudes about manufacture and about the nation. Writing to Stockton from Mount Vernon, Washington knew that his letter of August 31, 1788 (see appendix 1) would reach wide circulation among her friends and acquaintances and among the women who comprised her writing circle.[24] He commented explicitly on how women could serve the nation:

> And now that I am speaking of your Sex, I will ask whether they are not capable of doing something towards introducing fœderal fashions and national manners? A good general government, without good morals and good habits, will not make us a happy People; and we shall deceive ourselves if we think it will. A good government will, unquestionably, tend to foster and confirm those qualities, on which public happiness must be engrafted. Is it not shameful that we should be the sport of European whims and caprices? Should we not blush to discourage our own industry and ingenuity; by purchasing foreign superfluities and adopting fantastic fashions, which are, at best, ill suited to our stage of Society?[25]

Washington knew that Stockton would agree with the position he took, for he added, "I will preach no longer on so unpleasant a subject; because I am persuaded that you and I are both of a Sentiment." He knew, too, that she would circulate his thoughts widely. She had been involved in wartime relief efforts, collective efforts undertaken by women in the region to assist and relieve combatants and veterans, and she was convinced of the importance of the Federalist position.

Stockton responded, as she often responded to Washington's letters during these years, poetically. The following spring she sent him a poem that was soon printed as "To the President of the United States" in the

Federalist *Gazette of the United States* on May 13, 1789 (see appendix 2). The poem was occasioned by Washington's stops in Princeton and then Trenton, on his way from Mount Vernon to New York City in order to take office as president. Washington had left Mount Vernon on April 16, and with each new stop on his northward journey, the trip became a formalized, celebratory procession. Stockton poetically prophesied the new ways of managing the future that the new leader would propose. The poem opened:

> Oft times, when rapture swells the heart,
> Expressive silence can impart
> >   More full the joy sublime:
> Thus WASHINGTON, my wond'ring mind,
> In every grateful ardor join'd,
> >   Tho' words were out of time.

The central idea of the poem is captured in its opening lines: Washington's call to lead the country evoked something providential or otherworldly, so that the throngs of people surrounding his carriage as he entered each town were speechless in awe, indeed in a sense of sublimity, about the essentially timeless moment they were witnessing. The rest of the poem, like its opening, indicates the edifying formulation being constructed around the body of the general about to become the president in civil life. People of the new nation were, in exalting Washington, exalting themselves, claiming "an interest in his bays" in the scrolls of time.

As with her earlier poems to Washington, Stockton sought in this poem to account for the substitution of George Washington as leader of the people, rather than George III. Indeed, in Stockton's poems to Washington generally (ten are known; see appendix 3 for an example in epistolary form), Washington's nobility of character and his valor in war, his ability (characterized as manliness) to master complicated circumstances with spirit and grace, his qualities of temperance and fortitude—all contribute to the importance of Washington's becoming a substitute, as his "country's better genius," for George III, who had sent destruction (in the form of "hostile [Hessian] slaves") to his own English people in North America. By attaching the body of Washington, as "Hero" of the national throng, to the ideals of a confederated band, a "compact" of people, Stockton's poem worked very hard to proclaim that national unity would be a function of the "peculiar" blessings "of Heaven" to "these western climes," to "our selves and ... our race." The poem indicates that national unity would be a function of the leadership of George Washington. Such unity, too, was a necessary outcome, as written history would show, of "Nature['s]" taking "a turn" toward a new era. As Stockton framed it in this poem, the history of this moment had always been the destiny of this leader and his people.

Stockton was drawing upon common southern cultural attitudes, attitudes about self-mastery and transparent qualities of leadership, to create a federalist picture. By conceptualizing the ideal qualities of the nation she was attempting to describe, she was participating in the attempt to develop transparent cultural values of the nation and thus incite them into existence. Using neoclassical poetic models, classical references (to Aeneas particularly), European notions about *translatio studii* and *translatio libertatis*, and the dissenting Christian conception of the English colonies of North America fulfilling a providential destiny, Stockton capitalized on the cultural norms of the elite to articulate a poetics of nationhood, a statement about both the *process* of the making of a national bond and the *completion* or fruition of that process in the founding of a political compact that would bind a nation to itself and to a man, George Washington. In writing such encomia, Stockton was relying upon the tropes common in existing discourse regarding Washington's self-mastery, his ability to work with and lead others, and his reputation for honor, valor, and integrity.

Where Washington is concerned, Annis Stockton's is a fairly standard alignment of elite-group core values with the discursive poetic norms of her day. Washington was being continually celebrated that April of 1789 as he passed through towns from Mount Vernon to New York to take up the presidency there, and Stockton's poem marks his passage in Princeton. Yet Stockton's poetry does speak very explicitly, more explicitly than many other writings of her era, to what were then considered important concerns about identifying the qualities of an American "national character" and developing that national character around the ideals that Washington's administration would foster. Even so, like many women writers of her day, Stockton spoke to the centrality of women's participation in the formation of the nation, and she frequently, also like many women of her day, centered as the poetic muse in her political poetry the female figure of Columbia. Most often, though, Washington's figure is the focal point toward which all of Stockton's viewers' eyes and thoughts are directed.

The cultural values that Annis Stockton's poems spoke to were a constellation of several related tropes: the ideals of Whig country party politicians; the ideals of virtuous self-mastery converted to republican independency; the ideals holding that the leader of a nation should be sacralized and honored by the citizenry; and the overwhelming ideal that there was providential design evident in this particular kind of political outcome, an outcome in which "Nature" clearly "took a turn" "out of time." While we might not find all of these tropes so richly evident in the poems of every writer of her day, we can nonetheless place Stockton readily among the writers whose poetry spoke to elite-group Whig country political values, values that were obtained especially in the southern agrarian and plantation tradition, at the time when the ideology of the nation was being worked out in print.

Stockton's poems were quite widely distributed in print and in private reading circles, and they complemented the writings of other poets whose works were widely distributed. The very prevalence of this poetics would seem to indicate the successful instauration of the political values identified in this essay. In effect, however, this examination has only considered persons who were already convinced of the "truths" of the Whig tradition, people already convinced about the validity and viability of the core sets of values they were seeking to inculcate. The analysis, in other words, will find the outcomes it was already seeking, if it takes up only those writers who spoke, as Stockton did, from similar traditional core sets of values.

If the goal is to establish the extent to which Washington and the value system he represented was in process of becoming a model of "the nation," the test of the validity of such a position will be the extent to which all members of the presumed national community found value in that model. In this case in particular, questions arise: What happens in the writings of those in English America outside this white, landed, elite-group community? How prevalent for those outside the circles of a George Washington or an Annis Stockton were the values under discussion? How often did similar values appear in expressions by those not of Washington's or the Revolutionary and later the Federalist circles?

To address these questions, it will be useful to consider poems by an African in British North America, Phillis Wheatley, and by a British loyalist who removed to Canada during the Revolution, Jonathan Odell. To be sure, Phillis Wheatley occupied a relatively privileged position among Africans in British North America, although it is difficult to consider the state of being enslaved a privileged position. Wheatley was raised as a household servant, and she received much attention—and book learning—when at a very early age she evidenced her intellectual brilliance and verbal agility. Nonetheless, as an African in America, Wheatley did not occupy a position similar to Annis Stockton's, and as scholars have shown, Wheatley felt keenly the injustices of slavery. Jonathan Odell, for his part, felt the rebellion against England an injustice, perhaps in part because he was Anglican but also because he believed a separation from the English homeland and its values would be intolerable. A member of the elite in New Jersey, he agitated against the Revolution and finally fled to Canada to escape being harassed—or, worse, hanged—as a scoundrelly loyalist to Britain. By examining the writings of Wheatley and Odell, then, I hope to suggest the prevalence of the ideological positioning surrounding, indeed dependent upon, the figure of George Washington.

As agitation against Britain flourished during the 1770s, Phillis Wheatley was gaining a high reputation. Although the proposals to publish her first book of poems did not win in the colonies a sufficient number of signatures to encourage the printer to venture publication, Wheatley gained significant acclaim in England in 1773, while on tour there among people of state, evangelists, and abolitionists. Wheatley was in England at a time when abolitionists were beginning to win support among the people, those at the upper level and those too at the mercantile level who benefited from colonial trade and thus benefited from the labor of Africans, especially those in the staple colonies. Like Annis Stockton, Phillis Wheatley was gaining a wide readership and a great deal of support from friends and acquaintances. Her supporters in the colonies included, in addition of course to the Wheatley family and evangelist George Whitefield, a circle of people involved in supporting the situation of Africans in North America, a circle including the Newport, Rhode Island, evangelist and abolitionist Sarah Osborn, several African-born men, Bristol Yamma, John Quamine, and Newport Gardner, and another woman, the younger, African-born Obour Tanner, Wheatley's closest friend. But after her trip to London and the publication of her book, Wheatley's international circle of renown included wealthy London merchant Sir Brook Watson; William Legge, earl of Dartmouth; Benjamin Franklin; and abolitionists Selina Hastings, countess of Huntingdon, and Granville Sharp, noted antislavery advocate, among many others.[26] She served as a perfect example, in England, of the injustice of slavery in the English colonies. To men like Sharp, slavery in America "weakens the claim [of] natural Rights of our American Brethren to Liberty."[27] Phillis Wheatley was a good case in point.

During the summer of 1773, Wheatley returned to British North America a well-known figure in England but still a slave in Boston. Certainly the report of her London successes assisted her in finally receiving manumission later that year. As agitation continued, especially in New England, Phillis Wheatley as a recently freed African was especially well positioned to address the rhetorical issue of the colonials being slaves to a yoke of tyranny. In October 1775, Wheatley wrote a poem to Washington (see appendix 4), addressing the preparations afoot for war and the activities of the Continental Congress. Her poem, a strong statement about freedom, pointed to the freedom that war could create for Americans. She offered hope of Washington's success and concluded with the now famous lines

> Proceed, great chief, with virtue on thy side,
> Thy ev'ry action let the goddess guide.
> A crown, a mansion, and a throne that shine,
> With gold unfading, WASHINGTON! be thine.

The poem evoked in regular metrical cadences an aesthetic of the epic sublimity of wartime efforts. Like many of the poems by women, Wheatley's poem spoke of Columbia, but her representation of Columbia carries a particularly human and emotional quality, as the "anxious breast" of the female figure of Columbia (i.e., British North America) stands in both awe and alarm, filled with concern about "freedom's cause." Wheatley's poem located eventual freedom with current wartime, and it offered a prospect of "nations" viewing scenes before unknown. The armies of Columbia were gathering, Wheatley said, like the winds of Aeolus, in tempests and storms and upsurging ocean swells. "Or," shifting her metaphor to emphasize the numbers, "thick as leaves in Autumn's golden reign."

The poem placed Washington at the center of the "bright beams of heaven's revolving light" cast on his nation's "glorious toils." Apostrophized as "first in place and honours," "Fam'd for thy valour, for thy virtues more," he received the featured position as the leader of this "martial band" of "freedom's heaven-defended race." Wheatley's poem thus employed tropes common in poems to Washington, including the link associating the war with providential design and affiliating such design with Washington's first victory as an American hero, the Seven Years' War, when the French (the "Gallic powers") were defeated because of careful strategies by the colonials. As Samuel Davies had done in 1755 and as Benjamin Rush and others had recuperated the story in 1775, Wheatley was calling up a martial image of Washington that highlighted his virtue and his honor:

> Shall I to Washington their [the war band's] praise recite?
> Enough thou know'st them in the fields of fight.
> Thee, first in place and honours,—we demand
> The grace and glory of thy martial band.

> Fam'd for thy valour, for thy virtues more,
> Hear every tongue thy guardian aid implore!
> One century scarce perform'd its destin'd round,
> When Gallic powers Columbia's fury found;
> And so may you, whoever dares disgrace
> The land of freedom's heaven-defended race!

To the sublime nobility of Washington's figure, Wheatley contrasted "Britannia droop[ing] the pensive head" at the deaths arising from her own "cruel blindness to Columbia's state" of slavery to her tyranny.

The conventions Wheatley employed were typical in her day, except that, at least for readers aware of her successes in England, the insistence upon the word "freedom" must have carried particular import because of Wheatley's position as one who had only very recently been manumitted. Surely Wheatley herself understood the irony, for it was commonly spoken of in the London circles she had visited. Wheatley explored it in a letter written more than a year earlier to her Mohegan friend Samson Occom, remarking upon the "Absurdity of their Conduct" that leaders could cry out for liberty while keeping persons enslaved.[28] Surely the irony for someone in Wheatley's position bespoke the double meaning enslaved Africans would hear in her verse.

In the context of the situation that fall, winter, and spring in Virginia, Wheatley's incantations about freedom must have had significant resonance. In April 1775, John Murray, fourth earl of Dunmore, then serving as governor in Virginia, had pretended to offer emancipation to Africans; indeed, he tried to argue locally that this offer of freedom was itself the sole cause of the colonials' unrest. Such an offer of freedom if one remained British, not American, would have had significant reverberation for Phillis Wheatley, who had visited London and learned of serious emancipation efforts there. To be sure, a number of Africans and people of African descent were interested in loyalism to the Crown in return for freedom.[29]

It turned out that the offer of emancipation applied only to those who would fight the colonials. Probably like many Africans in English North America, especially those enslaved on southern plantations, Wheatley originally took seriously Dunmore's first offer of emancipation as a key cause of the war. This, at the very least, was what many enslaved Africans thought at the time the first announcements went out in 1775.[30] Perhaps Wheatley hoped that Washington would make emancipation a goal of his own: by mimicking Dunmore's offer he would undermine it, undercutting any particular association between freedom and partisanship with Britain. All of this rich context, in any case, suggests that Wheatley had to have been aware of the doubled message in her poetical uses of images of freedom.

For personal reasons, Wheatley must have had freedom very much on her mind in 1775. She was looking for patrons at this time because her key patron, Susanna Wheatley, had died in 1774. Phillis Wheatley was certainly aware that finding patrons in England was hampered by her continued residence in British North America during the wartime activities of the revolutionary congress and the agitation of colonial militias. The colonials had not favored the original publication of her book of poems in 1772–73, when her proposal for subscriptions failed. She needed their support now. She was in a difficult position, and her desire to win a reputation for her writing in English America provides an interesting backdrop to her poem to Washington written at this time. Instead of writing on British leaders living in England, as she had been doing in recent years, Wheatley announced, by writing this poem to Washington, that she would support the British Americans' cause.

Wheatley sent the poem to Washington in the fall of 1775, shortly after she wrote it. She was in Providence, Rhode Island, at the time, visiting her friend Obour Tanner, and thus avoiding British-occupied areas at Boston. Washington was in Cambridge, working with militia there.[31] He had been in the practice of getting encomia quickly into print, as he sometimes did with the poems of Annis Stockton, for instance. Yet he was busy in Cambridge that fall and winter, and he did not respond to Wheatley until December. During the winter, Washington forwarded the poem to his friend and former secretary Joseph Reed. In his letter of February 10, 1776, Washington seemed to deprecate the poem but claimed nonetheless that he would have published it himself, had he not been concerned that people would consider him vain. This seems to have been all the hint that Reed needed to get the poem published that spring. In March 1776 it appeared in Dixon and Hunter's *Virginia Gazette*, and in April it was picked up in Philadelphia, in Thomas Paine's *Pennsylvania Magazine*.

The timing and the locations of publication have relevance for this inquiry into nation-making imagery in the figure of George Washington. At the conclusion of her poem, Wheatley exhorted the "great chief" Washington: "Proceed . . . with virtue on thy side" and let Columbia guide "thy ev'ry action" so that "A crown, a mansion, and a throne that shine, / With gold unfading, WASHINGTON! be thine." The poet thus engaged the standard trope of Washington as the central figure in a divinely nurtured battle over freedom.

Such a message from an African—her African birth was featured in the heading of the printed versions—would have had significant import, especially in the Virginia of 1775–76. On the heels of Dunmore's proclamations of interest in enlisting Africans in exchange for postwar freedom, tenant farm workers and indentured laborers engaged in their own freedom movements. Landholders had been insisting on payments in specie, and laborers were feeling increasingly restive under pressure to produce without having sufficient resources for their own sustenance. Elite-group leaders feared revolt by enslaved Africans, and they saw the need for unity among whites at a time when poorer and laboring whites wanted to wrest control from the established landholders, whose overseers seemed to demand of them far more labor and debt repayment than they could actually provide. From the perspective of members of the elite group, the propaganda value of a poem that was pro-Washington and written by an African must have been wonderfully appealing. What better way to instruct nonelite people, African and ethnic English and mixed-group people, about their proper attitude and station in the world? Wheatley's poem could be used to create, validate, and promulgate the conception of Washington that was being instaurated more typically by the writings of elite-group people. The edification power of Wheatley's poem must have been quite high indeed. Enslaved Africans, as I have suggested, might have understood a different message in Wheatley's poem. We can only guess at what laboring people might have believed about this, if they read Dixon and Hunter's *Gazette* at all.

The key point here is a different one, though. To return to the original question—what happened in writings by persons outside the elite circle—it would seem, at least in the case of Phillis Wheatley, that outsiders might have found greater acceptance if they spoke the language of patriotism and affiliated their causes with Washington. Wheatley's poem, while a stronger because slightly different message about freedom, employed all of the tropes common in encomia to Washington, thus indicating both the prevalence of those images and their durability. Whether or not Phillis Wheatley herself fully believed in the sacral character of Washington and his cause, she effectually participated in the instauration of Washington and the core set of values his figural presence represented in terms of nation-formation discourse and the affiliation of that discourse with the person and the presence of George Washington. And there is indeed a chance that she thought Washington would consider the freeing of slaves—an even more compelling reason for Wheatley to have written such a poem at that time.

Like Phillis Wheatley and black people in the colonies, the loyalists (royalists, or Tories, those who did not wish to lose their colonial relationship with England, and some of whom were, of course, of African descent) were outside the center of power of the colonial elite interested in separating from England. What were the particular rhetorical appeals used by revolutionaries that loyalists found most worth attacking in their own writings? Loyalist writings provide telling evidence of the power of Washington's figure for the populace, especially because the loyalist writings reveal by negation the important differences between political ideologies espoused by revolutionaries and by loyalists. Where those who followed Washington tended to be willing to venture into a culture and a marketplace unattached to the home country, those who remained loyal to the Crown could not conceive of their social formation without the assistance and protection of British political agency.[32] As North Callahan has assessed the situation, the loyalists "believed from the first that they were right and that they were infinitely superior to their upstart opponents."[33] His point is harshly phrased but well taken. Phrased differently, loyalists, like many of their agitating neighbors, valued political and social stability and understood the hierarchies of power and social ties to Britain from which they personally benefited, whether as clergy, civil leaders, or mercantile agents.

New Jersey, a strong loyalist area, finally became untenable for Jonathan Odell, despite the leadership of then royal governor William Franklin. When even people like the Stocktons—who had proposed a moderate course until the early 1770s—decided in favor of a break from Britain, Odell considered his situation perilous. Odell, a physician and Anglican minister, first removed from New Jersey to New York and then eventually to New Brunswick, Canada. A person much admired in his day, Odell held values fairly representative of the loyalist values shared by many.[34] In his poem *The American Times*, published in New York by James Rivington in 1780 (see appendix 5), Odell cast a Juvenalian satirist's glare at the key men thought to have created the disturbances that had rent the communities where they lived, torn families apart, and fostered total anarchy. The men included a number of those involved in significant ways in the continental union of English colonies, but the chief conspirator against unity and peace was, as one might expect, George Washington.

In situating Washington as the key fomenter of the turmoil, Odell indicated the very centrality of Washington's reputation as the most important, reliable, and accountable leader of the Revolution. The strength of Washington's place among the Revolutionary agitators becomes clear in part 1 of *The American Times,* where Odell brings out onto the literary stage many of the men involved but saves Washington for last. By putting off the entrance of the one man readers would have considered most central to the action, Odell's poem heightens the reader's anticipation—and, in the process, heightens our understanding of the degree of aura surrounding George Washington. A torrent of abuse spews forth once Washington arrives on the poem's scene. This should come as no surprise, for, if Callahan's assessment is correct, "George Washington himself was their [the loyalists'] greatest nemesis."[35]

The measure of Washington's reputation can be taken from the level of opprobrium that Odell heaped upon his name and thus his character. Odell used terms of high abuse, terms serving as the fundamental opposites of the terms of quality used to describe Washington in pro-Washington and pro-agitation propaganda, and he even made an inverse reflection upon Washington's glory in battle during the Seven Years' War. As signals of the chaos Odell configured around Washington, "hell's music" and "infernal drums"—not the light of the heavens or the choral singing of the Muses or of angels—are called upon to suit the entrance of Washington upon the poet's imaginative scene:

> Strike up, hell's music! roar, infernal drums!
> Discharge the cannon—Lo! the warrior comes!
> He comes, not tame as on Ohio's banks,
> But rampant at the head of ragged ranks.
> Hunger and itch are with him—Gates and Wayne—
> And all the lice of Egypt in his train.
> Sure these are Falstaff's soldiers, poor and bare;
> Or else the rotten regiments of Rag-fair:
> Bid the French generals to their Chief advance,
> And grace his suite—O shame! they're fled to France.
> Wilt thou, great chief of Freedom's lawless sons,
> Great captain of the western Goths and Huns,
> Wilt thou for once permit a private man
> To parley with thee, and thy conduct scan?

Odell has called up the figure of hell and the devil—not fair "Columbia" or a "Lord of Hosts"—in order to speak about Washington. Characterized as the "great chief of Freedom's lawless sons," who "supported an atrocious cause / Against thy King, thy Country, and the laws," Washington is cast in Odell's poem as the single person most responsible for the attendant ruin of his country.

Odell here has employed an almost direct reversal of the view commonly held of Washington—that he was a virtuous and modest figure, significant enough to replace the foolish king, "manly" enough to make people across English America combine to support him, and stalwart enough to establish for the people a rule of law in place of rule by imperial or parliamentary pleasure. The pro-Washington poems employed devices that portrayed Washington, and all the fathers of the nation's rural landscape, as leaving the plow and the hearthside, sacrificing their security and family safety, in order to fight for their country. By contrast, Odell evoked an image of a countryside in pandemonium. To confirm his negating view, Odell invoked the deaths of innocent people, using the important figure of the broken family to create a rhetorical gesture shocking enough to combat the sentimental devices used in the pro-Washington poems. Odell concluded that Washington was the "Patron of villainy, of villains chief." He turned around the common metaphor of the Christian God's being on Washington's side, along with truth and virtue, offering instead a reversed image in which it was George Washington who should hide from "Truth's avenging sword."

In each instance, Odell systematically attempted to create a Washington who was the obverse of the Washington typically presented to readers in support of the Whig and Revolutionary position. The obvious poetic move to turn those positive tropes entirely into negative ones indicates the very strength of the impact of the cultural value system that was being instaurated around the body of Washington and thereupon sacralized as the values of the nation. That Odell selected these particular ways to abuse Washington marks the strength of the propaganda then in use to support Washington. That is, this negative example clarifies just how compellingly Washington and the value system he represented were producing the model of "the nation" and the imagery that that construction called "the American nation" would adhere to.

In taking up the most common images surrounding George Washington—as a man, a military leader, and a much admired cultural icon—Jonathan Odell's *The American Times*, like Phillis Wheatley's poem, works strategically to reinforce in the culture the importance of Washington and the cultural system he represented in the English American nation's construction of itself. That is, even when Washington was being denigrated, as in Odell's poem, the very import of the denigration depends upon a reader's ready knowledge of the existent imagery used to instaurate Washington as the American nation's leader. Surely the readers these two writers were addressing found additional messages to take to heart, but the evocative images employed by both Wheatley and Odell speak to the effective deployment of the dominant-group value system as it was in play during the era. Like the poems Annis Stockton wrote to George Washington, these writings provide an important index of the extent to which the cultural norms were readily accepted by many of the people who would make up the American nation.

POETICS OF NATIONAL MEMORY

In the configuration of Washington as a cultural icon of the new American nation, writers—and especially poets—of the day were, in effect, instaurating for commemoration sets of cultural values that can be associated with planter attitudes. George Washington and Martha Washington became prime representatives of the new national character, what finally became a rather elitist, federal character, that developed in the first decades of the federal republic. The new national situation of Washington's presidency centered southern planter cultural values, values that would become dominant-group cultural assumptions in the new era of federation. In the culture of the white southern planters, self-mastery, social mastery, and having a reputation for both of these attributes were of prime importance to the construction of masculine identity. George Washington, having emerged within this kind of cultural configuration, was an exemplary model of these cultural values, values that found a distinct affiliation with country party ideology in England. From the time of the Seven Years' War in North America, Washington stood out as a model of the virtuous and manly citizen such a culture of independency could produce. That model became the normative model for the nation as Washington was in the process of emerging as a leader of the United States, one every bit as dignified, cordial, sensible, and patriotic as the ideal and virtuous leader figured in hundreds of poems about manor households in old England.

I have attempted to show the ways in which these cultural attitudes, with George Washington taken as the greatest model of this constellation of values, entered literate discourse about "the American nation" between the 1750s and the 1780s and thus assisted a poetics of nationhood with Washington as the figural center of the new American nation. A supreme irony of the loyalists' situation was that, although they seem to have feared popular insurrection and populist control,[36] the presidency of Washington was one centrally involved with the retention of social stability through, as necessary, forced acquiescence to elite-group leadership and elite-group values. The ideology of American nationhood argued at once for the invention of new cultural values and the retention of those values held particularly dear to the leaders then in power.

To return to the point originally offered about John Adams, it would seem as if, indeed, the "whole fable, plot, and catastrophy" *was* a poetics of the actions of Franklin and of Washington. Adams was concerned about who should create history and what stories would be told. But regardless of who was creating the stories of "the nation," it seems that stories about Washington, stories revealing a collective memory of all kinds of persons, would drive the national story for years to come. Adams did, after his plaintive outburst, admit to Benjamin Rush that he didn't really mind that Washington was being featured. (He had different attitudes about Benjamin Franklin, but that's a different story I tell elsewhere.) After concluding that "No Nation can adore more than one man at a time," Adams offered this:

> It is a happy circumstance that the object of our devotion is so well deserving of it. That he has virtue so exquisite and wisdom so consummate. There is no Citizen of America will say, that there is in the world so fit a man for the head of the nation: from my soul I think there is not: and the question should not be, who has done or suffered most, or who has been the most essential and indispensable cause of the Revolution, but who is best qualified to govern us? Nations are not to sacrifice their future happiness to the ideas of historical Justice. They must consult their own weaknesses, prejudices, passions, Senses and imaginations as well as their reason.

If the question really had to do with who was most fit, Adams concluded, then the answer was in the man George Washington. Adams's is a telling reminder of the ways stories about men and nations can have their own meaning outside of the presumed actual events and occurrences that the stories purport to represent. People might have been, in Adams's view, retelling incorrect versions of the history of the American Revolution, but the national system that was emerging nonetheless would be, he admitted, invaluable to the future of the English American nation if connected with the very person of and the cultural patterns represented by George Washington.

APPENDIX 1

Letter of George Washington to Annis Boudinot Stockton,
August 31, 1788

This letter, indicating Washington's suggestion that Stockton and elite women generally could make significant contributions to the project of creating "national manners," is in *The Writings of George Washington*, ed. John C. Fitzpatrick, 39 vols. (Washington, D.C.: U.S. Government Printing Office, 1931–44), 30:75–77.

Mount Vernon, August 31, 1788.

I have received and thank you very sincerely, My dear Madam, for your kind letter of the 3d. instant. It would be in vain for me to think of acknowledging in adequate terms the delicate compliments, which, though expressed in plain prose, are evidently inspired by the elegant Muse of Morvan. I know not by what fatality it happens that even Philosophical sentiments come so much more gracefully (forcibly I might add) from your Sex, than my own. Otherwise I should be strongly disposed to dispute your Epicurean position concerning the œconomy of pleasures. Perhaps, Indeed, upon a self-interested principle, because I should be conscious of becoming a gainer by a different practice. For, to tell you the truth, I find myself altogether interested in establishing in theory, what I feel in effect, that we can never be cloyed with the pleasing compositions of our female friends. You see how selfish I am, and that I am too much delighted with the result to perplex my head much in seeking for the cause. But, with Cicero in speaking respecting his belief of the immortality of the Soul, I will say, if I am in a grateful delusion, it is an innocent one, and I am willing to remain under its influence. Let me only annex one hint to this part of the subject, while you may be in danger of appreciating the qualities of your friend too highly, you will run no hazard in calculating upon his sincerity or in counting implicitly on the reciprocal esteem and friendship which he entertains for yourself.

The felicitations you offer on the present prospect of our public affairs are highly acceptable to me, and I entreat you to receive a reciprocation from my part. I can never trace the concatenation of causes, which led to these events, without acknowledging the mystery and admiring the goodness of Providence. To that superintending Power alone is our retraction from the brink of ruin to be attributed. A spirit of accomodation was happily infused into the leading characters of the Continent, and the minds of men were gradually prepared, by disappointment, for the reception of a good government. Nor would I rob the fairer sex of their share in the glory of a revolution so honorable to human nature, for, indeed, I think you Ladies are in the number of the best Patriots America can boast.

And now that I am speaking of your Sex, I will ask whether they are not capable of doing something towards introducing fœderal fashions and national manners? A good general government, without good morals and good habits, will not make us a happy People; and we shall deceive ourselves if we think it will. A good government will, unquestionably, tend to foster and confirm those qualities, on which public happiness must be engrafted. Is it not shameful that we should be the sport of European whims and caprices? Should we not blush to discourage our own industry and ingenuity; by purchasing foreign superfluities and adopting fantastic fashions, which are, at best, ill suited to our stage of Society? But I will preach no longer on so unpleasant a subject; because I am persuaded that you and I are both of a Sentiment, and because I fear the promulgation of it would work no reformation.

You know me well enough, my dear Madam, to believe me sufficiently happy at home, to be intent upon spending the residue of my days there. I hope that you and yours may have the enjoyment of your health, as well as Mrs. Washington and myself: that enjoyment, by the divine benediction, adds much to our temporal felicity. She joins me in desiring our compliments may be made acceptable to yourself and Children. It is with the purest sentiment of regard and esteem I have always the pleasure to subscribe myself Dear Madam,

Your etc.

APPENDIX 2

Poem by Annis Stockton, "To the President of the United States," May 1789

This poem, published in the *Gazette of the United States*, May 13, 1789, had been sent to Washington in a letter dated May 1. Stockton probably wrote the poem in April. Note that Stockton adopted Washington's honorific appellation of her, "the Muse of Morven"—Morven being the name she had selected for the Stockton estate, based on the poems of Ossian—but she dropped that name in line 7 of this anonymously published poem.

To THE PRESIDENT of the UNITED STATES.

Oft times, when rapture swells the heart,
Expressive silence can impart
   More full the joy sublime:

Thus WASHINGTON, my wond'ring mind,
In every grateful ardor join'd,
   Tho' words were out of time.

The muse of ******'s peaceful shade,
Gave way to all the gay parade
   For transports of her own;
She felt the tear of pleasure flow,
And gratitude's delightful glow
   Was to her bosom known.

Triumphal arches—gratulating song,
And shouts of welcome from the mixed throng,
   Thy laurels can not raise.
We praise ourselves; exalt our name,
And in the scroll of time, we claim
   An int'rest in thy bays.

But erst on *Hudson*'s whit'ned plain,
Where the blue mists enshroud the slain,
   And Hero's spirits came;
   Anxious to seal thy future fate,
Each on his cloud, in awful state,
Pronounc'd thee good as well as great,
   And fill'd thy cup of fame.

While we the favorites of Heaven,
To whom these western climes are given,
   And halcyon days await
May bless our selves and bless our race
That God by his peculiar grace
   Sav'd thee to rule the state.

Fame as she flies, her trump shall sound,
To all the admiring nations round,
   And millions yet unborn,
Will read the history of this day,
And as they read will pause—and say
   HERE NATURE TOOK A TURN.

For in the annals of mankind,
Who ever saw a compact bind
   An empire's utmost bound;   40
Who ever saw ambition stand,
Without the power to raise her hand,
   While ONE the people crown'd.   *New-Jersey, May 1789.*

APPENDIX 3

Poem by Annis Stockton, "Epistle to General Washington,"
May 26, 1787

This poem in epistolary form is an example of the many poems Stockton frequently wrote to Washington. Referring to the dissensions caused by the federal convention, it asserts its hope that Washington will be able to conduct affairs of state to a peaceful and fruitful conclusion. The poem was entered into Annis Stockton's copybook of poems at the time she sent it to Washington, signed with her pen name, Emelia. It is reprinted from *Only for the Eye of a Friend: The Poems of Annis Boudinot Stockton*, ed. Carla Mulford (Charlottesville: University Press of Virginia, 1995), 144–46, by permission of the publisher.

           Morven the 26th of May 1787–
The timid muse reluctant to intrude—
In time so sacred spent in doing good—
Could hardly dare this freedom to assume.—
Did not your kindness cause her to persume.
The dear rememb'rance by my *brother* given—   5
To friendship grateful as the dew from heaven—
Stole on my soul most exquisitely sweet—
And made me every doubt and fear forget.
—Now string the harp I *cry'd* and tune the lyre—
For Washington once more my lays inspire—   10
Tell him his virtues are so deeply trac'd—
Upon my heart they can not be eras'd.—

No distance keeps you from my mental sight—
My Spirit hovers round you day and night—
While fancy leads me through the green retreats   15
The groves of Vernon and its silvan seats—
The murmering river, lawn, and rocky cell—
Where heavenly Contemplation loves to dwell.

Views the same objects—hails the silver moon—
Gliding thro aether to her highest noon—   20
Sees nature lead thee thro her sacred stores—
By mild philosophy unlock'd; her plants and plow,
All spread before thee emulous to show—
Their various properties and whence they flow.
And oft I follow to potomacks—shore—   25
Where you undaunted rocks and shelves explore—
Lay plans to make her channels deep and wide—
To extend th' blessings of her silver tide—
Amaz'd I view such works of usefulness—
And shrink to see exertion in excess—   30
Sapping a life by friendship held more dear—
Than to the plants the sun and vernal air.—
The Trytons in each gelid crystal grot—
Where ripening diamonds to perfection brought,
Pour on the dark abodes their lucid rays—   35
And imitate the Suns meridian blaze—
The river Gods thro all their coral groves—
And green hair'd Naids in their gay alcoves—
Astonish'd stand to see a mortal aim—
To sway a sceptre o'er their wat'ry plain.—   40

—But now far other cares thy mind expands—
One effort more thy Countries weal demands—
That glorious plan on deep foundations laid—
For which thou brav'ly fought, and many a heroe bled—
Wants energy to spread its blessings round—   45
And like a barque without a pilot found.—
System the soul of policy refin'd—
Should all the states in perfect union bind—
Our Nations Cement is the federal band—
The golden chain that links this favour'd land—   50
Which if kept bright, will more and more refine—
And Constitute a government devine:—

—But ah too well thy penetrating soul—
Foresaw the cloud and heard the thunder roll—
Saw local prejudice the land o'erwhelm—   55
The vessel wreak'd, and parted from its helm—

Warn'd us of danger—pointed out the mean—
T'avoid the horrors of the present scene—
How great the error that involves each state—
Tho blest with men illustrious good and great,   60
With spirit to Contrive and to Compleat—
The noblest schemes of mutual benefit—
With talents equal to Conduct a world—
We're left to chance and in confusion hurl'd—
By those whose honesty is all their boast—   65
But thro their want of skill our fame and empire lost—

Once more thou best of men thy powers exert—
Thy Counsel and thy zeal may yet avert—
The threatning danger ere it be too late—
And we without redress submit to fate—   70
                                        Emelia

APPENDIX 4

Poem by Phillis Wheatley, "To His Excellency General Washington," March 30, 1776

Phillis Wheatley sent this poem, with a letter (accurately reproduced when the poem was published, and printed below) during the fall of 1775, when she was in Providence, R.I., and Washington in Cambridge, taking command of the army there. Washington did not respond to Wheatley until December of that year. During the winter, Washington forwarded the poem on to his friend Joseph Reed. In his letter to Reed, Washington claimed that he would have published the poem himself, had he not been concerned that people would consider him vain. This seems to have been all the hint that Joseph Reed needed to make sure that the poem would be published that spring. It was printed in the *Virginia Gazette* (Dixon and Hunter), March 30, 1776, and then in the *Pennsylvania Magazine*, April 17, 1776.

TO HIS EXCELLENCY GENERAL WASHINGTON.

[The following LETTER and VERSES, were written by the famous Phillis Wheatley, the African Poetess, and presented to his Excellency Gen. Washington.

SIR,

I Have taken the freedom to address your Excellency in the enclosed poem, and entreat your acceptance, though I am not insensible of its inaccuracies. Your being appointed by the Grand Continental Congress to be Generalis-

simo of the armies of North America, together with the fame of your virtues, excite sensations not easy to suppress. Your generosity, therefore, I presume, will pardon the attempt. Wishing your Excellency all possible success in the great cause you are so generously engaged in. I am,
Your Excellency's most obedient humble servant, PHILLIS WHEATLEY.
Providence, Oct. 26, 1775.
His Excellency Gen. Washington.]

    Celestial choir! enthron'd in realms of light,
Columbia's scenes of glorious toils I write.
While freedom's cause her anxious breast alarms,
She flashes dreadful in refulgent arms.
See mother earth her offspring's fate bemoan,   5
And nations gaze at scenes before unknown!
See the bright beams of heaven's revolving light
Involved in sorrows and the veil of night!

The goddess comes, she moves divinely fair,
Olive and laurel binds her golden hair: 10
Wherever shines this native of the skies,
Unnumber'd charms and recent graces rise.

Muse! bow propitious while my pen relates
How pour her armies through a thousand gates:
As when Eolus heaven's fair face deforms,   15
Enwrapp'd in tempest and a night of storms;
Astonish'd ocean feels the wild uproar,
The refluent surges beat the sounding shore;

Or thick as leaves in Autumn's golden reign,
Such, and so many, moves the warrior's train.   20
In bright array they seek the work of war,
Where high unfurl'd the ensign waves in air.
Shall I to Washington their praise recite?
Enough thou know'st them in the fields of fight.
Thee, first in place and honours,—we demand   25
The grace and glory of thy martial band.
Fam'd for thy valour, for thy virtues more,
Hear every tongue thy guardian aid implore!
One century scarce perform'd its destin'd round,
When Gallic powers Columbia's fury found;   30

And so may you, whoever dares disgrace
The land of freedom's heaven-defended race!
Fix'd are the eyes of nations on the scales,
For in their hopes Columbia's arm prevails.
Anon Britannia droops the pensive head,   35
While round increase the rising hills of dead.
Ah! cruel blindness to Columbia's state!
Lament thy thirst of boundless power too late.

Proceed, great chief, with virtue on thy side,
Thy ev'ry action let the goddess guide.   40
A crown, a mansion, and a throne that shine,
With gold unfading, WASHINGTON! be thine.

APPENDIX 5

Poem by Jonathan Odell, *The American Times: A Satire in Three Parts*, 1780

Odell's long poem *The American Times* was published originally as a pamphlet by New York printer James Rivington, who at different times seems to have served as a spy for both the colonials and the supporters of the Crown. Odell himself was a well-known and outspoken supporter of the Crown. Here, from part 1 of the poem, are two excerpts, beginning with the opening.

PART I.

When Faction, pois'nous as the scorpion's sting,
Infects the people and insults the King;
When foul Sedition skulks no more conceal'd,
But grasps the sword and rushes to the field;
When Justice, Law, and Truth are in disgrace,   5
And Treason, Fraud, and Murder fill their place;
Smarting beneath accumulated woes,
Shall we not dare the tyrants to expose?
We will, we must—tho' mighty Laurens frown,
Or Hancock with his rabble hunt us down;   10
Champions of virtue, we'll alike disdain
The guards of Washington, the lies of Payne;
And greatly bear, without one anxious throb,
The wrath of Congress, or its lords the mob.
Bad are the Times, almost too bad to paint;   15

The whole head sickens, the whole heart is faint;
The State is rotten, rotten to the core,
'Tis all one bruize, one putrefying sore.
Here Anarchy before the gaping crowd
Proclaims the people's majesty aloud;   20
There Folly runs with eagerness about,
And prompts the cheated populace to shout;
Here paper-dollars meagre Famine holds,
There votes of Congress Tyranny unfolds;
With doctrines strange in matter and in dress,   25
Here sounds the pulpit, and there groans the press;
Confusion blows her trump—and far and wide
The noise is heard—the plough is thrown aside;
The awl, the needle, and the shuttle drops;
Tools change to swords, and camps succeed to shops;   30
The doctor's glister-pipe, the lawyer's quill,
Transform'd to guns, retain the power to kill;
From garrets, cellars, rushing thro' the street,
The new-born statesmen in committee meet;
Legions of senators infest the land,   35
And mushroom generals thick as mushrooms stand.
Ye western climes, where youthful plenty smil'd,
Ye plains just rescued from the dreary wild,
Ye cities just emerging into fame,
Ye minds new ting'd with learning's sacred flame,   40
Ye people wondering at your swift increase,
Sons of united liberty and peace,
How are your glories in a moment fled?
See, Pity weeps, and Honour hangs his head.

O! for some magic voice, some pow'rful spell,   45
To call the Furies from profoundest hell;
Arise, ye Fiends, from dark Cocytus' brink;
Soot all my paper; sulphurize my ink;
So with my theme the colours shall agree,
Brimstone and black, the livery of Lee.   50

They come, they come!—convulsive heaves the ground,
Earth opens—Lo! they pour, they swarm around;
About me throng unnumber'd hideous shapes,

Infernal wolves, and bears, and hounds, and apes;
All Pandemonium stands reveal'd to sight;   55
Good monsters, give me leave, and let me write:
They will be notic'd—Memory, set them down,
Tho' reason stand aghast, and order frown.

[Odell now submits several men to his poetical castigation, in this order: Livingston, Jay, Chase, R. Morris, G. Morris, Duer, Duane, Cooper, Hancock, J. Adams, S. Adams.]

Yet tho' the frantic populace applaud,   185
'Tis Satire's part to stigmatize the fraud.
Exult, ye jugglers, in your lucky tricks;
Yet on your fame the lasting brand we'll fix.
Cheat male and female, poison age and youth;
Still we'll pursue you with the goad of truth.   190
Whilst in mid-heav'n shines forth the golden flame,
Hancock and Adams shall be words of shame;
Whilst silver beams the face of night adorn,
Cooper of Boston shall be held in scorn.

Strike up, hell's music! roar, infernal drums!   195
Discharge the cannon—Lo! the warrior comes!
He comes, not tame as on Ohio's banks,
But rampant at the head of ragged ranks.
Hunger and itch are with him—Gates and Wayne—
And all the lice of Egypt in his train.   200
Sure these are Falstaff's soldiers, poor and bare;
Or else the rotten regiments of Rag-fair:
Bid the French generals to their Chief advance,
And grace his suite—O shame! they're fled to France.
Wilt thou, great chief of Freedom's lawless sons,   205
Great captain of the western Goths and Huns,
Wilt thou for once permit a private man
To parley with thee, and thy conduct scan?
At Reason's bar has Catiline been heard:
At Reason's bar e'en Cromwell has appear'd: 210
Successless, or successful, all must stand
At her tribunal with uplifted hand.
Severe, but just, the case she fairly states;
And fame or infamy her sentence waits.

Hear thy indictment, Washington, at large; 215
Attend and listen to the solemn charge:
Thou hast supported an atrocious cause
Against thy King, thy Country, and the laws;
Committed perjury, encourag'd lies,
Forced conscience, broken the most sacred ties; 220
Myriads of wives and fathers at thy hand
Their slaughter'd husbands, slaughter'd sons demand;
That pastures hear no more the lowing kine,—
That towns are desolate, all—all is thine;
The frequent sacrilege that pain'd my sight: 225
The blasphemies my pen abhors to write;
Innumerable crimes on thee must fall—
For thou maintainest, thou defendest all.

Wilt thou pretend that Britain is in fault?
In Reason's court a falsehood goes for nought. 230
Will it avail, with subterfuge refin'd
To say, such deeds are foreign to thy mind?
Wilt thou assert that, generous and humane,
Thy nature suffers at another's pain?
He who a band of ruffians keeps to kill, 235
Is he not guilty of the blood they spill?
Who guards M'Kean, and Joseph Reed the vile,
Help'd he not murder Roberts and Carlisle?
So, who protects committees in the chair,
In all their shocking cruelties must share. 240

What could, when half-way up the hill to fame,
Induce thee to go back, and link with shame?
Was it ambition, vanity, or spite,
That prompted thee with Congress to unite;
Or did all three within thy bosom roll, 245
"Thou heart of hero with a traitor's soul?"
Go, wretched author of thy country's grief,
Patron of villainy, of villains chief;
Seek with thy cursed crew the central gloom,
Ere Truth's avenging sword begin thy doom; 250
Or sudden vengeance of celestial dart
Precipitate thee with augmented smart.

> O Poet, seated on the lofty throne,
> Forgive the bard who makes thy words his own;
> Surpriz'd I trace in thy prophetic page   255
> The crimes, the follies of the present age;
> Thy scenery, sayings, admirable man,
> Pourtray our struggles with the dark Divan.
> What Michael to the first arch-rebel said,
> Would well rebuke the rebel army's head;   260
> What Satan to th' angelic Prince replied,
> Such are the words of Continental pride.
> I swear by Him, who rules the earth and sky,
> The dread event shall equally apply;
> That Clinton's warfare is the war of God,   265
> And Washington shall feel the vengeful rod.

NOTES

1. John Adams to Benjamin Rush, April 4, 1790, Papers of John Adams, Massachusetts Historical Society, reel 115.

2. Jay Fliegelman, *Declaring Independence: Jefferson, Natural Language, and the Culture of Performance* (Stanford: Stanford University Press, 1993), 2. Fliegelman's study, an excellent analysis with particular reference to Thomas Jefferson and the Declaration of Independence, examines the influential effects of language and personal self-representation upon the formation of "national" ideology in this era.

3. The term comes from the Greek *poiētikos* and the Latin *poeticus*, both of which are related to the process of invention and making.

4. Early studies of this anxiety appeared in the works of Gordon Wood, Jack P. Greene, and Rhys Isaac. See, for example, Wood's "Rhetoric and Reality in the American Revolution," *William and Mary Quarterly*, 3d ser., 23 (1966): 3–32; Greene's edition of *Landon Carter: An Inquiry into the Personal Values and Social Imperatives of Eighteenth-Century Virginia Gentry* (Charlottesville: University Press of Virginia, 1965), and his "Society, Ideology, and Politics: An Analysis of the Political Culture of Mid-Eighteenth-Century Virginia," in *Society, Freedom, and Conscience: The American Revolution in Virginia, Massachusetts, and New York*, ed. Richard M. Jellison (New York: Norton, 1976), 14–76. See also T. H. Breen, *Tobacco Culture: The Mentality of the Great Tidewater Planters on the Eve of Revolution* (Princeton: Princeton University Press, 1985). Excellent analyses of Virginia culture and the extent to which elite attitudes took substance from cultural anxiety are to be found in Jan Lewis, *The Pursuit of Happiness: Family and Values in Jefferson's Virginia* (Cambridge: Cambridge University Press, 1983), and Kathleen M. Brown, *Good Wives, Nasty Wenches, and Anxious Patriarchs: Gender, Race, and Power in Colonial Virginia* (Chapel Hill: University of North Carolina Press for the Institute

of Early American History and Culture, 1996). Additional useful sources include Michal J. Rozbicki, *The Complete Colonial Gentleman: Cultural Legitimacy in Plantation America* (Charlottesville: University Press of Virginia, 1998), and Daniel Blake Smith, *Inside the Great House: Planter Family Life in Eighteenth-Century Chesapeake Society* (Ithaca: Cornell University Press, 1980).

5. The best discussion of Washington and the cultural norms highlighted here occurs in Paul K. Longmore, *The Invention of George Washington* (Berkeley and Los Angeles: University of California Press, 1988).

6. Washington used an English translation of a French handbook.

7. *George Washington's Rules of Civility and Decent Behaviour in Company and Conversation*, ed. Charles Moore (Boston: Houghton Mifflin, 1926). A recent edition, introduced by Letitia Baldridge and annotated by Ann M. Rauscher, is published by the Mount Vernon Ladies' Association (1989). For a good discussion of the importance of these "rules" in Washington's everyday life, see Longmore, *Invention*, 1–16, esp. 6–7.

8. Bertram Wyatt-Brown, *Southern Honor: Ethics and Behavior in the Old South* (New York: Oxford University Press, 1982), passim. The issues are summarized well in Longmore, *Invention*.

9. Fliegelman explains the concepts well in the introduction to *Declaring Independence*, esp. 2–3. On transparency in the theatre, see my essay "Re-presenting Early American Drama," *Resources for American Literary Study* 17 (1990), 1–24.

10. See Breen, *Tobacco Culture*.

11. See Longmore, *Invention*, esp. 123–85. But see also Don Higginbotham, *George Washington and the American Military Tradition* (Athens: University of Georgia Press, 1985).

12. Washington tried repeatedly for a military commission from Britain, without success. Colonials were regularly discriminated against in terms of pay and military rank. See Longmore, *Invention*, and Higginbotham, *Military Tradition*.

13. The Resolves were printed in Rind's *Virginia Gazette*, August 4, 1774, p. 2, and the *Boston Gazette and Country Journal*, August 8, 1774, p. 2. Longmore treats the extent to which Washington's thinking developed along lines of country party ideology in *Invention*, 4–6, 171 ff., 184–85.

14. Longmore takes up this issue, *Invention*, 137. See, for example, Samuel Adams to Joseph Warren [?], September 25, 1774, *Letters of Delegates to Congress, 1774–1789*, ed. Paul H. Smith et al., 34 vols. (Washington, D.C.: U.S. Government Printing Office, 1904–37), 1:100.

15. Quoted in Longmore, *Invention*, 138.

16. Samuel Davies, *Religion and Patriotism the Constituents of a Good Soldier* (Philadelphia, 1755), 8–9.

17. Quoted in Longmore, *Invention*, 138–39.

18. Adams to Elbridge Gerry, June 18, 1775, *Letters of Delegates*, 1:504.

19. Silas Deane to Elizabeth Deane, June 16, 1775, *Letters of Delegates*, 1:494.

20. Breen, *Tobacco Culture*, 191. One might assume that successful planters

would be uninterested in joining in boycotts and nonimportation agreements. Yet as Breen has shown, the planter groups, heavily indebted to merchants in England, had clear reasons for wishing to be extricated from their economic obligations and requisite ties to England. Just a month before signing the nonimportation resolution of 1769, Washington wrote to George Mason on April 5 about the complicated psychology of indebted planters, caught between competing desires—the compulsion to order what they could not afford and the wish to reclaim a lost independence and be free of the system entirely. See *The Writings of George Washington from the Original Manuscript Sources, 1745–1799*, ed. John C. Fitzpatrick, 39 vols. (Washington, D.C.: U.S. Government Printing Office, 1931–34), 2:502–3; Breen, *Tobacco Culture*, 191–92.

21. As Breen has written, "When the great planters spoke of conspiracy or slavery, they were not mouthing abstractions borrowed from the writings of English Country authors. A source of their hyperbole—though perhaps not the only one—can be found in those private disappointments, humiliations, and misunderstandings recounted so poignantly in the letterbooks" (*Tobacco Culture*, 203).

22. Christopher Gadsden, "To the Planters, Mechanics, and Freeholders of the Province of South Carolina, No Ways Concerned in the Importation of British Manufactures" (June 22, 1769), in *The Writings of Christopher Gadsden, 1746–1805*, ed. Richard Walsh (Columbia: University of South Carolina Press, 1966), 83–84. Linda Kerber mentions Gadsden in her essay "'History Can Do It No Justice': Women and the Reinterpretation of the American Revolution," in *Women in the Age of the American Revolution*, ed. Ronald Hoffman and Peter J. Albert (Charlottesville: University Press of Virginia for the U.S. Capitol Historical Society, 1989), 18, and in her renowned study of Revolutionary women, *Women of the Republic: Intellect and Ideology in Revolutionary America* (New York: W. W. Norton, 1986), 36–38.

23. Kerber, "'History Can Do It No Justice,'" 18.

24. The introduction to my *Only for the Eye of a Friend: The Poems of Annis Boudinot Stockton* (Charlottesville: University Press of Virginia, 1995) explains the extent to which, especially for persons of Washington's and Stockton's status, letters were rarely private missives, unless both writers expressly insisted upon privacy.

25. Printed in *Writings of George Washington*, ed. Fitzpatrick, 30:75–77.

26. Wheatley's situation is widely discussed. For an understanding of the circles of friendships and how these served as mutually supportive communities, see James Oliver Horton and Lois E. Horton, *In Hope of Liberty: Culture, Community, and Protest Among Northern Free Blacks, 1700–1860* (New York: Oxford University Press, 1997), esp. 56–65, for Wheatley's situation.

27. Quoted in Horton and Horton, *In Hope of Liberty*, 58.

28. In the middle of a very important statement about freedom, Wheatley concluded that "in every Human Breast, God has implanted a Principle, which we call Love of Freedom; it is impatient of Oppression, and pants for Deliverance; and by the Leave of our Modern Egyptians I will assert, that the same Principle lives in us. God

grant Deliverance in his own way and Time, and get him honour upon all those whose Avarice impels them to countenance and help forward the Calamities of their Fellow Creatures. This I desire not for their Hurt, but to convince them of the strange Absurdity of their Conduct whose Words and Actions are so diametrically opposite. How well the Cry for Liberty, and the reverse Disposition for the Exercise of oppressive Power over others agree,—I humbly think it does not require the Penetration of a Philosopher to determine." The letter of February 11, 1774, to Samson Occom is in *The Collected Works of Phillis Wheatley*, ed. John C. Shields (New York: Oxford University Press, 1988), 176–77.

29. Studies of black loyalists include Ellen Gibson Wilson, *The Loyal Blacks* (New York: Capricorn, 1976); James W. St. G. Walker, *The Black Loyalists: The Search for the Promised Land in Nova Scotia and Sierra Leone, 1783–1870* (New York: Africana, 1976); and, among other works by Graham R. Hodges, his essay "Black Revolt in New York City and the Neutral Zone," in *New York in the Age of the Constitution, 1775–1800*, ed. Paul A. Gilje and William Pencak (Cranbury, N.J.: Associated University Presses, 1992), 20–48. See also Benjamin Quarles, *The Negro in the American Revolution* (Chapel Hill: University of North Carolina Press for the Institute of Early American History and Culture, 1991), and Sylvia R. Frey, *Water from the Rock: Black Resistance in a Revolutionary Age* (Princeton, N.J.: Princeton University Press, 1991).

30. See Woody Holton, *Forced Founders: Indians, Debtors, Slaves, and the Making of the American Revolution in Virginia* (Chapel Hill: University of North Carolina Press for the Omohundro Institute of Early American History and Culture, 1999), 133–63. Holton's is an excellent study of the intercultural tensions in the region and the reasons for those tensions.

31. Wheatley's and Washington's locations are discussed in Sidney Kaplan and Emma Nogrady Kaplan, *The Black Presence in the Era of the American Revolution*, rev. ed. (Amherst: University of Massachusetts Press, 1989), 183–85. See also Quarles, *Negro*, 46–47.

32. Among the many studies of loyalists, and in addition to the titles listed in note 29, these remain some of the best discussions of the complexities faced by loyalists: William H. Nelson, *The American Tory* (Oxford: Clarendon Press, 1961); North Callahan, *Royal Raiders: The Tories of the American Revolution* (Indianapolis: Bobbs-Merrill, 1963); Robert M. Calhoon, *The Loyalists in Revolutionary America, 1760–1781* (New York: Harcourt Brace Jovanovich, 1965); Wallace Brown, *The Good Americans: The Loyalists in the American Revolution* (New York: William Morrow, 1969); Carol Berkin, *Jonathan Sewall: Odyssey of an American Loyalist* (New York: Columbia University Press, 1974); and John E. Ferling, *The Loyalist Mind: Joseph Galloway and the American Revolution* (University Park: Pennsylvania State University Press, 1977).

33. Callahan, *Royal Raiders*, 245.

34. A useful study is Cynthia Dubin Edelberg, *Jonathan Odell, Loyalist Poet of the American Revolution* (Durham, N.C.: Duke University Press, 1987). Regarding

Odell's poetics, see, in addition to Edelberg, my essay-review of that book, "Loyal Verses, Tory Curses of the American Revolution," *New Jersey History* 106 (spring-summer 1988), 87–99.

35. Callahan, *Royal Raiders*, 246.

36. Some of the loyalist propaganda, especially that written by Anglican ministers, blamed the Revolution on the petty bureaucracies and republican individualism (Sons of Liberty associations, for instance) of New Englanders, who were inspired to their republican villainy by a culture of dissent inherited from the Puritans. This is one interesting line of the loyalist commentary that is entirely mixed up with the line pursued in this essay regarding Washington. For background on the issue, see Nelson, *The American Tory*, 176–90.

Part III

Free and Enslaved
Black Americans in
George Washington's South

Chapter 8

SLAVE FLIGHT

Mount Vernon, Virginia, and the Wider Atlantic World

PHILIP D. MORGAN AND MICHAEL L. NICHOLLS

In 1786 George Washington proposed purchasing six slaves, even though he had become aware that his Mount Vernon estate was, as he put it, "overstocked," and even though he claimed that he would never again buy slaves and indeed expressed "great repugnance" at the very idea. He had two essential requirements: the slaves must be young, healthy males and "none of them addicted to running away." Slave flight, Washington added for emphasis, "I abominate." And well he might, for between 1760 and his death in 1799, at least forty-seven of his and his wife's slaves—perhaps 7 percent of the slaves he owned and managed over his lifetime—ran away. Washington's first mention of a runaway was in 1760 when he paid 39s. 6d. for the capture of the dower slave Jemmy; thirty-nine years later, in the year of his death, he still wrestled with the problem, for he then discovered that his recently married waiting man Christopher Sheels planned an escape with his bride. In many of the years between 1760 and 1799, one or two of Washington's slaves were absent some of the time. No wonder Washington hated running away.[1]

This essay will first explore Washington's extensive experience with runaway slaves: his preemptory actions to thwart slave escapes; the unquenchable will to resist of his most inveterate fugitives; the two cases of collective flight, including the mass exodus of the Revolutionary War; flight northward in the early national era; and precise measurement of the extent of slave flight during the 1790s. Washington's exhaustive records permit cameo sketches of individual fugitives: intrepid Will Shag; incorrigible Coachman Jamey; newly arrived African Neptune with his filed teeth, close-shaved hairstyle, and distinctive scarifications; Harvey Washington, who joined an insurrection in Sierra Leone in 1800; intrepid Oney Judge, who ran away to New Hampshire and gave an interview about her experiences in the middle of the nineteenth century; and Hercules the cook, who escaped to Philadelphia. Thanks largely to Washington's assiduous record keeping, it is possible to provide arresting portraits of people usually anonymous in the historical record. A gallery of colorful individuals parade before us.[2]

Washington's experiences with runaway slaves pose a number of questions, the answers to which form the second part of the essay. Overall, did Washington have more or fewer runaways than other Virginia masters? Was Washington's loss of seventeen slaves in one mass escape during the Revolutionary War typical? Did fewer slaves run away in the early national than in the colonial years, as seems to have been the case at Mount Vernon? Finally, where does Virginia's experience with slave flight fit in the context of the larger Atlantic world? Did Virginia witness a large or small rate of slave flight? What accounts for Virginia's place in this larger Atlantic context?

George Washington always took slave flight seriously, and he usually adopted harsh actions to curtail it. One of his most decisive acts occurred in 1766 when, only two weeks after paying £2 for the capture of Tom, Washington dispatched him to St. Christopher in the West Indies. Although a gang foreman at Washington's River Farm and "exceeding healthy, strong, and good at the Hoe," Tom was, in his master's estimation, "both a Rogue & Runaway (tho. he was by no means remarkable for the former, and never practised the latter till of late)." Watchful to the last, Washington advised the schooner captain who transported Tom to the islands to "keep him handcuffed till you get to Sea" lest he attempt his escape. Faced with an experienced and inveterate fugitive, Washington resolved to export the problem.[3]

An even more notable runaway was Will Shag, a thirty-year-old, six-foot, "very full faced, and full eyed" Virginia-born slave. In 1771 the manager of Washington's York County estates moved Will, who "was allways Runaway," from an outlying quarter to the home estate in hopes that he "might do better." But Will Shag soon fled and passed as a freeman in Yorktown by the name of Will Jones. Although captured and put in the York County jail, Will managed to escape, before being apprehended a second time and transported to his home plantation. He there assaulted the white overseer who had him in his charge and escaped once more. He remained at large for about two months before some young slaves at another of Washington's quarters reported seeing him, and he was eventually taken "[a]sleep in the wo[o]ds." The following year, Will Shag fled yet again and stayed out another two months. Finally, in December, an exasperated Washington paid more than £13 to have Will transported to Port-au-Prince in St. Domingue.[4]

In 1773 another York County slave, Coachman Jamey, posed a difficult problem for James Hill, another of Washington's managers. Hill was at his wit's end in dealing with "one of the Greatest Raschals I ever lookd after in all my life," who left "without an angry word or a blow from any one." Hill complained to Washington that Jamey would do only as much work as he pleased and that he "corrupt[ed]" the other slaves. Put to ditching, presumably an activity beneath his station, Jamey expressed his distaste by running away. The manager proposed sending Jamey to the Eastern Shore, where he would not have access to "negro Blacksmiths in town" who could file off his "Iron spancels." Jamey remained at large for more than three months, killing hogs, stealing corn, and recruiting others to join him in hopes of getting the manager the sack. In the end, Hill used his overseers and a tracking dog to capture the fugitive. Jamey promised that he would not run away again, but Hill believed that there was "no dependence in him." If an Eastern Shore sojourn would not solve the problem, Hill proposed petitioning the General Court for permission to ship Jamey out of the colony.[5]

Washington sold runaways locally as well as internationally. By the summer of 1767, Washington had lost patience with Sam, a carpenter at Mount Vernon, who had run away at least four times in the previous five years. Apparently Sam continued to vex masters, for eleven years later George Noble of Frederick County, Virginia, advertised for his runaway slave, a "country-born" forty-year-old who knew "a little of the Carpenter's and Cooper's business, and took away some tools with him." Almost certainly this was the same Sam, for Noble mentioned that his slave had belonged to General Washington "some years ago, and was sold in Maryland to the late Dr. Leeper, who sold him to Mr. Geo. Fraser Hawkins." Incorrigible runaways like Sam probably found themselves sold from one master to another.[6]

A slave did not have to run away, just threaten to do so, to cause a master problems. In 1775, after gaining title to a black shoemaker who lived in Charles County, Maryland, across the Potomac River, Washington learned that "the Fellow would Run away immediately, for he was so attached to his Wife & children that he had repeatedly declared he had rather Die than leave them." The slave begged to be sold, as there was no chance of his wife and children accompanying him. The man was adamant that he would "much rather be hang'd than come to Virginia." When Washington's farm manager went to Maryland to see the slave, his family "either did not know or pretended they coud not tell where he was—but suppos'd he was looking out for some one to purchase him, or hire him." The manager persisted, elicited a promise from the shoemaker to make the trip, and remained convinced that he would show up, as "he has not the look of a Runaway Negroe." The shoemaker eventually arrived at Mount Vernon, but persuaded his new owner that he would "much rather be sold in Maryland than live in Virginia," and seems to have got his wish. Masters learned to deal with prospective as well as actual runaways. They also tried to read the likelihood of flight in a look, a gesture, or a slave's demeanor.[7]

Washington experienced two cases of group flight. The first occurred in 1761 when four Africans fled his Dogue Run farm. Neptune, with his filed teeth, close-shaved hairstyle, and scarifications in the form of "small Marks or Dots running from both Shoulders to his Waistband," was the most obviously African. He and Cupid were shipmates, having been bought from the same slave-trading vessel exactly two years previously, and both still spoke "very broken and unintelligible English." A "Countryman" of theirs, a man named Jack, also scarified with "Cuts down each Cheek, being his Country Marks," spoke quite good English "having been several Years in the Country." The last member of the group, the oldest, a man named Peros, may well have been the leader, for he had "little of his Country Dialect left" and was "esteemed a sensible judicious Negro." Nine years later, Peros or Parros ran away again, but this time more typically, as a solitary.[8]

During the Revolutionary War, Washington experienced a much larger mass exodus when a group of seventeen slaves, accounting for a third of all his runaways, joined the British. Their fate is instructive about the odds of escape. At no other point in the eighteenth century did slaves have a greater chance to escape Virginia than during this war. Opportunity beckoned Washington's slaves in spring 1781 when Captain Thomas Graves, the commander of HM sloop *Savage*, anchored in the Potomac close to Mount Vernon. Graves sent ashore a party of men who either attracted or cajoled fourteen men and three women from Mount Vernon. But Washington managed to recover at least six of the men in Philadelphia and two of the women after the siege of Yorktown. Only three slaves are known to have escaped with the British from New York in 1783: twenty-two-year-old Daniel Payne, twenty-year-old Deborah Squash, and forty-three-year-old hostler Harvey (or Henry) Washington. Thus a sixth of Washington's wartime escapees made it out of the state permanently, but half were retrieved.[9]

The later history of two slave fugitives who fled during the Revolutionary War captures some of the potential outcomes of such flight. The first is Harvey or Henry Washington, who left New York in 1783 for Nova Scotia. He, along with others, subsequently ventured to Sierra Leone. There, on Washington Hill, "he put into practice agricultural lessons," notes Christopher Fyfe, "he may have learnt at Mount Vernon before he left his master." In 1800 farmer Henry Washington joined an insurrection aimed at limiting the authority of governor and council in his adopted country. In a sense, Henry Washington was following in his former master's footsteps, but unfortunately for him the insurrection failed and he was expelled from the colony to the Bulom Shore. By contrast, eight years after the end of the war, a slave named Paul who met Washington at Elkridge Landing, north of Baltimore, had gained little from his Revolutionary escapades. Paul told Washington that he had been seized—"more probably runaway" to the British, interjected Washington—by troops under Lord Cornwallis. Put on board a British vessel, Paul was then captured by an American ship. Disembarking at Baltimore, he was sold to one Maryland master, who in turn sold him to his present owner at Elkridge. Paul wished to return to the estate from which he was taken, and Washington wrote on his behalf to his former Virginia master. Washington knew that Paul had a sister, Rose, still in Virginia. Henry Washington discovered freedom and even put his American ideals into practice; Paul found continued slavery in Maryland and preferred to return to Virginia.[10]

With the Revolutionary War over, the chances of permanent escape dwindled, except that by the 1790s escape northward did hold out the distant prospect of freedom. At least two Washington slaves availed themselves of the opportunity. The first was twenty-two-year-old Oney Judge, who had attended Martha Washington as a "body servant" since the age of ten, was the daughter of seamstress Betty, and had herself become a "perfect Mistress of her needle." In August 1796 she fled the Washington home in Philadelphia, made it to New York, and then took sail for Portsmouth, New Hampshire. Washington's protracted negotiations to retrieve Oney Judge (extending even to the year of his death) do not reflect well on him. Referring to her as a "mulatto girl" when she was a young adult, Washington spoke of her ingratitude, of her leaving "without the least provocation," of her being treated "more like a child than a Servant," and of her being duped by a Frenchman—the classic rationalizations of an aggrieved master. She responded eloquently that she had left of her own free will and from "a thirst for compleat freedom." She expressed affection for the Washington family, said that she might return to Virginia if guaranteed freedom, but that she "should rather suffer death than return to Slavery." Washington rejected Oney Judge's proposed bargain: granting her freedom would only "discontent her fellow servants" and reward unfaithful behavior, setting a "dangerous precedent." He wanted her put on board a vessel for Virginia, forcibly if necessary, but surreptitiously so as not to incite mob action. Ever attentive of his reputation, Washington wished above all to avoid public embarrassment. Oney Judge had other ideas: in January 1797 she married a free mulatto and settled down to life in New Hampshire.[11]

Oney Judge is the only eighteenth-century Virginia runaway slave who has left her own account of her actions. Many years after the event, in the mid-1840s, she gave interviews to the Reverend T. Adams and Benjamin Chase. The "nearly white" and "very much freckled" Mrs. Staines, as Oney Judge was then known, who "might easily pass for a white woman," did not know her age, although she said that she "was a large girl at the time of the revolutionary war"; both interviewers estimated that she was about eighty. If Washington was accurate in 1786 when he listed her as a twelve-year-old, she must have been a young girl by the end of the Revolutionary War and in her early seventies when she gave the interviews. She recalled that she was a chambermaid for Mrs. Washington and went to Philadelphia when Washington was elected president. She said that "she did not want to be a slave always, and she supposed if she went back to Virginia, she would never have a chance to escape." She spoke of taking passage in a ship to Portsmouth and there marrying a "colored sailor" by the name of Staines, with whom she had three children. After her marriage and the birth of her first child, and while her husband was at sea, Oney had a visit from one of Washington's emissaries, Burwell Bassett. At first he attempted to persuade her to return to Virginia, but "she utterly refused." She then learned he had orders to take her by force, so she fled to a free mulatto named Mr. Jack in Greenland, eight miles from Portsmouth, and remained there until her husband returned. Oney said that she "never received the least mental or moral instruction of any kind, while she remained in Washington's family." She also recalled "being given verbally, if not legally, by Mrs. Washington, to Eliza Custis, her grand-daughter," which helped prompt her flight because "she was determined never to be *her* slave." She foresaw continued enslavement, not manumission, in her future if she returned to Virginia.[12]

The second slave to seek freedom in the north was Hercules, Washington's chief cook. In March 1797, as Washington left Philadelphia to retire to private life at the end of his second presidential term, Hercules ran away rather than return to Mount Vernon. Eight months later Washington still lamented the inconvenience to his family caused by Hercules' departure, and feared he would therefore have to break his resolution "never to become the master of another Slave by *purchase.*" In January of the following year, Washington had still not heard of his cook's whereabouts, although he did not doubt that he was in Philadelphia. He proposed hiring somebody to investigate Hercules' haunts. Once again, as with Oney Judge, this tracking would have to be done surreptitiously, for if Hercules got wind of the plan he would elude capture. Hercules was never apprehended. In April 1797 a visitor to Mount Vernon conversed with Hercules' six-year-old daughter. Was she not upset at not seeing her father again? Back shot the reply: *"Oh! Sir, I am very glad, because he is free now."*[13]

Significantly, both the Washington slaves who escaped permanently in the 1790s did so not from Virginia but from Philadelphia. No Washington slave escaped from Virginia itself in that decade. Furthermore, Washington experienced barely half as many runaways in the 1790s as in the 1760s, though he owned about twice as many slaves in the last decade of the eighteenth century as he had in the 1760s. Slave flight at Mount Vernon declined in frequency over time. Moreover, most late-eighteenth-century runaways do not seem to have remained at large for extended periods. Flight had apparently become a harder, not an easier, proposition.[14]

For two years in the 1790s it is possible to be precise about the extent of slave flight at the Mount Vernon estate. In 1797 and 1798 James Anderson kept a detailed report of every farm and work activity at Mount Vernon. Each week he calculated the number of slave workers at each of the five farm sites and in each of the specialized work groups—carpenters, ditchers, spinners, and so on. For each farm and activity, he reckoned the number of days of labor devoted to each task; he noted any loss of labor, whether attributable to sickness or to absenteeism. In those two years Washington's labor force averaged 125 hands. Apart from Hercules the cook, who then resided in Philadelphia and was obviously not included in Anderson's records, just three slaves ran away: Joseph, one of the gardeners, for two days; thirteen-year-old Sophia at Dogue Run for six; and Caesar at Union Farm, who ran away three times—once for three, once for six, and once for forty-two days, for fifty-one days in all. In 1797 and 1798, then, 2 percent of Washington's adult slaves or 1 percent of all his slaves ran away. The labor lost to flight amounted to just 0.08 percent of the total labor of the Mount Vernon estate slaves. In this more precise accounting, running away seems an extremely minor issue at Mount Vernon.[15]

In the last decade of Washington's life, Caesar was his most notable local fugitive. Described as a "black negro," Caesar was in his late forties in the late 1790s. He was five feet seven or eight inches tall, had "a sharp aquiline nose," and was missing some of his front teeth. He usually dressed in homespun black and white. James Anderson, the farm manager, thought him a "plausible and artful" slave. Indeed, Caesar could both read and write, and he was especially well known in the neighborhood, for he "frequently" read or preached to the local blacks. During his longest absence—all of March and the first half of April of 1798—Caesar spent time at the other Washington farms in and about Alexandria, and at Dr. Stuart's town house and plantation in and near Georgetown. At this last place, apparently, he had relatives, although he had no reported family connection among the Washington slaves in 1799 when the estate was inventoried. According to Anderson, Caesar had not been punished before he left and faced no threats of punishment; his manager was at a loss to account for his absence. Perhaps, then, Caesar left to visit members of his family. He returned to Union Farm (or was captured) on the very day an advertisement offering a $25 reward for his delivery at Mount Vernon appeared in the Alexandria newspaper.[16]

Caesar and Christopher Sheels, the waiting man who planned an escape from Alexandria by vessel in 1799, reveal how Washington, even at the very end of his life, could never rest easy in dealing with the problem of runaway slaves. Slave flight continued to trouble the Washington estate. The year after Washington's death, the sixteen-year-old "bright mulatto" house slave Marcus, who formerly went by the name of Billy and perhaps reverted to it, ran away, probably trying to "pass for one of those Negroes that did belong to the late General Washington, and whom Mrs. Washington intends in the Fall of this year to liberate." Apparently Marcus or Billy, a dower slave ineligible for freedom by Washington's will, attempted very cleverly to pass himself off as one of Washington's nondower slaves who would be freed at Martha's death (or, as happened, when she went ahead and gave them their freedom earlier). Slave fugitives would haunt the Washington estate even after the general's death.[17]

Arguably more is known about the number, character, and life histories of runaway slaves in eighteenth-century Virginia than in any other part of the early Anglo-American world. The public sources are rich: advertisements in newspapers for both fugitives and captives, county court claims for capturing runaways, claims for capturing slaves presented to the legislature, claims for slaves taken by the British, and lists of evacuees during the Revolutionary War. From these diverse sources, more than 8,000 eighteenth-century Virginia runaway slaves are identifiable by name. Furthermore, by making allowance for missing records, it is possible to arrive at a plausible estimate of the total number of runaway slaves for the century. That count, based on public documents, is 14,000. From these varied public sources, between 1 to 2 percent of the Virginia slave population ran away during most decades of the eighteenth century (see table 1).[18]

In addition to these public accounts, the private records of individual

Table 1. Estimated Number of Runaway Slaves in Virginia, 1700–1799[1]

Years	Captives Returned[a]	Fugitives Sought[b]	Captives Offered[c]	Fugitives Claimed[d]	Total	Percent[e]
1700–1709	200	—[2]	—	—	200	1.2
1710–19	320	—	—	—	320	1.4
1720–29	410	—	—	—	410	1.2
1730–39	580	70	10	—	660	1.3
1740–49	680	260	20	—	960	1.1
1750–59	950	380	60	—	1390	1.1
1760–69	710	700	110	—	1520	0.9
1770–79	—	960	470	2840	4270	2.1
1780–89	—	1000	150	1900	3050	1.2
1790–99	—	1130	170	—	1300	0.4[3]
1700–1799	3850	4500	990	4740	14080	

Note: All figures have been rounded.
[a]Based on claims for apprehending runaways in Virginia county courts and in the House of Burgesses.
[b]Based on masters' newspaper advertisements for their runaways.
[c]Based on jailers' advertisements and occasional advertisements by individuals for captured runaways.
[d]Based on claims submitted by individual masters for slaves lost to the British and a list of evacuees who reported a Virginia residence.
[e]Runaways in a decade as percentage of mid-decadal slave population. E.g., in the 1710s the total of 320 runaway slaves represents 1.4 percent of the 23,250 estimated slaves resident in the colony in 1715.

masters permit rough approximations of the scale of running away on single estates. An approximate measure is thereby at hand to gauge the discrepancy between the number of runaways reported in advertisements and county claims and the number of runaways recorded on individual estates. Of course, individual owners experienced widely varying rates of slave absenteeism. Despite idiosyncrasies, private records promise to provide a rough guide to the underreporting inherent in public records.

Although no other eighteenth-century Virginia planter has left records so voluminous as Washington's, other rather more scattered materials suggest that the rates of slave flight at Mount Vernon were unexceptional. From 1742 to 1778 Landon Carter's fifty-five fugitives made seventy attempts to run away, averaging about two a year. In the 1760s about 3 percent of Carter's slaves ran away. From 1775 to 1795 Robert Carter of Nomini Hall's sixty runaways made twenty-six attempts at flight. Except for one Revolutionary War year, Robert Carter's runaways averaged about 5 percent of his slave population. Apart from a large group of slaves who went to the British in 1781, Thomas Jefferson reported just two eighteenth-century runaway slaves. In the early nineteenth century, when documentation on Jefferson's plantation operations becomes fuller, only fourteen slaves absconded, or 3 percent a decade. From 1769 to 1795 William Cabell, an Amherst County resident, recorded just six runaways in his extensive diaries—about 3 percent of the slaves he owned over the whole period.[19]

The numbers of runaway slaves evident from private records are therefore roughly double those drawn from public sources. Between 3 and 5 percent of slaves on individual Virginia estates ran away during most decades of the eighteenth century. Apparently, public records undercount the number of slave runaways by about a half. This supposition gains credence from the estimate of an historian of Jamaica who, on the basis of early-nineteenth-century evidence, found that the number of runaways at large may have been about twice the number captured, captured slaves being the ones most evident in public records. For the moment, then, the best rule of thumb would seem to be that the total number of runaways in a society was about double the number evident in the public records. For most of the eighteenth century, approximately two to four out of every hundred Virginia slaves ran away in any ten-year period.[20]

The Revolutionary War is the one major exception to these generalizations. In the ten years before the Revolution, public records indicate that roughly 1,500 Virginia slaves ran away, but during the seven years of warfare about 5,000 escaped to the British, and another 1,000 or so took advantage of the wartime chaos to flee their masters, either joining the patriot armies, visiting family, or attempting to pass as free. An almost sixfold increase in the annual rate of running away during the war years is notable. In spite of this impressive increase in the number of runaway slaves during wartime, only about 3 percent of Virginia's slave population escaped to the British.[21]

The first half of 1781—when Washington lost his seventeen slaves—represented the last great opportunity for Virginia slaves to abscond to the British, but the enemy incursions were limited in time and localized in space, thereby restricting the slaves' ability to desert. In January, Brigadier General Benedict Arnold's troops moved along the James River and, in the words of the Reverend James Madison, some Virginians "lost 40, others 30, every one a considerable Part of their Slaves." Not all did, however, for Robert Pleasants, the Quaker resident of Curles in Henrico County, had but two escapees. By April the action shifted to the Potomac River, where in nine days Robert Carter lost more than thirty slaves from his Coles Point quarter and George Washington lost his fourteen men and three women from Mount Vernon. But other owners escaped entirely: George Mason at Gunston Hall lost no slaves. In May and June the center of British attention again reverted to the James River. Edmund Pendleton described General William Phillips's plundering as "immence particularly in slaves"; Robert Honeyman thought the loss of slaves "inconceivable," as some plantations "were entirely cleared & not a single Negro remained." In June about 11 percent of Thomas Jefferson's slaves—eleven males and twelve females—fled to the British. The climax occurred when many slaves joined Cornwallis along the York River. Even then, however, John Parke Custis could report that he "had not received the least injury from the Enemy; although some of their parties had been within four miles of my brick house quarters" on the York River in New Kent County.[22]

Not all slaves who ended up with the British had voluntarily fled their masters, and some indeed voluntarily returned. Jefferson referred to Cornwallis carrying off his slaves. In claims for losses sustained during the war, masters mentioned roughly as many slaves being "taken or carried away" as "going off" or "absconding" or "escaping." Edmund Pendleton likened the British to African slavers sending out war parties to hunt for slaves to make up their cargoes. Many slaves returned to their masters before the war was over. Ten of the twenty-three slaves Jefferson lost to the British returned to him. A fifth of the slaves taken from Robert Carter's Coles Point quarter also returned. Perhaps Washington was more fortunate than most in retrieving over half of his wartime fugitives.[23]

Apart from the unusual events of the Revolutionary War, running away seems to have declined over time. In the colonial era, the largest number of escaped slaves, viewed as a percentage of the total slave population, occurred in the 1710s. Early in the eighteenth century, Africans constituted the largest proportion of Virginia's slave population, and they were always more prone to flight than native-born slaves. As the slave population creolized, the percentage of slaves who ran away declined, except of course during the Revolutionary War. In the 1760s the percentage of slave runaways dipped below 1 percent for the first time, and by the 1790s the proportion of runaway slaves in the Virginia slave population had fallen below 0.5 percent (see table 1). This is confirmation, then, that Washington's experience of having more runaways in the 1760s than the 1790s was typical.[24]

From the figures that are available for other New World colonial societies, Virginia seems to have had one of the lowest recorded rates of slave flight in British America. From slave registration records in the early nineteenth century—listing only inveterate fugitives for the most part, thereby supplying minimal counts—about 7–8 percent of the slave populations of Trinidad and Jamaica ran away per decade. An 1813 census of Dominica put runaways at over 2 percent of its slave population; even acknowledging that many runaways were repeat offenders, the proportion of fugitives in a ten-year period must have been well over 10 percent. In just one year, 1789, 6 percent of St. Croix's 22,000 slaves were absent. Newspaper counts of runaways also confirm Virginia as an exception. Edward Brathwaite calculates from advertisements of fugitives and workhouse reports on captives that late-eighteenth- and early-nineteenth-century Jamaica had over 3 percent of its slaves run away annually—an overestimate perhaps, but even if the figure should be halved, 15 percent of the island's slaves ran away each decade. South Carolina, with a slave population about one-third to one-half the size of Virginia's, had four times as many advertised runaways. Even Pennsylvania, which hardly ranks as a seething cauldron of slave discontent, seems to have had proportionately twice as many runaways as Virginia in the middle decades of the eighteenth century. Similarly, late-eighteenth-century New York, with a slave population less than one-tenth the size of Virginia's, averaged more advertised runaways a year.[25]

Individual estates in other Anglo-American societies also report much higher rates of slave absenteeism than their Virginia counterparts. On the Stapleton estate in early-eighteenth-century Nevis, two or three of the roughly 130 slaves ran away each year—about 20 percent per decade. In just one year in the middle of the eighteenth century, a quarter of the 42 slaves on a Jamaican livestock pen ran away at least once. Few Caribbean estates registered less than 10 percent of their slaves as runaway in a ten-year period, and many reported 20 percent or more. Whereas hardly any Virginia probate inventories mentioned fugitives, hundreds of Jamaican and South Carolina estate appraisers listed slaves who were "absent," "out considerable time," "slid away," or simply "run in the woods."[26]

In short, in spite of the varied sources that permit a rather full record of Virginia's runaways, the fugitive population seems to have been one of the smallest in relative terms in British America. Whether the measure is the official number of runaways calculated from captive lists, registration returns, and newspaper advertisements or the unofficial number drawn from the private records of individual planters, Virginia had a smaller percentage of slaves who were runaway than most other places.

What accounts for this Virginia exceptionalism? Clues are evident both in the character of Virginia's runaway population and the nature of Virginia's slave system. Furthermore, for the most part, Washington's experiences are broadly in line with wider societal patterns.

Gender is one key to Virginia's low rate of slave flight. In all New World runaway groups so far studied, men heavily outnumbered women, but few more so than in Virginia. The ratio of men to women among Virginia runaways—whether advertised fugitives, advertised captives, or captives in the county jails—was 7:1 or more. Among Washington's runaway slaves, the sexual imbalance was actually less than the Virginia norm, for men outnumbered women 4:1. This imbalance is all the more remarkable in that it derived from a slave population that had a higher percentage of women than most. By midcentury in the tidewater and a decade or two later in the piedmont, Virginia had about equal numbers of slave men and women. With few Virginia slave women running away, the overall rate of slave flight was correspondingly low.[27]

Many factors explain this gender pattern. Slave women's family connections—which were more extensive in Virginia than in most other colonies, in large part because Virginia's slave population grew from natural increase much earlier than others—tied women down. Women also faced greater odds than men when they ran away, not just because they were slowed by accompanying children, but because they were not commonly seen on the roads. Almost exclusively, slave men rather than women delivered messages, drove wagons and carts, operated watercraft, and practiced their skills from quarter to quarter. An itinerant black woman inevitably aroused suspicion. Only when wholesale flight—as to the British—was a real possibility did women run away in great numbers. Finally, the presence of a major town or city was crucial in attracting female fugitives. Many towns throughout the British American world contained more slave women than men; hawking goods, domestic service, seamstressing, and washhouses were almost entirely female preserves. Virginia, however, except for the last few decades of the eighteenth century, was notable for its lack of urbanization.[28]

A second explanation for Virginia exceptionalism was the extent of individual as opposed to group flight. Most New World fugitives were solitaries, people who ran away alone. Nevertheless, in most slave societies, a significant proportion of runaways fled in groups. In South Carolina and the Bahamas, for example, 40 percent of the advertised fugitives were members of groups. In Jamaica, the rate of group flight was probably even higher, for three in four recent African immigrants—always a significant segment of that colony's slave population—ran off with others. Virginia, by contrast, had one of the lowest rates of group flight. Throughout the eighteenth century, less than one-third of Virginia's advertised fugitives ran away with other slaves. Washington was typical of Virginia slaveowners in having just two groups of slaves run away, although less typical in that almost half of his runaway slaves fled in these two collective endeavors.[29]

In large part, the extent of group flight was connected to the number of Africans in the slave population. The third, and probably most important, explanation for Virginia exceptionalism was, therefore, the birthplace of its fugitives. All New World slave societies show a close correlation between Africans and high rates of flight, but Virginia was the first slave society in British America (and almost certainly in the New World more generally) to possess a creole or native-born majority among its slaves, and its fugitive population was predominantly composed of creoles. Again, Washington's experience was normal. Only five of Washington's forty-seven runaways are known to have been African; the vast majority were native-born slaves. Throughout the Anglo-American world there was a general decline in *marronage*, a direct product of the decrease in the proportion of African-born slaves.[30]

Fourth, the nature of the Virginia slave system inhibited slave flight. Washington owned many more slaves than the average Virginia owner, but he dispersed those slaves onto quite small units—larger than the norm in Virginia but not large by the standards of most other slave societies—usually overseen either by a white overseer directly or by a white manager indirectly, even occasionally by a slave overseer. In that sense, the experience of the typical Washington slave—living on a unit with twenty or thirty other slaves, under the close supervision of at least one white man—was fairly representative of the Virginia slave system. Washington was not pitted against three hundred slaves at Mount Vernon; rather, his white managers, tenants, and overseers confronted a score, or two score, slaves on a variety of separate farms and on outlying quarters. Washington's slaves were often involved in personal battles with overseers: Will Shag, a dower slave, beat his overseer in York County; Washington speculated that Frenches Paul might have absconded because of "a quarrel with, or threats from, his Overseer." The social control exercised by Washington and most other Virginia masters was broadly dispersed throughout Chesapeake society.[31]

This diffuse social control not only deterred slaves from flight but also helped capture fugitives. Most of Washington's runaways seem to have been caught fairly soon after their departures. His accounts are dotted with payments of a few shillings here, a few shillings there, occasionally a pound or two for the capture of a fugitive. Sometimes the capturers were fellow slaves: Washington paid Abraham Barnes's Davy ten shillings for the capture of Boson, and two of George Mason's slaves apprehended another of Washington's runaways. Far more often he paid neighboring whites: five shillings to William Ransom of Fairfax County, a pound to Leonard Milsford, and two to the Reverend Charles Green. Local whites brought him his fugitives or brought news of them: Christmas Meekins of New Kent returned Breechy; two whites reported seeing runaway Sam. Thus Washington, like other Virginia masters, depended on fellow slaveholders and nonslaveholders and even occasionally slaves to reclaim his runaways. He also depended on public agencies. He paid £3 7s. 3d. in prison fees in Maryland for runaway Neptune, and 180 pounds of tobacco to the public for the apprehension of Jemmy. Washington was not averse to hiring people to go after his fugitives. And he used the newspaper: in 1761 he advertised in the *Maryland Gazette* for his four runaway Africans; ten years later he was "at home all day a writing Letters & Advertisements of Harry who run away." All told, nine Washington runaways merited newspaper advertisements. Washington or his managers also resorted to public outlawry: Will Shag could have been shot on sight, no questions asked. In all of these ways, an individual master got support from his neighbors.[32]

In sum, most Virginia runaway slaves were male, solitary, and native-born. To a large degree, Virginia's low rate of slave flight is explained by these characteristics: although slave women comprised close to half the population, very few of them ran away; although a significant minority of Virginia slaves fled in the company of others, group running-away was uncommon; and although Africans showed a propensity for flight in Virginia as elsewhere, they were heavily outnumbered by creoles, who were on the whole more sedentary. Furthermore, the characteristics of Virginia's slave system—most notably, a white majority, small plantations, resident whites, and the co-option of all slaveholders, many nonslaveholders, and even some slaves as informal policemen—prevented many slaves from fleeing and facilitated their capture when they did.

Although creolization, family ties, and the nature of Virginia's slave system dampened the number of runaway slaves, these factors also helped to ensure that those who fled were knowledgeable, purposeful, and directed. Virginia runaway slaves may have been proportionately one of the smallest runaway populations in the New World, but they were also one of the most sophisticated. Judged by their masters' advertisements, Virginia fugitives were highly conversant with white ways, quite ingenious in remaining at large within the broader society, and most adept at exploiting the weaknesses of Virginia's slave system.

Virginia's runaway slaves were more skilled than most. Virginia's advertised runaways comprised a larger proportion of tradesmen and privileged slaves than any other comparable population so far studied. In this too, Washington's experience was representative. A quarter of his forty-seven runaway slaves held posts outside the fields: he had an overseer, a foreman, a brickmaker, a hostler, a cooper, a weaver, a gardener, a house servant, a coachman, a cook, and a needlewoman abscond, and he had good reason to think that a shoemaker and a waiting man might join them. Providing training in a skill might co-opt a slave, but it also gave that slave the wherewithal to oppose the system. Despite the formidable powers available to masters, some slaves refused to be intimidated. Gang foreman Tom, seamstress Oney Judge, and Hercules the cook—to single out just three of Washington's skilled slaves—proved particularly resourceful foes.[33]

Some runaway slaves in Virginia were intimately acquainted with whites, because they were their direct descendants. Mulattoes made up a much larger proportion of the advertised runaway population than they did in the broader slave population. By the time of the Revolution, perhaps one of twenty Virginia slaves was a mulatto but about one of five advertised fugitives was of mixed racial origin. It is not known how many mulattoes there were at Mount Vernon, but certainly Washington had at least two mulatto fugitives (Oney Judge and Marcus) and perhaps a third (Christopher Sheels married a mulatto and may well have been a mulatto himself). Mulattoes tended to be extremely self-possessed. Argyle, resident in Hampton, loved to drink; he "was very bold in his Cups" but, even more ominously for his master, "dastardly when sober." Mulattoes could more readily pass as free, as in the case of a fugitive mulatto woman, Rachel, who was "uncommonly white." Oney Judge, who could also pass for white, personifies this pattern. But even so-called Negro slaves possessing a light complexion might also pass as free. Thus the master of a twenty-two-year-old "Negro Man" could surmise that, "as he is yellow, he may attempt to impose on the Publick for a free Man." Another "negro man," Jacob, "rather inclined to a yellowish complexion," was thought to be passing as free by "lurking about Queen's Creek, being much acquainted with the free mulattoes in that neighborhood."[34]

Apart from skin color and skills, perhaps the most obvious way in which Virginia fugitives acquired white ways was their proficiency in the English language. Most common was the description "smooth-tongued," which, though not offered as a compliment, yet spoke well of the slaves' ability to manipulate the dominant language. Some Virginia runaways had mastered the art to an impressive degree: John Wilson was "sober and smooth in his discourse"; Joe had "a fine smooth address"; and Davy spoke "softly and civilly." The ultimate compliment went to George Quacca, who had "a masterly speech," but Jacob had similar aspirations, for he liberally sprinkled the words "moreover and likewise" into his conversation. By the late eighteenth century, when Virginia slaves were moved out of the region in large numbers, their new owners often referred to their "Virginian" speech. In some cases the new masters located the accent more precisely. Thus King, "born and hired on the Borders of Virginia" had "the Accent peculiar to the lower sort of those People," while Jack spoke "the language of a Back Country Negro." Usually, though, the ascription was general: Elijah, Virginia-born, spoke "with the accent of that country"; nineteen-year-old Sealy, brought from Baltimore into South Carolina, spoke "the Virginia language"; and William had "the Virginia accent." Some runaways were so assimilated that they were classified as Virginians by their speech.[35]

Another testament to the abilities of Virginia runaways was the long time that generally elapsed between escape and advertisement. On average, masters waited eighty days after their slaves had absconded before advertising. This average figure is a little misleading, biased upward as it is by a few extraordinarily long delays. Nevertheless, although almost half of the fugitives were advertised within a month of their departure, a third eluded capture for three months or longer before their masters resorted to a public announcement. Two conclusions seem warranted. First, advertising was a measure of last resort. Masters contacted likely destinations, made local searches of known haunts, and relied on sightings before going public. When George Washington's Natt ran away in August 1767, he was seen "once or twice" in the same month. Like many another Virginia master, Washington was no doubt confident of apprehending his fugitive. The anticipation of a quick recovery or even a voluntary return of the runaway delayed the placing of a newspaper notice. Second, the long delay between escape and advertisement points to the ability of many runaways to remain at large for long periods. Of Washington's slaves, Coachman Jamey was absent from at least February through May 1773 and yet merited no advertisement.[36]

One key to these extended absences was the presence of supportive kin and friendship networks. Slave kin were probably more widely scattered in eighteenth-century Virginia than in all other New World plantation societies, in part because the colony's slave population was the first to grow rapidly by natural means, and in part because the small size of estates, their continual division through sale and inheritance, and the extensive westward migration of tobacco farming continually broke up slave families. The importance of sales is confirmed by the personal history of many advertised runaways, a quarter of whom were mentioned as having former owners, even though most fugitives were only in their late teens and early twenties. Furthermore, about one in three Virginia fugitives was said to be making for family, friends, or former residences. The example of fifty-year-old Tony and his forty-year-old wife, Phillis, is instructive. They lived in Fauquier County, nestling up against the Blue Ridge Mountains. Both had been born in Lancaster County, located at the far tip of the Northern Neck. They had known at least one previous owner in the piedmont, a Culpeper County resident. Over the course of their married life, they had raised several children, only to have them sold and dispersed throughout Culpeper, and even further west, into Frederick and Augusta Counties in the Shenandoah Valley. In 1770 the couple ran away, perhaps to visit one of their many progeny, though possibly to their birthplace, their master surmised, since Tony "always expressed an uncommon desire to return there."[37]

The ability of Virginia fugitives to remain at large may also help explain why a significant number of them did not stop at one flight. At least one-tenth of advertised runaways managed more than one escape. In contemporary parlance, the unquenchably rebellious were described as notorious runaways, addicted to flight, many times outlawed, great villains, ingenious renegades, slaves of daring and resolute character, and so on. The incorrigible runaways came from all ranks, but creoles and mulattoes were more likely to be inveterate fugitives than Africans. If anything, Washington experienced disproportionately more recurrent runaways than the average Virginia master. Most of his runaways managed only one flight, but one-fifth fled more than once—Sam four times, Caesar and Frenches Paul three times, Coachman Jamey and Will Shag many times.[38]

Inveterate fugitives such as Coachman Jamey and Will Shag were part of a select group, for, by all accounts, proportionately fewer slaves absconded in Virginia than in most other New World colonies. A large part of the explanation seems to reside in the precociously creole character of Virginia's slave population. Yet at least some of these same creoles cleverly exploited the weaknesses of Virginia's slave system: they took advantage of the mobility of many male slaves; they put the knowledge acquired through their skills and privileges to good use, and certainly a use their masters had never intended; they manipulated their linguistic proficiency for their own ends; they relied on extensive networks of kin and friends to remain at large for long periods; and they ran away again and again. Above all, they provoked their masters—and none more so than George Washington.

In the last years of his life, Washington was despondent about the future of slavery in Virginia. In 1797, hearing of a friend's loss of a slave through flight, Washington expressed his "opinion [that] these elopements will be MUCH MORE, before they are LESS frequent." He actually experienced proportionately fewer runaways in the late eighteenth century than earlier, but perhaps Washington was thinking less of the scale of the problem than of the sheer persistence of certain individuals, their high degree of skills, and their new destinations. After all, in the 1790s he lost two of his own slaves to freedom in the north. Perhaps this loss led him to emphasize that absconders "should never be retained, if they are recovered, as they are sure to contaminate and discontent others," although this statement was also an articulation of his longstanding policy of selling troublemakers. Perhaps too Washington had simply wearied of his constant attention to the problem of slave flight: the Will Shags, the Sams, the Frenches Pauls, and the Caesars no doubt had sapped his willpower. Whatever the reason, reflection on slave elopements encouraged Washington to hope that the Virginia legislature would gradually abolish slavery. Such an act would "prevent much further mischief," he concluded.[39] No matter how small the overall number of runaway slaves, how little the labor time they actually denied an estate, they had their impact. In Washington's case, they helped convince him that slavery had no future.

NOTES

1. *The Writings of George Washington from the Original Manuscript Sources, 1745–1799* (hereafter *Writings*), ed. John C. Fitzpatrick, 39 vols. (Washington, D.C.: U.S. Government Printing Office, 1931–44; online at etext.virginia.edu/washington/fitzpatrick, 29:56, 116–18, 37:367–68; *The Papers of George Washington: Colonial Series* (hereafter *Col. Ser.*), ed. W. W. Abbot et al., 10 vols. (Charlottesville: University Press of Virginia, 1983–95), 6:271; *The Papers of George Washington: Retirement Series* (hereafter *Ret. Ser.*), ed. Dorothy Twohig et al., 4 vols. (Charlottesville: University Press of Virginia, 1998–99), 4:310–11. We would like to thank Dorothy Twohig and Bill Abbot for allowing us to use the files of the Washington Papers and the yet-to-be-edited electronic transcriptions of the materials (which extend from the colonial period to 1787 but omit the Revolutionary War era) at the University of Virginia. Philander Chase, the present editor, kindly offered assistance at a later stage. He doubts that there are more instances of runaway slaves in the Washington materials than we have found, but notes that he and his associates are only now researching the financial papers in depth. We have simply guessed that, over his lifetime, Washington owned between two and three times the number of slaves he possessed at his death.

2. In recent years, the word "runaway" has been considered inappropriate because it is the master's term and delegitimates the act of escaping from bondage. By using the term, we accept no such connotations. Rather, we agree that slaves who took flight were liberating themselves, at least for a time. We mean by runaway no more nor less than fugitive or escapee. We use all three terms synonymously. For a general study, focusing on the period 1790–1860, see John Hope Franklin and Loren Schweninger, *Runaway Slaves: Rebels on the Plantation* (New York: Oxford University Press, 1999).

3. *Col. Ser.*, 7:441, 453–54. For a more cursory and flattering view of Washington's attitude toward runaways, see Ulrich B. Phillips, *American Negro Slavery: A Survey of the Supply, Employment and Control of Negro Labor as Determined by the Plantation Regime* (1918; Baton Rouge: Louisiana State University, 1966), 285–86.

4. *Col. Ser.*, 8:520–21, 529.

5. *Col. Ser.*, 9:171–74, 231–33.

6. *Col. Ser.*, 7:107, 109, 235–36, 439–40, 494–95. Although, as the editors note, there were two Sams belonging to Washington in the 1760s, one a carpenter and the other a field hand, the later advertisement by Noble (*Maryland Journal and Baltimore Advertiser*, January 27, 1778) seems a strong indication that Washington's runaway Sam was a skilled slave.

7. *The Papers of George Washington: Revolutionary War Series* (hereafter *Rev. War Ser.*), ed. Philander D. Chase et al., 12 vols. to date (Charlottesville: University Press of Virginia, 1985–), 2:478, 570, 3:126, 129, 130, 188, 270. Washington faced a similar problem in 1787 when he took Neptune on trial as an apprentice bricklayer. Neptune was unhappy at being removed from his wife, and ran away. Washington

then agreed to hire Neptune by the month. See *The Diaries of George Washington* (hereafter *Diaries*), ed. Donald Jackson and Dorothy Twohig, 6 vols. (Charlottesville: University Press of Virginia, 1976–79), 5:131; *Writings*, 29:199; John Lawson to GW, March 17, April 2, 18, 25, 1787, Washington Papers.

8. *Col. Ser.*, 7:65–68. Another shipmate relationship surfaced in 1786 when Washington asked whether Simon would like to return to Mount Vernon to work as a carpenter alongside Sambo, his shipmate (Sambo had been one of the seventeen to join the British in 1781); Simon declined to be moved (*Diaries*, 4:326–27).

9. *Writings*, 22:14 n; Marquis de Chastellux, *Travels in North America in the Years 1780, 1781, and 1782*, ed. Howard C. Rice Jr., 2 vols. (Chapel Hill: University of North Carolina Press, 1963), 2:597; *The Papers of George Washington: Confederation Series*, ed. W. W. Abbot, Dorothy Twohig, et al., 6 vols. (Charlottesville: University Press of Virginia, 1992–97), 1:55. Earlier in the war, Lund Washington noted that he feared the running away of white servants more than of black slaves (*Rev. War Ser.*, 2:480, 3:129). Apparently he had cause, for in July 1776 three of Washington's servants ran to the British; see *Naval Documents of the American Revolution*, vol. 5, ed. William James Morgan (Washington, D.C.: U.S. Government Printing Office, 1970), 1250.

10. Sylvia R. Frey, *Water from the Rock: Black Resistance in a Revolutionary Age* (Princeton: Princeton University Press, 1991), 198; Christopher Fyfe, *A History of Sierra Leone* (London: Oxford University Press, 1962), 63, 84–85; Ellen Gibson Wilson, *The Loyal Blacks* (New York: Capricorn, 1976), 52, 85, 395–96; *The Papers of George Washington: Presidential Series*, ed. Dorothy Twohig et al., 9 vols. to date (Charlottesville: University Press of Virginia, 1998–), 7:59–61.

11. *Writings*, 35:201–2, 296–98; Joseph Whipple to Oliver Wolcott Jr., September 10, October 4, December 22, 1796, *Ret. Ser.*, 4:237–38 (copies of these letters were also kindly sent us by Valerie Cunningham of Portsmouth, New Hampshire). Miss Oney Gudge married a Mr. John Harris on January 8, 1797, according to New Hampshire Town Records, Greenland, vol. 1, 1749–1820, New Hampshire State Library, Concord, as cited in Fritz Hirschfeld, ed., *George Washington and Slavery: A Documentary Portrayal* (Columbia: University of Missouri Press, 1997) 116–17; but all later information points to a (second?) marriage to a mulatto sailor named Staines. For Oney's age and parentage, see *Diaries*, 4:277–78. The year before, Washington speculated that his slave Frenches Paul of Union Farm had left Virginia by water or land in the company of a slave belonging to Mr. Dulany. Washington offered to join Dulany in the expense of recovering the slaves, but "would not have my name appear in any advertisement" (*Writings*, 34:153–54).

12. John W. Blassingame, ed., *Slave Testimony: Two Centuries of Letters, Speeches, Interviews, and Autobiographies* (Baton Rouge: Louisiana State University Press, 1977), 248–50, and the *Portsmouth Weekly*, June 2, 1877, which reprints the Rev. T. Adams's story from the *Granite Freeman*, May 1845. For more on Oney Maria Judge or Ona Staines, see M. O. Hall, *Rambles about Greenland in Rhyme* (1900; Hampton, N.H.: Peter E. Randall, 1979), 200. The last two references are kindly supplied by Valerie Cunningham.

13. *Ret. Ser.*, 1:27–28, 469–70, 2:16, 60; Stephen Decatur Jr., *Private Affairs of George Washington, from the Records and Accounts of Tobias Lear, Esquire, His Secretary* (Boston: Houghton Mifflin, 1933), 296–97; Louis Philippe, King of France (1830–48), *Diary of My Travels in America*, trans. Stephen Becker (New York: Delacorte, 1977), 32. Washington also heard from his sister about two of her "Principal hands" who had absconded apparently to Philadelphia "as they have a thought in geting there thay will be free" (Betty Washington Lewis to GW, February 9, 1794, Washington Papers).

14. In the 1760s he had fifteen runaway slaves (one ran four times, three twice) and in the 1790s eight runaway slaves (two ran three times, one twice).

15. We have analyzed all the available farm reports in the Washington Papers. These are systematic for 1785–87 and 1789–99, but for most years there are only a few weekly reports still extant. For 1797 and 1798, all but one week survives. We have analyzed the loss of labor attributable to running away for every surviving farm report; we found comparable figures to those reported for 1797 and 1798. Sophia was the daughter of Sylla (or Sillar or Priscilla) who had herself run away in 1794 and 1796. See *Ret. Ser.*, 4:535.

16. James Anderson, *Columbian Mirror and Alexandria Gazette*, April 14, 1798; *Ret. Ser.*, 4:536.

17. James Anderson, *Columbian Mirror and Alexandria Gazette*, April 22, 1800; *Ret. Ser.*, 4:529, where Marcus is listed as a house servant and as a dower slave.

18. For a full description of these sources and the precise numbers of runaways drawn from them, see Philip D. Morgan and Michael L. Nicholls, "Runaway Slaves in Eighteenth-Century Virginia: A New World Perspective" (MS in preparation).

19. Landon Carter's total comprises forty-one named and seven unnamed runaways in *The Diary of Colonel Landon Carter of Sabine Hall, 1752–1778*, ed. Jack P. Greene (Charlottesville: University Press of Virginia, 1965), seven in county court claims (but two refer to a slave who is also mentioned in the diary and is therefore not counted again), and three advertisements (one of whom is likewise a slave also mentioned in the diary). Landon Carter had seven known runaways in the 1760s. If we assume about ten in all and put his total number of slaves at three hundred, then this number is 3 percent. The Robert Carter references are too voluminous to cite individually, but were compiled from his letterbooks and daybooks at Duke University, his daybooks and journals at the Library of Congress, the Carter Family Papers and account books at the Virginia Historical Society, and the Emmet Collection (microfilm) at the Colonial Williamsburg Research Department. Robert Carter had 350 slaves in 1772, 410 in 1784, and 509 in 1791; from 1775 to 1795 he probably possessed at least 600 slaves; see Louis Morton, *Robert Carter of Nomini Hall: A Virginia Tobacco Planter of the Eighteenth Century* (Williamsburg: Colonial Williamsburg, 1941), 100. Lucinda Stanton generously compiled the information on Jefferson's runaway slaves in a Monticello Research Department memorandum, June 1993. Jefferson owned about two hundred slaves during the 1810s and had six known runaways. The William Cabell Commonplace Books, 1769–95, are at the Virginia Historical Society. It is quite possible that Cabell failed to report all his

runaway slaves, particularly those on outlying quarters, and five years of the diary are missing.

20. Orlando Patterson, *The Sociology of Slavery: An Analysis of the Origins, Development and Structure of Negro Slave Society in Jamaica* (Rutherford, N.J.: Fairleigh Dickinson University Press, 1969), 262. For a more sophisticated, but as yet inconclusive, wrestling with this problem, see David Geggus, "On the Eve of the Haitian Revolution: Slave Runaways in Saint Domingue in the Year 1790," *Slavery and Abolition*, 6 (1985): 114–17.

21. For much higher estimates, see Gary B. Nash, *Race and Revolution* (Madison, Wis.: Madison House, 1990), 57, 59, 60, and Frey, *Water from the Rock*, 211; but cf. Allan Kulikoff, *Tobacco and Slaves: The Development of Southern Cultures in the Chesapeake, 1680–1800* (Chapel Hill: University of North Carolina Press, 1986), 418.

22. Rev. James Madison to James Madison, January 18, 1781, *Papers of James Madison*, ed. William T. Hutchinson and William M. E. Rachal, 17 vols. (Chicago: University of Chicago Press, 1962–91), 2:293; Robert Pleasants to General Arnold, January 30, 1781, Robert Pleasants Lettercopy Book, photostats, College of William and Mary; David Jameson to Madison, *Papers of James Madison*, 3:15–16; Robert Carter to commanding officers, October 30, 1781, Robert Carter Letterbook IV, Duke University, 137–39; *Writings*, 22:14, and see also Ralph Wormeley Jr. to Secretary of State, August 8, 1783, CO 5/1344, fol. 376, Public Records Office (the Wormeleys lost twelve men and two boys in early June 1781); George Mason to Delegates, April 3, 1781, *Papers of James Madison*, 3:55; Edmund Pendleton to Madison, May 7, 1781, ibid., 3:111; diary of Robert Honeyman, May 11, 1781, Library of Congress; John Parke Custis to George Washington, July 11, 1781, in Billy J. Harbin, "Letters from John Parke Custis to George and Martha Washington, 1778–1781," *William and Mary Quarterly*, 3d ser., 43 (1986): 290. In July 1781 Fanny Tucker at her plantation near Farmville was grateful that the presence of hundreds of British light horse did not provoke any of her slaves to desert; see Mary Haldane Coleman, *St. George Tucker: Citizen of No Mean City* (Richmond: Dietz Press, 1938), 65, as cited in Benjamin Quarles, *The Negro in the American Revolution* (Chapel Hill: University of North Carolina Press, 1961), 121.

23. Claim of Alice Taylor, October 24, 1789, Executive Papers, September-October 1789, Library of Virginia, and see also "Losses Sustained from [British] from May 23, 1783," Records of the General Assembly, Office of the Speaker, Correspondence, MSS, Library of Virginia; Edmund Pendleton to William Woodford, June 21, 1779, Pendleton Letters, University of North Carolina; Edwin Morris Betts, ed., *Thomas Jefferson's Farm Book, with Commentary and Relevant Extracts from Other Writings* (Princeton: Princeton University Press, 1953), 29, 503–5, and *Papers of Thomas Jefferson*, ed. Julian Boyd et al., 28 vols. to date (Princeton: Princeton University Press, 1950–), 6:224; Robert Carter to Commanding Officers who now have the care of sundry negro slaves, and to Mr. Garland Moore, October 30, 1781, Letterbook IV, Robert Carter Papers, Duke University, 137–39, 141.

24. Cf. Jean B. Lee, *The Price of Nationhood: The American Revolution in Charles County* (New York: W. W. Norton, 1994), 216.

25. B. W. Higman, *Slave Populations of the British Caribbean, 1807–1834* (Baltimore: The Johns Hopkins University Press, 1984), 387; Michael Craton, *Testing the Chains: Resistance to Slavery in the British West Indies* (Ithaca: Cornell University Press, 1982), 368; N.A.T. Hall, "Maritime Maroons: *Grand Marronage* from the Danish West Indies," *William and Mary Quarterly,* 3d ser., 42 (1985): 482; Edward Brathwaite, *The Development of Creole Society in Jamaica, 1770–1820* (Oxford: Clarendon Press, 1971), 201–2; Philip D. Morgan, "Colonial South Carolina Runaways: Their Significance for Slave Culture," *Slavery & Abolition* 6 (1985): 57; Billy C. Smith, "Runaway Slaves in the Mid-Atlantic Region during the Revolutionary Era," in *The Transforming Hand of Revolution: Reconsidering the American Revolution as a Social Movement,* ed. Ronald Hoffman and Peter J. Albert (Charlottesville: University Press of Virginia, 1996), 199–230; Shane White, *Somewhat More Independent: The End of Slavery in New York City, 1770–1810* (Athens: University of Georgia Press, 1991), 140–41.

26. Keith Mason, "The World an Absentee Planter and His Slaves Made: Sir William Stapleton and His Nevis Sugar Estate, 1722–1740," *Bulletin of the John Rylands University Library of Manchester* 75 (1993): 128; Philip D. Morgan, "Slaves and Livestock in Eighteenth-Century Jamaica: Vineyard Pen, 1750–1751," *William and Mary Quarterly,* 3d ser., 52 (1995): 47–76; J. R. Ward, *British West Indian Slavery, 1750–1834: The Process of Amelioration* (Oxford: Clarendon Press, 1988), 198; J. Harry Bennett, *Bondsmen and Bishops: Slavery and Apprenticeship on the Codrington Plantations of Barbados, 1710–1838* (Berkeley and Los Angeles: University of California Press, 1958), 26–28; Brathwaite, *Creole Society,* 202, who reports an average of seven runaways per year in 1792–97, and Michael Craton, *Searching for the Invisible Man: Slaves and Plantation Life in Jamaica* (Cambridge: Harvard University Press, 1978), 153, who reports three a year from 1783 to 1797 (we have assumed an average of five a year out of a total population of about five hundred); B. W. Higman, *Slave Population and Economy in Jamaica, 1807–1834* (Cambridge: Cambridge University Press, 1976), 180. Many Jamaican inventories list runaways; we count sixty-five colonial South Carolina inventories that recorded a total of 118 runaways. To date we know of only two Virginia inventories that mention a runaway—that of John Herbert, July 15, 1760, Chesterfield County Will Book 1, 391–98, and that of Clement Read, June 4, 1764, Lunenburg County Will Book 2, 278, both in the Library of Virginia.

27. This information is reported in full in Morgan and Nicholls, "Runaway Slaves in Eighteenth-Century Virginia." On the number of women in the Virginia slave population, see Kulikoff, *Tobacco and Slaves,* 11; Kulikoff, "A 'Prolifick' People: Black Population Growth in the Chesapeake Colonies, 1700–1790," *Southern Studies* 16 (1977): 405–6; Philip D. Morgan and Michael L. Nicholls, "Slaves in Piedmont Virginia, 1720–1790," *William and Mary Quarterly,* 3d ser., 46 (1989): 211–51. The Virginia runaway slave population remained heavily dominated by men, 6:1 in the advertisements for 1,227 adult slaves in the Richmond *Enquirer* between 1804 and 1828; see Stanley W. Campbell, "Runaway Slaves," in *Dictionary of Afro-American Slavery,* ed. Randall M. Miller and John David Smith (Westport, Conn.: Greenwood

Press, 1988), 649–52. The one colony that had a runaway slave population as heavily dominated by men as Virginia's was neighboring North Carolina; see Marvin L. Michael Kay and Lorin Lee Cary, *Slavery in North Carolina, 1748–1775* (Chapel Hill: University of North Carolina Press, 1995), 258.

28. On sex ratios in towns, see, for example, Higman, *Slave Population*, 118, and Philip D. Morgan, "Black Life in Eighteenth Century Charleston," *Perspectives in American History*, n.s., 1 (1984): 190.

29. Captive advertisements, by their very nature, generally fail to mention a runaway's companions, so studies that include these in their statistics report rather low rates of group running-away, e.g., 33 percent and 30 percent in colonial Georgia, according to Marvin L. Michael Kay and Lorin Lee Cary, "Slave Runaways in Colonial North Carolina," *North Carolina Historical Review* 63 (1986): 21, and Betty Wood, *Slavery in Colonial Georgia, 1730–1775* (Athens: University of Georgia Press, 1984), 176. Morgan, "Colonial South Carolina Runaways," *Slavery & Abolition* 6 (1985): 72, found that 36 percent of all fugitives and captives fled in groups but 40 percent of fugitives fled alone. In the Bahamas 39 percent of fugitives ran in groups, say Michael Craton and Gail Saunders in *Islanders in the Stream: A History of the Bahamian People*, vol. 1, *From Aboriginal Times to the End of Slavery* (Athens: University of Georgia Press, 1992), 367. For more on group running-away in South Carolina—though with no information on the number of group runaways as a proportion of all runaways—see Michael P. Johnson, "Runaway Slaves and the Slave Communities in South Carolina, 1799 to 1830," *William and Mary Quarterly*, 3d ser., 38 (1981): 418–41. For the Jamaican information, but unfortunately again with no information on the number of group runaways as a proportion of all fugitives, see Michael Mullin, *Africa in America: Slave Acculturation and Resistance in the American South and the British Caribbean, 1736–1831* (Urbana: University of Illinois Press, 1992), 291. For one of the lowest rates of group flight so far reported, see White, *Somewhat More Independent*, 139.

30. This information on birthplace is fully reported in Morgan and Nicholls, "Runaway Slaves in Eighteenth-Century Virginia."

31. *Col. Ser.*, 8:520; *Writings*, 34:135. Paul was about thirty years old, "a stout, square-built fellow, six feet high; he has big full mouth, large cross eyes, and slow spoken" (William Pearce, *Columbian Mirror and Alexandria Gazette*, March 12, 1795).

32. *Col. Ser.*, 6:405 (Davy), 6:456 (Mason's slaves), 6:444 (Ransom); 7:6 (Green), 7:67 (Maryland prison fees), 7:213 (public), 7:268–69 (Breechy), 7:494 (Sam); 8:520–21 (Milsford and outlawry of Shag); *Maryland Gazette*, August 20, 1761; *Diaries*, 3:45 (Harry).

33. This information is fully reported in Morgan and Nicholls, "Runaway Slaves in Eighteenth-Century Virginia." It is also a major theme of Gerald W. Mullin, *Flight and Rebellion: Slave Resistance in Eighteenth-Century Virginia* (New York: Oxford University Press, 1972).

34. Jacob Wray, *Virginia Gazette* (Dixon & Hunter), November 4, 1775; B. Middleton, *Virginia Independent Chronicle* (Davis), July 9, 1788; Thomas Huson, *Vir-*

ginia Gazette (Purdie & Dixon), May 26, 1774; John Seawell, *Virginia Gazette* (Purdie), November 7, 1777, supplement.

35. William Black, *Virginia Gazette* (Purdie & Dixon), December 13, 1770; John Gordon, *Virginia Gazette* (Purdie), May 29, 1778; Robert Beverley, *Virginia Gazette or American Advertiser* (Hayes), July 9, 1785; George Hope, *Virginia Gazette and Weekly Advertiser* (Nicolson), November 5, 1785; David Hoops, *Virginia Gazette* (Dixon & Hunter), March 30, 1776; Stephen Drayton, *South Carolina Gazette*, April 11, 1774; Andrew Fornea, *State Gazette of South Carolina*, April 18, 1785; Peter Lepoole, *South Carolina and American General Gazette*, August 21, 1776; Randal Eldredge, *City Gazette* (Charleston), August 17, 1790; Roger Smith Jr., ibid., July 15, 1797. Over half of advertised Virginia fugitives with stated language skills were said to speak English (and other European languages) well.

36. *Col. Ser.*, 8:18–19; for coachman Jamey, see note 4. One of the few previous studies of runaways that explore the time between a runaway's escape and an advertisement is Wood, *Slavery in Colonial Georgia*, 171. She finds that 58 percent of advertisements were placed within a month of escape. The comparable figure for Virginia is 45 percent. The less dispersed nature of settlement in Georgia—i.e., ease of access for the advertiser—may be one explanation for the difference, but the greater incidence of running away in that colony was probably also important. Faced by many runaways and a rapidly growing black population, Georgia masters resorted to newspapers rather quickly.

37. Cuthbert Bullit, *Virginia Gazette* (Rind), November 8, 1770. Former owners were mentioned in 681, or 28 percent, of the advertisements for the 2,474 fugitives.

38. The information on recurrent runaways is fully reported in Morgan and Nicholls, "Runaway Slaves in Eighteenth-Century Virginia."

39. *Writings of Washington*, 36:2.

Chapter 9

"UNDER THE COLOR OF LAW"

The Ordeal of Thomas Jeremiah, a Free Black Man,
and the Struggle for Power in Revolutionary South Carolina

WILLIAM R. RYAN

> Must ethnic groups accept the dominant patriotic criterion of what is a "contribution" so as to gain the respect they deserve? Black Loyalists, black neutralists, or blacks who simply ran away were concerned for their personal freedom, no less than black patriots.
> —Alfred F. Young[1]

> In exploring the revolutionary South, I have discovered that most historians have no understanding of the civil struggle that shattered most of the region during the war years, and that little serious thought has been given to how the rather unpopular Whig elites managed to retain their authority during the period's incredible turmoil. None of the relevant interpretations—progressive, neo-Whig, or New Left—are very helpful in explaining either the pattern of wartime social disruption or political behavior.
> —Ronald Hoffman[2]

Historians have traditionally shied away from the experience of South Carolina in the American Revolution.[3] So much so that in 1981 Jerome J. Nadelhaft proclaimed that the history of Revolutionary South Carolina had in fact been abandoned. "For almost 200 years," Nadelhaft contended, serious scholars had directed their attention northward, leaving South Carolina "to military historians and laymen, who each praising his or her own hero, crossed and recrossed the state with eighteenth century armies and besieged readers with books about battles, campaigns, and high ranking officers."[4] While Nadelhaft's assertion is drastically oversimplified, it unfortunately contains a great deal of truth. Whether out of covert racism, New England exceptionalism, or the misconception that simply not enough sources exist, surprisingly little is known, or written, about the history of Revolutionary South Carolina. As Nadelhaft rightly points out, "while partisan generals such as Francis Marion, Andrew Pickens, and Thomas Sumter have been the subjects of biographies, the civilian leaders, and the political and constitutional events they participated in, remain obscure."[5] South Carolina's role in the war that brought George Washington to prominence remains poorly understood, and the impact of the largest segment of the Carolina population—African-Americans—is even less well known.[6]

This is particularly unfortunate in that African-Americans may have had a greater stake in the outcome of the Revolutionary War than anyone else. As Peter H. Wood once declared, "No group had less formal power, or a larger potential interest in the unraveling of social relationships than Afro-Americans."[7]

Indeed, by the mid-to-late eighteenth century, black Americans had a great deal of practical experience with the concepts of slavery and freedom. Unlike their white patriot counterparts who were steeped in the traditions of republican Rome and England's seventeenth-century commonwealth, blacks knew firsthand what the loss of liberty entailed. As Wood points out, they *did not need* to resort to abstract Enlightenment models or a white spillover in order to conceive of revolutionary ideology.[8] The presence and behavior of an insurgent black populace, especially in the south, would add a racial dimension to the War for Independence—one that was often reflected in the strategies, debates, and actions of whites on both sides.

The notion of a three-way tug of war is not a new one. First articulated in several articles by Peter H. Wood in the mid-1980s, and later elaborated by Sylvia Frey and Robert Olwell, this explanatory concept has revealed much about social dynamics that bound masters, slaves and subjects together.[9] Although these scholars, and several others including Benjamin Quarles, Herbert Aptheker, Sidney Kaplan, and Philip Morgan, have done much to illuminate the study of early Afro-American history, there remains much to learn.[10] While countless studies have been devoted to the extraordinary crucible of slavery, the experience of free blacks in the Revolutionary South is still very much a mystery.[11]

In this essay, a trial and execution serve as lenses for viewing the frenzied atmosphere of Charlestown, South Carolina (Charleston after August 13, 1783), during the spring and summer of 1775. By examining the ordeal of Thomas Jeremiah, a free black harbor pilot accused of plotting a slave insurrection, the essay will shed light on the three-way struggle for power that took place among blacks, Whigs, and Tories on the eve of the American Revolution.[12] Jeremiah's trial and the circumstances of his death provide an ideal test case for the notion of a "three-way tug of war" and give a profound sense of how one black man with money and slaves "experienced" the hostile climate of Revolutionary South Carolina.

At some point during the mid-eighteenth century, Thomas Jeremiah obtained his freedom and began to distinguish himself as one of the most prominent blacks in the Charlestown community.[13] As he left no diary or papers of his own, little is known about his existence. If not for the controversy surrounding his trial and execution, we would know virtually nothing about the man. Although much about his life remains obscure, it is clear from the few available records that Jeremiah was the possessor of a number of talents. According to the last royal governor of South Carolina, Lord William Campbell, Jeremiah's "publick services were universally acknowledged, particularly in cases of fire, where by his skill and intrepidity he had often been remarkably useful." In addition to his duties as a firefighter and protector of property, "Jerry," as he was often called by contemporaries, made a successful living by transporting soldiers and "piloting in Men-of-War."[14] As an accomplished boatbuilder and the proprietor of a lucrative fishing business, Jeremiah managed to acquire a modicum of fame and a substantial estate. Eventually he would become a slave owner himself, employing a number of men in the fish market as well as on the wharves of the Cooper River.[15] Fueled by a capacity for self-promotion and an ability to capitalize on his public image, Jeremiah was able to augment an already sizable reputation. In 1768, for example, an edition of the *South Carolina Gazette* contained the heading "The Negro Jerry (well known for his extinguishing of fires) has just completed a Well-Boat, in order to supply the inhabitants of [Charlestown] with Live Fish every day."[16]

Jeremiah's competence was well known and often discussed by the white community. Lord Campbell, for example, observed that he "had by his industry acquired a property upwards of £1000 sterling, was in a very thriving situation, had several slaves of his own, who he employed in fishing, and was one of the best pilots in the harbor." Another contemporary, royal surgeon George Milligen, estimated that Jeremiah was worth "six or seven hundred pounds sterling." According to historian Philip Morgan, Jeremiah was one of the wealthiest blacks in pre-Revolutionary America.[17]

Regarded as one of the best firefighters in the city and one of the most knowledgeable boatmen in the harbor, Jerry earned the respect of his own community as well as a number of prominent white allies. Undoubtedly, the pilot blurred and frequently transcended the boundaries of race that were becoming ever more sharply drawn during the course of his lifetime. Yet the same skills that initially brought him success and notoriety would ultimately make him a target of white suspicion. As a man who had long worked with battleships and fire, Jeremiah must have appeared to be the most plausible and potentially dangerous link between the Royal Navy and the black majority.[18]

Although he never fit the traditional profile of a radical, Jerry was certainly a complex figure. His paradoxical relationship to the white power structure is perhaps best illustrated by an incident that occurred in 1771. On July 17 Jeremiah was convicted, for reasons unknown, of assaulting a white ship captain by the name of Thomas Langer—a bold action for a black man living in the pre-Revolutionary South—and was sentenced to an hour in the pillory and ten lashes with a whip. In consideration of his widely acknowledged public deeds, however, Lieutenant Governor William Bull granted him a pardon.[19] Four years later, when open conflict broke out between England and the colonies, the fisherman would not be so lucky.

On the eve of the Revolutionary War, the entire eastern seaboard felt the increasing strain of the three-way tug of war between patriots, loyalists, and African-Americans. However, it was in the colony of South Carolina with its unique black majority that these tensions became most acute.[20] The racial demography of that province in the eighteenth century, and of the low country in particular, fostered a palpable air of suspicion among the white minority and hostility on the part of enslaved blacks.[21] For the entire colony below the Cherokee territory in 1775, there were roughly 107,300 African-Americans (almost all of whom were enslaved), 71,600 whites, and 500 Native Americans.[22] In the low country, where the black majority was most apparent, enslaved blacks outnumbered whites during the mid-1770s at a rate of four to one—80,000 to 20,000.[23] And within individual parishes along the coastal waterway, the population disparity was often far greater. In 1762, for example, St. John's Berkeley Parish was inhabited by more than a thousand adult male slaves and only seventy-six adult white males.[24] Even in Charlestown, where the racial imbalance was less pronounced, residents of African descent continued to outnumber their European counterparts well into the eighteenth century. Philip Morgan estimates that 5,833 enslaved blacks, 24 free blacks, and 5,000 whites resided in the colonial capital during the 1770s.[25] It should therefore come as no surprise that in the early months of 1775, when rumors proliferated of a British intent to collaborate with the colony's black majority, fear became endemic among the white "revolutionary" populace.

Such rumors were substantiated on Wednesday, May 3, 1775, when a letter arrived from Arthur Lee, the American correspondent in London, notifying the wealthy merchant planter Henry Laurens of a design by the British administration to foment insurrections among the African slaves of the province.[26] Five days later, the brigantine *Industry*, captained by Edward Allen, arrived in Charlestown from Salem, Massachusetts, carrying a copy of the *South Carolina Gazette*—the first published account of the battles in Lexington and Concord.[27]

News of the outbreak of war in Massachusetts and of the British administration's so-called black plan threw "the people into a great ferment" and precipitated the opening of the second session of South Carolina's Provincial Congress.[28] Since 1720 the Commons House of Assembly and the various offices of the royal government had been the only recognized symbols of authority.[29] But now there were two entities "within the colony" vying for legitimacy and sovereignty. The problem of allegiance, a contentious issue since the Stamp Act, was now a primary concern.

Out of fear and a desire for unity, Whig leaders in the General Committee banded together and on May 11 drafted an "association" to be signed by all white men of property. Despite their unanimous approval of the document, the authors decided to delay its ratification until the opening session of the Provincial Congress.[30] Even at this early stage, however, it is evident that British-inspired or British-assisted slave revolts were foremost in the minds of the General Committee members, who explicitly referred to "the dread of instigated Insurrections at home" as a cause "sufficient to drive an *oppressed* people [white patriots] to the use of Arms."[31]

In June, as members of the South Carolina Provincial Congress began to consider measures for the defense of the colony, a fissure became apparent in the attitudes of patriot leaders. A secret communiqué from Alexander Innes, who had landed in Charlestown on April 19 to make preparations for the arrival of a new royal governor, to Secretary of State for the Colonies William Legge, second earl of Dartmouth, reported that "the Opulent and Sensible . . . are opposed by a numerous body of the Low and Ignorant, led by a few desperate Incendiaries, who have nothing to lose, and some hot headed Young Men of fortune whom it will be difficult to restrain."[32]

When the unanimously approved draft of the Association was brought before the General Assembly on Saturday, June 3, it immediately sparked controversy. Moderate and more conservative patriots, among them Henry Laurens, called for an ancillary statement of "Duty and Loyalty to the King," while radical "incendiaries" such as the Reverend William Tennant wished to hold all nonsignatories "inimical to the Liberty of the Colonies." Likening the Association to "an Athanasian test," Laurens argued that the document would "anathematize good men" and turn friends and neighbors into enemies. Despite these objections, however, the following day (George III's birthday) the document was signed by the 170 members in attendance and ordered dispersed among the parishes.[33]

On Monday, June 5, the question of naval defense was brought before the General Assembly. Radicals such as William Henry Drayton were convinced that the most efficient way to ward off an impending attack by sea would be to sink vessels in the channels of Charlestown harbor and effectively blockade the entire waterway. The "more opulent" members of the house, namely those with a stake in shipping and trade, regarded the plan as extremely dangerous and utterly irrational. Although he did not say so at the time, Laurens feared that the proposal to obstruct the harbor would have drastic long-term consequences. The merchant was convinced that the blockade would permanently ruin the harbor and drain the city of nine-tenths of its prosperity. The planter estimated that the measure had the potential to cost the province half a million pounds sterling and to make the port of Charlestown into "a second Antwerp on the Schelds." Such an action, Laurens predicted, not only would raise the ire of Britain but would make the patriot party an object of derision around the world.[34]

As the debate over the blockade ran its course, a motion was put forth by the radical faction to "immediately purchase & fit out" the *Maria Wilhelmina* in order to secure the harbor's entrance. The vessel, captained by William Williams, had been docked in Charlestown harbor since April 4.[35] The radical party wanted to equip the boat with "50 guns in order to keep out any of his Majesty's Ships of War." According to Henry Laurens, there were even "some whispers" about seizing the *Tamar*, also stationed at the port, and using her for the same purpose. The latter proposal, made by a "violent advocate," reportedly touched off a "clamor" and "dialogue" in the house which "forced" Laurens to intervene. According to the patriot leader, "the Question was put & passed in the Negative by so great a majority as all the difference between 11 Yeas & about 180 Nays—In consequence of that disappointment a long train of Armed Schooners, Fortifications, & the intended Blockade of the Channels into this Harbour, all the effects of Fear, & Zeal in a delirium was postponed and laid aside."[36]

That same day, a motion was put forward to oppose the landing of William Campbell, the newly appointed royal governor. Vehemently opposed to the measure, the ever cautious Laurens asked: "what is to become of Lord W.C. and his Suite?" The merchant reportedly argued that such "conduct would be ungrateful, inhumane, & answer no other end but Shewing that of ill temper." As a concession to Drayton and other "firebrands," harbor pilots such as Thomas Jeremiah were ordered by the congress not "to board or bring in any Man of War or Transport Ship." Despite the numerous objections of more conservative committee members, the order was eventually confirmed. Embarrassed by the designs of the more ardent patriots, Laurens consoled himself by asserting, "His Lordship will certainly find a Way into the Harbour without the aid of our Pilots."

Although we can only speculate, the heated debates that transpired during the first week of the Provincial Congress may have prompted "conservatives" within the patriot party to search for a scapegoat—one whose punishment would simultaneously deter an increasingly insurgent black majority, discourage harbor pilots from collaborating with the British Navy, and pacify a growing number of radicals intent on "destroying" the lucrative waterway of Charlestown harbor.[37]

When news began to circulate that Campbell was on his way to Charlestown, neither whites nor blacks had any idea of what to expect.[38] As the frenzied second session of the congress was still under way, Captain Innes wrote: "The Governor is expected every hour, and although he can do very little, yet I hope his presence with the King's ship under his Command may afford some countenance to the King's friend's, and will I know embarrass the other party, who have at present a clear field."[39] Local merchant and patriot Josiah Smith observed that the entire colony was "in a Ticklish situation" on account of "numerous Domesticks" who had been "deluded by some villainous Persons into the notion of being all set free" upon the arrival of the new governor.[40] This sentiment was reportedly shared by a group of Charlestown slaves, who, according to Drayton, "entertained ideas that the present contest [with Britain] was for obliging" their masters "to give them liberty."[41] Shortly before the governor reached Charlestown harbor aboard the sloop of war *Scorpion*, Smith observed that Campbell's arrival was a frequent topic of discussion among the slaves of the province. The merchant was intensely distressed, claiming that such "common talk" among slaves made them act with impertinence. Mr. Smith took comfort, however, in the fact that the Provincial Congress was issuing certificates to the amount of one million pounds, to raise a force of "Two thousand Men Horse and food," for the purposes of keeping those "mistaken creatures in awe" and warding off "coercive" British troops.[42]

Around the same time, the *South Carolina Gazette and Country Jour-*

nal made an optimistic report that companies of militia were patrolling regularly, "the salutary Consequences of which are every Day more apparent; The nightly meetings and Riots of the Negroes are entirely suppressed."[43] According to Henry Laurens, Charlestown was filled with "the daily & nightly sound of Drums and Fifes." These harrowing sounds, Laurens told his son, awakened "a Spirit in the people" and resolved them "to do all in their power to resist the force & stratagems of the British Ministry."[44]

When Governor Campbell finally arrived on the evening of Saturday, June 17, it did not take him long to realize that his presence was unwelcome.[45] Not only was the sloop he arrived in, HMS *Scorpion*, "detained off the Bar until the loss of one tide," the vessel was expressly prohibited from entering the harbor until the next day, when the patriot-imposed "restraint upon Pilots was taken off."[46] The following afternoon Campbell was received on the steps of the Exchange Building with minimal fanfare and feigned enthusiasm.[47] Normally the arrival of such a prominent public official would occasion large crowds and elaborate ceremony. Yet on this day "the citizens for the most part preserved a sullen silence," as John Drayton recalled:

> They made no *feu de joie*, as had ever been usual in such a case; neither was there the loud and hearty acclamation of citizens, when his commission as Governor was publicly read before him, from the portico of the Exchange. Whatever acclamation was made, was trivial. ... No gentlemen as was customary, awaited his Excellency's landing; or attended his parade, along the streets—save only three Placemen Councilors including the Chief Justice Gordon and Assistant Judge Gregory; three other Assistant Judges, Savage, Fewtrell and Coslett; the Colonel of the Militia—the Collector, Robert Dalway Haliday—the Clerks of the Council, James Simpson, and Common Pleas, James Trail; and some officers of the *Scorpion:* the whole of the escort did not exceed fifteen persons.[48]

The gentlemen of Charlestown were not the only ones to slight the newly appointed royal governor. Lieutenant Governor William Bull, the acting royal overseer of the colony for years, adamantly refused to see Campbell and conveniently neglected to attend his reception.[49] Yet the most unexpected affront to His Lordship was probably one that came from a member of the patriot rank and file on Sunday, June 18.

That evening "just about dusk," Campbell and his personal secretary, Captain Alexander Innes, proceeded on foot through the city. As they turned down Meeting Street and approached the State House, the pair came upon a large company of artillery—the same group of militia raised by the Provincial Congress to suppress "instigated slave insurrections." Although most of Meeting Street was barricaded, the governor found a narrow opening and proposed to go between the guns and the wall. But "in commencing this passage," as Drayton recalled, Campbell was hailed by the sentinel on duty, Thomas Harvey, who would not let him pass. Innes immediately rebuked the young officer, informing him that he was in the presence of the royal governor. Reportedly the sentinel replied, "I am not to know the Governor," and refused to let Campbell and his secretary through. "His Excellency then found himself obliged to quit the pavement: and in doing so" asked the sentinel's name. Without hesitation the soldier replied, "Harvey at your service!" Campbell may have thought of himself as "the Representative of Majesty" in the "unhappy province" of South Carolina, but at that moment he must have realized once and for all that his authority as governor was stillborn.[50]

In a letter to the colonial secretary, Lord Dartmouth, Campbell attributed his chilly reception to the intelligence sent by patriot correspondent Arthur Lee. According to Campbell, Lee was responsible for circulating rumors that "the Ministry had in agitation not only to bring down the Indians on the Inhabitants of this Province, but also to instigate and encourage an insurrection among the slaves." The royal governor was astonished to find that it was reported and "universally believed, that to effect this plan 14,000 Stand of Arms were actually on board the *Scorpion*, the Sloop of War" he arrived in. According to the governor, "the cruelty and savage barbarity of this scheme were the conversation of all Companies." Campbell could scarcely believe "the flame" engendered by this rumor among "all ranks and degrees," lamenting that "no one dared venture to contradict the intelligence conveyed from such respectable authority."[51] The governor's trusted friend Chief Justice Thomas Knox Gordon, a loyalist barrister from Ireland, was convinced that Whigs propagated reports of black insurrection to justify the augmentation of military resistance.[52] George Milligen, Campbell's physician and a fellow loyalist, on the other hand, was convinced that these pervasive rumors could be traced back to the Association and its explicit reference to "instigated insurrections."[53]

According to Milligen, "the people" had been made "to believe that His Majesty's ministers and other servants instigated their slaves to rebel against their masters and to cut their throats."[54] Like Campbell, Milligen was astonished that no one questioned the veracity of these reports, which he claimed were taken as "strong as proofs of Scripture writ," especially by "the ignorant and unwary." As far as the surgeon was concerned, the mob's "fears" and weak "distractions of mind" made it particularly vulnerable to the recent efflorescence of patriot propaganda. Especially seductive, Milligen argued, were the widely circulated tales of plantation slaves who "had refused to work" and of domestics who had "gone and murdered their masters and families." The doctor was convinced that the Whigs had manufactured accounts of blacks obtaining arms and hiding in the woods in order to turn the white populace toward the Revolutionary cause.[55] Such accounts were bolstered by news items like the one on Monday, May 29, in the *South Carolina Gazette* reporting that "there is gone down to Sheerness, seventy-eight thousand guns and bayonets, to be sent to America, to put into the hands of N*****s [Negroes], the Roman Catholics, the Indians and Canadians; and all the . . . means on earth used to subdue the colonies."[56]

During that same week, patriot Michael Hubart testified to the Committee of Safety against Catholic loyalists James Dealy and Laughlin Martin. As John Drayton recounts the story, Hubart testified that on Friday, June 2, James Dealy entered the residence of one Thomas Nicoll in King Street and proclaimed that "good news had come to town." When asked what the "good news" was, Dealy replied that "a number of arms" were "sent over to be distributed amongst the Negroes, Roman Catholics, and Indians." Hubart told Dealy that he thought it was "very bad news that Roman Catholics and Savages should be permitted to join and massacre Christians," whereupon Dealy struck his breast and swore that "he was a Roman Catholic, and that he had arms, and would get arms and would use them as he pleased."[57]

Hubart returned to his home. After some time, James Dealy appeared at Hubart's door with a certain Laughlin Martin and one A. Reed. After sitting down and engaging in small talk, Laughlin Martin arose and asked, "So, Mr. Hubart, you'll not allow Roman Catholics to carry guns?"[58] Hubart informed Martin that his circumstances were too meager to forbid any party or sect to carry arms. Martin proceeded to damn Hubart for a "false faced villain" and ordered Dealy to drag him out of his house and tear him to pieces in the street. Dealy held Hubart by the throat while Martin brandished a blade. Hubart dropped to his knees and pleaded for his life, at which time Martin vowed to God that he would cut off Hubart's head if he did not beg for Dealy's pardon. Hubart apologized and Martin exclaimed that he was a Roman Catholic and vowed to God that he would cut off the head of anyone who said he should not carry arms. Afterward, Hubart claimed, he witnessed Martin drinking with Dealy and Reed and overheard them toasting to "the Damnation of the Committee and their proceedings."[59]

On the morning of Wednesday, June 7, Charlestown residents awoke to the "repeated alarms of the popular Bell." Heeding the summons, Henry Laurens reluctantly made his way to the State House. When the merchant planter arrived, he found that "the call was to collect a proper Court for trying, condemning and executing a sentence on, two impudent fellows who had not only refused to Subscribe to the Association but threatened vengeance against the whole Country by exciting an insurrection." While most members of the congress, including Laurens, reportedly "preserved their dignity" by ignoring the matter and went about their usual business, "some of the lower people" including William Henry Drayton "set up a judge and called witnesses." Within less than an hour, on the basis of Hubart's testimony, the Secret Committee of the Council of Safety ordered that James Dealy and Laughlin Martin be tarred and feathered.

The following day, Laurens reported that he witnessed from his "windows the shocking spectacles put into a cart and driven up and down the Broad Street." The patriot leader expressed his disapproval of the scene and told his son, "I need not describe my feelings to you on this occasion."[60] According to another eyewitness, Captain Innes, "this very *well-timed* piece of Justice was attended with the happiest effects, no one since daring even to think of refusing to swallow anything that may be offered."[61] In his study of the Charlestown artisans, historian Richard Walsh observes that "for the first time, the people saw the mob at its worst."[62]

Having thoroughly shamed "the shocking spectacles," the Secret Committee ordered that the men be put on board a vessel aptly named the *Liberty* and banished indefinitely. At the last moment, however, Martin was reprieved through the intercession of his friends and allowed to remain in Charlestown pending a public apology. Dealy would not be as fortunate. On the day that Martin's plea appeared in the *South Carolina Country Journal,* his loyalist friend was whisked away to England.[63]

While Charlestown's patriot authorities deliberated over the Dealy and Martin incident, news appeared that a band of several blacks had looted "a schooner loaded with goods," taking "nothing else but [gun] Powder."[64] Knowing full well that the Council of Safety was going to interrogate and arrest a number of blacks in connection with the incident, Henry Laurens called a meeting of his brother's slaves and "admonished them to behave with great circumspection in this dangerous time, [and] set before them the great risque of exposing themselves to the treachery of pretended friends and false witnesses if they associated with any [unfamiliar] Negroes."[65]

Loyalists were convinced that the incarceration of blacks by the Council of Safety was part of a deliberate ploy on the part of patriots to substantiate the mob's fears of instigated insurrection. According to Campbell, because the widely reported threats of Indian incursions never materialized, patriots needed "to have recourse to the instigated insurrection amongst their slaves, effectually to gain the point proposed, and they could not be long at loss for pretexts to establish this."[66] George Milligen argued that the white populace became increasingly skeptical about the constant "reports of country insurrections among the Negroes," and many were beginning to doubt "the truth of instigations being used." In order to "carry on the tragedy, several Negroes were taken up on suspicion and were committed to the prison where there is a workhouse for them."[67]

Amid this environment of accusation and suspicion, Thomas Jeremiah found himself in a precarious situation. On June 16, 1775, "a Negro Man Slave" named Jemmy, "the Property of Mr. Peter Croft," testified before the patriot Council of Safety at Charlestown that several weeks earlier at Prioleau's Wharf (near the city's fish market) his brother-in-law, a "free Negro" by the name of Thomas Jeremiah, had pulled him aside and asked if he would be willing to smuggle guns to a runaway named Dewar. According to the witness, these guns were to be distributed by the runaway and "placed in Negroes hands to fight against the [white] inhabitants of the province." To make matters worse, the prime suspect had allegedly boasted about having a large stockpile of gunpowder and had proclaimed himself "the Chief Command[er] of the Negroes."[68]

These accusations were corroborated by a second slave witness, named Sambo, who reported that "two or three months earlier"—that is, just before news had reached Charlestown of the battles in Lexington and Concord—while he was working on [Fitz]simmon's Wharf, the suspect had approached him and asked if he had heard "anything of the war" that was "coming." When the witness declared that he had not yet heard the news, the suspect assured him that "a great war" would most certainly be "coming soon." The dockworker asked, "What shall we poor Negroes do?" The suspect reportedly advised him to set a "schooner on fire, jump on shore and join the [British] soldiers" and added that "the war was com[ing] to help the poor Negroes."[69]

In a letter written on Sunday, June 18, patriot leader Henry Laurens told his son of the slave depositions: "Trials of Several Negroes charged of plotting an insurrection have been conducted this Week I mean the past Week." Laurens wrote that "Jerry the pilot" was "among the most criminal" and that "two or three white people" were "committed to prison on strong Negro Evidence." According to the merchant planter, just as the committee was about to adjourn, Council of Safety members received a letter from a Mr. Oliver Hart declaring that one of his female slaves and "another [belonging] to Joshua Ward Esq. could make very ample discoveries." Laurens noted that both women were immediately ordered into custody to be examined the following day.[70] Of the slave witnesses, loyalist George Milligen would later write: "I am well informed that the witnesses against him declared him innocent, that the evidence they had given against him was not true and given only to save themselves from a whipping, the only punishment they were told would be inflicted on Jerry."[71]

The validity of such scant testimony given by prisoners facing harsh punishments must have been hard to assess, but it did not prevent the Council of Safety from taking swift action. Within days Thomas Jeremiah was arrested, brought to the workhouse in the northwestern corner of the city, and put into solitary confinement.[72] On Thursday, June 22, the committee appointed by the Provincial Congress to investigate reports of black insurrection was ordered to summon freeholders to try Jeremiah under the Negro Act of 1740.[73] The following day Laurens reported to his son that "one or two Negroes" were sentenced to be "severely flogged and banished." Laurens noted that "the white men suspected will be set at large, nothing is brought in evidence against them, yet tis said that the populace are determined to drive them out of the country."[74]

Relieved that the white suspects were exonerated, but puzzled by the committee's apparent "leniency" toward the black suspects, Laurens declared that "if they deserve any punishment, nothing less than death should be the sentence, & at this critical time no pardon or mitigation should be granted." Laurens was vexed by the reluctance of freeholders to enforce the Negro Act, which would necessarily entail the sentence of execution for plotting slave rebellion. The planter was confident, however, that the committee would eventually find individuals willing to apply the harsh set of statutes. He told his son there was "no danger in this, in a town where the Inhabitants are as suddenly blown up by apprehensions as Gun powder is by Fire."[75]

Laurens's observations were on the mark. Within a few days, all obstacles were removed, and Jeremiah was brought before two justices and five freeholders under the Negro Act. According to Campbell, "after sitting a week, and taking uncommon pains to get evidence, no proof could be produced to convict him, or [to] give sufficient grounds to believe any attempt of the kind they pretended to fear was ever intended." The matter was put on hold—but, as the governor noted, "Jerry was order'd to be remanded to prison and his tryal resumed two months afterwards, by which time they hoped to procure more evidence."[76] According to Milligen, around the end of June the black suspects were "dismissed excepting two," who were "remanded to the workhouse till further proof could be got against" them.[77]

The primary sources illuminating Jeremiah's ordeal reveal little about the two months that he spent in the Charlestown workhouse. However, it seems that the incarceration of a black suspect had the effect of temporarily ameliorating white anxieties. At the end of June, Laurens wrote to his son in England, "Jerry is Still to take his trial but he is not in close confinement—this was relaxed as the people's fears abated."[78] In July the plantation owner Gabriel Manigault, also writing to kin in England, observed: "We have been alarmed by idle reports that the Negroes intended to rise, which on examination proved to be of less consequence than expected, however a Strick[t] watch has been kept for fear of the worst."[79] His grandson would later write back to Charlestown, "I am very glad to find by Grandpa's Letter, that there was not so much reason to be afraid of the Negroes, as was first suspected."[80]

By mid-August 1775, however, the tensions between African-Americans, patriots, and loyalists were once again out in the open. On Friday, August 11, Jeremiah was tried for the second and final time. During the course of this second trial under the same court, Jeremiah allegedly committed perjury. According to Laurens, when first confronted with accusations by a runaway slave named Jemmy, Mr. Jeremiah "denied that he knew his person," although upon further inquiry it was revealed that the man was in fact his brother-in-law.[81] It was on this ground that Jeremiah was finally found guilty. For his suspected treason, he was sentenced to be hanged and publicly burned on the following Friday, August 18.

Infuriated by the ill treatment of several royal officers (including the tarring and feathering of a British soldier named George Walker), determined to restore order, and hoping to protect "all other peaceable and faithful subjects," royal governor Campbell reportedly waited "two or three days" to receive a petition in favor of a pardon for Thomas Jeremiah.[82] When none appeared, he requested a meeting with Justice of the Peace John Coram for the morning of Wednesday, August 16, in order to discuss "the proceedings against this poor man, and the whole of the evidence." Before the meeting commenced, Coram gave Campbell a copy of the slave depositions and the "notes of the evidence" against Jeremiah. Reportedly, Campbell's blood "ran cold" when he read the grounds on which "they had doomed a fellow creature to death." Realizing that without a petition from one of the patriot judges he would not be able to save the prisoner, Campbell expressed to Coram "in the strongest terms" his sense of "the weakness of the evidence." The governor entreated Coram "for his own sake" and that of his fellow judges to get a petition signed by them. In addition to this request, Campbell ordered Coram to meet with the royal judges and the attorney general and "lay the affair before them" so that they could evaluate the legality of the patriot decision and report back to the governor the following evening.[83]

While it is impossible to know what transpired during this encounter, at noon Coram was dismissed. According to Henry Laurens, the justice then "voluntarily acquainted the people that his Lordship had recommended to him to procure or promote a petition in behalf of the Criminal, and that in speaking of the Evidence had said, 'the People should consider the Consequence of executing him upon such Evidence in case the times should alter.'"[84]

Word spread rapidly of a bitter confrontation between Coram and the royal governor, and it was soon leaked that Campbell was trying to stay Jeremiah's execution. Laurens wrote that the alleged remark made by the governor "greatly affected the mind of those to whom it was repeated" because it played on patriot apprehensions and made them acutely aware of the dangers inherent in such an openly rebellious stance against "the Representative of Majesty."[85]

"Whilst this was transacting," Campbell would later recall, "my attempting to interfere in the matter raised such a Clamor amongst the People, as is incredible, and they openly declared that if I granted the man a pardon they would hang him at my door." As rumors continued to spread and recriminations continued to fester, Campbell received a letter from "a man of the first Property in the Province, who had always express'd great friendship."[86] According to Campbell, the letter represented in "the strongest terms, the dreadful consequences that would attend my pardoning him" and concluded with "the remarkable expression, that it would raise a flame all the water in Cooper River would not extinguish."[87]

The following morning, Thursday, August 17, Coram openly confronted Governor Campbell over the perceived threat. According to Laurens, "The Justice persisted in the declaration to Lord William's Face, His Lordship said he had mistaken him some how or other—but Mr. Coram is clear & positive & was very prudently cautious."[88]

At twelve noon, Campbell met with the Reverend Robert Smith, Anglican rector of St. Phillip's Charlestown, in the home of the wealthy Charlestown merchant Miles Brewton.[89] Although Smith was a devoted patriot, he had become intrigued by Jeremiah's story over the course of the past few months.⁹⁰ At several points between the end of June and the middle of August, the minister conferred with Jeremiah and his brother-in-law, Jemmy, and spoke to them at great length about their involvement in the "crime."⁹¹

During the meeting with Campbell on the afternoon of the seventeenth, Smith reportedly told the governor "that he attended the Black [meaning Jeremiah] as much from a desire to ascertain the reality of an instigated insurrection as from the motives of humanity." According to Campbell, Smith "used every argument every art to draw him to confession, endeavoring to make him contradict himself in the many conversations he had with him but in vain." Smith also informed Campbell that Jeremiah's behavior "was modest and his conversation sensible to a degree that astonished him." When asked about the impending execution, Jeremiah reportedly told the rector "that he was perfectly resigned to his unhappy, undeserved fate." Moreover, "He was in a happy frame of mind and prepared for death." According to Campbell, "Mr. Smith concluded this afflicting story with acquainting me, that the wretch [Jemmy, who was] one of the evidences against Jerry, and condemn'd with him, retracted what he had said against him, and voluntarily declared his innocence."⁹² Based on their conversation, that afternoon Smith applied to Campbell for Jemmy's pardon, and the governor decided to redouble his efforts to save the accused.

Meanwhile, John Coram and a freeholder by the name of Daniel Cannon laid the affair before the royal judges and the attorney general as Campbell had requested.⁹³ Chief Justice Thomas Knox Gordon and Attorney General James Simpson conferred with the justices Edward Savage, William Gregory, John Fewtrell, and Charles Matthew Coslett and proceeded to examine the verdict made by the Whig committee. Given the sentence of death looming over Jeremiah's head, the royal officials knew that they had to report back to the governor as quickly as possible.⁹⁴ Yet it appears that they had difficulty reaching a decision, and in fact the governor found himself receiving not one report but three. The first, drawn up on the evening of the seventeenth by Gordon, Savage, Simpson, and Gregory, favored Jeremiah's acquittal. It argued that the Negro Act of 1740 was "an Act of a very penal nature," which required "a strict and literal construction." The judges opined that the only part of the Negro Act that made the crime of attempting to raise an insurrection a capital offence was section 17. In that section, the judges wrote, "The Words are 'And every Slave who shall raise or attempt to raise an Insurrection in this Province, shall upon conviction suffer Death.'"⁹⁵ Because Jeremiah was "a *free Ne-*

gro and not a slave," they argued, the critical seventeenth section did not and could not apply. The judges claimed that the "makers of the Law, cou'd never have had it in contemplation to include Free Negroes in the said recited words of the 17th section, because in many parts of the Act there is a plain and palpable distinction made between *Slaves* and *Free Negroes.*" They contended that in the "very preceding sixteenth section" free blacks were mentioned and were "subjected to the [same] pains of death" as slaves. "Had it been the intention of the Legislature" to have included free blacks in the all-important "subsequent section, they cou'd never have so immediately forgot them."

The four judges also noted that because free blacks were not mentioned in the seventeenth section, they could only be "punishable for an attempt to raise an Insurrection, in a like manner as white men." Moreover, the judges argued, "a bare attempt to raise an Insurrection evidenced *only by words without any overt Act in consequence of them*" could not be construed as "a levying of War within the meaning of the Act of Parliament passed in the 25th year of King Edward the 3rd and consequently" did not "amount to Treason." The royal authorities concluded that the patriot "Justices and Freeholders in the present case" had indeed "mistaken the Law" and that the sentence of death passed by them upon Jeremiah was "illegal."[96] A similar line of argument would later be made by George Milligen, who claimed that because Jeremiah "was free and a Christian and possessed of property to the amount of six or seven hundred pounds sterling, . . . he ought to have been tried by the King's court and a jury."[97]

That same evening, Justice Charles Matthew Coslett put forth a very different interpretation of the legality of Jeremiah's trial. The justice began by stating that although Coram did accede to Campbell's command by laying "before the Judges and His Majestie's Attorney General the Evidence," he "very incorrectly declared that the Witnesses were examined at different times and always confirmed what they had said on their first examination." Coslett recollected that barristers in England "could not make any report *viva voce* Evidence which we ourselves had not heard, and that it was always the Judge who heard and saw the Witness examined who reported to his Majesty."[98] Yet, despite Coslett's stance against the committee's faulty use of evidence and improper procedure, the justice agreed with Coram's decision.[99]

Coslett argued that the Negro Act was indeed applicable to "free Negroes." He grounded his opinion entirely on the fourteenth section of the statute, specifically the section that stated that "the evidence of any free Indian or Slave with Oath shall be allowed and admitted in all cases against any free Negroes, Indians, & c. and all Crimes and Offenses committed by free Negroes & c. shall be proceeded in, heard, tried and adjudged by the Justices and Freeholders appointed by this Act for the trial of slaves in a like manner as is hereby directed for the trial of Crimes committed by Slaves any Law &c to the Contrary."[100] The construction Coslett put on the clause was that the Whig justices and freeholders were within their rights "to try and convict all free Negroes for any crime which a slave under this Act can be tried or convicted for except in the 29th section where free Negroes are fined only for harboring slaves."

Coslett conceded that the seventeenth section only used the term *slave* and never actually referred to free blacks, but he stated that "if it is not to be construed that free Negroes are liable to the same punishment for this same offense, they will not be punishable at all under this Law or any that I know of."[101] Coslett rested his decision primarily on South Carolina's unique racial demography. Surely he must have had the black majority in mind when he argued that "the peculiar circumstances of this Province would never permit the Legislature to make any difference in the punishment of a slave and a free Negroe in an offense of so enormous a nature," especially when one was "at least as equally dangerous as the other." Coslett conceded that the Negro Act was indeed a penal statute, which ought to be taken strictly, but noted that in "the 53rd section: it is enacted that all Clauses therein contained shall be construed most largely for the promoting and carrying into Execution this Act." Coslett concluded his report to Campbell by making an explicit reference to the black majority. "Besides, I could not help reflecting, that there was a vast multitude of slaves and free Negroes, Mullatoes &c in the Province, and that it might be of the most fatal consequence to the lives and properties of the white Inhabitants, if these fellows once got into their heads that free Negroes &c were not punishable under this Act for such an enormous crime."[102]

Lord Campbell eventually received a third opinion from his divided legal panel. The opinion submitted by Justice John Fewtrell can only be described as neutral. Not only was the report strikingly evasive, it was also submitted two days late. Fewtrell began by stating the obvious, namely that "the Legislature of the Province" based its opinion on the Negro Act of 1740.[103] According to Fewtrell, the act gave the justices and freeholders the power to "examine Witnesses and other evidence & *finally* hear and determine the matter brought before them." According to the justice, "another section" of the Negro Act gave the colonial authorities "power in Cases Capital to mitigate the Sentence, except for the homicide of a white person, to corporal punishment in such discretion as they see fit." Invoking *stare decisis,* Fewtrell cited a precedent from 1751 that provided "Justices and Freeholders" with the power to mitigate punishment and concluded that "such full power being placed in the Justices & Freeholders in Criminal Matters . . . takes away all jurisdiction from the Judges & that they cannot anyways interfere."[104]

It is unclear what Campbell thought of Coslett's and Fewtrell's opinions, but when the governor spoke with Gordon, Savage, Simpson, and Gregory on the evening of Thursday, August 17, he became disheartened. Despite the favorable opinion given by the four judges, the men informed Campbell that "they were well assured his death was determined on" and told the governor that it might be improper for him to intervene. In his letter to Dartmouth, Campbell remarked, "I leave your Lordship to conceive of the poignancy of my agony and distress on this occasion. I was almost distracted, and wished to have been able to fly to the remotest corner of the Earth from a set of Barbarians who are worse than the most cruel Savages any history described."[105]

Henry Laurens's description of the royal judges' reports was somewhat caustic. The merchant planter later told his son that the law by which Jeremiah "was tried was called into question, the Judges & Attorney General were called on for their opinions, & for a while those Sages were pleased to aver that a Free Negro was not amenable to that Act." He added that one of the judges even "threw the Magna Charta in the faces of the people—but loose opinions would not pass & the Gentleman dared not venture to Subscribe to a declaration which must have called something more valuable than their Law knowledge into question."[106]

At six o'clock that evening, Governor Campbell pardoned Jemmy in accordance with the Reverend Robert Smith's request, and ordered Smith "to attend the [patriot] Committee then sitting."[107] The governor would later inform Lord Dartmouth that he believed Smith's reputation as a virulent patriot would have some influence on the Council of Safety and cause them to change their minds. At precisely seven o'clock, Campbell sent Smith's report to John Coram and to Henry Laurens and scripted personal letters to both of them asking them to rethink the sentence of execution.[108]

Campbell deliberately "wrote in such terms" as he "hoped might rouse their consciences."[109] In his letter to John Coram, Campbell declared: "In case of Blood I wave *Ceremony,* I would even give up *Dignity* to Save the Life of an Innocent Man. Consider it Seriously Sir, lay it before your Brother Justice, and the Freeholders, between God & your own consciences be it, I take every Holy Power to witness I am innocent of this Mans death upon your heads be it, for without your interposition, I find I cannot Save him."[110] In the letter to Laurens, Governor Campbell openly informed the merchant that he was trying to appeal to his feelings for "the Representative of Majesty in this unhappy Province."[111] In a further effort to rouse the patriot leader's conscience, the governor called on Laurens to think of "the weight of Blood," and—apparently protesting the recent letter of warning which may have come from Laurens—concluded "I am told I cannot attempt to save this Man without bringing greater Guilt on this Country than I can bear even to think of."[112]

Laurens received the letter at 9 P.M. on Thursday, August 17, while "Sitting in the Chair of the Committee" and "offered it immediately as a matter proposed." The governor's letter and Smith's report were then read aloud, but when the members of the Committee "heard the Contents, they utterly refused to take them under Consideration."[113] Laurens would later claim that "the retraction by Jemmy could have no weight with Men who would give themselves time to consider that his first Evidence was corroborated by two other witnesses, that a Sambo who was the main Witness would not retract & that Jerry when he was first confronted by Jemmy positively denied that he knew his person—that he knew the Man although upon enquiry it clearly appeared that they were old acquaintance[s] & nearly allied by Jerry's connection as a husband to the other man's sister."[114]

Although Henry Laurens refused to intervene on Jeremiah's behalf, out of "good manners" and a love of "plain dealing," he drafted a response to the governor shortly after the hearing drew to a close at half past ten o'clock. Mr. Laurens later told his son that the rebuttal to Lord Campbell was "done in haste & very late at night," claiming that he failed to express "his thoughts so clearly as he might have done at a little more leisure." This rebuttal, coming on the eve of Jeremiah's execution, touched off a set of harsh exchanges between the merchant planter and Campbell's private secretary, Alexander Innes, which according to Laurens himself gave the patriot leader "Some pain."[115]

In his first letter to the governor, Laurens claimed that he had not "heard the Evidence fully against Jerry" and would not declare the man innocent or guilty. Laurens implied that a sort of underhanded plea bargain had been made to the detriment of justice. "If the retraction of Evidence by one who had been admitted an accomplice & after he had secured his own pardon and Reward, was to be admitted at the Old Bailey many Rogues would escape Punishment and many of his Majesty's Proclamations [would] prove worse than Nugatory, but such a retraction I also presume would not even be listen'd to in a case where there had been another firm Evidence." The patriot leader declared that "the unhappy man in Question was found Guilty after a fair Legal trial, that the Justices and freeholders were unanimous in their opinion of his Guilt." He argued that the alarm of "the people" was justified, given the "Calamitious Situation of this Colony under the threats of Insurrection" and "the strong proofs" that "they are possessed of."[116]

Lord Campbell offered no direct response. However, in the early hours of the morning on Friday, August 18—the day Jeremiah was to be executed —Alexander Innes scripted a quick riposte to Laurens's allegations.[117] Campbell's secretary informed Laurens that the "Confession of the Wretch Jemmy" was voluntary and "made to Mr. Smith before His Lordship knew such a person was even under Confinement." Innes informed Laurens, "No application was made to the Governor in his [Jemmy's] behalf till past 12. Yesterday. his Excellency signed the Pardon at 6 O Clock and by desire of Mr. Smith, Jemmy is now ignorant of it, unless Mr. Coram to whom Mr. Nesbitt was obliged to apply for such information as was necessary to enable him to draw the Pardon has acquainted him with it." Noting that Laurens had "omitted inclosing Mr. Smiths Conversation with the wretched Creature," which the governor had previously asked him to return, the secretary requested that he enclose the rector's report in his next letter.[118]

Later that morning, at half past seven o'clock, Laurens responded by sending an envelope to Innes containing Smith's account of Jemmy's recantation, along with a hostile retort. He accused Campbell of threatening Coram during the meeting that had taken place two days before. The merchant planter concluded by informing Innes that Jemmy was "a liar of the most abominable order of Liars" and that his testimony was not to be given much credit.[119]

That afternoon Innes sent a response, noting that Laurens had "mistaken Jemmy for Jerry." Innes repeated that "no application was made for Jemmy till 12 Yesterday" and "that till that time his Excellency did not know Jemmy was under Confinement." Changing his tone somewhat, the secretary declared, "How cruel then that Suggestion in Mr. Laurens Letter of last Night, that either pardon or reward was offered to procure his recantation." Innes then told Laurens that if he still doubted the point, he should consult Mr. Smith, whose testimony would surely "satisfy." Innes conceded that he thought Jemmy was "the most Abominable of Liars" and informed Laurens that the "persons of both wretches" were unknown to him. Addressing the alleged statement that Campbell made to Coram regarding what might happen to "the people" should the times change, Innes claimed that "his Excellency . . . never made use of that expression." The secretary defended Campbell by asserting that his attempt to intervene on Jeremiah's behalf was rooted only in "what proceeded from Humanity Justice and Mercy." The governor's assistant was quick to add that had Campbell been convinced of Jeremiah's guilt, "his Lordship would have been the last Man . . . to save him from the Punishment due to a Crime of so *Black* a dye." The secretary's concluding remarks were no doubt designed to elicit guilt. Begging Laurens's pardon, Campbell's assistant declared, "the horrid Scene will soon be closed and this Matter decided by that Eternal God to whom all hearts are open & before whom the most Secret thoughts cannot be hid."[120]

In spite of Campbell's best efforts, on the afternoon of August 18, Thomas Jeremiah was brought before the gallows, strung up by a noose, and "burned to ashes" for all to see. While there are no eyewitness accounts of the spectacle, the varied crowd of onlookers must have harbored conflicting emotions.[121] Jerry reportedly "asserted his innocence to the last, behaved with the greatest intrepidity as well as decency, and told his implacable, and ungrateful Persecutors, God's judgement would one day overtake them for shedding his innocent blood."[122] Milligen, who may have been in attendance or may have heard about the event ex post facto, recalled, "Jerry met death like a man and a Christian, avowing his innocence to the last moment of his life." "Surely," the doctor would conclude, "there is no murder so cruel and dangerous as that committed under the appearance of law and justice."[123]

Shortly after Jeremiah was executed, Laurens sent a final letter to Innes.[124] The letter, which was somewhat apologetic in tone, began with a concession by the patriot leader. Laurens admitted that in his last letter to the secretary he had indeed "mistaken the name of Jemmy for Jerry." The patriot leader claimed that he now understood that "no application was made in favor of the former till Yesterday Noon" and solemnly declared that he never intended to "Complain of a Want of Candour" on Innes's part. Laurens informed Innes that he did not mean "an unkind Suggestion" when referring to "the inefficacy of retracted Evidence after a fair trial." He conceded that at "a Court of Oyer and Terminer in Great Britain" there are cases where "His Majestys Proclamations not only Pardon but Rewards are offered to accomplices for discovering their Confederates." Laurens argued that such practices were common, citing what he called a proverb—"the greatest rogue turns Kings Evidence." He then denied that he "by any means intended to Infer from thence that Pardon and Reward had been offered to Jemmy by the Governor or by his authority directly or indirectly."

Laurens again denied that Campbell had ulterior motives for attempting to "save the Life of Jerry," but at the same time declared "I now believe Jerry was Guilty and I am fully persuaded that the Governor and you are so open to Conviction that I should have no difficulty in bringing you both to be of my opinion on this he[a]d." Laurens admitted that he "was till this morning unacquainted with particular circumstances" and "had avoided the knowledge of the whole of this horrible Insurrection Report as much as possible." Laurens concluded the letter and the correspondence by claiming that he was "in hopes of having steered clear of an affair which in the sequel has given me some uneasiness. but I learn the Scene is closed! Justice is satisfied! I beg our correspondence on this disagreeable Subject may here end."[125]

At some point that afternoon, Campbell received a long-awaited response from the patriot-dominated Commons House of Assembly. In addition to informing the governor that he was "wasting" their time with "pathetic" complaints, the members of the house attempted to justify the harsh punishments inflicted on Thomas Jeremiah:

> When civil commotions prevail, and a people are threatened both with internal and external dangers, they would be unwise not to entertain a certain jealousy of intestine foes; and take every precaution to guard against their secret machinations. For this purpose, the inhabitants of this Colony have been impelled to adopt certain measures, which although not warranted by any of the written laws; yet in our apprehension, are more justifiable and constitutional than any of the late acts of the British Administration. . . . In times like the present, when a whole continent is engaged by one arduous struggle for their civil liberties; if individuals will wantonly step forth and condemn measures universally received and approved; they must abide the consequences. It is not in our power in such cases to prescribe limits to popular fury.[126]

The following day, Saturday, August 19, Governor Campbell wrote to Dartmouth in a state of frenzy. "Your Lordship will I am sure excuse my warmth when I acquaint you, that yesterday under the color of the law they hanged and burned, an unfortunate wretch, a Free Negro of considerable property, one of the most valuable & useful men in his way in the Province, on suspicion of instigating an Insurrection, for which I am convinced there was not the least ground, I could not save him my Lord! the very reflection Harrows my Soul! I have only the comfort to think I left no means untried to preserve him. They have now dipt their hands in Blood, God only knows where it will end."[127]

For white contemporaries both in and out of South Carolina, the Jeremiah affair seems to have become a major item of news.[128] Evidence suggests that there were heated polemics both for and against his innocence on either side of the Atlantic, with opinions split along factional lines.[129] Royal governor Thomas Hutchinson of Massachusetts, for instance, was well aware of Jeremiah's trial and of the Negro Act itself, and described both as overt examples of patriot tyranny.[130] In contrast, white patriots in South Carolina such as Henry Laurens saw the case of Thomas Jeremiah as a prime example of what could—and should—happen to a black upstart who had overstepped his bounds, exceeded his station, and conspired against provincial authority. Whigs in South Carolina were also intensely attuned, however, to the various ways in which the affair would be received by contemporaries—so much so that on Sunday, August 20, the day after Campbell first wrote to Dartmouth about the affair, Henry Laurens sent to his son in London a detailed account of the trial in order to contradict "false reports" and lies "which may be, among others, propagated to the prejudice of the poor Carolinians."[131]

In early October, John Laurens reported back to his father that the "story of the Negro man Jerry" was indeed a frequent topic of discussion, opining that the widely known English version of the affair would have a highly detrimental effect on attitude toward the "character of our countrymen for justice and humanity."[132] The prevailing loyalist take to which the young Laurens alluded was no doubt derived from the observations of Lord Campbell, who had sent word to England on Saturday the nineteenth and again on Thursday the thirty-first of August that Jeremiah's trial was a travesty of justice, the judicial murder of an innocent man who as an industrious pillar of the seaport community had become the victim of "numberless arts" and "notorious falsehoods propagated" by provincial elites to whip up the frenzy of the mob.[133]

As the fall progressed, the three-way struggle for power between blacks, Whigs, and Tories intensified. On Friday, September 15, Lord Campbell was forced to dissolve the royal government, taking refuge aboard the *Tamar*. Lingering in Charlestown harbor and attempting to conduct the affairs of state from a dilapidated sloop, Campbell would receive much-needed assistance from a black pilot named Scipio Handley (who must have known Jeremiah) as well as from other African-American boatmen who refused to be intimidated by patriot discipline and saw the British side as the most likely path to freedom.[134]

In early November the radical William Henry Drayton replaced Laurens as president of the Second Provincial Congress, and the blockade that conservatives long feared became a reality. In an ironic twist, the blockade provoked the British to action. On Saturday, November 11, as patriots began to sink vessels in Charlestown harbor, the British warships *Tamar* and *Cherokee* fired on the patriot schooner *Defense*, thus precipitating the revolution in South Carolina.[135]

Up and down the eastern seaboard, the deeply held fears of collaboration between black pilots and British forces also came to fruition. Like Campbell, Governor Dunmore of Virginia and Governor Martin of North Carolina each established rival governments offshore. Relying heavily on African-American know-how, the British employed black seafarers in a number of capacities. As sailors, spies, messengers, marauders, and counterrevolutionaries, the blacks who crossed over to enemy lines during the summer and fall of 1775 would become active participants in the Revolutionary conflict—despite the machinations of patriot authorities. Athough it was designed to pacify black loyalism and placate the radical wing of the patriot party, in the end, Jeremiah's execution functioned more as a catalyst than a deterrent.

NOTES

1. Albert F. Young, afterword to *The American Revolution: Explorations in the History of American Radicalism*, ed. Alfred F. Young (De Kalb: Northern Illinois University Press, 1976), 274.

2. Ronald Hoffman, "The 'Disaffected' in the Revolutionary South," in *The American Revolution*, ed. Young, 274.

3. Notable exceptions include Robert M. Weir, Jerome J. Nadelhaft, and Robert Olwell.

4. Jerome J. Nadelhaft, *The Disorders of War: the Revolution in South Carolina* (Orono: University of Maine at Orono Press, 1981), ix.

5. Ibid.

6. Peter H. Wood, "'Liberty Is Sweet': African-American Freedom Struggles in the Years before White Independence," in *Beyond the American Revolution: Explorations in the History of American Radicalism*, ed. Alfred F. Young (De Kalb: Northern Illinois University Press, 1993), 152.

7. Peter H. Wood, "'Impatient of Oppression': Black Freedom Struggles on the Eve of White Independence," : 11.

8. Wood, "'Liberty Is Sweet,'" 152.

9. See Peter H. Wood, "'The Dream Deferred': Black Freedom Struggles on the Eve of White Independence," in *In Resistance: Studies in African, Caribbean, and Afro-American History*, ed. Gary Y. Okihiro (Amherst: University of Massachusetts Press, 1986), 166–87; "Impatient of Oppression," 10–16; "Liberty Is Sweet," 149–72. See also Sylvia R. Frey, *Water from the Rock: Black Resistance in a Revolutionary Age* (Princeton: Princeton University Press, 1991); Robert Olwell, *Masters, Slaves and Subjects: The Culture of Power in the South Carolina Low Country, 1740–1790* (Ithaca: Cornell University Press, 1998).

10. For pioneering works on the role of blacks in the Revolution, see Benjamin Quarles, *The Negro in the American Revolution* (Chapel Hill: University of North Carolina Press, 1961); Herbert Aptheker, *American Negro Slave Revolts* (New York: Columbia University Press, 1943); Sidney Kaplan and Emma Nogrady Kaplan, *The Black Presence in the Era of the American Revolution*, rev. ed. (Amherst: University of Massachusetts Press, 1989); Philip D. Morgan, *Slave Counterpoint: Black Culture in the Eighteenth-Century Chesapeake and Lowcountry* (Chapel Hill: University of North Carolina Press, 1998).

11. One book that stands out, however, is Ira Berlin, *Slaves Without Masters: The Free Negro in the Antebellum South* (New York: Pantheon, 1975).

12. A number of authors have mentioned the story of Thomas Jeremiah or analyzed some aspect of it. Among these are Peter H. Wood, Robert M. Weir, Robert Olwell, Sylvia Frey, Philip Morgan, Ray Raphael, Pauline Maier, David M. Zornow, and Peter Linebaugh and Marcus Rediker. All of these authors have drawn upon, and occasionally added to, a slim number of primary sources that shed light on the incident. I have benefited greatly from earlier assessments in developing this essay. For the sake of clarity, however, my citations will be to the primary sources themselves, rather than to modern authors who have also used them.

13. See Certificate of Freedom, August 4, 1748, Miscellaneous Records GG 354, South Carolina Archives. (I am grateful to Robert M. Weir for this reference.) See also Philip D. Morgan, "Thomas Jeremiah," in *American National Biography*, ed. John A. Garraty and Mark C. Carnes, 24 vols. (New York: Oxford University Press, 1999), 12:1.

14. Lord William Campbell to Secretary of State William Legge, second earl of Dartmouth, August 31, 1775, British Public Record Office Transcripts, vol. 35, 184–215, South Carolina Archives (hereafter BPROT), 35:202. With the Great Fire of 1740 fresh in their minds, eighteenth-century Charlestonians venerated firefighters as guardians of the public weal and of private property. After 1740, Charlestown residents rapidly made important advances in protecting their city from conflagration. In fact, Charlestown was one of the first colonial cities to take steps toward a paid fire department. Although not as well paid for their services as whites, black firefighters, according to Carl Bridenbaugh, did receive compensation. "Negroes received but ten shillings for turning out"; for working one of the city's five fire

engines, the African-American firefighters in Charlestown received an additional ten shillings per hour. Unlike white firefighters, however, blacks who refused to answer the cry of fire and the call of duty received thirty-nine lashes with a whip. See Carl Bridenbaugh, *Cities in Revolt: Urban Life in America, 1743–1776* (New York: Alfred A. Knopf, 1955), 105.

15. Campbell to Dartmouth, August 31, 1775, BPROT, 35:196.

16. See *South Carolina Gazette*, July 20, 1768. Jeremiah also made the news in less favorable contexts as when he had a boating accident in the winter of 1755. See the *South Carolina Gazette*, February 13, 1755. I am grateful to Robert M. Weir for these references. See also Robert M. Weir, *Colonial South Carolina: A History* (Columbia: University of South Carolina Press, 1983), 200–201.

17. See Dr. George Milligen to Lord Dartmouth, September 15, 1775, *Documents of the American Revolution, 1770–1783* (hereafter *DAR*), ed. K. G. Davies, 21 vols. (Shannon: Irish University Press, 1972–), 11:110; Morgan, "Thomas Jeremiah."

18. See Campbell to Dartmouth, August 31, 1775, BPROT, 35:196. Laurens wrote to his son John, who was in London, that "the fellow had Money & many friends among people of his own Color, Some among the White"; see Henry Laurens to John Laurens, August 20, 1775, *The Papers of Henry Laurens* (hereafter *(PHL)*, ed. Philip M. Hamer, George C. Rogers Jr., David R. Chesnutt, et al., 15 vols. to date (Columbia: University of South Carolina Press, 1968–), 10:320. According to John Drayton, "the charge on which he was executed, was a conspiracy to excite an insurrection of the slaves, and to set fire to Charlestown. It was also said the principal charge was, that Jerry said 'If the British ships come here, he would pilot them over the Charlestown Bar.' Jerry was a Pilot"; see John Drayton, *Memoirs of the American Revolution: from its commencement to the year 1776, inclusive; as relating to the State of South-Carolina: and occasionally refering to the States of North-Carolina and Georgia*, 2 vols. (Charleston, 1821), 2:24.

19. Miscellaneous Records, book RR, 239, August 17, 1771, and book oo, 215, 264, 624, South Carolina Department of Archives and History, Columbia; Morgan, "Thomas Jeremiah."

20. Wood, "The Dream Deferred," 172; Frey, *Water from the Rock*, 56.

21. Conditions for overt confrontation between whites and blacks had been building for generations, occasionally erupting into open violence, as in the Stono Rebellion of 1739. Heightened social and political tensions during the decade that followed the Stamp Act controversy of 1765 increased the prospects for further conflagration by the spring of 1775.

22. Wood, "Changing Population," 38. In 1775, Dr. George Milligen-Johnston, then surgeon to His Majesty's forces, arrived at a similar number when he surmised that "the number of white inhabitants had increased to 70,000" and that "the number of negroes had like wise increased to 100,000"; see "Additions [of 1775]" to his pamphlet *A Short Description of the Province of South Carolina* (London, 1770), reproduced in *Colonial South Carolina: Two Contemporary Descriptions by Governor James Glen and Doctor George Milligen-Johnston*, ed. Chapman J. Milling (Columbia: University of South Carolina Press, 1951), 109. For an alternative estimate,

see Peter A. Coclanis, *The Shadow of a Dream: Economic Life and Death in the South Carolina Low Country, 1670–1920* (New York: Oxford University Press, 1989), 63–68. According to Coclanis, the total population of South Carolina in 1770 was 124,244, with 49,066 whites and 75,178 blacks, so African-Americans comprised 60.51% of the total population.

23. Olwell, *Masters, Slaves and Subjects,* 32.

24. The statistics for St. John's Berkeley Parish are from David Morgan Knepper, "The Political Structure of Colonial South Carolina, 1743–1776" (Ph.D. diss., University of Virginia, 1971), 36, cited in Robert Olwell, "'Domestic Enemies': Slavery and Political Independence in South Carolina, May 1775–March 1776," *Journal of Southern History* 55, no. 1 (1989): 22.

25. Philip D. Morgan, "Black Life in Eighteenth-Century Charleston," *Perspectives in American History,* n.s., 1 (1984): 188.

26. Frey, *Water from the Rock,* 56.

27. See *South Carolina Gazette,* May 12, 1775.

28. The first session took place January 11–17, 1775. The opening of the second session took place on Thursday, June 1, 1775. See a letter from the General Committee, Charlestown, to delegates for South Carolina at Philadelphia, May 8, 1775, *PHL,* 10:114nn. 2, 4; John R. Alden, ed., "John Stuart Accuses William Bull," *William and Mary Quarterly,* 3d ser., 2 (July 1945): 318.

29. Although somewhat dated, the best description of the royal government is still Edward McCrady, *The History of South Carolina under the Royal Government 1719–1776* (New York: Russell and Russell, 1899).

30. The Provincial Congress was the patriot legislative body, the General Committee was the patriot council of state, the Council of Safety was the patriot executive body, and the Secret Committee was a radical wing of the Council of Safety, composed of five members.

31. See Henry Laurens to John Laurens, May 15, 1775, *PHL,* 10:118–19.

32. Captain Innes, a Scotsman, arrived in Charlestown on April 19, 1775. He would serve Governor Campbell as a personal secretary and send home secret reports on political developments to Lord Dartmouth. See Innes to Dartmouth, June 10, 1775, in B. D. Bargar, "Charles Town Loyalism in 1775: The Secret Reports of Alexander Innes," *South Carolina Historical Magazine* 63 (1962): 133.

33. The Athanasian Creed, named for the fourth-century Alexandrian bishop St. Athanasius, affirms Christian beliefs in the Trinity and the Incarnation. Laurens's objection arose from the fact that the creed is prefaced and concluded with the assertion that salvation is impossible without strict adherence to these doctrines. Adopted in 1662 by the Church of England, the creed was printed immediately before the litany in the Book of Common Prayer. See Henry Laurens to John Laurens, June 8, 1775, *PHL,* 10:172–79, 323n. 7; *Wells's Register together with an Almanack for the Year of Our Lord 1775 by George Andrews, esq.,* 12th ed. (Charleston, 1775): 89–94; *South Carolina Historical Magazine* 34 (1933): 198.

34. Clearly the patriot leader knew his history. His allusion was to an incident

that occurred during the Spanish occupation of the Low Countries in the 1580s. To ward off an impending Habsburg attack, the Dutch sank vessels in the Scheldt River and ruined the thriving port of Antwerp. The city's trade suffered for years. The Antwerp harbor (unbeknownst to Laurens) would not reopen until 1792, when France cleared the Scheldt River. See Henry Laurens to John Laurens, May 30, 1775, *PHL*, 10:158–60, 163, 165. See also E. H. Kossmann, *The Low Countries, 1780–1940* (Oxford: Clarendon Press, 1978), 14–15, 21.

35. The *Maria Wilhelmina* arrived April 4 from New York. She had begun loading for Gosport by April 18, was cleared for sailing by June 2, but remained "windbound" for several weeks. The vessel finally sailed after July 28. See *South Carolina General Gazette*, April 7, 18, June 2, 9, 16, 30, July 28, 1775; Arthur Middleton to William Henry Drayton, Council of Safety, August 5, 1775, in "Correspondence of Arthur Middleton," *South Carolina Historical and Genealogical Magazine*, no. 27 (July 1926): 124–25.

36. The man-of-war *Tamar*, captained by Edward Thornbrough, operated on the Carolina station from May 5, 1772, until March 30, 1776, when the vessel sailed for Halifax. See Henry Laurens to John Laurens, June 8, 1775, *PHL*, 10:165; *South Carolina Historical Magazine* 71 (1970): 169.

37. The debate over the blockade would continue throughout the summer and into the fall. On July 30, for example, Laurens wrote to his son, "Yesterday we concluded upon, no plan, to do what I esteem in our circumstances worse than nothing, to 'Fortify Charlestown or to put it in some posture of defense,' this I say will be worse than doing nothing, for diverse reasons which are obvious & for one which is invincible but I am not at liberty to divulge it—the Council of Safety have been constantly persecuted into a Consent, by a few persons who have been constantly pushing for ruinous measures which they call vigorous—a little time will Shew their error, but the Consequences may be fatal to Charlestown" (*PHL*, 10:256). As we shall see, radicals in the party would ultimately have their way.

38. Wood, "The Dream Deferred," 175–76.

39. Innes to Dartmouth, June 10, 1775, in Bargar, "Charles Town Loyalism," 133.

40. Josiah Smith Jr. to James Poyas, May 18, 1775, and Smith to George Appleby, June 16, 1775, in Josiah Smith Letter Book, Southern Historical Collection, University of North Carolina; Jeffrey J. Crow, "Slave Rebelliousness and Social Conflict in North Carolina, 1775 to 1802," *William and Mary Quarterly*, 3d ser., 37 (January 1980): 84–85n; Wood, "The Dream Deferred," 175–76; Olwell, *Masters, Slaves and Subjects*, 230.

41. Drayton, *Memoirs*, 2:179–80; Olwell, *Masters, Slaves and Subjects*, 230.

42. Josiah Smith to George Appleby, June 16, 1775, in Josiah Smith Letter Book, Southern Historical Collection, University of North Carolina; Milligen to Dartmouth, 110.

43. *South Carolina Gazette and Country Journal*, June 13, 1775; Alden, "John Stuart," 318–19; Peter Wood, "'Taking Care of Business' in Revolutionary South Carolina: Republicanism and the Slave Society," in *The Southern Experience in the*

American Revolution, ed. Jeffrey J. Crow and Larry E. Tise (Chapel Hill: University of North Carolina Press, 1978), 282.

44. Henry Laurens to John Laurens, May 15, 1775, *PHL*, 10:119.

45. By his own account, Campbell was agitated and embarrassed by the reception: "Three Councillors could barely be found to admit me into my office: Mr. Gordon, the chief justice; Mr. Irving, the receiver general; and Mr. Gregory one of the Judges" (Campbell to Dartmouth, July 2, 1775, *DAR*, 11:32).

46. Henry Laurens to John Laurens, June 18, 1775, *PHL*, 10:183–84.

47. Ibid.; George C. Rogers, *Charleston in the Age of the Pinckneys* (Columbia: University of South Carolina Press, 1980), xiii.

48. This tiny retinue of loyalists, along with secretary Alexander Innes and Dr. George Milligen, were virtually the governor's only allies in South Carolina. As we shall see, Gordon, Gregory, Fewtrell, and Coslett would later report to Campbell during his efforts to pardon Thomas Jeremiah. See Drayton, *Memoirs*, 1:257–58; Campbell to Dartmouth, July 2, 1775, *DAR*, 11:32.

49. "I have not seen or heard from the lieut.-governor: ever since my arrival he has remained at his country house [Ashley Hall] about 12 miles from town without favoring me with the smallest attention or giving the least assistance to government. I should have been extremely sorry had I been conscious to myself of personally deserving from Mr. Bull so pointed and contemptuous a neglect, but in the present case I have only to lament that a gentleman who for so many years has filled an important station with credit to himself and advantage to his country should treat the commission of his Sovereign with such studied disrespect.... Such my lord is the present distracted state of this province, such the very difficult and embarrassed state in which I find myself, abandoned by the lieut-governor, without a Council, without support of any kind" (Campbell to Dartmouth, July 2, 1775, *DAR*, 11:34).

50. Drayton, *Memoirs*, 1:257.

51. Campbell to Dartmouth, August 31, 1775, BPROT, 35:192–93.

52. Loyalist Claims Memorial, Public Record Office (London), Audit Office, class 12, vol. 51, fol. 289, cited in Wood, "Liberty Is Sweet," 162.

53. Milligen to Dartmouth, 110; see Campbell to Dartmouth, August 31, 1775, BPROT, 35:191; Transcripts of the Manuscript Books and Papers of the Commission of Enquiry into Losses and Services of the American Loyalists ... made for the New York Public Library (1900), microfilm, 55:331–43, cited in *PHL*, 10:324n. 8.

54. Milligen to Dartmouth, 110. Such reports were prevalent in other colonies. Toward the end of the summer, for example, a patriot preacher in Maryland would write, "The governor of Virginia, the captains of the men of war, and mariners have been tampering with our Negroes; and have nightly meetings with them; all for the glorious purpose of enticing them to cut their masters' throats while they are asleep. Gracious God! that men noble by birth and fortune should descend to such ignoble base servility"; see "Extracts of a Letter from a Clergyman in Maryland to his Friend in England," August 2, 1775, in *American Archives*, ed. Peter Force, 4th ser. (Washington, D.C., 1837–46), 3:10, cited in Hoffman, "Disaffected," 281. See also Wood, "Taking Care of Business," 279.

55. Milligen to Dartmouth, 110. According to an official report made by the British Administration in 1776, "The newspapers were full of Publications calculated to excite the fears of the People—Massacres and Instigated Insurrections were in the mouth of every Child"; see Alden, "John Stuart," 318–19.

56. *South Carolina Gazette,* May 29, 1775, cited in Olwell, *Masters, Slaves and Subjects,* 229; Wood, "Liberty Is Sweet," 166.

57. Drayton, *Memoirs,* 2:300.

58. Drayton, *Memoirs,* 2:301. According to Laurens, Martin was an "under Wharfinger" of "Some Credit in Town" (Henry Laurens to John Laurens, June 8, 1775, *PHL,* 10:167).

59. Drayton, *Memoirs,* 2:301.

60. Henry Laurens to John Laurens, June 8, 1775, *PHL,* 10:168.

61. Innes to Dartmouth, June 10, 1775, in Bargar, "Charles Town Loyalism," 133.

62. Richard Walsh, *Charleston's Sons of Liberty: A Study of the Artisans, 1763–1789* (Columbia: University of South Carolina Press, 1959), 71.

63. On June 13 Martin's apology appeared in the *South Carolina Country Journal,* and on that same day Captain John Lasley set sail for Bristol in the *Liberty* with James Dealy on board. See Henry Laurens to John Laurens, June 8, 1775, *PHL,* 10:168n. 11.

64. Joseph Manigault to Gabriel Manigault, June 4, 1775, Manigault Family Papers, South Caroliniana Library, University of South Carolina, cited in Olwell, *Masters, Slaves and Subjects,* 230.

65. The merchant planter remarked that the "poor creatures" were "sensibly effected and with many thanks promised to follow my advice and to accept the offer of my protection" (Henry Laurens to James Laurens, June 7, 1775, *PHL,* 10:162–63).

66. Campbell to Dartmouth, August 31, 1775, *DAR,* 11:195.

67. Milligen to Dartmouth, 110.

68. Campbell to Dartmouth, August 31, 1775, BPROT, 35:215.

69. Ibid., 216.

70. Henry Laurens to John Laurens, June 18, 1775, *PHL,* 10:185.

71. Milligen to Dartmouth, 111.

72. Henry Laurens to John Laurens, June 23, 1775, *PHL,* 10:191–92.

73. *Extracts from the Journals of the Provincial Congresses of South Carolina, 1775–1776,* ed. William Edwin Hemphill and Wylma Anne Wates (Columbia: University of South Carolina Press, 1960), 66.

74. Henry Laurens to John Laurens, June 23, 1775, *PHL,* 10:191.

75. Ibid.

76. Campbell to Dartmouth, August 31, 1775, BPROT, 35:197.

77. Milligen to Dartmouth, 110. The other black who remained under suspicion must have been Jemmy, who was later sentenced to death along with Jeremiah but was pardoned on Thursday, August 17, the day before his scheduled execution.

78. Henry Laurens to John Laurens, June 23, 1775, *PHL,* 10:191–92.

79. "The Papers of Gabriel Manigault," *South Carolina Historical Magazine* 64 (January 1963): 2, cited in Wood, "Taking Care of Business," 283.

80. Letter from Woodmanstone, England, September 5, 1775, Manigault Family Papers, cited in Wood, "Taking Care of Business," 283.

81. Henry Laurens to John Laurens, August 20, 1775, *PHL*, 10:321.

82. At two o'clock in the afternoon on Saturday, August 12—the day after the sentence of Jeremiah was handed down—George Walker, the Tory "gunner of Ft. Johnson" was seized for making an "insolent speech against the patriot cause." Like Jeremiah, Walker may have been targeted for his strategic occupation. See "Correspondence of Arthur Middleton," *South Carolina Historical and Genealogical Magazine* 27 (July 1926): 126, 129; Milligen to Dartmouth, 113.

83. Campbell to Dartmouth, August 31, 1775, BPROT, 35:198–99.

84. Henry Laurens to John Laurens, August 20, 1775, *PHL*, 10:331.

85. Ibid., 331–34.

86. This could have been Miles Brewton, a wealthy Charleston resident and member of the Commons House, or it may have even been Henry Laurens. See Campbell to Dartmouth, August 31, 1775, BPROT, 35:199.

87. Ibid.

88. Henry Laurens to John Laurens, August 20, 1775, *PHL*, 10:334.

89. Ibid., 330. The Brewton House, a Georgian mansion built between 1765 and 1769, is located at 27 King Street. Brewton allowed Campbell to stay there for several months while the governor's mansion at 34 Meeting Street was being prepared. See M. Victor Alper, *America's Heritage Trail: South Carolina, North Carolina, Virginia: A Tour Guide to Historical Sites of the Colonial and Revolutionary War Period* (New York: Macmillan, 1976), 25, 27.

90. Robert Cooper, rector of St. Michael's, may have also tried to intervene on Jeremiah's behalf. According to Laurens, "both Clergymen" visited him frequently and "became solicitous for him." The Anglican Laurens was probably angered by the fact that two priests from his own church provided a black man with counsel and assistance. He wrote to his son, "Your uncle knows that that Sort of Duty had been generally left to the Dissenting Ministers when White Men were under Sentence of Death" (Henry Laurens to John Laurens, August 20, 1775, *PHL*, 10:320).

91. Campbell to Dartmouth, August 31, 1775, BPROT, 35:200.

92. Ibid., 201.

93. Ibid., 198–99. Milligen claimed that a Daniel Cannon "about the end of June" summoned him and ordered him to subscribe to the Patriot Association. When Milligen refused, Cannon told the surgeon he could "expect to be treated agreeable to the rules of sound policy" (Milligen to Dartmouth, 111).

94. Campbell to Dartmouth, August 31, 1775, BPROT, 35:199.

95. Ibid., 208.

96. Ibid., 209–10.

97. Milligen to Dartmouth, 110.

98. Campbell to Dartmouth, August 31, 1775, BPROT, 35:211.

99. Ibid., 211–12.

100. Ibid.

101. Ibid., 212–13.

102. Ibid., 213.

103. This may have been a mistake. Fewtrell probably meant the Council of Safety (the executive) and not "the Legislature of the Province," which was actually the Provincial Congress.

104. Fewtrell submitted his report in writing to Lord Campbell on Saturday, August 19, the day after Jerry's execution. See Campbell to Dartmouth, August 31, 1775, BPROT, 35:214.

105. Ibid., 199–200.

106. Henry Laurens to John Laurens, August 20, 1775, *PHL*, 10:320.

107. According to a letter written by Alexander Innes, which Laurens sent to his son, Smith applied for a pardon for Jemmy that day at noon, but Campbell did not sign it until 6 P.M. See ibid., 330; Campbell to Dartmouth, August 31, 1775, BPROT, 35:201.

108. Ibid., 201–2. See also Henry Laurens to John Laurens, August 20, 1775, *PHL*, 10:321.

109. Campbell to Dartmouth, August 31, 1775, BPROT, 35:201.

110. This letter was later given to Laurens, who referred to it as a "very extraordinary Letter from the 'Representative of Majesty.' Attempting to prove a Negative—charging two Justices & three Freeholders with the shedding of Innocent blood—because after a fair & patient hearing, they were unanimously of opinion that Jerry was Guilty" (Henry Laurens to John Laurens, August 20, 1775, *PHL*, 10:334).

111. This line in particular aggravated Laurens a great deal, and he would later mockingly refer to Campbell by that epithet.

112. Henry Laurens to John Laurens, August 20, 1775, *PHL*, 10:328.

113. Campbell to Dartmouth, Charlestown, August 31, 1775, 201; Henry Laurens to John Laurens, August 20, 1775, *PHL*, 10:329.

114. Ibid., 321.

115. Ibid., 321, 330.

116. Ibid., 329.

117. Laurens's response to Innes's letter was sent out at 7:30 A.M. Considering that Innes's initial letter was also written that day, the secretary must have penned it in the wee hours.

118. Henry Laurens to John Laurens, August 20, 1775, *PHL*, 10:330–31.

119. Ibid., 331.

120. Ibid., 332.

121. Milligen to Dartmouth, 111; Campbell to Dartmouth, August 31, 1775, BPROT, 35:196. As Peter Wood notes, "Among white residents of Charleston, neither his accusers nor his defenders could fully comprehend the meaning of his life and death. But fellow blacks, both enslaved and free, must have sensed his real and symbolic importance in a powerful way" ("Taking Care of Business," 286–87).

122. Campbell to Dartmouth, August 31, 1775, BPROT, 35:202.

123. Milligen to Dartmouth, 111.

124. Henry Laurens to John Laurens, August 20, 1775, *PHL*, 10:333–34. No spe-

cific time is given, but the letter was sent by Laurens on the afternoon of the eighteenth from the Charlestown district of Ansonburgh.

125. Ibid., 334.

126. Drayton, *Memoirs*, 2:20–21.

127. Campbell to Dartmouth, August 19, 1775, *The Manuscripts of the Earl of Dartmouth*, comp. Royal Commission on Historical Manuscripts, 3 vols. (London: Eyre and Spottiswoode for HMSO, 1887–96), 2:353–55.

128. See the December 16, 1775, edition of the *Public Advertiser* (London), cited in *PHL*, 10:450n. 2. It is impossible to know what black opinion was regarding the matter, but news traveled quickly through the black community. In September of 1775, for example, two low-country whites remarked that the "Negroes have a wonderful art of communicating Intelligence among themselves." Apparently African-American communication networks could "run [news] several hundreds of miles in a week or a fortnight." The case of Thomas Jeremiah may have been an important topic of discussion for African-Americans up and down the coast. See entry of September 24, 1775, in John Adams, *Diary and Autobiography*, ed. L. H. Butterfield, 4 vols. (Cambridge: Harvard University Press, Belknap Press, 1961), 2:182–83.

129. John Laurens to Henry Laurens, October 4, 1775, *PHL*, 10:450.

130. Thomas Hutchinson, *The Diary and Letters of His Excellency Thomas Hutchinson . . .*, ed. Peter Orlando Hutchinson, 2 vols. (Boston: Houghton, Mifflin, 1884–86), 1:543.

131. Henry Laurens to John Laurens, August 20, 1775, *PHL*, 10:321–22.

132. According to John, Englishmen had the wrong opinion about the Jeremiah trial: "The affair of the negro man Jerry has been quite differently represented here. I shall set it in a proper light whenever it occurs here in conversation, for according to the prevailing story the character of our countrymen for justice and humanity would suffer very much" (John Laurens to Henry Laurens, October 4, 1775, *PHL*, 10:450).

133. Campbell to Dartmouth, August 31, 1775, BPROT, 35:191. Returning to England in the fall of 1775 on the *Eagle*, Milligen may have also spread the story.

134. For information on Scipio Handley, see Memorial of Scipio Handley, Transcripts of the Manuscript Books and Papers of the Commission of Enquiry into Losses and Services of the American Loyalists . . . made for the New York Public Library (1900), microfilm, 53:166–67; Public Record Office (London), Audit Office, class 13, vol. 119, fol. 431. For information on a slave named Shadwell who escaped to the *Tamar*, see a letter from the Council of Safety to Captain Edward Thornbrough, October 28, 1775, *PHL*, 10:504–5.

135. Henry Laurens to William Manning, November 14, 1775, *PHL*, 10:509n. 2.

Part IV

George Washington
and Southern Indians

Chapter 10

GEORGE WASHINGTON, DRAGGING CANOE, AND SOUTHEASTERN INDIAN RESISTANCE

PETER H. WOOD

In the spring of 1865, with the war over and the martyred president laid to rest, James Russell Lowell composed his lengthy "Commemoration Ode." It was drafted for the commencement ceremonies at Harvard College, and it became remembered for its tribute to Abraham Lincoln.[1] The poet mused that Nature, in creating Lincoln, had set aside "her Old-World moulds . . . / And choosing sweet clay from the breast / Of the unexhausted West," had produced a man whom Lowell called, in a famous line, the "New birth of our soil, the first American." In terms that the graduating seniors would readily have understood, their mentor reminded them of Lincoln:

Here was a type of the true elder race,
And one of Plutarch's men talked with us face to face.

If Lincoln had any rival for the poet's honor of "the first American," it would undoubtedly be either Thomas Jefferson, who died on the fiftieth anniversary of his Declaration of Independence, or George Washington, the man we honor through this publication, who died more than two hundred years ago in December 1799. They too can be considered "Plutarch's men"; each would have been worthy of treatment by the founder of the western biographical tradition.

Plutarch was the Greek-born historian who lived and wrote in the Roman Empire of Trajan and Hadrian at the beginning of the second century A.D. He not only compiled engaging profiles of ancient leaders from previous centuries, but he also pioneered in the art of comparative history. He chose to pair his profiles in a series of "parallel lives," matching a famous

Greek, such as Alexander, with an important Roman, such as Julius Caesar. He composed nearly two dozen pairs, and the device allowed him to examine similar characters, comparable professions, or analogous situations. Some of the juxtapositions were less provocative and convincing than others; Nicias and Crassus, for example, had little in common "except that both men were rich and both suffered a great military defeat at the end of their lives."[2] Nowadays the format of sketching parallel lives is rarely practiced, but it remains a potentially powerful and suggestive device for prompting us to scrutinize a period, a problem, or a personality from several perspectives. Such a comparison, whether obvious or surprising, can allow a reader to connect the familiar to the foreign, to compare the known to the less well known, and to reexamine the commonplace while exploring new territory. It can shed new light on the individuals being contrasted and on the different circumstances in which they lived.

With this in mind, I want to examine briefly the parallel lives of two eighteenth-century Americans. One is the best-known and most thoroughly documented individual of the era: the commander of the revolutionary Continental Army and the first president of the United States. Since few Americans have prompted more books and articles than the master of Mount Vernon, I will limit my observations about this familiar and fascinating figure, except to draw out a comparison with another person, the Cherokee leader known as Tsi'yu-gûnsi'ni, often called Dragging Canoe. While no significant individual from the Revolutionary era is so justifiably prominent as George Washington, no one remains more totally and unjustifiably obscure than Dragging Canoe.

It would be hard to exaggerate this contrast. George Washington, or at least a plausible and partial image of him, is always with us—in courthouses and legislatures, in banks and malls, in schools and libraries. We invoke him in our speeches and sermons; we carry him around in our wallets and pocketbooks. On the other hand, Dragging Canoe, who was also a bold soldier and respected leader at the center of a revolutionary struggle, remains utterly unknown to most Americans. The reasons for this are hardly obscure. Dragging Canoe and his followers failed in their Herculean effort where Washington and his supporters succeeded, and historical prominence is one of the spoils of victory. The Cherokee people, whether militant or accommodationist, were battered by the onslaught of white soldiers, speculators, and settlers in the late eighteenth century, while the Virginia planter gentry, epitomized and often led by George Washington, managed to extract themselves from a tight and untenable situation in the 1770s and emerge as a dominant and controlling force in American society by the 1790s.³ Virginia gentlemen nearly monopolized the presidency of the new United States for several generations, and it was President Andrew Jackson, another self-made southern planter, general, slaveholder, and Indian fighter, who saw to the forced "removal" of most of the Cherokee people from their southern homeland in the 1830s.

Clearly, these men lived in different and often opposing worlds, and yet their worlds overlapped considerably, even if the two individuals never met face to face. For if it is true that only "six degrees of separation" link all of us in present times, Americans two centuries ago were often joined by only two or three degrees of separation. Each man knew someone, who knew someone, who knew the other well. To cite one example, the Quaker naturalist William Bartram from Pennsylvania, known among southeastern Indians as "Puc Puggy" or "the Flower Gatherer," was hiking through the Nantahala Gorge toward Cherokee country in the summer of 1775 when he encountered "a company of Indians, all well mounted on horse back," heading in the opposite direction toward Charleston. At their head was the small, distinguished figure of Dragging Canoe's father, the famous Cherokee chief Attakullakulla, also called the Little Carpenter, on his way to meet with his British friend John Stuart,⁴ the Indian Superintendent for the region.⁵ Bartram exchanged greetings with the respected elder statesman, and later, after he returned to his garden on the Schuylkill River outside Philadelphia, he wrote about the meeting in recounting his journey. One of the members of the Constitutional Convention who visited Bartram's garden in the summer of 1787 was the knowledgeable, and critical, husbandman from Mount Vernon, who wrote in his diary for June 10, "Rid to see the Botanical gardens of Mr. Bartram which tho' stored with . . . curious plants, trees and shrubs . . . , many of which are exotic, was not laid out with much taste."⁶ In 1791 President Washington subscribed to buy a copy of Bartram's published *Travels*, although, in accordance with his usual policy, he declined to have the volume dedicated to him.⁷

If Dragging Canoe appears at all in history books, it is usually in reference to a famous comment predicting a "dark and bloody" ground, which he made during negotiations at Sycamore Shoals on the Watauga River in March 1775, several months before William Bartram encountered his father. Half a dozen land speculators from North Carolina, associated in a private company and led by Judge Richard Henderson, were attempting to purchase control of a huge tract of Cherokee land by inducing older chiefs, such as Attakullakulla and Oconostota, to sign it over illegally in exchange for six wagonloads of badly needed goods, reputedly valued at £10,000. At such meetings, young warriors usually deferred to their elders and joined the consensus that traditionally prevailed among Indian negotiators, but Dragging Canoe broke with this expected pattern and spoke out in defiance of his own father. He was painfully aware that the Proclamation of 1763 forbidding colonial settlement west of the Appalachian Divide had been violated repeatedly, and he knew that subsequent compromises reached in the treaties of Fort Stanwix and Hard Labor in 1768 and of Lochaber in 1770 had been ignored. Therefore he refused to see his kinsmen give up another 27,000 square miles of Cherokee land, covering most of the modern state of Kentucky, without putting up a serious fight.

Unable to prevent the transaction, Dragging Canoe broke with those negotiating the deal, chastising elders and speculators alike in an impassioned speech that represented his own Declaration of Independence:

> We had hoped that the white men would not be willing to travel beyond the mountains.... Now that hope is gone. They have passed the mountains, and have settled upon Cherokee land. They wish to have that usurpation sanctioned by treaty. When that is gained, the same encroaching spirit will lead them upon other land of the Cherokees. New cessions will be asked. Finally the whole country, which the Cherokees and their fathers have so long occupied, will be demanded, and the remnant of Ani-Yunwiya, "The Real People," once so great and formidable, will be compelled to seek refuge in some distant wilderness. There they will be permitted to stay only a short while, until they again behold the advancing banners of the same greedy host. Not being able to point out any further retreat for the miserable Cherokees, the extinction of the whole race will be proclaimed. Should we not therefore run all risks, and incur all consequences, rather than submit to further laceration of our country? Such treaties may be alright for people who are too old to hunt or fight. As for me, I have my young warriors about me. *A-waninski*, I have spoken.[8]

The following day he remained present as the land purchase was signed. "You have bought a fair land, but there is a dark cloud hanging over it," Dragging Canoe told Henderson. "You will find its settlement dark and bloody."[9]

He would never take part in another parley with white intruders. Instead, he led his young warriors in a brief war against the Virginians that had disastrous repercussions. Undaunted, in March 1777 he withdrew southwestward with some five hundred followers to Chickamauga Creek on the Tennessee River near modern-day Chattanooga.[10] They established a community of five towns not far from where the states of Georgia, Alabama, and Tennessee now converge, and he invited members of other beleaguered Indian nations to come to Chickamauga from all directions to join in a resistance movement that lasted for two decades. According to an excellent dissertation written more than three decades ago at Mississippi State University, Dragging Canoe showed "unwavering determination to fight and resist the invasion, takeover, and occupation of traditional Cherokee hunting grounds." The author, James Pate, observed that by the time of the war chief's death on March 1, 1792,

> He had never agreed to the surrender of any Cherokee lands nor had the Cherokee who followed him, that were known as the Chickamauga. His thin red line on the Tennessee had gained many adherents since the early days along Chickamauga Creek. He died with his forces intact and ready to continue his struggle against the ever increasing "Virginians." His tactics and strategy had paid rich dividends and many of the leaders in the new government in Philadelphia had heard of the Chickamauga of the Five Lower Towns.[11]

If leaders such as Washington and his secretary of war Henry Knox "had heard of the Chickamauga," why is it that we have not? Why do textbooks, when discussing frontier affairs and Indian relations during the first years of the republic, invariably concentrate on the Old Northwest rather than the Old Southwest? They never fail to mention the defeats suffered by General Josiah Harmar in 1790 and General Arthur St. Clair in 1791, or the successful retaliation of General Anthony Wayne's troops at the Battle of Fallen Timbers three years later, leading to the Treaty of Greenville in 1795. One excellent current textbook, after recounting Indian resistance north of the Ohio, says of the southern region only: "Old internal frictions grew nastier. . . . Murder and clan revenge plagued the tribes, and depression and suicide became more common. The use of alcohol, which had been a scourge on Indian societies for two centuries, increased. Indian males spent more time in their villages and less on the hunt, and by most accounts they drank more and grew violent."[12] While this depressing thumbnail sketch contains much that is valid, it makes no mention of the fact that serious and consistent efforts at armed resistance were under way for an entire generation, led by Dragging Canoe and residents of the five lower towns, who considered themselves to be the Ani-Yunwiya, the Real People, who kept alive the spirit of the Cherokee ancestors.

In part, the persistent imbalance in the assessment of Native American resistance above and below the Ohio represents a broader imbalance regarding northern and southern history that is all too familiar to southerners. To oversimplify slightly, the older more numerous universities in the northeast, with bigger budgets and richer archives, have long been staffed by learned but provincial historians who have encouraged generations of their students to concentrate on what is close and familiar, ignoring the early South generally, and particularly the broad region that Claudio Saunt at the University of Georgia, in an excellent recent book on the Creek Indians, calls the Deep South Interior.[13] One can look in vain for references to Dragging Canoe and the Chickamauga in most books on the so-called opening of the trans-Appalachian West,[14] at least until the appearance in 1992 of *A Spirited Resistance,* Gregory Dowd's important volume subtitled "The North American Indian Struggle for Unity, 1745–1815."[15] Besides the Pate dissertation just mentioned, historians have had little to draw upon in expanding this picture apart from an intriguing 1938 volume on the Cherokee by John P. Brown that featured Dragging Canoe in a chapter called "The Savage Napoleon."[16] Fortunately we have an excellent recent article about Dragging Canoe by historian Jon Parmenter in a volume entitled *The Human Tradition in the American Revolution,* containing essays on diverse contemporary figures.[17]

As we all know—or used to know before the creation of Presidents' Day—George Washington was born on February 22, 1732, in Westmoreland County, Virginia. The date was actually February 11, but reforming the English calendar in 1752 by moving all dates ahead eleven days meant that in adulthood Washington observed February 22 as his birthday, and subsequent generations have followed suit.[18] If Washington's birth is uncertain by days, Dragging Canoe's is uncertain by years, in part because his son, known as Young Dragging Canoe, also appears in the record.[19] Both Brown and Pate, after examining conflicting evidence, suggest that he was in his early forties at the time of the Henderson Purchase in 1775 and that his father was then in his seventies. This would mean that Dragging Canoe was born not long after the Little Carpenter's return from a Cherokee diplomatic mission to London in 1730, and Pate goes so far as to suggest that the war chief of the Chickamauga was sixty when he died in March 1792.[20] If so, then these two principled southern leaders appear to have been born within a year—perhaps even within months or weeks—of one another.

Geographically they were somewhat farther apart, one growing up in the Virginia Tidewater and the other in the Overhill Cherokee village of Chotte, located beside the Little Tennessee River amid the Great Smoky Mountains on the western side of the Appalachian chain, near modern

Knoxville in what is now Monroe County, Tennessee.[21] But the lore surrounding their childhoods—even if taken figuratively rather than literally—suggests that both boys experienced and relished the appealing climate of the Upper South, thriving outdoors in the bountiful and hard-to-imagine countryside of the premodern era. Washington's adoring and fanciful biographer Parson Weems was probably not entirely off track to suggest that George at an early age was already good with a hatchet—perhaps too good.[22] And it is quite plausible that as a youth, before becoming a surveyor, George already had enough strength, and enough spare change, to toss a coin across a river. Similarly, Dragging Canoe, according to Parmenter, is said to have "earned his name as a young boy by literally dragging a canoe across a portage in order to accompany his father's war party against the Shawnees (who ironically would later become his closest allies)."[23]

Both men, like so many other persons in the eighteenth century, had contracted the dreaded smallpox virus in their early years. And both survived, carrying always the scars that were a common reminder of the disease, but also carrying the immunity that would protect them from later lethal outbreaks of the sickness. Washington was nineteen when he accompanied his elder half-brother, Lawrence, who was suffering from tuberculosis, on a sojourn to Barbados in September 1751. It was his only voyage outside North America, and it nearly proved fatal. In early November the brothers received a dinner invitation from a high-ranking British officer that they felt compelled to accept. "We went—" Washington wrote in his diary, "myself with some reluctance, as the smallpox was in his family." It was indeed, and after the predictable thirteen-day incubation period, George scrawled in his diary, "Was strongly attacked with the small Pox."[24] He lapsed into a sickly silence for nearly a month, taking up his pen again in mid-December.

According to biographers, Washington later "bore only several very light scars on his nose,"[25] but it is interesting to speculate about the history of the North Atlantic world during the second half of the eighteenth century if this young planter had died in 1751 instead of 1799. It is equally intriguing to consider the other side of the coin—what might have happened if he had never had this sobering brush with smallpox. A recent book by historian Elizabeth Fenn suggests convincingly that among the most significant and farsighted moves of his military career were two that showed his keen awareness of smallpox and its wartime implications. First, when he took command of the Continental Army at Cambridge in July 1775, he made an immediate decision to quarantine swiftly any soldiers who came down with smallpox, setting up a smallpox hospital at Fresh

Pond outside Cambridge and forbidding healthy soldiers from going fishing in the vicinity. Second, he later gave timely orders to inoculate the troops, first at Morristown and then during the grim winter respite at Valley Forge in the early months of 1778.[26]

Dragging Canoe's bout with smallpox had come much earlier in life, probably at the age of six or seven, when the chances of survival are considerably better than for small children under two or for older adults over fifty. His run-in with the fearful disease left large visible scars, and perhaps some psychological ones as well. According to Parmenter, "contemporary descriptions of his pock-scarred face suggest that he survived the devastating smallpox epidemics that ravaged the Cherokee in the late 1730s."[27] Smallpox did indeed have a crushing impact on Cherokee villages in those years.[28] "About the year 1738," James Adair recalled after spending decades among the southeastern Indians, "the Cheeroke received a most depopulating shock, by the small pox . . . ; it was conveyed into Charlestown by the Guinea-men, and soon after among them by the infected goods." Finding that their traditional remedies could not stem the contagion, Cherokee medicine men, according to Adair, "broke their old consecrated physic-pots" in utter frustration, "imagining they had lost their divine power by being polluted; and shared the common fate of their country." Even for those adults who survived, the shame of disfigurement was so great that many committed suicide. It is correct to say that the Cherokee population was literally decimated (that is, at least one person died of every ten), and in certain towns Adair may have been correct to report that the epidemic "reduced them almost one half, in about a year's time."[29]

Surviving this scourge gave Dragging Canoe the immunity to pass safely through the next deadly recurrence of smallpox, when it raced through Cherokee villages once again during the Cherokee-English War of 1759–60.[30] The invading commander, South Carolina governor William Henry Lyttelton, found that smallpox had "raged for some Time before our Arrival in the *Indian* Town and killed about everyone it attacked."[31] A second invasion under Archibald Montgomery burned a series of Cherokee villages, beginning with the prominent town of Keowee. "The surprise was complete; and the Indians so terrified that their resistance was trifling," boasted one officer. "Doubtless numbers perished in the flames and the smallpox was in their towns and we came upon them like lightning,"[32] destroying crops and food supplies as well as homes and people. Seeing his people defenseless, weakened by yet another horrifying smallpox epidemic, must have left an indelible impression on the young warrior. Dragging Canoe, fully as much as Washington, understood the devastating effects of the disease by the time he emerged as a military leader after 1775.

By the mid-1770s both men already had substantial military experience leading men in combat, and both, now in their early forties, had watched stoically as older, more cautious leaders appeared to compromise basic principles and the well-being of their society in order to maintain a tenuous peace. As tensions mounted and the stakes rose higher, towns and even families were divided, often along generational lines, as Dragging Canoe discovered firsthand at Sycamore Shoals in 1775. That same year, Washington witnessed many similar splits, such as the one between Edmund Randolph, age twenty-two, and his father, the prominent Williamsburg lawyer John Randolph, who left Virginia with his wife and daughters for England. Young Edmund chose to stay put, joining Washington as an aide-de-camp in 1775–76 and then serving as the youngest member of Virginia's state constitutional convention before becoming the state's first attorney general and then a Virginia delegate to the Continental Congress from 1779 to 1782. He served as the state's governor from 1786 to 1788, dealing directly with bitter Cherokee protests from the west, and he became a delegate to the Constitutional Convention in 1787, though he voted against the Constitution in the state's ratifying convention. Under Washington, he was the attorney general from 1789 to 1794 and the secretary of state from 1794 to 1795.

In the years following 1775 both Washington and Dragging Canoe demonstrated impressive leadership skills against formidable odds. The primary military task for each was to confront and engage enemy forces that were more numerous and better equipped and that, if pressed, could draw on seemingly endless reserves of men and supplies. At New York in the summer of 1776, Washington had only 19,000 men to confront more than 30,000 in the invading army, many of them Hessian mercenaries. His forces suffered defeat on Long Island in August and evacuated Manhattan in September, surrendering Fort Washington and abandoning Fort Lee in October. By December the American Army had retreated before General William Howe across New Jersey; thousands of men had been captured—including Charles Lee, Washington's second in command—and thousands more had deserted. As the remainder straggled across the Delaware River into Pennsylvania, one general suggested that it might be time to "bargain away the Bubble of Independency for British Liberty well secured."[33] Only Washington's surprising strike back across the Delaware on Christmas night restored morale and extended the struggle. It was a move that Dragging Canoe would have understood and respected.

During the second half of 1776 the Cherokees were also facing an invasion and retreating in the face of overwhelming odds. After armies from North and South Carolina and Georgia destroyed and pillaged scores of

Valley and Middle towns, a Virginia force of 2,200 men under Colonel William Christian set out to destroy the less accessible Overhill towns, now swamped with refugees and short of food and ammunition. Able to muster only 700 men, the Cherokees, like Washington's Continentals, were obliged to withdraw in October before superior forces. Crossing the French Broad River on October 15, Christian ignored the peace feelers of beleaguered and accommodating Cherokee chiefs; instead the Virginians ransacked undefended Overhill towns, destroying 50,000 bushels of corn and more than 10,000 bushels of potatoes, pilfering livestock, and forcing hundreds of refugees to take flight. Just as General Howe hoped to capture Washington, Colonel Christian hoped that the accommodationists, led by Oconostota, the Raven, and Attakullakulla, would surrender up Dragging Canoe as an assurance of peace. But they refused this demand, stating plausibly that they lacked sufficient influence, and Dragging Canoe was absent when Christian opened peace talks the following year.[34]

During those negotiations, held at Fort Patrick Henry on the Long Island of the Holston in July 1777, Old Tassel, perhaps speaking in part for Dragging Canoe, assessed the situation in an extended speech.

> It is surprising that when we enter into treaties with our fathers the white people, their whole cry is more land.... What did you do? You marched into our towns with a superior force. Your numbers far exceeded us, and we fled to the stronghold of our woods, there to secure our women and children. Our towns were left to your mercy. You killed a few scattered and defenseless individuals, spread fire wherever you pleased, and returned to your own habitations. . . .
>
> We wish, however, to be at peace with you, and to do as we would be done by. We do not quarrel with you for the killing of an occasional buffalo or deer on our lands, but your people go much farther. They hunt to gain a livelihood. They kill all our game; but it is [considered] very criminal in our young men if they chance to kill a cow or a hog for their sustenance when they happen to be in your lands.
>
> The Great Spirit has placed us in different situations. He has given you many advantages, but he has not created us to be your slaves. We are a separate people! He has stocked your lands with cows, ours with buffalo; yours with hogs, ours with bears; yours with sheep, ours with deer. He has given you the advantage that your animals are tame, while ours are wild and demand not only a larger space to range, but art to hunt and kill them. They are, nevertheless, as much our prop-

erty as other animals are yours, and ought not to be taken from us without our consent, or for something of equal value.[35]

Dragging Canoe, meanwhile, was not present to hear these words. Throughout the winter his forces had continued their raids, even striking within two miles of Fort Patrick Henry. But in March 1777 he led his strategic retreat to Chickamauga, denouncing the peace treaties that were being arranged with separate coastal states and mocking as "Virginians" rather than true Cherokees those Indians, including his own father, who continued to bargain with the white invaders rather than withdraw and fight. "Thus despite the great setbacks suffered in the late summer and fall of 1776," Pate concludes, Dragging Canoe demonstrated that a core of "the Overhill Cherokee were still a game adversary who possessed the ability to inflict losses.... He declared that his own followers were 'Ani-yuniwiya,' the Real People. But for the next seventeen years, everyone knew his followers to be the 'Chickamauga.'"[36]

Having bought time with their initial maneuvers, both Washington and Dragging Canoe now settled in to conduct long and arduous struggles. Because each found himself playing David to the enemy Goliath, both men were obliged to expand their warrior roles. They repeatedly displayed leadership skills beyond the battlefield in necessary ways, and it is worth looking briefly at some of the specific and parallel ways in which they did this. I count at least six.

First of all, in dire circumstances early in the struggle, they each demonstrated their mettle, as already suggested, by rallying beleaguered forces and proving their will to persist indefinitely. It was a skill that each would use repeatedly in subsequent years.

Secondly, faced with continuing fear and dissension among their own people, they each labored to overcome strong opposition and deep internal divisions. We know well of the efforts among his own jealous officers to second-guess Washington on the battlefield, and we recall the secret cabals in Congress to have him replaced as commander-in-chief. His pen was required to be at least as mighty as his sword, as he carried on a large and varied correspondence to justify his decisions, protect himself from slander and disinformation, and shore up the support necessary to continue the fight. Dragging Canoe too had to cajole and sway his countrymen, though he was obliged to use speeches and messages rather than notes and letters. There is general agreement that Cherokee oratory in this era was enormously clear, strong, and persuasive.[37] His father, Attakullakulla, was known as the Little Carpenter in part because he was a logic chopper, a skilled craftsman with words who could put together a tight argument with smooth interlocking sentences, as others might notch logs to build a solid cabin. But in his younger years he had fought as well; likewise Dragging Canoe, though called by circumstances to fight, could speak as well as his father. How else could he have argued the Little Carpenter to a standoff with regard to Cherokee foreign policy?

Thirdly, Washington and Dragging Canoe each in his own way had a skill, apparently, for attracting and utilizing individuals who could be helpful to the cause and whose active support might lead to further support at a later time. With Washington, we think of the young marquis de Lafayette and the energetic "baron" von Steuben, of Pulaski and Kosciuszko, of de Kalb and Duportail.[38] We know less about Dragging Canoe's support, both internal and external, but it is interesting to consider the talks delivered by his Cherokee associates, the old Corn Tassel and Tuskegetchee, or the Long Fellow. These two leaders disavowed the Chickamaugas and positioned themselves as trustworthy negotiators with the Virginians. In June 1787, when Washington was at the Constitutional Convention in Philadelphia, his former aide Edmund Randolph was serving as governor of Virginia. Randolph had written to these powerful middlemen as their "elder brother," chastising them for the hostile actions of the Chickamaugas; on June 12 at the Indian town of Chota they delivered angry formal speeches in response.

Corn Tassel spoke first. "It is well known that I have done everything in my power to keep peace In my land and hold fast all the treaties and Good Talks and Keep my young men from doing mischief, and I wish I had no greater cause to Complain than you have." The chief continued, "It is well known that you have Taken almost all our Country from us without our consent. That Don't seem to satisfy my Elder Brother, but he still Talks of fire and sword." Then the Long Fellow spoke. He professed friendship and distanced himself from Dragging Canoe, asserting: "I stand up like a wall between bad people and my Brothers, the Virginians." He conceded that he had "formerly Loved War, and lived at Chicamogga," but he contended that for the past "six winters" he had worked to prevent the Creeks and Chickamaugas "from Doing mischief." Still, he added pointedly that he commanded influence in twenty Cherokee towns, and if Virginia continued its incursions, he would be obliged, reluctantly, to "Look for new friends."[39]

Fourthly, in order to help offset the steep odds against them, Washington and Dragging Canoe each went beyond recruiting individuals and toiled to develop workable alliances between nations, even where it involved former enemies. In 1778 Washington, who is often credited with having personally inaugurated a global war against France a quarter century earlier, worked hard to secure, maintain, and utilize an alliance with the French monarchy. It was not easy for either side, as countless stories attest. Washington risked his life, for instance, when he sailed out of Chesapeake Bay in 1781 to pay his respects to Admiral de Grasse, only to endure three days of wind and storms in a small open launch on his precarious return trip.[40] Dragging Canoe also negotiated constantly for support, not only from the British but from the Spanish, the Creek, the Chickasaw, the Delaware, and others. The Shawnee, against whom he and his father had fought in earlier days, became his strongest allies. A recent history of the Shawnee notes: "Between 1779 and 1790 the Shawnee village of Chillicothe on the Little Miami River was attacked five times and completely destroyed on four of those occasions. Shawnee victims were often scalped by American soldiers; prisoners were subjected to torture and even burned at the stake."[41] It was logical, therefore, for Dragging Canoe to send warriors north to help protect the Shawnee, and for them to send fighters south to augment the Chickamauga.

Fifthly, confronted by chronic shortages, each leader invested enormous time and energy in the mundane work of obtaining the food, clothing, and armaments necessary to sustain the struggle. Washington's efforts to procure much-needed supplies from all quarters are well known, and Dragging Canoe's exertions were even greater, if only because his straits were more desperate. He traveled personally to meet with the British in Mobile and Pensacola, and he sent delegations to the Spanish in New Orleans and St. Louis pleading his cause. So long as Washington's war in the East continued, Dragging Canoe was able to obtain a steady flow of gunpowder, but when that conflict ended, his problems increased. Success in the field after 1788 was more than offset by the continuing scarcity of fresh resources.

Finally, when faced with repeated pressure to accommodate or to alter course, they both refused to compromise and continued to fight for their beliefs. Washington, we recall, not only stood up to and outlasted the forces of the strongest empire in the world, but he also took on and bested his own officer corps when necessary. His understated showdown at Newburgh, New York, in 1782 with the disgruntled, headstrong, and self-interested members of his own staff, at the moment when a military coup loomed as a real threat, was one of the high points of his career as a leader.[42] Dragging Canoe, we can infer indirectly, must have shown an equally strong will and single-mindedness of purpose. After all, he managed to sustain a more difficult and desperate cause against even greater odds for a far longer time. Indeed, as we have seen, when the Cherokee leader finally died in March 1792, President Washington himself was fully aware of his ongoing resistance movement. Throughout the remainder of that election year, there was increasing pressure on the chief executive, both from certain sectors of the frontier and from various members of Congress, to address the problem. In December Congressman Abraham Clark of New Jersey went so far as to introduce a motion, eventually defeated, calling upon the president "(if he shall judge it expedient) to carry offensive operations against the Indians of the five lower Cherokee towns called Chickamauga."[43]

In the end, perhaps, it is one overriding difference between the two men from opposite sides of the Appalachian Divide that stands out most strongly, a difference that concerns their relation to the land itself. Washington moved readily from skilled surveyor to successful planter, and from expansive planter to speculator par excellence. He strove to excel at everything he did, and he proved to be at least as patient, shrewd, aggressive, and successful in acquiring real estate as he was in the art of war. The vast scope of his investments in western land and the tactics he used to procure them have been almost as well documented as they have been warmly debated.[44] It was apparently a skill that ran back several generations. In his four-volume biography of the first president, James Flexner describes the paternal great-grandfather, John Washington, who arrived in Virginia in the third quarter of the seventeenth century. "Having a passion for acreage," Flexner reports, "he used a legal trick to pull the soil out from under an Indian village. This earned him the tribal name Caunotaucarius (town-taker), which that long-memoried people were later to apply by inheritance to his great-grandson."[45]

If the Washingtons were, like many of their neighbors, "town-takers" almost by definition, Dragging Canoe and his clan were "town-savers," dedicated to protecting Cherokee villages and the ancestral hunting grounds that surrounded and supported them. The cause was worthy, but ill-fated. The last buffalo in the Appalachian region was killed within several years of Dragging Canoe's death. The demise of the eastern buffalo serves as a milepost, confirming the spread of what Alfred Crosby has described as a Neo-Europe. Pressing inland from the Atlantic coast came an onslaught of European people bringing new economic values and strange domesticated animals. For the newcomers, the sheer weight of their numbers made them strong.[46] The entire region of modern-day Tennessee and Kentucky had contained fewer than 100 white persons when Dragging Canoe was born and scarcely 2,000 at most when he withdrew from the parley at Sycamore

Shoals in 1775. When he died in 1792, there were more than 70,000 Europeans and 15,000 Africans newly arrived in the region, and their numbers were escalating every week. "In other words, more than 80,000 persons, both free and enslaved, had poured into one segment of the vast interior region within [seventeen] years (not to mention thousands more who were now residing in the mountains of extreme western Virginia and North Carolina). Suddenly the total population had jumped more than twenty-five times in little over a decade, and this proved only a prologue to the influx that was still to come."[47]

Dragging Canoe was laid to rest at Running Water Town, between Lookout Mountain and the Tennessee River, seven years before his contemporary George Washington was buried overlooking the Potomac. Was the war chief of the Chickamauga as great a patriot and leader as the master of Mount Vernon? We might as well ask whether Josh Gibson was as great a hitter as Ty Cobb; we shall never know, for they played in different leagues. Suffice it to say both were extraordinary individuals from separate, and eventually opposing, worlds. Both, to use an eighteenth-century phrase, would have been "worthy of the ancients." Upon encountering either one of them, I suspect that we would believe, in the words of Lowell's couplet,

> Here was a type of the true elder race,
> And one of Plutarch's men talked with us face to face.

NOTES

1.
Great captains with their guns and drums,
Disturb our judgment for the hour,
  But at last, silence comes;
These are all gone, and, standing like a tower,
Our children shall behold his fame,
  The kindly, earnest, brave, foreseeing man
Sagacious, patient, dreading praise, not blame.

See Merrill D. Peterson, *Lincoln in American Memory* (New York: Oxford University Press, 1994), 32.

2. Plutarch, *Fall of the Roman Republic: Six Lives by Plutarch*, trans. Rex Warner (London: Penguin, 1958), 8.

3. See Woody Holton, *Forced Founders: Indians, Debtors, Slaves, and the Making of the American Revolution in Virginia* (Chapel Hill: University of North Carolina Press, 1999).

4. Attakullakulla had helped to save Stuart's life in a dramatic episode at Fort Loudoun during the English-Cherokee War in 1760, and they remained firm friends. See John Richard Alden, *John Stuart and the Southern Colonial Frontier* (Ann Arbor: University of Michigan Press, 1944), 118; J. Russell Snapp, *John Stuart and the Struggle for Empire on the Southern Frontier* (Baton Rouge: Louisiana State University Press, 1996), 56–57, 86–87, 198.

5. Attakullakulla knew the path well: as a young man in 1730 he had even sailed from Charleston to London, where he and a delegation of six other Cherokees visited fairs and cathedrals, posed for their picture in European clothing, and on June 18 had "the honor to kiss the hands of his Majesty" George II during a ceremony for Knights of the Garter at Windsor Castle, where the delegation appeared in Indian garb with bows in their hands, feathers in their hair, and spots of red, blue, and green paint on their faces and shoulders. See Carolyn Thomas Foreman, *Indians Abroad, 1493–1938* (Norman: University of Oklahoma Press, 1943), 45–46. See also James C. Kelly, "Notable Persons in Cherokee History: Attakullakulla," *Journal of Cherokee Studies* 3 (winter 1978): 2–34; William O. Steele, *The Cherokee Crown of Tannassy* (Winston-Salem: John F. Blair, 1977).

6. Quoted in Joseph Kastner, *A Species of Eternity* (New York: Knopf, 1977), 112.

7. Francis Harper, ed., *The Travels of William Bartram: Naturalist's Edition* (New Haven: Yale University Press, 1958): xxii. The encounter is described in Harper, 230–31, and in the original *Travels* at 364–65. Bartram mistakenly dates his journey as 1776.

8. John P. Brown, *Old Frontiers: The Story of the Cherokee Indians from Earliest Times to the Date of Their Removal to the West, 1838* (Kingsport, Tenn.: Southern Publishers, 1938), 10.

9. Brown, *Old Frontiers*, 11.

10. James Paul Pate, "The Chickamauga: A Forgotten Segment of Indian Resistance on the Southern Frontier" (Ph.D. diss., Mississippi State University, 1969), 80–81.

11. Pate, "The Chickamauga," 206–7.

12. John M. Murrin et al., *Liberty, Equality, Power: A History of the American People*, 2d ed. (Fort Worth: Harcourt Brace, 1999), 252.

13. Claudio Saunt, *A New Order of Things: Property, Power, and the Transformation of the Creek Indians, 1733–1816* (New York: Cambridge University Press, 1999).

14. See, for example, Francis S. Philbrick, *The Rise of the West, 1754–1830* (New York: Harper and Row, 1965); Jack M. Sosin, ed., *The Opening of the West* (Columbia: University of South Carolina Press, 1969). A slight exception is Reginald Horsman, *Expansion and American Indian Policy, 1783–1812* (East Lansing: Michigan State University Press, 1967), which contains three pages (76–78) on the Chickamauga. This book was reprinted as a paperback in 1992 by the University of Oklahoma Press, with a new preface by the author. His later book *The Frontier in the Formative Years, 1783–1815* (New York: Holt, Rinehart and Winston, 1970) contains one mention of the Chickamauga (11) and no reference to Dragging Canoe.

15. Gregory Evans Dowd, *A Spirited Resistance: The North American Indian*

Struggle for Unity, 1745–1815 (Baltimore: The Johns Hopkins University Press, 1992). Subsequent books that reflect this broader perspective include Tom Hatley, *The Dividing Paths: Cherokees and South Carolinians through the Era of Revolution* (New York: Oxford University Press, 1993); Gregory A. Waselkov and Kathryn E. Holland Braund, eds., *William Bartram on the Southeastern Indians* (Lincoln: University of Nebraska Press, 1995); Colin G. Calloway, *The American Revolution in Indian Country: Crisis and Diversity in Native American Communities* (New York: Cambridge University Press, 1995); Daniel K. Richter, *Facing East from Indian Country: A Native History of Early America* (Cambridge: Harvard University Press, 2001).

16. Brown, *Old Frontiers*, chap. 1. See also E. Raymond Evans, "Notable Persons in Cherokee History: Dragging Canoe," *Journal of Cherokee Studies* 2 (winter 1977): 230–39, and "Was the Last Battle of the American Revolution Fought at Lookout Mountain?" *Journal of Cherokee Studies* 5 (spring 1980): 30–40. Related articles of interest in the same journal include Helen Hornbeck Tanner, "Cherokees in the Ohio Country," *Journal of Cherokee Studies* 5 (spring 1978): 94–102, and James C. Kelly, "Oconostota," *Journal of Cherokee Studies* 3 (fall 1978): 221–38.

To put the Cherokee situation in broader context, see James H. O'Donnell III, *Southern Indians in the American Revolution* (Knoxville: University of Tennessee Press, 1973), and *The Cherokees of North Carolina in the American Revolution* (Raleigh: North Carolina Department of Cultural Resources, 1976); Francis Jennings, "The Indian's Revolution," in *The American Revolution: Explorations in the History of American Radicalism*, ed. Alfred F. Young (De Kalb: Northern Illinois University Press, 1976): 319–48; John Shy, "British Strategy for Pacifying the Southern Colonies, 1778–1781," in *The Southern Experience in the American Revolution*, ed. Jeffrey J. Crow and Larry E. Tise (Chapel Hill: University of North Carolina Press, 1978): 155–73; James H. O'Donnell III, "The South on the Eve of the Revolution: The Native Americans," in *The Revolutionary War in the South: Power, Conflict, and Leadership: Essays in Honor of John Richard Alden*, ed. W. Robert Higgins (Durham: Duke University Press, 1979): 64–78; Edward Cashin, "'But Brothers, It Is Our Land We Are Talking About': Winners and Losers in the Georgia Backcountry," in *An Uncivil War: The Southern Backcountry during the American Revolution*, ed. Ronald Hoffman, Thad W. Tate, and Peter J. Albert (Charlottesville: University Press of Virginia, 1985), 240–75.

17. Jon W. Parmenter, "Dragging Canoe (Tsi'yu-gûnsi'ni), Chickamauga Cherokee Patriot," in *The Human Tradition in the American Revolution*, ed. Nancy L. Rhoden and Ian K. Steele (Wilmington, Del.: Scholarly Resources, 1999), 117–37.

18. Flexner, *George Washington*, 12n.

19. This kind of long-standing confusion surrounding a figure on the margin of mainstream American history is not uncommon. For generations persons writing about the Virginia slave rebel Nat Turner—including novelist William Styron—assumed that the person who took down and published Turner's famous "Confession" after the Southampton Revolt of 1831 was the elderly lawyer Thomas R. Gray. But in 1978 the research of Thomas C. Parramore made clear that it was his much

younger and very different son of the same name. See Peter H. Wood, "Nat Turner: The Unknown Slave as Visionary Leader," in *Black Leaders of the Nineteenth Century*, ed. Leon Litwack and August Meier (Urbana: University of Illinois Press, 1988): 21–40, 325.

20. Pate, "The Chickamauga," 206. See also Brown, *Old Frontiers*, 9n.

21. Harper, *Travels of William Bartram*, 391.

22. Mason L. Weems, *The Life of Washington*, ed. Marcus Cunliffe (1804; reprint, Cambridge: Harvard University Press, 1962), 10–12.

23. Parmenter, "Dragging Canoe," 119.

24. George Washington, *The Daily Journal of Major George Washington, in 1751–2: Kept While on a Tour From Virginia to the Island of Barbadoes, With His Invalid Brother, Maj. Lawrence Washington, Proprietor of Mount Vernon on the Potomac*, ed. Joseph M. Toner (Albany, N.Y.: Joel Munsell, 1892), 40, 53.

25. James Thomas Flexner, *George Washington: The Forge of Experience, 1732–1775* (Boston: Little, Brown, 1965), 50.

26. Elizabeth A. Fenn, *Pox Americana: The Great Smallpox Epidemic of 1775–1782* (New York: Hill & Wang, 2001), 47–48, 98–103. Fenn argues that, in carrying out variolation, Washington and his army "had pulled off the first large-scale, state-sponsored immunization campaign in American history" (102).

27. Parmenter, "Dragging Canoe," 118.

28. Peter H. Wood, "The Impact of Smallpox on the Native Population of the Eighteenth-Century South," *New York State Journal of Medicine* 87 (January 1987): 30–36.

29. James Adair, *Adair's History of the American Indians* (1775; reprint, Ann Arbor: University of Michigan Press, 1966), 244–45.

30. The epidemic eventually spread to Charleston, as infected colonial troops returned from the interior. See Suzanne Krebsbach, "The Great Charlestown Smallpox Epidemic of 1760," *South Carolina Historical Magazine* 97 (January 1996), 30–37; Hatley, *The Dividing Paths*, 123–30.

31. George Milligen, *A Short Description of the Province of South Carolina* (London, 1779), 190, quoted in Hatley, *The Dividing Paths*, 123.

32. Letter of James Grant (Montgomery's second in command) to William Bull, reprinted in the *South Carolina Gazette* of June 7–16, 1760.

33. Quoted in Murrin et al., *Liberty, Equality, Power*, 207.

34. Pate, "The Chickamauga," 70–76.

35. Brown, *Old Frontiers*, 166–67.

36. Pate, "The Chickamauga," 77, 81.

37. See William Strickland, "Cherokee Rhetoric: A Forceful Weapon," *Journal of Cherokee Studies* 2 (fall 1977): 375–84.

38. Don Higginbotham, *The War of American Independence: Military Attitudes, Policies, and Practice, 1763–1789* (New York: Macmillan, 1971), 214.

39. *Calendar of Virginia State Papers and Other Manuscripts: ... Preserved in the Capitol at Richmond*, vol.4, ed. William P. Palmer and Sherwin McRae (Richmond: R.V. Derr, 1884), 306–7.

40. James Thomas Flexner, *George Washington in the American Revolution, 1775–1783* (Boston: Little, Brown, 1967), 450.

41. Jerry E. Clark, *The Shawnee* (Lexington: University Press of Kentucky, 1977), 88. Clark does not mention the Chickamauga or Cherokee in his discussion. "In 1782 the Shawnee were joined by the Delaware, Wyandot, Miami, Ottawa, Chippewa, and Mingo in a confederacy to drive the settlers from Kentucky and Ohio. Their first confederated battles took place at Bryan Station and Blue Licks, Kentucky, in August of 1782. They were repulsed at Bryan Station, but when pursued to Blue Licks they defeated a militia led by Daniel Boone. In 1792 Henry Knox, secretary of war, claimed that the sole cause of the continuing war was the unprovoked aggression of the Shawnee and their confederated tribes. Certainly there are numerous accounts of Shawnee aggression against the Kentucky and Ohio settlers; but that these attacks were unprovoked is certainly not the case" (87–88).

42. Flexner, *Washington in the American Revolution*, 4–5, 486–95, 500–508, 511–13. See also James Thomas Flexner, *George Washington and the New Nation, 1783–1793* (Boston: Little, Brown, 1969), 146n, 234–35; Higginbotham, *War of American Independence*, 405–11, 439.

43. Quoted in Pate, "The Chickamauga," 224.

44. See Thomas P. Slaughter, *The Whiskey Rebellion: Frontier Epilogue to the American Revolution* (New York: Oxford University Press, 1986), chap. 5.

45. Flexner, *Forge of Experience*, 10.

46. Alfred Crosby, *Ecological Imperialism: The Biological Expansion of Europe, 900–1900* (New York: Cambridge University Press, 1986).

47. Peter H. Wood, "The Changing Population of the Colonial South: An Overview by Race and Region, 1685–1790," in *Powhatan's Mantle: Indians in the Colonial Southeast*, ed. Peter H. Wood, Gregory A. Waselkov, and M. Thomas Hatley (Lincoln: University of Nebraska Press, 1989), 35–103, esp. 38–39, 84–88; quote from 87–88.

Chapter 11

CREEKS AND AMERICANS
IN THE AGE OF WASHINGTON

ROBBIE ETHRIDGE

With the march of the Spanish conquistador Hernando de Soto through the American South, and even before, southeastern Indian history began to play itself out in a larger world. But the interactions between southern Americans and the Indians in the late eighteenth century were not solely ones of political nor military sparring between the great leaders of both. Nor were the interactions fundamentally economic ones between dependent and independent actors. Rather, the interactions that forged the American South were largely interactions between the regular folk living in or near Indian territory. Deep-rooted ideological and cultural differences generally marked the two groups, but their proximity to one another ensured daily, taken-for-granted interactions and relations. Still, Creek and American relations, no matter how cooperative, friendly, intimate, and mutually beneficial, were played out in the larger context of American westward expansion. Westward expansion had always lain at the heart of Euro-American and Indian relations, and this, in turn, guaranteed that hostility and suspicion would come to characterize most dealings between the two and would culminate, quite regularly, in outbreaks of violence. This hostility permeated regular encounters between Indians and Americans on the southern frontier, which meant that daily life was underlain by a contradiction—both Indians and frontier Americans knew and depended on one another, yet they fundamentally distrusted one another.

The territory of the Creek Confederacy, the well-known epithet for the eighteenth-century Muskogees, as the Creeks called themselves, ran from the Oconee River in present-day Georgia to the Tombigbee River in present-day Alabama. The Creek Confederacy was a collection of towns under a loose political organization.[1] The core of the confederacy consisted of towns with people who spoke Muskogean, but the Creek Confederacy was a known refuge for dislocated people speaking various non-Muskogean languages who were allowed to establish their own towns within the Creek Confederacy's territory.[2] By the end of the eighteenth century, the Creeks divided themselves into two divisions—the Upper Creeks who lived on the Tallapoosa, Coosa, and Alabama Rivers in present-day Alabama, and the Lower Creeks who lived on the lower Chattahoochee and Flint Rivers in present-day Georgia. Seventy-three towns, ranging in size from as few as ten or twenty families to more than two hundred families, comprised the Confederacy—forty-eight Upper Creek towns and twenty-five Lower Creek towns.[3]

The age of George Washington is perhaps one of the best-documented periods for the Creeks. The years after the American Revolution had been tumultuous ones. Alexander McGillivray, the son of a Creek woman and a Scottish trader, emerged as a strong and central leader of the Creeks. McGillivray's rise to power among the Creeks is a story full of unusual twists and turns in Creek politics and cannot be fully told here.[4] He died in 1793, leaving a legacy of intrigue, duplicity, resentment, and harsh retaliations against the Georgians he had always hated. With his death, the situation between the Creeks and the state of Georgia was explosive. President Washington knew that the Creeks mistrusted the federal government and that they deplored the Georgia government.[5] The southern Indian agent, James Seagrove, was ineffectual and terrified of the Indians, and he could not deal with the situation. Washington recognized the need to replace him with a man the Creeks could learn to trust. In 1796 he found such a man in Benjamin Hawkins, who had a reputation for fairness and justness in his dealings with the Indians, and whom he soon appointed temporary agent to the southern Indians.[6]

At the time of his appointment, Hawkins was not a newcomer to Indian affairs. As a North Carolina senator he had served on committees appointed to investigate certain Indian affairs; he had served as a United States commissioner in the 1785 Treaty of Hopewell with the Cherokees; he had been an unofficial observer at the negotiations for the 1790 Treaty of New York with the Creeks; and he had served as a United States commissioner in the 1796 Treaty of Colerain with the Creeks.[7] Hawkins had an interest in Indian life beyond the negotiating of Indian treaties. Hawkins and his friend Thomas Jefferson exchanged letters on a wide array of topics on Indian life as well as on scientific farming, agricultural experiments, and gardening.⁸ Once in the South, Hawkins compiled numerous word lists in Choctaw, Cherokee, and Creek for Jefferson, who was intensely interested in Indian languages.⁹ Hawkins lived and worked among the Creeks for twenty years and left a large volume of written correspondence and other documents on Creek life and Indian affairs in the South.

One of Hawkins's primary objectives as Indian agent was to implement the "plan for civilization." The plan for civilization, as a means of addressing the so-called Indian problem, appealed to Hawkins and other prominent intellectuals and federal officials for many reasons. The plan for civilization, essentially, aimed to turn the Indians into Euro-American-style yeoman farmers. The idea was to provide the southern Indians with domesticated animals such as hogs, cows, and sheep and manufactured implements of agriculture, especially the plow, and to teach them to become herdsmen and agriculturalists, growing cash crops such as cotton and wheat and driving their herds to seaports or frontier markets. Through such changes, the southern Indians would become self-sufficient farmers, able to clothe and feed themselves, yet also able to participate in the market economy, exchanging agricultural and herd surpluses for manufactured items.

The United States understood that transforming the southern Indians into herdsmen and commercial farmers meant they would no longer rely on the hunt and therefore would not need as much hunting territory.¹⁰ Thus, as whites needed more land, the Indians would be more willing to sell. The plan for civilization, although quite controversial among the Creeks, actually conformed to many aspects of Creek life at the time. For one, the Creeks were farmers, and had been for thousands of years. The main difference here was that Creek women, not men, were the farmers, and the plan for civilization called for the men to give up the hunt and pursue agriculture. Creek men, although showing strong resistance in this matter, in fact were already facing diminishing returns from commercial hunting.

After the American Revolution, the Creeks faced unprecedented economic, political, and social challenges because the deerskin trade in which they had been involved for more than a hundred years was rapidly declining. The reasons for this decline are multiple. For one thing, the American Revolution completely disrupted the southern Indian trade. European traders who had lived and worked among the Creeks for decades had close ties with England and took the loyalists' side in the conflict. Afterward, in defeat, many of them had their property confiscated, fled to Europe, or in some cases were hanged. Plus, the Treaty of Paris prohibited commercial arrangements between the United States and Britain, and transatlantic commerce came to a temporary halt. The lines of credit and banking between the former colonies and Britain, which had been fundamental to the Indian trade, deteriorated beyond repair.[11] Equally important, commercial trading and hunting had also caused a crash in the white-tailed deer population in the South.[12] With this decline, the Creeks found that they had to find economic alternatives to the deerskin trade. They could not now simply extricate themselves from the larger world or the world market, so they needed to find other avenues to the commercial market. Many Creeks turned to commercial farming, but most turned to ranching.

Although some Creeks began acquiring cows and hogs in the early years of colonization, it was not until after the American Revolution and with the decline in the deerskin trade that they began owning them in any number.[13] Ranching was a relatively easy alternative to the deerskin trade.[14] It functioned to keep the formal trade economy afloat, and switching commodities from deerskins to livestock could be done within the well-established methods of the trade system. The number of cattle and hogs in Creek territory by the turn of the nineteenth century is not known. However, there is every indication that the numbers were high. Most Creeks, men and women, owned some kind of livestock—if nothing more than a horse. Hawkins lists almost every town as having herds of livestock, and some individual herds ranged from 30 to 150 head, and were "spread over the whole nation."[15] So, although he encountered other obstacles, on the issue of raising cattle and hogs Hawkins found the Creeks well on the road to becoming ranchers at the time of his arrival in the Creek Confederacy in 1796. The Creeks did not keep cows and hogs for home consumption. Although they did acquire a taste for beef and pork, they raised cattle and hogs mostly for sale to Euro-Americans.[16] It was not unusual then in Creek country to come across a herd of cows or hogs being driven to port cities such as Savannah, Pensacola, or Mobile.

Livestock also became an item that figured prominently in a growing discrepancy in privately owned material items. In other words, at the turn of the nineteenth century a thin strata of wealthy, usually mestizo, elite were emerging as a dominant political and economic sector. One measure of their wealth and economic influence was the size of their livestock herds, although these men and women were more planters than ranchers, as they were usually engaged in various commercial agrarian pursuits.[17] Even so, ranching was not limited to the elite. Ranching required neither a large labor force nor any special technology. The livestock were free-ranging, which meant that the animals required little maintenance for most of the year. And almost anyone could be involved, because ranching did not appreciably alter the hunting and agricultural cycle of labor requirements.[18]

Ranching did alter Creek gender roles, though, by more fully incorporating women into the market economy. Many women realized profits from ranching by selling meats to foreign visitors and travelers, which kept the activity within their well-defined roles in the Creek economy. But women also became engaged in the formal trade economy by selling their hogs and cattle on the hoof. With this money they garnered a purchasing power that had heretofore been denied them. Hawkins noted that many women had begun to buy slaves with the profits from their ranching activities, and others had enlarged the number of animals in their herds.[19]

Because ranching was widespread, we also see a changing settlement pattern. Creek towns usually were located within the alluvial floodplain of major streams. They were typically nucleated, meaning that there was a town center surrounded by households. The town center was the public space, and it held the rotunda, the square ground, and the town plaza. The rotunda was a large, round semi-subterranean structure, and the square ground was an open courtyard surrounded by four open "cabins" situated in a square pattern.[20] All important assemblies of the ranked warriors, weather permitting, took place in the square ground, and it was the focus of all formal public events. The rotunda was used as a meeting place in inclement weather.[21] The town plaza was a large open area, demarcated by a low earthen embankment, and people gathered here to socialize, play games, dance, and perform certain ceremonies. The households, which were courtyard compounds consisting of three or four buildings surrounding an open area, were tightly clustered around the town center.[22]

By the late eighteenth century, people began to move away from the town centers and the major rivers. Since Creek ranchers allowed their animals to free-range, and as the natural forage around the major population centers began to show signs of depletion, more and more people fanned across the country, settling farmsteads on the alluvial floodplains of smaller streams, away from the town centers, and ranging their livestock in the hinterlands.[23] So instead of diminishing their needs for land, as the proponents of the plan for civilization had hoped, the new husbandry insured that the Creeks would continue to need and occupy all of their territory. The Creek ranching complex was part of the larger frontier economy as also practiced by frontier Americans. It should not be surprising, then, that the settlement patterns of both the Creeks and the late-eighteenth-century American frontier farmers should be similar, as both vied for the exact same resources, in this case good rangelands and floodplain soils.

The American southern frontier settlers are barely known, although recent scholarship has gone far in debunking many of the myths and stereotypes usually associated with the American frontier.[24] At the time of Hawkins's arrival in the Creek Confederacy, the people on the southern frontier were a mixed lot—Scots, English, Irish, Spanish, German, French, and American farmers migrating from Virginia, Pennsylvania, the Carolinas, and other more northern states. As Hawkins wrote to Thomas Jefferson, "at the moment I am writing I can hear the languages of Scotch, French, Spanish, English, African, Creek, and Uchee."[25] But as the nineteenth century got under way, the diversity of immigrants diminished until they were mostly people born and reared in America.[26]

The demographic profile of these settlers is of young nuclear families with high birth rates.[27] They lived on single-family farmsteads consisting typically of two-room log cabins and one or two outbuildings for storage, with few material possessions.[28] Few families used the plow. Most adopted the Indian techniques of swidden farming, using only a digging stick and hoe with no fertilization.[29] Their crops were identical to those of the Creeks—corn was the staple, supplemented by sweet potatoes, squashes, beans, melons, peas, and so on. Frontier men hunted deer, bear, rabbit, opossum, squirrel, and other wild animals for meat.[30] Because swidden agriculture requires easily turned soil, their farms usually stretched along the alluvial plains of waterways, much like the farmsteads of Indian families who had moved out of the towns.[31] They also were highly mobile. They stayed at their farms until the soils grew unproductive, usually after ten to fifteen years. They then sold their land and moved on, usually farther into the interior as Indian lands were ceded.[32]

These American farmers grew enough to feed themselves, with a minor amount of surplus to sell at the trade house or to barter with Indians and free blacks. These families did not have the land or labor to engage in large-scale commercial agriculture. The best they could do was to devote some small patches to cotton and/or tobacco, which were their main commercial crops.[33] Apparently frontier American hunters engaged in the pelt trade only at the most minimal level. The Creeks may have objected to Americans hunting for peltry.[34] The farmsteaders' real commercial interests lay with ranching. Most families owned at least a horse or two for transportation, and a small herd of cattle and hogs, which provided their major market commodity. Some families were large ranchers, reportedly owning herds in the hundreds and even thousands.[35] Like Creek livestock, American-owned livestock were free-ranging. Livestock were raised primarily for the market, although pork and beef constituted some of the family's meat protein. Cows were rarely used for their milk products.[36]

Although farmsteads were usually dispersed, frontier families still understood themselves to be part of a community, although their definition of such usually fell along different lines than we use today. For instance, people sometimes described themselves as living in a "neighborhood," which meant a group of families living at a distance from each other but along a particular stream or in some other distinctive geographic area.[37] In cases where a town was nearby, people defined themselves as being citizens of that town, even though it may have been miles away. The towns usually were the county or territorial seats. They were widely spaced, ramshackle frontier affairs that could barely be called towns.[38] Only a few people actually lived in them. Most of the people who claimed town citizenship lived in the surrounding areas, on their farms and ranches.[39]

The boundary lines dividing Creek country and United States territory marked the legitimate line of separation, but Indians, whites, and blacks routinely penetrated far beyond these lines so that there was, in fact, no real boundary between the Creeks and the Americans. People passed between the Creek and American territories continuously and quite easily despite some efforts by federal officials to control the comings and goings of people. Creeks and the frontier Americans forged pervasive economic connections because each depended on the other for various goods that were hard to come by on the frontier. Creek visitors to American farmsteads brought items such as wild meats, baskets and buckskins to trade for cloth, metal pots and pans, trinkets, ammunition, difficult-to-find foodstuffs such as coffee, flour, and sugar, and any other items that a frontier family could spare. But most frontier homesteaders were not wealthy and did not have large quantities of goods to exchange. Plus, Creek men and women could only afford to barter their surpluses. These sorts of exchanges then were small, but they were necessary because of the irregular access to commercial goods on the frontier and because of the risks and unpredictability of subsistence farming and hunting.[40]

Frontier Americans and Creeks were engaged in many forms of exchange, not only economic ones. As we saw, southern frontier farmers adopted Indian agricultural methods and crops. They also learned from the Indians herbal remedies and fused their folklore with Indian mythology and tales.[41] Friendships formed, as did marriages and business partnerships, most notably between gangs of horse thieves comprised of red, white, and black.[42] Genetic exchanges took place through sexual liaisons and intermarriage, which also promoted an exchange of ideas and lifeways, and permanent residences of Creeks in American towns and vice versa. Creek men and women were constantly visiting settlers to drink, socialize, and stage various competitions such as horse and foot races. Frontier

Americans likewise regularly crossed into Creek territory to visit with friends and family and to barter. Even in the larger port cities such as Pensacola, Mobile, and New Orleans, Creek men and women from the interior could be found trading and visiting. Some Creeks chose to reside near frontier towns, where they became a part of the town citizenry.[43] Likewise, many white and black men and women chose to reside in the Creek Confederacy, marrying Creeks and raising mixed households.[44]

Such mingling, exchanges, and interactions between Creeks and Americans were daily, taken-for-granted affairs that did not necessarily arouse suspicions and animosities. The interactions were not between aliens—Indians and frontier Americans were not strangers to one another. They knew each other well; they had common troubles and triumphs; and their lives were more similar than we may realize. Despite boundary lines and many distinctions of habit, their world was a single one composed of their interactions and reliance on one another. This world, however, was built on the unstable foundation of westward expansion. American frontier families may have constituted the leading edge of western expansion, but acquisition of Indian land was driven by wealthy land speculators. These men, most of them prominent government officials, incessantly pushed for land cessions, and they clearly and consciously understood that the American frontier family must play the role of "the villains who did the dirty work—deplored by government—of corrupting, cheating, terrifying, and extinguishing both the Indians and their claims."[45]

During the age of Washington and in the first few decades afterward, the Creeks made three major land cessions. In the 1796 Treaty of Colerain, which confirmed the 1790 Treaty of New York, the Creeks ceded the lands roughly between the Ogeechee and Oconee Rivers in Georgia. The 1802 Treaty of Fort Wilkinson ceded a portion of land between the Oconee and Ocmulgee Rivers. And in the Treaty of 1805, also known as the Treaty of Washington, the Creeks sold the remaining section of land between the two rivers, making the boundary between the Creek Confederacy and Georgia roughly the Ocmulgee River.[46] By 1805 even Secretary of War Henry Dearborn was weary of dealing with the incessant demands for land by the southern states, Georgia in particular. He wrote Hawkins: "If the Ocmulgee can once be established as the boundary, I trust I shall not live long enough to hear any contention for any other boundary line between Georgia and the Creek Nation."[47]

Land sales were always accompanied by a strong Creek opposition. Land cessions could only be given by the consent of the Creeks as a whole, but in reality such a consensus was impossible to attain. Whereas a majority of Creeks may have agreed to a cession, some agreeing through pressure, those who did not agree were not compelled to conform to any treaty stipulations nor to respect any new boundary lines. In the Creek Confederacy, those in positions of authority, the town headmen, could only lead by persuasion and popular consensus. They had no powers of coercion and little punitive authority, although Hawkins and other federal and state officials endeavored to empower their governing bodies, especially the National Council, with such.[48] The leading legislative principle was blood revenge, or blood for blood, to be carried out by the members of a wronged person's clan.[49] In short, the Creeks had no authority structure to control the actions of any who opposed national policy. And under the principles of blood revenge, headmen who had signed the treaties often felt themselves in personal danger from those in opposition, especially if the headmen endeavored to punish anyone for actions taken against a cession.[50]

Hawkins, other Americans, and some Creeks labeled those opposing a land sale, roads, the plan for civilization, or any other American proposition as "the opposition." Hawkins believed that this opposition, although only loosely organized, was determined to thwart the plan for civilization and to foment general unrest. This is difficult to validate. At times, the opposition appears to have acted as an organized resistance. Some sort of Creek council could apparently mobilize warriors to intimidate frontier Americans so that they would be too frightened to pass through Creek territory. In 1798, for example, some Upper Creek warriors plundered a party of South Carolinians en route to Tensaw. When Hawkins interrogated the men, they told him that they robbed the whites because their passage was "irregular and that they had been advised to do it in order to stop whites from traveling through Creek lands."[51] In 1802 more than eight hundred white people reportedly ventured through Creek territory without the proper papers. At the time, Hawkins had been at a prolonged meeting with the Choctaws, Chickasaws, and Cherokees and, according to Hawkins, the whites took advantage of his absence to pass through. Creek headmen contemplated sending out warriors to frighten the travelers and put a halt to the passage. Hawkins's assistants, the white trader Timothy Barnard and the Creek headman Alexander Cornells, speaking on Hawkins's behalf in his absence, persuaded the headmen not to act but to wait for Hawkins's return, at which time he would get the situation under control.[52]

Another act of apparent organized resistance occurred when Creek warriors arrested and disarmed a road survey crew who were cutting a section of the Federal Road, which a Creek Council had reluctantly agreed might be cut through their territory.⁵³ Only after much assurance on Hawkins's part did the Creek warriors release the crew unharmed.⁵⁴ Creek warriors habitually killed American postal riders (another reluctant concession by the Creeks) unless they were Creek riders, in which case they would simply take the mail pouch and send the rider to complete his route. In either case the mail was stopped, and this appears to have been the aim of the Creek resistance.⁵⁵

Organized resistance also occurred when Creek warriors would thwart the running of boundary lines. Those who opposed a land sale commonly attempted to prevent running of the boundary lines by ambushing the surveying parties. These parties were usually composed of the surveyors, American and Creek observers, or commissioners, whose job was to see that the lines were run in accordance with treaty stipulations, and Creek warriors and American soldiers who acted as guards. Opposition warriors would ambush the surveyors, take their instruments, horses, and anything else they fancied, and, more often than not, leave some guards injured or dying from wounds incurred in the raid.⁵⁶ Once, while running the boundary for the Treaty of Colerain, a Creek commissioner was crippled for life from a wound in a raid.⁵⁷

Such tactics delayed the running of the lines and prompted Hawkins, under military escort, to call emergency meetings with Creek headmen and representatives from the opposition, if they would come.⁵⁸ The Creek headmen who had signed the treaty were then left to settle their differences with the opposition. If not, Hawkins offered military invasion as the alternative.⁵⁹ Hawkins's strategy usually proved effective, and most boundary lines were eventually run to completion. The exception was the line between Spain and the United States, as stipulated in the 1795 Treaty of San Lorenzo. In this case the Seminoles, who never once met with Hawkins, successfully prevented the running of the boundary for two decades.⁶⁰

Others on the frontier shared Hawkins's notion that the opposition was organized, as evidenced by the case of Appy Howard. Appy Howard was a settler in Camden County, Georgia. On June 5, 1807, she swore a deposition recounting Samuel Greene's death. According to Mrs. Howard, two Creek men approached her house on the morning of May 8, asking for breakfast. She bade them to eat, and afterwards they departed "seemingly well pleased." Later that afternoon, the same men returned for dinner. She asked them to eat, and during the course of the meal, while she had gone outside to fill a plate from the pot on the fire, the two Creeks shot her neighbor, Mr. Greene, who was dining with them. Mrs. Howard fled with her two-month-old son when one of the Creeks approached her "with his gun clubbed as if to knock her down." The two men then took everything in the house.

Later, when asked if she knew why the two Creek men killed Greene, she swore "that there was not any offence offered the said Indians by the said Greene, or herself, or by any other person in the settlement to her knowledge, or to any other Indian whatever."[61] She believed the motive was robbery. Even so, with Greene's death, the settlers in the county were considerably alarmed because they did not know if "it was a thing done by the desire of the nation or the act of a few villains."[62]

It is doubtful that the opposition was as highly organized, precise, and disciplined a group as the Camden County residents or Hawkins believed. More likely, it was composed of various individuals whose sentiments regarding America and land cessions fluctuated. Certainly some people were unwavering in their hatred of America and Americans, and these people perhaps formed a core around which others, depending on their current opinions and interests, coalesced. Much hostility undoubtedly resulted from personal vendettas, blood revenge, retaliations for perceived personal wrongs, and private or criminal motives. Hawkins and other Americans, however, understood any hostile activity by the Creeks to be an anti-American statement.

Creek headmen sometimes manipulated this perception of an organized Creek resistance to Creek benefit. For instance, during one meeting regarding the land cession for the Treaty of Fort Wilkinson, Hawkins told the Creek headman Efau Haujo that as the game was gone and as the United States would not be forthcoming with presents as in the past, he saw no other way for them to support themselves but to sell their lands.[63]

That evening, an unidentified headman, probably Efau Haujo, replied to Hawkins in confidence that there was another recourse of which Hawkins had not thought:

> The old Chiefs and their associates in opposition are of opinion that if we reject the new order of things, order the agent and the Blacksmiths and ass't to leave the nation, stop travelling of all white people through their land, and let the horse thieves worry the frontier for a while, the government will change its plan, revive the old mode of presents for the sake of peace and court, caress and accommodate their wants and those of their adherents.

The headman continued that whereas he did not agree with this, the idea was gaining ground among many people.[64]

At other times, Creek headmen denied the existence of an organized resistance and disavowed any responsibility whatsoever for depredations against whites—they singled out ungovernable young men as the cause of their troubles.⁶⁵ Federal and state officials likewise blamed American depredations against the Creeks on "rash young men" or "mad men" who had no respect for law or international pacts. Such was the diplomatic language of the time, and both American officials and Creek headmen had been saying this since the beginning of the eighteenth century.⁶⁶

Generally speaking, Creek resistance was located at the individual level, in particular in individual reprisals against various forms of trespassing and squatting, or intrusions, as they were called at the time. The most common type of trespassing was the use of Creek lands by white border settlers for hunting, fishing, and grazing, all of which were considered a form of intrusion. In 1796, when Hawkins moved to Creek territory, Timothy Barnard remarked that the Creeks were more peaceable than he had ever known.⁶⁷ In previous years the Creeks and Georgians had been "continually in a state of war," and border settlers had retreated to the more secure coastal regions.⁶⁸ By 1800, however, American westward migration had resumed apace, and with it the tensions. White settlers, whose farms were in United States territory and therefore legal, still broke the law by crossing into Creek territory to hunt, fish, or to graze their livestock. The hunting trips of white men did not last months like those of Creek hunters, but they were fairly regular excursions and usually ranged into Creek lands.⁶⁹ The Creeks, already suffering from a shortage of white-tailed deer, resented these white hunters further depleting the game. According to Creek headmen, whites "destroyed the game" and ate all of the bear when they came into Creek territory.⁷⁰

As we have seen, white hunters were not responsible for the dearth of white-tailed deer in the South at this time. However, Creek headmen insisted that white hunters overhunted the deer, and they pointed to the common practice of night hunting by white hunters as proof of overkill.⁷¹ In night hunting, hunters used torches to blind and confuse deer, thus making the animals easier to kill and increasing the number of deer harvested. In an early measure of conservation, some southern states had outlawed night hunting for this very reason after the deer population in the coastal regions declined.⁷²

Frontier settlers also trespassed on Creek lands when fishing and cutting timber. They built fish traps in the rivers and hauled away large loads of fish, undermining another vital food source of the Creeks.⁷³ Timber harvesting roused complaints because it was a blatant violation of treaty stipulations. It also meant that whites instead of Creeks were garnering the profits from timber sales, on top of bringing whites into Creek territory.[74]

Grazing of free-ranging livestock and attendant thefts were, by far, the most frequently voiced Creek complaint against American settlers, and vice versa. Creek hunters killed or stole American-owned livestock that had strayed over the line, an occurrence so reportedly frequent that "the whites cannot count on their stock as an income."[75] At the talks for the Treaty of Colerain in 1796, Georgia sought compensation to its citizens for "thefts" at the hands of Creeks. As the Georgia commissioners were enumerating their complaints, the Creeks in attendance "rarely asserted; remained generally silent." When the Georgia commissioners began complaining about Creek hogs straying into Georgia territory, "they all laughed." The Tuckabatchee headman Big Warrior saw some irony in Georgia settlers complaining about straying hogs. Later, while dining with the commissioners, Big Warrior asked for a roll longer than that used by the commissioners, so that he could list all of the offenses of Georgians against the Creeks.[76]

Everyone realized that "a mere mathematical line in the woods" could not prevent the livestock from ranging.[77] Much of the boundary between Creek territory and the state of Georgia was a river, the Oconee—and, with the Treaty of Fort Wilkinson, the Ocmulgee River. Because livestock congregated at shallow river shoals to eat the moss for its salt content, it was only natural that livestock strayed across the rivers. Frontier ranchers understood this, and some people even attempted, with little success, to block crossing points, although how they did so is not described.[78]

Straying livestock created problems because both Creeks and Americans crossed into the other's territory searching for the strays. On both sides, the search parties went armed and, more often than not, managed a few thefts themselves while looking for their own wandering livestock. In addition, white thieves regularly moved through Creek country preying on hunting and traveling parties, although they rarely penetrated far enough into Creek country to raid a town or farmstead. Having armed groups of Creeks and Americans roving the woods was alarming to all involved and contributed to the mounting tensions. Hawkins and many Creek headmen sought a peaceable method of rounding up strays and curbing the rampant thefts.[79]

Chance meetings in the woods between Creeks and Americans were so dangerously explosive that many people carried vouchers of good character and/or intent from prominent frontier whites such as Hawkins or Barnard.[80] Hawkins even tried to issue hunting passes to Indians so that everyone in the woods could be accounted for.[81] But he could not enforce such decrees, as one case made clear. In 1794 a group of Chehaws (Lower Creeks) crossed the Oconee River (the boundary line) to steal horses. On the way back, they ambushed a militia group that had been sent to pursue them, and they killed several of the white men. As if to flaunt their deed, the Chehaws posted on a tree, beneath which lay the mutilated bodies of the white men, a voucher attesting to their good character and firm friendship to America, written by Timothy Barnard. Barnard later denied issuing the voucher, insisting that it was a forgery.[82]

Hawkins also decreed that no American was to enter Creek territory without a passport signed by him.[83] Even then, many ignored the passport requirement or forged passes.[84] Besides, these frontier people were knowledgeable forest travelers and could evade Hawkins's watchful eye by taking one of the many "little blind paths" through Creek country.[85] When some Creeks stepped up the harassment of white travelers, Hawkins banned traffic altogether until a solution could be found.[86] He requested that military checkpoints be established along the full length of the Federal Road to insure that only legal travelers passed, but his request was never honored.[87] In 1811 Hawkins attempted to reassure the Creeks that only military personnel would be using the roads and these soldiers were under strict orders to behave correctly.[88] Neither Hawkins nor the Creeks had much faith in this promise nor in his efforts to control the traffic through Creek country.. Even as late as 1811, the Shawnee warrior Tecumseh appears to have moved into and out of Creek country quite easily.[89]

Another form of intrusion was that of American settlers illegally establishing whole towns in Indian territories. This form of intrusion was limited to a few settlements, most notably Wofford's settlement in Georgia and Muscle Shoals in Tennessee. In both of these cases, American settlers moved onto lands supposedly ceded by the Indians, but the titles were of dubious legality. Also in both of these cases, powerful land speculators such as William Blount of Tennessee financed the settlement and sheltered the settlers from federal legal actions. As for the state level, land speculators controlled the southern state governments at this time, and therefore state governments actually sanctioned and abetted such illegal settlements.[90] To their way of thinking, with American settlements already established, state officials could point to the problems of removing the settlers and thus pressure the Indians for these particular tracts of land.

At Muscle Shoals, John Chisholm, the agent of William Blount, oversaw and promoted the settlement. The land was said to have been ceded by the Cherokees in the 1785 Treaty of Hopewell, but once the boundaries were drawn, the town was still on Cherokee lands. The Cherokees wanted the town removed to United States territory, and they forced the settlers to leave several times. Chisholm, however, persuaded the occupants to return after each removal. Muscle Shoals was occupied and abandoned many times until the Cherokees finally relented and ceded the land in 1816.[91]

Wofford was settled prior to the Treaty of Holston in 1791 between the United States and the Cherokees. But once the lines were surveyed, the town was found to be in Indian territory and in an area to which both the Creeks and Cherokees laid claim. The Creeks and Cherokees pressed Hawkins to have the settlers removed. This proved difficult to do. For one thing, the contested Creek/Cherokee claim had to be resolved, which took more than a year. Even then, it was resolved only because the Creeks, disgusted with the interminable delays, eventually renounced their claim and washed their hands of the matter.[93] The Cherokees were left pushing for the removal of the settlement. By this time Wofford, which was actually a mixed settlement of Indians, white Americans, and black slaves, was firmly entrenched, and several farms were flourishing, which made the inhabitants that much more resistant to moving. The affair came to the notice of the War Department, which conducted a thorough investigation and found the Cherokee claims to be legitimate. Thus began a long debate as to the best way to remove the settlers.[93]

The Cherokees wanted the whole town immediately abandoned. But the War Department insisted that such a move would be ruinous to the inhabitants, as they would lose that year's crops. The problem was compounded because several families were of mixed white-Indian marriages. The Cherokees agreed to let settlers stay, with no restrictions, in those cases where the marriage was between an Indian man and a white woman, but white men married to Indian women could stay only so long as the men "behaved themselves." There was also some question about what to do with the "old" and "new" settlers. The Cherokees agreed to let the old settlers, presumably the original inhabitants, stay until their crops were in. The most recent arrivals had to leave immediately. But all of the settlers refused to leave, even after receiving stern instructions from the War Department to do so. Hawkins eventually ordered a military detachment to Wofford to dislodge the farmers, only to have them return later.[94] In 1804 the United States finally purchased the land on which Wofford stood, although its ownership was still in dispute as late as 1812.[95]

The Creeks had similar problems with American settlements, but there is little documentation relating to these matters. In 1805 Hawkins reported to Secretary of War Henry Dearborn that some white settlements were forming on Creek lands between the headwaters of the Oconee and Ocmulgee Rivers. Hawkins suggested that the settlers be immediately removed by military force because their presence would certainly pose problems in the impending negotiations for the Treaty of 1805.[96] In this case the Creeks complained about the settlement in the treaty talks, but apparently the lands were included in the 1805 land cession.

More typically, intrusions onto Creek lands consisted of single families moving into disputed borders or onto Indian lands. Some of these settlers bought their land from individual Creeks who were not authorized to make private land sales. The settlers must have known such sales were illegal, but they pressed their claims when asked to move.[97] In other cases the Creeks, collectively and individually, extracted fees from Americans for various land uses. For instance, by treaty, any farmsteader who wished to cut timber on Creek lands had to pay them for the privilege.[98] The Creeks insisted that Americans pay for the use of grazing or agricultural lands. In some cases, the Creeks allotted a piece of land to American farmers for a fee. In 1807, for example, Naniabe Island, which was actually a cove at the fork of the Tombigbee and Alabama rivers, became the focus of a dispute between the Choctaws and the Upper Creeks. Some white farmers were cultivating the island, and the Choctaws requested that their agent, Silas Dinsmoor, ask the farmers for the rent due the Choctaws.[99] When the Upper Creeks heard about this, some headmen sent a letter to the Choctaws explaining their position according to what "their ancestors said about the island."[100] The Creeks asserted that they had initially gained possession of the land through conquest and that subsequently they had given the island to John Stuart, the British superintendent for Indian affairs. Then, in the 1776 Treaty of Pensacola the island was ceded to the British. But since the 1776 treaty was negated with the American Revolution, the land reverted to the Creeks, not the Choctaws, and it was the Creeks who had rights to any rental fees. They were asking for fifty cents an acre. In this same letter, the Creeks stated their policy simply as "if you see any whites on Indian land you can ask for rent."[101]

For grazing, the fee was twenty-five cents per head of cattle and fifty cents per horse.[102] The Creeks likewise expected payment for the grazing on Indian lands of any livestock belonging to the military forts and the American trading houses, and Hawkins apparently also paid for grazing privileges when his personal stock wandered off his homestead on the Flint River.[103] To whom these sorts of fees went is unclear. In 1798 Efau Haujo stated that only the nation, not individuals, had the right to grant grazing rights to Americans. Efau Haujo made this remark in a complaint about this rule being broken. Individuals were selling timber, grazing, and other use rights to Americans and collecting the fees for themselves.[104]

Needless to say, when American land claims came under contest, all of these things had to be sorted out, which was no easy task. When such a situation came to Hawkins's attention, he duly submitted a report to the War Department, requesting authorization for an investigation into the legality of the claim.[105] The investigations were time-consuming because the information was usually faulty and imprecise and because every piece of evidence had to be verified in some way. For example, in 1803 Hawkins received information about a Mrs. Durant who had purchased some Indian lands on her own. Even the most basic facts had to be determined—Hawkins had to first find out whether she was white or an Indian. Secretary Dearborn instructed Hawkins to have her arrested if she were white, but that if she were an Indian to not do anything as "we have no control over her."[106] It is uncertain how this case was resolved, if at all.

Even if one could manage to get some reliable information on the basic facts, many other things conspired to impede investigating legal titles to land. For example, when Hawkins wanted to conduct such an investigation, he had to call a meeting of Creek town representatives, which entailed sending runners to inform men throughout Creek territory to meet at an appointed time. It also involved obtaining some sort of legal deed from the American settlers, which was difficult since most informal land deals were verbal agreements. If there was no deed, Hawkins had to go through a lengthy process of taking depositions from the American settlers and their neighbors.[107] Once all the information had been gathered, Hawkins then had to sort through the conflicting claims, confer with Creek headmen, and somehow resolve the issue.[108] Because of such problems, Hawkins submitted petitions only for those American farmers and ranchers who he believed held some justifiable claim that warranted an investigation. For squatters who moved over the boundary in flagrant violation of the law, Hawkins refused to intercede.[109]

Hawkins continually complained about such intrusions, and the Creeks grew restless as they saw more and more squatters illegally crossing the line. The federal government had responded early on in the proclamations of the Continental Congress by making intrusions of any sort illegal, but the enforcement of such laws was always lackadaisical.[110] In the South, military garrisons stood at the Indian–United States borders to ward off intruders. Although the Creeks did not want an American army in their country, some Creek headmen and others welcomed a United States military presence on the borders because they believed only this would stop the intrusions without involving the Creeks in a general war.[111] It also meant that the Creeks, as all of the southern Indians, depended on United States recognition and enforcement of Indian land rights.

By treaty, Hawkins had the authority to send a military detachment to forcibly eject any intruders. The arrangements for sending such deputations are cloudy. Hawkins, as the leading United States military authority in Indian territory, could order such an expedition, but the costs were above ordinary expenses, and the soldiers and officers expected extra pay. For example, in 1808 Hawkins ordered Captain Boote to remove the Wofford settlers, as requested by the Cherokees. After several months' delay, Boote sent word to Hawkins and the Cherokees that he had not yet proceeded because he had no money.[112] On another occasion, Hawkins paid Captain Timothy Freeman and his deputation two dollars a day to make the rounds of Georgia squatters and collect rental fees as the Creeks had requested.[113] The federal government never allocated the money to maintain an adequate military or police effort to stop intrusions. The southern military outposts were so few, so ill manned, and so impoverished as to be useless.[114] The War Department, never generous to Hawkins's office anyway, did not allocate sufficient funds for military evictions. This was not lost on the Creeks, who despite treaty stipulations and promises and despite Hawkins's assertion that they "readily distinguish between intruders on their rights and the federal government," realized that the federal government did not seem disposed to stop the intrusions.[115]

The frontier Americans, faced with eviction from their farms, resisted forced removal even though they knew their settlements on Indian lands were illegal. They resented Hawkins. They perceived him as favoring the Creeks over themselves and increasingly questioned the Creeks' rights to the land.[116] They took their complaints to the state governments, and, because the subject of states' rights was so sensitive, the federal government was reluctant to interfere.[117] By law, intruders could be ejected, but any claims they made on Indian lands and any depredations they committed against the Creeks were state issues. Georgia and Tennessee had laws against squatting, theft, murder, and so on, but in Georgia and Tennessee, Indian testimony was not allowed in a court of law, automatically invalidating any Creek claims against citizens of these states. Hawkins appealed to the War Department to do something to change these state laws since, no matter how many oaths and depositions he collected from Creek complainants, the law hampered getting legal proof and blocked the prosecution of American criminals.[118]

In 1809 Governor Irwin of Georgia finally issued a proclamation whereby anyone caught hunting, cutting cedar, building fish traps, or driving stock on Creek lands was subject to a hundred-dollar fine or six months' imprisonment.[119] Irwin had agreed to issue the proclamation only after Hawkins and a deputation of Creeks visited the governor with the express aim of getting such an injunction. Four months later, Hawkins wrote to Secretary of War William Eustis that the proclamation was ineffectual, in that it had stopped the intrusions only for about a month.[120]

The trip to see Governor Irwin was prompted by the intrusions of Captain Roderick Easley, whose case exemplifies the legal difficulties of removing squatters as well as the impudence and arrogance that state-supported trespassing engendered. Easley and a few other men built cow pens, cleared and farmed some land, and built a "dairy establishment" across the Creek line at High Shoals in Georgia. The Creeks sent numerous warnings to Easley, and Hawkins ordered him off the land several times.[121] For three years Easley ignored the Creeks and Hawkins. He told Hawkins he had legal title to the land, but he could not show any legal proof when Hawkins finally went to High Shoals to confront him.[122] Creek headmen, at Hawkins's behest, agreed to seek redress through the proper American channels. This is why they made the trip to Governor Irwin.

Even after Irwin's proclamation was issued, Easley refused to budge. Hawkins sent Captain Smith to arrest Easley and to destroy his establishment.[123] Easley's case was brought before the Attorney for the United States for the District of Georgia, William B. Bulloch, in Milledgeville.[124] Hawkins offered to appear in court on the Creeks' behalf since they were not allowed to do so.[125] When Hawkins arrived at Milledgeville on the court date, Easley and his partners jumped bail and "forfeited their recognizance."[126] Actually, Easley and his partners did not risk much, since under Georgia law their crime was only a misdemeanor.[127] The Easley incident, according to Hawkins, was the third time intruders had been removed by military force and the first time they had been handed over to the civil authority.[128] This was in 1810 and reflects only too well the federal and state governments' lax attitude toward intrusions.

When the intrusions continued and even increased, and with the dawning realization that the federal government could not or would not stop them, Creek warriors increasingly took matters into their own hands, raiding and harassing border settlers and especially squatters. An indication of the tension under which these families lived occurred when Hawkins and others were tracking a group of American outlaws. When Hawkins's party approached a farmstead, the family quickly "fled and left their house open."[129]

One of the most serious consequences of trespassing, squatting, and Indian raiding was a killing. Both Creeks and frontier Americans killed each other with alarming regularity. The motives for violence of this kind were varied. Some killings occurred by accident. Sometimes a man or woman got caught in a spray of bullets during a robbery attempt. Some people killed for vengeance. Sometimes vigilante groups, operating outside the law, executed people suspected of some offence. Some people killed out of sheer meanness and psychopathic behavior. Some killed for land. Some killed as part of a resistance to American encroachment. With every killing, the friends, family, or clan members of the slain sought punishment for the killers in their own ways.

In 1802 Hawkins and some Creek headmen discussed the problem of trying to settle these "debts of blood" between the Creeks and Americans. First there were some preliminary discussions concerning a land cession to Georgia as part of the Treaty of Fort Wilkinson. After addressing several other matters, Efau Haujo commented that the Creeks had never received restitution for the murder of Davey Cornells.[130] Cornells and a party of Creeks and Americans were en route to Colerain on the St. Marys River in Georgia to deliver a bundle of letters to James Seagrove, the Indian agent at the time. Creek headmen were relaying the letters to convey some recent deliberations among themselves concerning a series of retaliatory raids between some Cowetas, Chehaws, and Yuchis and some settlers on the Oconee River. Just outside Colerain, a Georgia militia group attacked the Indian party, killing Cornells, two other Creek men, and a fourteen-year-old boy who had come along to tend the horses. The Georgia government maintained that Cornells was a known horse thief and murderer and that he was shot on sight because of his past deeds.[131] Efau Haujo told Hawkins that Cornells was not a horse thief "but a man with a white flag."[132] Efau Haujo's reference to the white flag indicated Cornells's good will since, to the Creeks, white symbolized peace and good intentions. And because Georgia showed no inclination to punish Cornells's murderers, the Creeks had little faith in Georgians and saw no need to bend to their demands for land.

Hawkins, irritated by Efau Haujo's use of this old incident to block the treaty, retorted by enumerating the many deaths of Americans at Creek hands. A black woman was murdered in Cussetah. A man in Cumberland, Tennessee, was killed without provocation. Some Cussetahs had killed a white man in revenge; some Yuchis had done the same. In sum, "five debts were due the whites."[133] Tuskenehau Chapco of Cussetah countered that the black woman was killed in revenge for a white man killing a Creek hunter. Furthermore, even Hawkins acknowledged that the slayings by the Cussetahs and Yuchis were in revenge for some whites killing an Indian commissioner and wounding several others, including another headman. To the Creek headmen, the Creeks owed no debt of blood to Georgia.[134]

Such harangues over the balance sheet of the "debt of blood" happened at every Creek-American treaty negotiation. Despite all endeavors to impose some legal order on the frontier, frontier Americans and Creeks alike sought redress in blood for blood. The dangers in the doctrine of blood for blood were palpable. Timothy Barnard once reflected that "if people remember these old grudges we shall never have peace."[135] Barnard expressed a common sentiment. Hawkins and Creek headmen counseled patience to agitated relatives of slain Creeks on several occasions. In 1797, for example, Fusihatchee Mico reported to Hawkins that the brothers of a slain Creek man were preparing to seek vengeance among the whites. Hawkins immediately sent a runner to the brothers with a message beseeching them to calm down and let him handle the matter. By asking the brothers to come to him so that he could speak directly with them, he managed to defuse the situation.[136] Then in 1799 some Creek hunters killed a white man near the Ocmulgee River. Word of the killing quickly spread to other Creek hunting parties in the vicinity, and all feared that armed white men would flood the woods in reprisal. The women and children were sent back to the towns; a runner was dispatched to inform Hawkins of the affair, and the men prepared to defend themselves. In their message to Hawkins, the men asked him to assure the white people that they wished no trouble and that they would "cause justice to be done on this account."[137] Presumably this meant that the men would hand over the slayers to Hawkins or else themselves put the men to death. That same year, a Yuchi man killed a white man named Brown, and Hawkins insisted that the headmen have the Yuchi executed. The Yuchi man fled to the Shawnees, and the executing warriors did not pursue him. In the words of Tustunnuggee Emaultau of Tuckabatchee, one of the headmen appointed to execute the Yuchi man, "Some of us talked of killing one of his family and putting an end to the business, but were restrained by your [Hawkins's] orders."[138] This was an important departure from the usual code of blood revenge wherein the death of a clan member could substitute for the death of the actual individual responsible for the wrong. In blood revenge, the issue was the reinstatement of balance, not the punishment of the wrongdoer.

The Creeks knew, and in case they forgot Hawkins repeatedly reminded them, that if they did not turn over the people responsible for violations against Americans, the United States government would hold the whole Creek Confederacy accountable for the deeds.[139] This made it imperative for Creek headmen, now charged with preventing hostilities and punishing wrongdoers, to attempt to punish the persons responsible for such offences. Since the Creeks were dependent on the federal government to protect and acknowledge their land rights, they also feared turning the president against them by not punishing those guilty of crimes against Americans, and they knew friendly relations between them and the settlers would keep the president, and other white officials, favorably disposed toward them.[140] Finally, and most important, their land was at stake. If the headmen could not control the activities of their people, "the Creeks would be beaten and compelled to give up a portion of their land as the price for peace."[141] As Tussekia Mico of Cussetah said, "It will not do for us to lose our land for a few mad men."[142] Once, Hawkins copied into his journal a letter from an unnamed relation of Sinnajijee of Tuckabatchee. Sinnajijee had scalped a Mrs. Smith of Tombigbee. Mrs. Smith survived the assault and returned to Georgia. Still, Sinnajijee's relation was fearful of retaliation. He informed Hawkins that he had convinced his family that Sinnajijee must die for the offence and that he had sent some warriors to kill him, which they had done. Sinnajijee's relation hoped Hawkins would relay the message to the white people around Tombigbee.[143] This unnamed Creek man then sent a message to the warriors of the Upper and Lower towns that "they must take heart, follow the example I have set and let us free our land from guilt to save it."[144] Sinnajijee's relation knew, as every Creek man and woman knew, that the price for killing Americans, ultimately, would be their lands and their political sovereignty.

Frontier Americans understood the larger implications of killings as well, and some hoped to use it to their own advantage. In 1803, for instance, some Creek hunters sent a runner to Hawkins with an alarming message. A white person had killed a Creek. More important, the American settlers near Ocmulgee were extremely belligerent and "threatened to kill them for their land."[145] The women and children were ordered to return home, and the warriors remained near the Ocmulgee, waiting to hear from Hawkins. Hawkins immediately dispatched a letter to Governor Milledge of Georgia for information on the Ocmulgee settlers and to see if Milledge had deployed the Georgia militia for some reason and failed to inform Hawkins. A bit later Hawkins managed to calm the situation, but obviously everyone was fearful that a war was about to begin or already had begun.[146] As Mrs. Anna Vansant reported in her deposition regarding her husband Isaac's death, "The doctrine in her neighborhood was, let us kill the Indians, bring on a war, and we shall get land."[147]

An American-Creek war was not an unreasonable fear. Both the Creeks and the Americans knew full well that war was a real possibility. Everyone knew that the Georgia and Tennessee governments were only waiting for an excuse to invade Creek territory and drive them off their land. The Creeks faced a terrible contradiction. They were not wholly certain that they could win a war with America, so peace was imperative. But the Creeks loathed intruders and saw them as the harbingers of more land cessions. And if neither the United States federal nor state governments could control the intruders, then the Creeks would. Many Creeks lashed out at American settlers in an attempt to terrorize the frontier, stop the intrusions, and thereby stop westward expansion. Such terrorism was impossible to stop, because peace and lawfulness were impossible to attain on a frontier in which neither Indians nor American authority held any power to control the rank and file. Efau Haujo recognized this when he once pointedly observed, "I do the best I can but all I do is nothing. I look around every way and I see nothing but trouble and difficulties."[148]

Creek men and women vacillated between extremes in their opinions of Americans. On the one hand, many Creeks and Americans were business partners, friends, spouses, fathers, and mothers. On the other hand, and according to James Adair, who knew the southern Indians well, they were "so strongly attached to, and prejudiced in favor of their own colour, that they think as meanly of the whites as we possibly can do of them."[149] Bernard Romans put it more succinctly: "No nation has so contemptible an opinion of us as them."[150] It is no wonder that the southern frontier was a place of great paradoxes. Creek men and women moved easily between red, white, and black in their daily lives, and in many cases melded their lives with those of frontier Americans as in the mixed settlement of Wofford and in their own mixed population. And in the blink of an eye, one of those same Creeks could vow to kill every American he or she saw. For the Creeks, every frontier American in some way represented the aim of a larger America to take away their lands and to destroy them as a people; it was impossible to separate individual Americans from the larger forces working against them. By 1813 it would be impossible to separate those Creeks counseling conciliation with America from these forces as well. The result would be the Creek civil war known as the Red Stick War.

NOTES

1. I have chosen to refer to the people who made up the Creek Confederacy as Creeks instead of Muskogeans or Muscogulges, names that were also used historically and in some writings on the Creeks, because "Creeks" is the most common

reference in the historical documents, it is the one that contemporary people recognize, and it is the name contemporary Creek Indians use.

2. The Creek Confederacy as a functioning political unit has never been thoroughly examined. The anthropologist John R. Swanton first attempted to put some order to our understanding of the Creek Confederacy; see his *Social Organization and Social Usages of the Indians of the Creek Confederacy* (Washington, D.C.: U.S. Bureau of American Ethnology, 1928). Using more modern historical and archaeological methods, Vernon J. Knight gives an outline of its formation and Michael Green gives an account of its workings in the political and legal fight against removal; see Michael D. Green, *The Politics of Indian Removal: Creek Government and Society in Crisis* (Lincoln: University of Nebraska Press, 1982), and Vernon James Knight Jr., "The Formation of the Creeks," in *The Forgotten Centuries: Indians and Europeans in the American South, 1521–1704*, ed. Charles Hudson and Carmen Chaves Tesser (Athens: University of Georgia Press, 1994), 373–92. Most recently Claudio Saunt, in *A New Order of Things: Property, Power, and the Transformation of the Creek Indians, 1733–1816* (Cambridge: Cambridge University Press, 1999), examines the transforming effects of wealth on the political system of the Creeks during the eighteenth century. Steven Hahn's *Invention of the Creek Nation: A Political History of the Creek Indians in the South's Imperial Era, 1540–1763* (Lincoln: University of Nebraska Press, forthcoming), examines the rise of the Creek Confederacy as a cohesive political unit.

3. These figures are taken from a modern map of the Creek Confederacy, ca. 1800, that I compiled; see Robbie Ethridge, *Creek Country: The Creek Indians and Their World* (Chapel Hill: University of North Carolina Press, 2003).

4. McGillivray's letters have been collected in Alexander McGillivray, *McGillivray of the Creeks*, ed. John Walton Caughey (Norman: University of Oklahoma Press, 1938). For various aspects of McGillivray's career and life, see Kathryn E. Holland Braund, *Deerskins and Duffels: The Creek Indian Trade with Anglo-America, 1685–1815* (Lincoln: University of Nebraska Press, 1993); Saunt, *A New Order*; J. Leitch Wright Jr., *Creeks and Seminoles: The Destruction and Regeneration of the Muscogulge People* (Lincoln: University of Nebraska Press, 1986).

5. Florette Henri, *The Southern Indians and Benjamin Hawkins, 1796–1816* (Norman: University of Oklahoma Press, 1986), 61–111.

6. As a part of the 1790 Trade and Intercourse Act, a law passed by the U.S. Congress to regulate Indian affairs, the Indians east of the Mississippi were divided into a northern and southern district with a federally appointed Indian agent for each district. Hawkins was appointed to replace James Seagrove as agent for the southern district; see Francis Paul Prucha, *American Indian Policy in the Formative Years: The Indian Trade and Intercourse Acts, 1790–1834* (Cambridge: Harvard University Press, 1962).

7. Benjamin Hawkins was a North Carolinian who at twenty-eight years of age began a successful career in politics, serving in the North Carolina state legislature and later as a state representative to Congress for fifteen years. By the time of his

appointment as Indian agent in 1796, Hawkins was around forty years old. Two biographies have been written about Hawkins, Henri's *Southern Indians* and Merritt B. Pound's *Benjamin Hawkins: Indian Agent* (Athens: University of Georgia Press, 1951). Most of Hawkins's writings have been published in *Letters of Benjamin Hawkins, 1796–1806* (Savannah: Georgia Historical Society, 1916); *The Letters, Journals, and Writings of Benjamin Hawkins*, ed. C. L. Grant, 2 vols. (Savannah: Beehive Press, 1980); *A Sketch of the Creek Country in the Years 1798 and 1799* (1848. reprint, New York: Kraus, 1971). The Hawkins family was a prominent North Carolina family that produced many statesmen, including a governor. The Hawkins Family Papers are at the Southern Historical Collection, Library of the University of North Carolina at Chapel Hill; additional collections are at the North Carolina Department of Archives and History, Raleigh.

8. Thomas Jefferson Papers, Library of Congress, Manuscript Division, Washington, D.C.

9. Benjamin Hawkins to Thomas Jefferson, "A Comparative Vocabulary of the Muskogee or Creek, Chickasaw, Choctaw, and Cherokee Languages, 1800," American Philosophical Society Library, Philadelphia.

10. President Jefferson on Indian Trading Houses, January 18, 1803, *Documents of United States Indian Policy*, ed. Francis Paul Prucha, 2d ed. (Lincoln: University of Nebraska Press, 1990).

11. For a comprehensive examination of the rise and decline of the deerskin trade during the eighteenth century, see Braund, *Deerskins and Duffels*.

12. Charles Hudson argues that the southern deer population was so seriously diminished as to be the major cause of the decline of the deerskin trade; see Hudson, "Why the Southeastern Indians Slaughtered Deer," in *Indians, Animals and the Fur Trade: a Critique of Keepers of the Game*, ed. Shepard Krech III (Athens: University of Georgia Press, 1981), 168–70. One argument against Hudson's conclusion is in Gregory A. Waselkov, "The Eighteenth-Century Anglo-Indian Trade in Southeastern North America," in *New Faces of the Fur Trade: Selected Papers of the Seventh North American Fur Trade Conference*, ed. Jo-Anne Fiske, Susan Sleeper-Smith, and William Wicken (East Lansing: Michigan State University Press, 1998), 193–222. Waselkov believes that because white-tailed deer are so fecund, rebounding so quickly from population depletion, shortages of deer for commercial purposes were short-lived. He further argues that one should examine the decline of the trade in light of the changes in the European market and the increasing interest of the southeastern Indians in economic alternatives like ranching, rather than ascribing it to a simple decline in the deer population. I conclude that the deer population had, in fact, crashed, if only temporarily, and that this crash, combined with distressed commercial factors, led to the demise of the skin trade; see Ethridge, *Creek Country*.

13. Hawkins lists almost every town as owning livestock *Letters of Benjamin Hawkins*, 285–316.

14. Vernon James Knight Jr., *Tukabatchee: Archaeological Investigations at an Historic Creek Town, Elmore County, Alabama, 1984*, Report of Investigations, no.

45 (Moundville: University of Alabama Office of Archaeological Research, 1985), 181.

15. *Letters of Benjamin Hawkins*, 583.

16. Gregory A. Waselkov and Marvin T. Smith, "Upper Creek Archaeology," in *Indians of the Greater Southeast: Historical Archaeology and Ethnohistory*, ed. Bonnie G. McEwan (Gainesville: University Press of Florida, 2000), 242–64; Knight, *Tukabatchee*, 180–82; Ethridge, *Creek Country*; Saunt, *A New Order*, 47–50.

17. Saunt, in *A New Order*, explores the emergence of private property and an elite class among the Creeks.

18. *Letters of Benjamin Hawkins*, 15.

19. Ibid., 353, 387, 553.

20. Albert James Pickett, *History of Alabama, and Incidentally of Georgia and Mississippi, from the Earliest Period* (Charleston, S.C.: Walker and James, 1851), 98; Louis LeClerc de Milfort, *Memoir; or, A Cursory Glance at My Different Travels and My Sojourn in the Creek Nation*, ed. John Francis McDermott, trans. Geraldine de Courcy (1802; reprint, Chicago: Donnelley, 1956), 95; *Letters of Benjamin Hawkins*, 317–18.

21. William Bartram, *William Bartram on the Southeastern Indians*, ed. Gregory A. Waselkov and Kathryn E. Holland Braund (Lincoln: University of Nebraska Press, 1995), 181; *Letters of Benjamin Hawkins*, 319; John Pope, *A Tour through the Southern and Western Territories of the United States of North-America, the Spanish Dominions on the River Mississippi, and the Floridas, the Countries of the Creek Nations, and Many Uninhabited Parts* (1791; reprint, New York: Charles L. Woodward, 1888), 56; Bernard Romans, *A Concise Natural History of East and West Florida*, ed. Kathryn E. Holland Braund (Tuscaloosa: University of Alabama Press, 1999), 93. Also see Craig T. Sheldon Jr., "Upper Creek Architecture at Fusihatchee," in *Archaeological Excavations at the Early Historic Creek Indian Town of Fusihatchee (Phase I, 1988–1989)*, ed. Gregory A. Waselkov, John W. Cottier, and Craig T. Sheldon Jr. (Auburn, Ala.: University of Auburn Department of Sociology and Anthropology, 1990), 45–76; Harold A. Huscher, *Historic Lower Creek Sites*, Georgia State Archaeological Site Manuscript Files, no. 182 (Athens: University of Georgia, 1958), 41; Charles Hudson, *The Southeastern Indians* (Knoxville: University of Tennessee Press, 1976), 221–22; Frank G. Speck, "The Creek Indians of Taskigi Town," *Memoirs of the American Anthropological Association* 2 (1907): 112.

22. Craig T. Sheldon Jr., "Historic Creek 'Summer' Houses of Central Alabama," paper presented at the Annual Meeting of the Society for American Archaeology, Nashville, April 4, 1997; Allan D. Meyers, "Household Organization and Refuse Disposal at a Cultivated Creek Site," *Southeastern Archaeology* 15, no. 2 (1996): 132–44; Diane Silvia Mueller, "Intrasite Settlement at the Historic Creek Town of Hickory Ground (1EE89), Elmore County, Alabama (1990–1991)," *Journal of Alabama Archaeology* 41, no. 2 (1995): 107–34; Gregory A. Waselkov, "Historic Creek Architectural Adaptations to the Deerskin Trade," paper presented at the Southeastern Archaeological Conference, New Orleans, October 22, 1988; Waselkov and

Smith, "Upper Creek Archaeology," 254–55. For an illustration of a Creek house, see Bartram, *Southeastern Indians*, 154. By the turn of the nineteenth century, some Creeks were building log cabins modeled after the American frontier style. These were basically horizontal, notched log constructions made of unhewn logs with roofs of bark and gable end chimneys. These houses became more and more popular throughout the first decades of the nineteenth century, and by the time of removal, most Creeks lived in them; for descriptions, see Captain Basil Hall, *Travels in North America in the Years 1827 and 1828*, 3 vols. (Edinburgh: Cadell, 1829), 3:290; Adam Hodgson, *Letters from North America, Written During a Tour in the United States and Canada* (London: Hurst, Robinson, 1824), 143–55; A. Levasseur, *Lafayette in America in 1824 and 1825; or, Journal of a Voyage to the United States*, trans. J. D. Godman (Philadelphia: Carey and Lea, 1829), 73. However, few of these have been found archaeologically; see Waselkov and Smith, "Upper Creek Archaeology," 254–55.

23. *Letters of Benjamin Hawkins*, 290–314; Ethridge, *Creek Country*. The archaeology also confirms this change in settlement patterns; see Robert W. Benson, *Cultural Resources Survey for FY91/FY92 Timber Harvesting Compartments and Testing Site MTA-2, Fort Benning, Alabama and Georgia*, report, Army Corps of Engineers, Savannah District and Fort Benning (Athens, Ga.: Southeastern Archaeological Services, Inc., 1994); Daniel T. Elliott et al., *Up on the Upatoi: Cultural Resources Survey and Testing of Compartments K-6 and K-7, Fort Benning Military Reservation, Georgia* (Environmental Management Division, Fort Benning, 1996); C. G. Holland, "A Mid-Eighteenth Century Indian Village on the Chattahoochee River," *Florida Anthropologist* 27 (1974): 31–46; Knight, *Tukabatchee*, 9–19; R. Jerald Ledbetter and Chad O. Braley, *Archaeological and Historical Investigations at Florence Marina State Park, Walter F. George Reservoir, Stewart County, GA* (Atlanta: Georgia Department of Natural Resources, 1989); Tim S. Mistovich and Vernon James Knight Jr., *Excavations at Four Sites on Walter F. George Lake, Alabama and Georgia*, Report of Investigations, no. 49 (Moundville: University of Alabama Office of Archaeological Research, 1986); Tim S. Mistovich and David W. Zeanah, *An Intensive Phase II Survey of Selected Areas of the Coosa River Navigation Project*, Report of Investigations nos. 35 and 38, vols. 3–4 (Moundville: University of Alabama Office of Archaeological Research, 1983); Marvin T. Smith, *Historic Period Indian Archaeology of Northern Georgia*, University of Georgia Laboratory of Archaeology Series, no. 30, (Athens: University of Georgia, 1994); Gregory A. Waselkov, "Changing Strategies of Indian Field Location in the Early Historic Southeast," in *People, Plants, and Landscapes: Studies in Paleoethnobotany*, ed. Kristen J. Gremillion (Tuscaloosa: University of Alabama Press, 1997), 179–94; Gregory A. Waselkov, *Coosa River Valley Archaeology: Results of a Cultural Resources Reconnaissance*, report to Army Corps of Engineers, Mobile District, 2 vols. (Auburn, Ala.: Auburn University Department of Sociology and Anthropology, 1980); Gregory A. Waselkov, *Lower Tallapoosa River Cultural Resources Survey, Phase I Report* (Auburn, Ala.: Auburn University Department of Sociology and Anthropology, 1981);. Waselkov, Cottier, and Sheldon, *Archaeological Excavations*; Nancy Marie White, Stephanie J. Belovich and David S. Brose, *Archaeological Survey at*

Lake Seminole, Jackson and Gadsden Counties, Florida; Seminole and Decatur Counties, Georgia, Archaeological Research Report, no. 29 (Mobile, Ala.: Cleveland Museum of Natural History for the U.S. Army Corps of Engineers, Mobile District, 1981).

24. The American frontiersman has been lionized in both popular and scholarly writings. Frederick Jackson Turner, in the early twentieth century, typified the American frontiersman as a rugged individualist, averse to authority of any kind, fiercely independent, and democratically minded. Turner—who, incidentally, barely mentioned Native Americans—posited that American pioneers embodied the American spirit, and indeed they gave birth to it. According to Turner, as these people entered the eastern woodlands, their European habits of mind were exorcised by the sheer necessities and hardships of settling a remote and untamed wilderness. Turner's thesis has become the basis of much stereotyping and mythmaking as well as scholarly debate. See Frederick Jackson Turner, *The Frontier in American History* (New York: Henry Holt, 1920). More modern scholarship has refined considerably the Turner thesis. For a sampling of recent scholarship about the southern frontier, see Andrew R. L. Cayton and Fredrika J. Teute, eds., *Contact Points: American Frontiers from the Mohawk Valley to the Mississippi, 1750–1830* (Chapel Hill: University of North Carolina Press, 1998); Joyce E. Chaplin, *An Anxious Pursuit: Agricultural Innovation and Modernity in the Lower South, 1730–1815* (Chapel Hill: University of North Carolina Press, 1993); Wilma A. Dunaway, *The First American Frontier: Transition to Capitalism in Southern Appalachia, 1700–1860* (Chapel Hill: University of North Carolina Press, 1996); Daniel H. Usner Jr., *Indians, Settlers, and Slaves in a Frontier Exchange Economy* (Chapel Hill: University of North Carolina Press, 1992).

25. *Letters of Benjamin Hawkins*, 341.

26. Usner, *Indians, Settlers, and Slaves*, 180.

27. Terry G. Jordan and Matti Kaups, *The American Backwoods Frontier: An Ethnic and Ecological Interpretation* (Baltimore: The Johns Hopkins University Press, 1989), 66.

28. Hall, *Travels*, 3:271.

29. James C. Bonner, *A History of Georgia Agriculture, 1732–1860* (Athens: University of Georgia Press, 1964), 95; Jordan and Kaups, *The American Backwoods Frontier*.

30. The foodways of the southern frontier family have yet to be compiled; this list of foodstuffs is taken from observers' accounts such as William Bartram, *Travels through North and South Carolina, Georgia, East and West Florida, the Cherokee Country, the Extensive Territories of the Muscogulges, or Creek Confederacy, and the Country of the Chactaws* (1791; reprint, New York: Penguin, 1988), and Romans, *Concise Natural History*. The most detailed analysis of historical southern foodways is Sam Bowers Hilliard, *Hog Meat and Hoecake: Food Supply in the Old South, 1840–1860* (Carbondale: Southern Illinois University Press, 1972), but it deals primarily with the antebellum period.

31. Benson, *Cultural Resources Survey*; Jordan and Kaups, *The American Back-*

woods Frontier, 123; R. Douglas Hurt, *Indian Agriculture in America: Prehistory to the Present* (Lawrence: University Press of Kansas, 1987), 39; Paul Starrett, *Appraisal Report: Lands in Southern Georgia and Southeastern Alabama Ceded by the Creek Nation, before the Indian Claims Commission, Docket No. 21, Valued as of August 9, 1814* (Washington, D.C.: Government Printing Office, 1957), 46–47; Clarence L. Ver Steeg, *Origins of a Southern Mosaic: Studies of Early Carolina and Georgia* (Athens: University of Georgia Press, 1975), 45–62.

32. Jordan and Kaups, *The American Backwoods Frontier.*

33. Joseph P. Reidy, *From Slavery to Agrarian Capitalism in the Cotton Plantation South: Central Georgia, 1800–1880* (Chapel Hill: University of North Carolina Press, 1992), 20–21.

34. Timothy Barnard to James Seagrove, March 26, 1793, "Unpublished Letters of Timothy Barnard, 1784–1820," typescript by Louise F. Hays, 1939, Georgia State Department of Archives and History, Atlanta (hereafter cited as Barnard/GDAH), 135. Stephen Aron makes a similar argument for the Kentucky frontier white hunters' lack of participation in the skin trade; see Aron, "Pigs and Hunters: 'Rights in the Woods' on the Trans-Appalachian Frontier," in Cayton and Teute, *Contact Points*, 175–204.

35. Mills Lane, comp., *The Rambler in Georgia* (Savannah: Beehive Press, 1973), 61.

36. Bonner, *Georgia Agriculture*; Lewis Cecil Gray, *History of Agriculture in the Southern United States to 1860*, 2 vols. (1932; reprint, Gloucester, Mass.: Peter Smith, 1958); Hilliard, *Hog Meat.*

37. Eliza A. Bowen et al., *Chronicles of Wilkes County, Georgia from Washington's Newspapers 1889–1898*, ed. Mary Bondurant Warren (Danielsville, Ga.: Heritage Papers, 1978); Ellis Merton Coulter, *Old Petersburg and the Broad River Valley of Georgia: Their Rise and Decline* (Athens: University of Georgia Press, 1965); Charles Danforth Saggus, "A Social and Economic History of the Danburg Community in Wilkes County, Georgia" (M.A. thesis, University of Georgia, 1951).

38. For a sampling of eighteenth- and early-nineteenth-century travelogues, see Lane, *The Rambler in Georgia.*

39. For a detailed narrative of a late-eighteenth-century southern frontier town, see Coulter, *Old Petersburg*. Basil Hall in his *Travels* has several colorful descriptions of frontier towns; for a picture he drew of Columbus, Georgia, as a frontier town, see his *Forty Etchings, from Sketches made with the Camera Lucida, in North America, in 1827 and 1828* (London, 1830), plate 26.

40. Such exchanges are difficult to document because they largely occurred in informal and unrecorded interactions, but in looking over eyewitness accounts and the Creek trade ledgers, one can see that these exchanges were common; see Romans, *Concise Natural History*; *Letters of Benjamin Hawkins*, 328–39; Richard Thomas, "His Book, Begun November 21, 1796," in *Letters of Benjamin Hawkins*, 448–500; also, from Record Group 75, Records of the Bureau of Indian Affairs, National Archives and Records Service, Washington, D.C. (hereafter cited as NA, RG 75), the following: entry 5, Records of the Office of Indian Trade, Creek Factory, Invoice and

Letterbook, 1803–1804, 1816–1822; entry 6, Records of the Office of Indian Trade, Creek Factory, Memorandum Book, 1807–1813; entry 9, Records of the Office of Indian Trade, Creek Factory, Journals, 1805–1824; entry 42, Records of the Office of Indian Trade, Creek Factory, Correspondence, 1795–1814; entry 43, Records of the Office of Indian Trade, Creek Factory, Creek Factory, Letters Sent, 1795–1816; entry 47, Records of the Office of Indian Trade, Creek Factory Journals, 1801–1820; entry 50, Records of the Office of Indian Trade, Creek Factory, Ledger of Hawkins's Accounts, 1808–1814; entry 52, Records of the Office of Indian Trade, Creek Factory, Miscellaneous Accounts, 1795–1816; entry 1065, Records of the Office of Indian Trade, Field Office Records, Records of the Creek Agency, East, Correspondence and Other Records, 1794–1818. See also Usner, *Indians, Settlers, and Slaves*.

41. W. O. Tuggle, *Shem, Ham and Japheth: The Papers of W. O. Tuggle*, ed. Eugene Current-Garcia and Dorothy B. Hatfield (Athens: University of Georgia Press, 1973).

42. Robbie Ethridge, "Horse Stealing as an Informal Economic Strategy on the Late Eighteenth Century Southern Frontier," paper presented at the 1993 Annual Meeting of the American Society for Ethnohistory, Bloomington, Ind., November 3–6, 1993.

43. Much of this interaction and daily encounters between red and white is documented in "Creek Indian Letters, Talks, and Treaties, 1705–1839," typescript by Louise F. Hays, 1939, and "Indian Letters, 1782–1839," typescript by Louise F. Hays, 1940, Georgia Department of Archives and History, Atlanta (hereafter cited as Creek Letters/GDAH and Indian Letters/GDAH, respectively).

44. Caleb Swan in 1790 estimated that three hundred whites lived in the Creek Confederacy; see Caleb Swan, "State of Arts and Manufactures, with the Creek Indians, in 1791," in *Information Respecting the History, Condition and Prospects of the Indian Tribes of the United States*, ed. Henry Rowe Schoolcraft, 6 vols. (Philadelphia: Lippincott, Grambo, 1852–57), 263. Many of these were traders who had married Indian women and chosen to reside in Creek country; see Braund, *Deerskins and Duffles*. However, many blacks also resided in Creek country either as slaves or as free blacks; see Kathryn E. Holland Braund, "The Creek Indians, Blacks, and Slavery," *Journal of Southern History* 57 (1991): 601–36, and Ethridge, *Creek Country*, 129–32. Saunt, in *A New Order*, explores the changing role of black slaves in the Creek Confederacy as the Creeks came to conceive of them as private property. Finally, white women were also present among the Creeks either as captives or as Creek men's wives who had decided to live among their husbands' people; see Ethridge, *Creek Country*.

45. Prucha, *American Indian Policy*, 186–87; Henri, *Southern Indians*, 85, 83–92, provides an excellent treatment of the influence of land speculation on southern Indian affairs.

46. Entry 108, Ratified Indian Treaties, 1722–1869, Record Group 11, General Records of the United States Government, National Archives and Records Service, Washington, D.C.

47. Henry Dearborn to Hawkins, June 28, 1805, entry 2, Records of the Office of the Secretary of War Relating to Indian Affairs, Letters Sent, 1800–1824, NA, RG 75.

48. Ethridge, *Creek Country*, 289–323; this is in contrast to Saunt, who argues (*A New Order*, 1, 164–85) that the National Council, controlled by a mestizo elite, could exert its control "over every Creek person."

49. Hudson, *The Southeastern Indians*, 229–32. The principles of blood revenge among the Creeks have not been thoroughly investigated, but they probably followed those of the Cherokee, well documented in John Phillip Reid, *A Law of Blood: The Primitive Law of the Cherokee Nation* (New York: New York University Press, 1970).

50. *Letters of Benjamin Hawkins*, 494, 508.

51. Ibid., 182.

52. Ibid., 406.

53. For a history of the Federal Road, see Henry DeLeon Southerland Jr. and Jerry Elijah Brown, *The Federal Road Through Georgia, the Creek Nation, and Alabama, 1806–1836* (Tuscaloosa: University of Alabama Press, 1989).

54. *Letters of Benjamin Hawkins*, 578.

55. Ibid., 507, 587; Southerland and Brown, *Federal Road*, 22–32.

56. *Letters of Benjamin Hawkins*, 157, 578; Timothy Pickering to Capt. John Eaton of Wilkerson, November 6, 1795, Creek Factory Correspondences, 1795–1814, entry 42, NA, RG 75.

57. *Letters of Benjamin Hawkins*, 157–59.

58. Ibid., 159, 260.

59. Ibid., 260, 271.

60. Also known as Pinckney's Treaty, this is the treaty that established the Thirty-first Parallel as the boundary between Spain and America. The line existed only in the abstract, partly because of Seminole resistance and partly because of the many contested Spanish and American claims along this border; see Thomas D. Clark and John D. W. Guice, *Frontiers in Conflict: The Old Southwest, 1795–1830* (Albuquerque: University of New Mexico Press, 1989), 41, 43, 68.

61. Creek Letters/GDAH, 716, 719.

62. Ibid., 716.

63. *Letters of Benjamin Hawkins*, 360.

64. Ibid., 360.

65. Ibid., 588; June 11, 1800, JO/APS.

66. Newton D. Mereness, ed., *Travels in the American Colonies* (New York: Macmillan, 1916), 178; Henri, *Southern Indians*, 141.

67. Barnard to Edward Price, March 27, 1799, entry 42, NA, RG 75.

68. This had been McGillivray's campaign against Georgia. Creek hostilities during this time were fearsome and widespread. McGillivray's warriors robbed and killed settlers and destroyed their farms. Georgia retaliated by invading Creek territory, killing seventeen people at the Flint River town of Padjeeligau, burning Oktelleoconee (Burnt Village), and killing a Creek peace emissary, Davey Cornells,

after he had shown his white flag. After McGillivray's death in 1793, hostilities subsided so that by 1796, the year of Hawkins's appointment, the southern frontier was relatively peaceful, as Barnard stated. The earlier years of terror, however, had left their imprint on the psyche of both the Creeks and the white settlers; some particulars of these disturbances can be found in Robert Woodruff, *Journal of a Trip Through New York, New Jersey, Pennsylvania, Delaware, Maryland, Virginia, North Carolina, Rhode Island, Massachusetts, South Carolina, Georgia, as Clerk to John Ansley, December 17, 1785–May 1, 1788* (Philadelphia: Independence National Historical Park, n.d.); Creek Letters/GDAH, 325–28, 338, 339, 344–48; Barnard to Seagrove, July 2 and 3, 1793, Barnard/GDAH, 188, 192b; Barnard to Major Henry Gaither, July 7, 1793, Barnard/GDAH, 197; Moses Barnett, William Dawson, James McLeod, October 25, 1753, Creek Letters/GDAH.

69. For a detailed description of frontier American hunting, see Aron, "Pigs and Hunters."

70. James White to Thomas Pinckney, May 24, 1787, *The New American State Papers: Indian Affairs*, gen. ed. Thomas C. Cochran, 13 vols. (Wilmington, Del.: Scholarly Resources, 1972), 24; June 9, 1802, JO/APS.

71. *Letters of Benjamin Hawkins*, 608; "Hawkins' Journal for the Treaty of Colerain, June 24, 1796," *New American State Papers*, 119–54; Creek Chiefs to Jefferson, November 3, 1805, Daniel Parker Papers, Historical Society of Pennsylvania, Philadelphia (hereafter cited as Parker Papers/HSP).

72. Albert E. Cowdrey, *This Land, This South: An Environmental History* (Lexington: University Press of Kentucky, 1983), 57; Timothy Silver, *A New Face on the Countryside: Indians, Colonists, and Slaves in South Atlantic Forests, 1500–1800* (New York: Cambridge University Press, 1990), 94–97. Night hunting is still illegal in most southern states; for a social history of hunting in the South, see Stuart A. Marks, *Southern Hunting in Black and White: Nature, History, and Ritual in a Carolina Community* (Princeton: Princeton University Press, 1991).

73. June 9, 1802, JO/APS; Chiefs of National Council to Hawkins, May 30, 1810, in James F. Doster, *The Creek Indians and Their Florida Lands*, 2 vols. (New York: Garland, 1974), 18–19.

74. "Hawkins' Journal for the Treaty of Colerain, 1796," in Cochran, *New American State Papers*, 119–54; *Letters of Benjamin Hawkins*, 460, 529, 608.

75. Early County to the Governor of Georgia and Benjamin Hawkins, 1808, entry 1065, NA, RG 75.

76. "Report on Negotiations with Indians in Georgia, 1797," in Cochran, *New American State Papers*, 133.

77. Dearborn to Hawkins, February 19, 1803, entry 5, NA, RG 75.

78. Thomas, "His Book," 491.

79. Ibid.; *Letters of Benjamin Hawkins*, 184, 496.

80. *Letters of Benjamin Hawkins*, 137; entry for June 7, 1798, *Benjamin Hawkins' Letterbook, May 1798–September 1801, 1802* (Philadelphia: Independence National Historical Park, n.d.).

81. *Letters of Benjamin Hawkins*, 169, 275.
82. James Adams, Affidavit Respecting Indians, 1794, Barnard/GDAH, 236; Report of Dr. Frederick Dalcho to the troops of the U.S. in Georgia, May 10, 1794, Barnard/GDAH, 233.
83. *Letters of Benjamin Hawkins*, 126.
84. Ibid., 550; Dearborn to William Davies, James Wilkinson, and Benjamin Hawkins, July 22, 1801, and William Eustis to Hawkins, July 20, 1811, entry 2, NA, RG 75.
85. Creek Chiefs to Jefferson, November 3, 1805, Parker Papers/HSP.
86. *Letters of Benjamin Hawkins*, 409.
87. Dearborn to Davies, Wilkinson, and Hawkins.
88. Eustis to Hawkins.
89. *Letters of Benjamin Hawkins*, 591, 604.
90. Henri, *Southern Indians*, 43, 194–95, 305; James Wilkinson to Governor Josiah Tatnell, June 10, 1802, entry 1, Records of the Office of the Secretary of War Relating to Indian Affairs, Letters Received, 1800–1823, NA, RG 75; June 9, 1802, JO/APS.
91. Henri, *Southern Indians*, 43, 194–95, 305.
92. Wilkinson to Tatnell.
93. June 9, 1802, JO/APS.
94. *Letters of Benjamin Hawkins*, 542; and, from entry 1, NA, RG 75: General Wilkinson to a Deputation of the Cherokee Nation, June 10, 1802; Amahuskasata (Dreadful Water), Calauesta (Hatchet), and Coatahu (Badger's Son) reply, June 27, 1802; Return J. Meigs to William Eustis, December 20, 1811; W. R. Carnes, Roderick Easley, B. Harris, and Howell Cobb, June 29, 1802.
95. Henri, *Southern Indians*, 224–25, 229, 252; Return J. Meigs to Secretary of War, December 20, 1811, and August 25, 1812, entry 1, NA, RG 75.
96. Dearborn to Hawkins, June 28, 1805, entry 2, NA, RG 75.
97. *Letters of Benjamin Hawkins*, 460, 767; Dearborn to Hawkins, January 24, 1803, and June 28, 1805, entry 2, NA, RG 75.
98. *Letters of Benjamin Hawkins*, 336; John Innerarity, "The Creek Debtors to John Forbes & Company, Successors to Panton, Leslie & Company: A Journal of John Innerarity, 1812," *Florida Historical Quarterly* 9 (1930): 76.
99. Creek Chiefs to Choctaw Nation, October 3, 1804, Parker Papers/HSP.
100. Ibid.
101. Ibid.
102. *Letters of Benjamin Hawkins*, 556.
103. Abstract of Provisions, Fort Wilkinson Treaty, 1802, entry 52, NA, RG 75.
104. *Letters of Benjamin Hawkins*, 183.
105. Ibid., 460, 529, 767.
106. Dearborn to Hawkins, January 24, 1803, entry 2, NA, RG 75.
107. Dearborn to Hawkins, January 24, 1803, and June 28, 1805, ibid.; *Letters of Benjamin Hawkins*, 460, 529, 767. Creek Letters/GDAH and Indian Letters/GDAH also contain many such depositions.

108. *Letters of Benjamin Hawkins*, 504.
109. Ibid., 767.
110. Proclamation of the Continental Congress, September 22, 1783, *Documents of United States Indian Policy*, 3.
111. Barnard to Seagrove, May 12, 1793, Barnard/GDAH, 165; *Letters of Benjamin Hawkins*, 499; June 11 and 16, 1802, JO/APS.
112. *Letters of Benjamin Hawkins*, 542.
113. Ibid., 556. In fact, Hawkins lists many such transactions in his ledger books; see entry 49, Records of the Office of Indian Trade, Creek Factory, Journal of Transactions with Benjamin Hawkins, 1808–1814, NA, RG 75.
114. We do not yet have a full reckoning of frontier military life, but the conditions were deplorable. In fact, soldiers thought being stationed in a southern garrison was the worst possible assignment. The garrisons were ramshackle affairs, leaky, cold, and generally uncomfortable. Rations were always meager and the pay was low. The southern military outposts figure prominently in the Creek Indian trade papers; see especially entry 53, Records of the Office of Indian Trade, Creek Factory, Records of the Fort Wilkinson Garrison, 1795–1801, NA, RG 75; also entries 5, 6, 9, 42, 43, 47, and 1065. We know somewhat more about colonial frontier military life, since archaeologists have excavated some colonial frontier forts in the South; see Gregory A. Waselkov, "Recent Archaeological and Historical Research," introduction to *Fort Toulouse: The French Outpost at the Alabamas on the Coosa* by Daniel H. Thomas (1960; reprint, Tuscaloosa: University of Alabama Press, 1989), vi–xli; Marshall W. Williams, *A Memoir of the Archaeological Excavation of Fort Prince George, Pickens County, South Carolina Along with Pertinent Historical Documentation*, Research Manuscript Series no. 226 (Columbia: South Carolina Institute of Archaeology and Anthropology, University of South Carolina, 1998); Jay Higginbotham, *Old Mobile: Fort Louis de la Louisiane, 1702–1711* (1977; reprint, Tuscaloosa: University of Alabama Press, 1991).
115. *Letters of Benjamin Hawkins*, 107, 409.
116. Ibid., 148.
117. "Report on Negotiations with Indians of Georgia, 1797," in Cochran, *New American State Papers*, 118–62; "Message on Negotiations with the Southern Indians, 1801," ibid., 178–84; "Message on Negotiations of Creek Treaty and Compact, 1812," ibid., 184–201.
118. Proclamation, July 19, 1790, Barnard/GDAH, 109–10; *Letters of Benjamin Hawkins*, 504.
119. *Letters of Benjamin Hawkins*, 555.
120. Ibid., 556.
121. Ibid., 574.
122. Ibid., 560.
123. Ibid., 574.
124. Ibid., 574, 601.
125. Ibid., 574.
126. Ibid., 578.

127. Ibid., 578.
128. Ibid., 578.
129. Ibid., 143.
130. Efau Haujo 1802, JO/APS.
131. *Letters of Benjamin Hawkins,* 314; Barnard to Seagrove, July 2 and 3, 1793, Barnard/GDAH, 188, 192b; Barnard to Gaither, July 7, 1793, Barnard/GDAH, 197; Moses Barnett, William Dawson, James McLeod, October 25, 1753, Creek Letters/GDAH. Cornells's murder is documented in Creek Letters/GDAH: Barnard to Seagrove, June 20, 1793, 325–28; Deposition of James Kirby, July 22, 1793, 338–39; Proceedings of the Court of Inquiry, October 26, 1793, 344–48.
132. Efau Haujo 1802, JO/APS.
133. June 12, 1802, JO/APS.
134. Ibid.
135. Barnard to Patrick Carr, April 13, 1784, Barnard/GDAH, 28.
136. *Letters of Benjamin Hawkins,* 145.
137. Ibid., 280.
138. Ibid., 140.
139. Ibid., 120.
140. Ibid., 478.
141. Ibid., 263.
142. Thomas, "His Book," 491.
143. *Letters of Benjamin Hawkins,* 422.
144. Ibid., 422.
145. Ibid., 452.
146. Ibid., 452.
147. Ibid., 102.
148. Ibid., 417.
149. James Adair, *Adair's History of the American Indians,* ed. Samuel Cole Williams (1775; reprint, Johnson City, Tenn.: Watauga Press, 1930), 1.
150. Romans, *Concise Natural History,* 97.

Chapter 12

GEORGE WASHINGTON AND THE "CIVILIZATION" OF THE SOUTHERN INDIANS

THEDA PERDUE

In 1796 George Washington wrote his "beloved Cherokees" a letter in which he described the "path" that could "make life comfortable and happy" for them as well as their white neighbors. He urged them to keep livestock, not only for their own use, but also "to sell to the White people." Adoption of the plow promised to "vastly increase . . . crops of corn" and enable the production of wheat, flax, and cotton, which, he told them, "you may sell to the White people, or have it made up by your own women into cloathing for yourselves. Your wives and daughters can soon learn to spin and weave." He promised to provide spinning wheels, looms, and plows, along with an agent to conduct instruction in their use, and medals for those who excelled at cultural transformation. Furthermore, Washington proposed that the Cherokee Nation follow the example of the United States and send "one or two of its wisest counsellors" from each town "to talk together on the affairs of your nation."[1] The economic and political changes that Washington recommended to the Cherokees formed the core of his policy for Native peoples south of the Ohio River, and he envisioned creating a similar society, mirroring that of the United States, among other Indian nations.

Washington's social engineering reflected new ideas about men and women that were emerging in England and America.[2] The political ideology of republicanism enhanced gender divisions; at the same time it muted class distinctions.[3] That is, as white men became more equal to each other, the gap between them and women—as well as people of color—widened. Washington reveled in the equalizing effect militias had on American men. He described the militia called into federal service to suppress the Whiskey Rebellion in western Pennsylvania in 1794: "It has been a spectacle displaying to the highest advantage the value of republican government to behold the most and least wealthy of our citizens standing in the same ranks as private soldiers."[4] The militias, of course, were a male institution. In European culture, military service, along with land ownership, traditionally had been an essential component of citizenship. With land more widely available in the United States than in England and with militias providing an opportunity for at least the illusion of military service, American men enjoyed relatively easy access to the obligations incumbent upon and the opportunities available to citizens. At the same time, women did not perform militia service, and the common-law tradition of *femme coverture* restricted their ability to hold land independently.[5] States gradually abolished property requirements for voting by men, but they moved to exclude formally both women and African-American men from the franchise. As white men became more equal, they distanced themselves from women and African- Americans; as class receded in political importance, gender and race became more pronounced.

In women's history, scholars have described this new relationship between men and women as "separate spheres" and have pointed to the ways in which this gender segregation created "bonds of womanhood" that ultimately spawned the women's rights movement.[6] Scholars are now beginning to examine constructions of masculinity in this period.[7] By looking at Washington's Indian policy, we can learn something about how the father of his country conceived of appropriate roles for men and women.

The ideas that shaped Washington's Indian policy came from diverse sources. A widely accepted Enlightenment understanding of human difference provided an ideological bedrock on which to construct policy. In the eighteenth century, American natural historians and philosophers attributed cultural differences—including dress, housing, cuisine, language, religion, technology, and artistic and literary achievement—to environment, both physical and intellectual, rather than to innate characteristics. Through education, even the most "savage" human could become "civilized." By "civilized," of course, these enlightened men meant like themselves—rational, republican, agricultural, literate, entrepreneurial, patriarchal, and Christian. As ethnocentric as this view is, it offered hope for Native people, unlike the racism that began to shape American Indian policy in the late 1820s and 1830s that led to the removal of 100,000 Indians from the South. Racism denied the possibility of change—"once an Indian, always an Indian"—while the Founding Fathers' environmental explanations of difference touted not only the possibility but the feasibility of transforming Indians into people who could be assimilated into the American family.[8]

In the Confederation period (1781–89), however, Washington's ideas about Indians and the frontier emanated from the surveyor's transit, the entrepreneur's balance sheet, and the general's strategic plan rather than from the philosopher's salon. In response to a petition from officers of the Continental Army requesting land grants, he recommended the settlement of soldiers and their families on the frontier: "A Settlement formed by such Men would give security to our frontiers, the very name of it would awe the Indians, and more than probably prevent the murder of many innocent families, which frequently, . . . fall the hapless Victims to savage barbarity." The safety of women and children was not the general's only concern. He believed that the demographic pressure of white settlers and the strain on natural resources, in particular on forage for deer, promised to make life so miserable for Native people that they would willingly surrender their lands and "remove into the illimitable regions of the West."[9] Correspondence with General Philip Schuyler, reported in a letter to James Duane, only confirmed his belief that settlements were the most practical approach to disposing of the Indian problem: "Every advantage that could be expected or even wished for would result from such a mode of procedure[;] our Settlements would be compact, Government well established, and our Barrier formidable. . . . the Indians . . . will ever retreat as our Settlements advance upon them and they will be as ready to sell; as we are to buy; That it is the cheapest as well as the least distressing way of dealing with them, none who are acquainted with the Nature of Indian warfare, and has ever been at the trouble of estimating the expence of one, and comparing it with the cost of purchasing their Lands, will hesitate to acknowledge."[10] Never one to mince words, Washington concluded: "The gradual extension of our Settlements will as certain cause the Savage as the Wolf to retire; both being beasts of prey tho' they differ in shape."[11] Native people, he suggested, acted from instinct instead of reason; passion rather than plan shaped their behavior.

Washington recognized that unruliness also extended to many of his countrymen who pushed into the backcountry. Settling soldiers on the frontier promised to protect public lands from being "over run with Land Jobbers, Speculators, and Monopolizers or even with scatter'd settlers." Ignoring his own role in land speculation, Washington characterized these people as the antithesis to disinterested citizens of the republic: "The People engaged in these pursuits without contributing in the smallest degree to the support of the Government, or considering themselves as amenable to its Laws, will involve it by their unrestrained conduct, in inextricable perplexities, and more than probable in a great deal of Bloodshed."[12] Washington knew well the human and financial cost of encroachments on Native land, and he sought to spare the fledgling government the enormous expense of endless Indian wars. Piecemeal, strife-torn expansion, however, offended Washington's sensibilities on another level: Washington abhorred disorder. He feared "overspreading the Western country ... by a parcel of Banditti, who will bid defiance to all authority," and believed that "discipline and arrangement are to be calculated upon in preference to brute force."[13] He decried the "unrestrained conduct" on both sides of the frontier as antithetical to republican values.

Until order prevailed, Washington urged that the government establish trading houses to promote the military and diplomatic loyalty of Native peoples, like the Creeks and Choctaws, who continued to trade and presumably treat with the British operating out of Spanish territory. Washington believed that honest men in the employ of, or at the very least licensed by, the United States "would fix them strongly in our Interest."[14] Washington thought that the purchase of European manufactured goods with deerskins in the South and beaver pelts in the North dominated Native economies, and he had misgivings about the health of societies grounded in trade. Although he promoted a diversified economy in his own country, including foreign trade, he questioned "whether the luxury, effeminacy, and corruptions which are introduced along with it; are counterbalanced by the convenience and wealth which it brings with it."[15] The linkage of effeminacy with corruption places it in opposition to disinterest, that hallmark of republican virtue, and suggests that Washington associated civic virtue with masculinity. Dependence on trade and the absence of discipline and restraint emasculated Native men. Only a self-sufficient agricultural economy and republican political institutions could elevate Native men above savagery and, at the same time, make them real men.[16]

To be real men, therefore, Native hunters and warriors had to become "civilized." Although Washington had little interest in "civilization" at first, he gradually began to entertain the possibility. In 1783 he received a letter from Selina Hastings, countess of Huntingdon, proposing the settlement of pious English emigrants near the Indians "as a means of civilizing the Savages, and propagating the Gospel among them." In a letter to Sir James Jay, he replied that her ideas met with his "highest approbation," although he had misgivings: "That love of ease, impatience under any sort of controul, and disinclination to every kind of pursuit but those of hunting and war, would discourage any person possessed of less piety, zeal and philanthropy than are characteristick of Lady Huntingdon." Nevertheless, he forwarded her plan to the president of Congress with the suggestion that it could "be made subservient to valuable political purposes." In particular, he favored "the encrease of population by orderly and well disposed characters, who would at once form a barrier and attempt the conversion of the Indians without involving an expense to the Union." He expressed concern, however, that the emigrants would be "Monarchical people . . . unmixed with republicans" living in proximity to British Canada. A further impediment to the project was the unavailability of public land, which the federal government planned to grant to veterans or sell to replenish the treasury. Washington, however, had a solution to this problem: "I submit as a dernier resort, for your Ladyships information and consideration, a gazette containing the terms upon which I have offered several tracts of Land (the quantity of my own in that country, and which lie as convenient to the Western Tribes as any in that territory.)"[17]

Washington's interest in land extended beyond his ownership of vast western tracts. Like the other Founding Fathers, Washington believed that widespread landholding promoted civic virtue and protected the republic. Those who owned land had a vested interest in preserving the checks and balances that protected property, as well as life and liberty. The United States had an obligation to acquire land for "Young People who are growing up, and strangers who are coming from other Countries."[18] Land was a commodity to be bought and sold, and Washington thought that Indian land should be purchased rather than seized: "In a word there is nothing to be obtained by an Indian War but the Soil they live on and this can be had by purchase at less expence, and without that bloodshed, and those distresses which helpless Women and Children are made partakers of in all kinds of disputes with them."[19] Treaties foisted on Native people during the Confederation period, so-called "treaties of conquest," had disastrous results that led to frontier unrest and renegotiations in the South and a costly Indian war in the North. By the time of the Constitutional Convention, the nation desperately needed a new Indian policy. The Constitution did both little and much. In its sole reference to Indians, the Constitution gave Congress the power to "regulate Commerce with foreign Nations, and among the several States, and with the Indian tribes."[20] This clause empowered the federal government—not the states or individual citizens—to purchase Indian land. The Constitution made possible the implementation of Washington's ideas.[21]

Washington expected Indians to sell. But many Native peoples did not want to part with their lands, particularly on terms they realized were unfavorable and failed to provide adequate guarantees to the land they retained. The Creeks, in particular, rejected three treaties negotiated by unauthorized individuals with the state of Georgia between 1783 and 1786, and when the federal government sent commissioners to negotiate a new agreement that recognized those cessions, the Creeks refused. When the United States finally obtained a legitimate treaty with the Creeks in 1790, the Creeks regained some of the ceded territory and received a substantial annuity for the rest. The Cherokees protested the Treaty of Holston, negotiated in 1791, and won additional financial considerations. But these concessions to the Creeks and Cherokees included novel provisions. So that these nations "may be led to a greater degree of civilization, and to become herdsmen and cultivators, instead of remaining a state of hunters," the treaties promised that "the United States will from time to time furnish gratuitously the said nation[s] with useful domestic animals and implements of husbandry."[22]

Washington's support for the countess of Huntingdon's plan to Christianize and "civilize" the Indians had stemmed primarily from the strategic advantage of settling non-Indians on the frontier and the possibility of selling land for the scheme. Furthermore, the countess had proposed a philanthropic endeavor, not a government-financed program. These treaties cast "civilization" in a very different light by making it a national policy and merging it with Washington's original conception of Indian-white relations. Conceived and implemented by Secretary of War Henry Knox, the "civilization" program sought to make Native people more amenable to land sales by instilling in them "a love of exclusive property." Knox believed that "this might be brought about by making presents, from time to time, to the chiefs or their wives, of sheep and other domestic animals" and providing agents to "teach the use of them." He also recommended gifts of "silver medals and gorgets, uniform clothing, and a sort of military commission" in which the recipients "retained an exclusive property."[23] In order to become "civilized," Native people had to recognize and appreciate land as a commodity to be bought and sold. Knox regarded the southern Indians as particularly appropriate for his plan.

Washington, Knox, and others who developed and implemented Indian policy in the early republic believed that Native people did not have a proper sense of ownership for several reasons. First of all, Native people owned land in common; that is, land title was vested in the nation as a whole, not in the individuals who lived on it and used it for farming and hunting. Secondly, the possessory right to improved land, land under cultivation, seemed to rest with women rather than men. Southern Indians were both matrilineal and matrilocal: they traced kinship through women only, not bilaterally as Europeans did, and husbands lived in the houses of their wives. Women rather than men did most of the agricultural labor, they controlled the product of that labor and engaged in the sale of produce, and dwellings and fields descended from mothers to daughters rather than from fathers to sons. Finally, Native men in the South seemed to have no proprietary right to their wives or children. For them to develop a real sense of property, Native men had to gain control over their own families.

Washington addressed his letter to the Cherokees to men only: he used the possessive pronoun "your" before "women," "wives," and "daughters." As historian Joan Wallach Scott has written, "Gender is a primary way of signifying relationships of power," and by decoding its meanings, we can come "to understand the complex connections among various forms of human interaction."[24] Linda Kerber phrased it another way: "An ideology that takes enormous pains to *exclude* women is, by that very fact, an ideology that is interactive *with* women."[25] In this case, Washington's failure to address women directly made an important point: he wanted Cherokees to understand that, in a "civilized" society, women belonged to men, and that women had no official standing with the United States except through men.

The hierarchical arrangement that Washington imposed on Native societies ran counter to their own gender conventions. The relationships between men and women among southern Indians varied from the egalitarian Cherokees to the relatively subservient role of women in Creek society. Among all southern peoples, however, matrilineal kinship and matrilocal residence conveyed status, autonomy, and even power on Native women. The eighteenth-century trader Alexander Longe commented that among the Cherokees "the women rule the roost and wear the breeches."[26] The egalitarianism that Washington had admired in a republican militia applied only to the absence of class distinctions and did not extend into the household. Men headed households; they conquered and subdued women. Washington, for example, congratulated an old friend on his marriage by noting that "like a prudent general, he had reviewed his *strength*, his arms, and ammunition before he got involved in an action," and advised him "to make the *first* onset upon his fair del Toboso, with vigor, that the impression may be deep, if it cannot be lasting, or frequently renewed."[27]

The preeminent place of Native women in their domestic relations shocked non-Native observers. Native men did not own the houses where they lived with their wives and children. Furthermore, they did not have an exclusive hold on their wives' sexuality, and their marriages were often of short duration. In the event of a divorce, men had no claims on their children, who in a matrilineal society were blood relatives of their mothers and not their fathers. John Lawson, the early observer of Native people in eastern North Carolina, observed: "The Children always fall to the Women's Lot; for it often happens, that two *Indians* that have liv'd together, as Man and Wife, in which time they have had several Children; if they part and another Man possess her, all the Children go along with the mother and none with the Father."[28] Thomas Nairne wrote of the Creeks: "A Girles Father has not the least hand or concern in matching her. . . . Sons never enjoy their fathers place and dignity."[29] If men had no proprietary interest in their mates or rights to their offspring, if they could not establish patriarchal order in their own households, what hope did they have for developing a sense of ownership of land?

Disarray in family life also translated into political anarchy. The Founding Fathers regarded families as nurseries for civic virtue, and the absence of order and discipline in Native families explained the savagery of Native societies. The matrilineal clan ties that women conveyed to their children held Native nations together and preserved internal order through the exercise of blood vengeance. Elias Boudinot, the highly acculturated Cherokee editor, echoed the views of late-eighteenth-century thinkers when, decades later, he linked blood vengeance to "ignorance and barbarism."[30]

The power of women, therefore, transcended Native households and corrupted the public political arena. James Adair, the eighteenth-century trader, interpreted the absence of Cherokee sanctions against unfaithful wives as evidence that the tribe had a "petticoat government." The failure of men to control women's sexuality elevated women to positions of power over men, an unnatural political hierarchy.[31] Women exercised considerable political influence through their clans, their roles in religious rituals, and, among the Cherokees, their right to speak in council. The very nature of Native politics made participation by women possible. Towns were the locus of power, councils sought consensus, and debates of important issues often lasted for weeks or even months. In these ongoing debates, women had ample opportunity to influence the outcome, even if they never spoke publicly. Furthermore, the public role of women in political dramas almost certainly unnerved Europeans. In southeastern Native societies, for example, women decided the fate of war captives.[32] Among all southern Indians, women performed the ritual of torture and adopted those captives who were spared. Early South Carolina treaties with the Cusabo bore the signatures of "women captains."[33] In the initial Choctaw negotiations with the United States following the American Revolution, Choctaw women symbolically adopted the United States commissioners in a public ceremony at the Hopewell Treaty conference. Without such participation, an alliance could not be cemented.[34] Women, therefore, were an essential part of politics.

The rules of international relations governed the interaction between Native nations and the United States. The Constitution lumped them together with foreign powers (as well as the states). Under the Constitution, however, only Native nations, not individuals, could transfer land from Native control to United States jurisdiction. Because Native people had little concept of delegated power—they sought consensus—identifying individuals with whom to negotiate often proved problematic, especially in land transactions. Native people did not delegate to anyone the power to sell land. The eighteenth-century historian Alexander Hewatt explained: "Each individual looked upon himself as the proprietor of all the lands claimed by the whole tribe, and bound in honor to defend them. . . . No Indian, however great his influence and authority, could give away more than his own right to any tract of land."[35] The republican government that Washington proposed in his letter to the Cherokees eliminated this difficulty. Washington assumed that the "wisest counsellors" would be men and that they would conduct major business such as land sales at their annual meetings. This centralization of power moved decision making from clans and towns, where all people including women had influence, to a new political institution more susceptible to United States manipulation. Excluding women from decisions about land became increasingly important as white settlers encroached on fields and villages as well as hunting grounds. Women had a vested interest in the fields they farmed and the matrilineal homesteads that comprised villages, and the scanty evidence we have for women's views on land cessions suggests that they were less amenable to land sales than men.[36] Removing them from political positions of power and from domestic ones went hand in hand.

One way to eliminate women from politics and make them submissive to their husbands at home was to circumscribe their economic productivity. As Washington supposed, southern Indians did engage in trade, that source of "luxury, effeminacy, and corruptions." Native men exchanged deerskins for European manufactured goods, including guns and ammunition, fabrics, and metal tools, which became increasingly important in Native life. But agriculture, the work of women, remained central to the economy and to the religious life of Native peoples in the South. Men, in other words, engaged in hunting, an occupation that the Founding Fathers associated with savagery, and in trading, which they suspected might be contrary to republican values and masculine virtue, while women toiled at that most ennobling enterprise, the cultivation of the soil. By farming the land, women legitimized their claim to it in a way that men could not under both Native conceptions of ownership and European legal doctrines.[37] Native peoples found little fault with the concept of land title vesting in women. The naturalist William Bartram noted that among Native southerners "marriage gives no right to the husband over the property of his wife," and early recorded laws recognized that women, whether married or not, held property apart from men.[38] For Europeans, however, property ownership entitled women to militia service, citizenship, and equality. A more contrary world could not be imagined. The treaties negotiated in 1790 and 1791 simply ignored the prominent role of agriculture in Native economies by characterizing the Creeks and Cherokees as living "in a state of hunters." Washington's Indian policy sought to convert men into farmers and women into housewives whose husbands controlled their productivity. This division of labor and balance of power was no less than what the Father of His Country wanted for his own people.

Washington sought to subdue Native people and to acquire their land by subordinating women to men. Certainly, he and his advisors saw "civilization" as a humane policy that perhaps would lead to the assimilation of Indians into the population of the United States, but the primary objective was always land acquisition. Washington had no sympathy for cultural differences, because they threatened to thwart United States expansion. But Washington also believed that "savagery" must give way to "civilization," and "civilization" rested on a relationship between men and women that made women subordinate at home, powerless in the political arena, and peripheral to an agricultural economy. His Indian policy speaks volumes not just about his attitudes toward Native people but also his conception of the appropriate role of women in the republic.

No sooner had the United States forced most Choctaws and Chickasaws from their homes in Mississippi than in 1839 the state passed the nation's first married women's property act. The purpose may well have been the protection of a father's bequest from a daughter's impecunious and profligate husband. This measure, however, was an important step in dismantling the ideological and legal structure on which disfranchisement of women rested, and it became a major demand of the women's rights movement that emerged in the 1840s. Decades later, the *Albany Law Review* praised the revision of laws to protect the property of married women and noted that the model for such progressive legislation came from the

Choctaws. Washington had tried to change Native gender roles to create a "civilized" society. Native people ultimately pointed the way toward making "civilized" society more just. Dramatic culture change and loss of their homelands were the legacies of Washington's Indian policy for Native people; a more inclusive and equitable society has been the legacy of Native people for the rest of us.

NOTES

1. *Cherokee Phoenix,* 20 March 1828.

2. See Linda K. Kerber, *Women of the Republic: Intellect and Ideology in Revolutionary America* (Chapel Hill: University of North Carolina Press, 1980).

3. Joan Gunderson, "Independence, Citizenship, and American Revolution," *Signs: Journal of Women in Culture and Society* 13 (1987): 59–75.

4. Sixth Annual Address, 19 November 1794, *A Compilation of the Messages and Papers of the Presidents,* ed. James D. Richardson, 10 vols. (New York: Bureau of National Literature, 1897), 1:158.

5. Linda K. Kerber, "The Paradox of Women's Citizenship in the Early Republic: The Case of *Martin vs. Massachusetts,* 1805," in *Toward an Intellectual History of Women: Essays* (Chapel Hill: University of North Carolina Press, 1997), 266.

6. See Nancy F. Cott, *The Bonds of Womanhood: "Woman's Sphere" in New England, 1780–1835* (New Haven: Yale University Press, 1977).

7. See Michèle Cohen, *Fashioning Masculinity: National Identity and Language in the Eighteenth Century* (London and New York: Routledge, 1996); Mark E. Kann, *A Republic of Men: The American Founders, Gendered Language, and Patriarchial Politics* (New York: New York University Press, 1998); Dana D. Nelson, *National Manhood: Capitalist Citizenship and the Imagined Fraternity of White Men* (Durham: Duke University Press, 1998)

8. Robert F. Berkhofer Jr., *The White Man's Indian: Images of the American Indian from Columbus to the Present* (New York: Alfred A. Knopf, 1978), 33–69.

9. George Washington to the President of Congress, 17 June 1783, *The Writings of George Washington from the Original Manuscript Sources, 1745–1799,* ed. John C. Fitzpatrick, 39 vols. (Washington, D.C.: U.S. Government Printing Office, 1931–44), 27:17–18.

10. Washington to James Duane, 7 September 1783, *Writings,* 27:136.

11. Ibid., 27:140.

12. Ibid., 27:133.

13. Ibid., 27: 136–37; Washington to Sir Edward Newenham, 29 August 1788, 30:71.

14. Washington to Duane, 7 September 1783, 27:138.

15. Washington to James Warren, 7 October 1785, *Writings,* 30:290.

16. The Treaties of Hopewell with the Cherokees (1785), Choctaws (1786), and Chickasaws (1786) included the provision that "citizens of the United States, shall

have liberty to go to any tribe or towns" within those nations to trade until Congress took action to regulate trade. See Charles J. Kappler, ed., *Indian Treaties, 1778–1883* (1904; reprint, Mattituck, N.Y.: Amereon House, 1972), 10, 13, 16.

17. Washington to Sir James Jay, 25 January 1785, *Writings*, 28:41–44; to the President of Congress, 8 February 1785, 28:67–71; to the countess of Huntingdon, 27 February 1785, 30 June 1785, 28:86–91, 180–81.

18. Washington to James Duane, 7 September 1783, *Writings*, 27:135.

19. Ibid., 27:140.

20. Article 1, section 8.

21. See Reginald Horsman, *Expansion and American Indian Policy, 1783–1812* (East Lansing: Michigan State University Press, 1967), 3–103.

22. Kappler, *Indian Treaties*, 28, 31.

23. Knox to Washington, 7 July 1789, *American State Papers, Class II: Indian Affairs*, 2 vols. (Washington, D.C.: Gales and Seaton, 1832), 1:53–54. Knox noted that the British had given medals in the South and "the Southern Indians are exceedingly desirous of receiving similar gifts from the United States."

24. "Gender: A Useful Category of Analysis," *American Historical Review* 91 (1986): 1053–75.

25. Linda K. Kerber, "'I Have Don ... much to Carrey on the Warr': Women and the Shaping of Republican Ideology after the American Revolution," in *Toward an Intellectual History*, 104.

26. Alexander Longe, "A Small Postscript on the Ways and Manners of the Indians called Cherokees," ed. David H. Corkran, *Southern Indian Studies* 21 (1969): 30, 32.

27. Washington to Reverend William Gordon, 20 December 1784, *Writings*, 28:15. The bridegroom was Col. Joseph(?) Ward.

28. John Lawson, *A New Voyage to Carolina*, ed. Hugh Talmage Lefler (Chapel Hill: University of North Carolina Press, 1967), 192.

29. Alexander Moore, ed., *Nairne's Muskhogean Journals: The 1708 Expedition to the Mississippi River* (Jackson: University Press of Mississippi, 1988), 33, 45.

30. *Cherokee Phoenix*, 18 February 1829.

31. James Adair, *Adair's History of the American Indians*, ed. Samuel Cole Williams (Johnson City, Tenn.: Watauga Press, 1930), 153.

32. Theda Perdue, *Cherokee Women: Gender and Culture Change, 1700–1835* (Lincoln: University of Nebraska Press, 1998), 38–39.

33. Chapman J. Milling, *Red Carolinians*, 2d ed. (Columbia: University of South Carolina Press, 1969), 30.

34. Warren Gregory O'Brien, "Choctaws in a Revolutionary Age: A Study of Power and Authority, 1750–1801" (Ph.D. diss., University of Kentucky, 1998), 131–32.

35. Alexander Hewatt, *An Historical Account of the Rise and Progress of the Colonies of South Carolina and Georgia*, 2 vols. (London, 1779), 1:67.

36. Petitions by Cherokee women in 1817, 1818, and 1831 are published in Theda

Perdue and Michael D. Green, eds., *The Cherokee Removal: A Brief History with Documents* (Boston: Bedford Books, 1995), 124–26. Also see Perdue, "Cherokee Women and the Trail of Tears," *Journal of Women's History* 1(1989): 14–30.

37. Emer de Vattel was the major eighteenth-century legal theorist. See his *The Law of Nations, or, Principles of the Law of Nature Applied to the Conduct and Affairs of Nations and Sovereigns* (Dublin: L. White, 1787).

38. William Bartram, "Observations on the Creek and Cherokee Indians, 1789," *Transactions of the American Ethnological Society* 3, pt. 1 (1853), 66; *Laws of the Cherokee Nation: Adopted by the Council at Various Periods* (Tahlequah, C.N.: Cherokee Advocate Office, 1852), 10.

CONTRIBUTORS

Martin Brückner is assistant professor of English literature with a secondary appointment at the Center of American Material Culture Studies at the University of Delaware. His published work includes articles on geography, cartography, nationalism, and American literary culture in journals such as *American Quarterly* and *English Literary History*. He is currently completing a book entitled *National Geographics: Land and Literacy in Early America*.

Robbie Ethridge is McMullan Assistant Professor of Southern Studies and assistant professor of anthropology at the University of Mississippi. She is coeditor with Charles Hudson of *The Transformation of the Southeastern Indians, 1540–1760* and author of the forthcoming volume *Creek Country: The Creek Indians and Their World, 1796–1816*. She is currently researching the early colonial experience of the Chickasaws and their participation in the Indian slave trade.

Tamara Harvey is assistant professor of English at the University of Southern Mississippi. She has written articles on Anne Bradstreet, Sor Juana Inés de la Cruz, and Patience Boston, and is currently working on a book entitled *Modesty's Charge: The Body and Feminist Tactics in Seventeenth-Century American Women's Discourse*.

Don Higginbotham is Dowd Professor of History at the University of North Carolina at Chapel Hill. He is author and editor of a number of books, including three on Washington: *George Washington and the American Military Tradition* (1985), *George Washington Reconsidered* (2001), and *George Washington: Uniting a Nation* (2002).

Warren R. Hofstra is Stewart Bell Professor of History at Shenandoah University in Winchester, Virginia. He is author of *The Planting of New*

Virginia: Shenandoah Valley Landscapes, 1700–1800 (2003) and *A Separate Place: The Formation of Clarke County, Virginia* (1986) as well as editor of several essay collections on regional history and the Shenandoah Valley. He also directs the Community History Project of Shenandoah University.

Philip D. Morgan is professor of history at The Johns Hopkins University. His most recent book is *Slave Counterpoint: Black Culture in the Eighteenth-Century Chesapeake and Lowcountry* (1998).

Carla Mulford is associate professor of English at Pennsylvania State University. Founding president of the Society of Early Americanists, she has recently published an anthology, *Early American Writings*, and is currently working on a manuscript tentatively titled *Benjamin Franklin and the Ends of Empire*.

Michael L. Nicholls is associate professor of history at Utah State University. His most recent publications include articles on the urban free blacks of early Virginia in *Virginia Magazine of History and Biography* and on African-American freedom suits in postrevolutionary Virginia in *Slavery and Abolition*.

Greg O'Brien is associate professor of history at the University of Southern Mississippi. He is author of *Choctaws in a Revolutionary Age, 1750–1830* (2002), and his 2001 article "The Conqueror Meets the Unconquered: Negotiating Cultural Boundaries on the Post-Revolutionary Southern Frontier" was awarded the biennial Fletcher M. Green and Charles W. Ramsdell Award for the best article in the *Journal of Southern History*.

Theda Perdue is professor of history at the University of North Carolina at Chapel Hill. She is author of *Slavery and the Evolution of Cherokee Society, 1540–1866* (1979), *Native Carolinians* (1985), *The Cherokee* (1989), *Cherokee Women: Gender and Culture Change, 1700–1835* (1998), and *"Mixed Blood" Indians: Racial Construction in the Early South* (2002); coauthor of *The Columbia Guide to American Indians in the Southeast* (2001); editor of *Nations Remembered: An Oral History of the Five Civilized Tribes* (1980), *Cherokee Editor* (1983), *The Cherokee Removal* (1995), and *Sifters: Native American Women's Lives* (2001); and coeditor of *Southern Women: Histories and Identities* (1992) and *Hidden Histories of Women of the New South* (1994).

William R. Ryan is a graduate student in history at Duke University. He is currently researching the role of common people in the American Revolution and the English Civil War.

David S. Shields is McClintock Professor of Southern Letters at the University of South Carolina. He is an historian of early American literature and culture and edits the journal *Early American Literature*.

Daniel H. Usner Jr. is professor of history at Vanderbilt University. He is the author of *Indians, Settlers, and Slaves in a Frontier Exchange Economy* (1992) and *American Indians in the Lower Mississippi Valley* (1998).

Sophie White received her doctorate in the history of art from the Courtauld Institute of Art, University of London, and teaches in the Gender Studies program at the University of Notre Dame. Her research centers on French colonial Louisiana and investigates issues of gender, consumerism, and the role of dress and appearance in managing race, class, and ethnic encounters in a colonial context.

Peter H. Wood is professor of history at Duke University. He is author of *Black Majority* (1974) and *Strange New Land* (2002), coeditor of *Powhatan's Mantle: Indians in the Colonial Southeast* (1989), and coauthor of *Created Equal* (2003).

INDEX

Abarca y Bolea, Pedro Pablo de, Conde de Aranda, 23–24, 34
Adair, James, 266, 300, 320
Adams, Abigail, 129, 131–32, 135
Adams, John, 132, 155–56, 161, 177
Adams, Rev. T., 202
Addison, Joseph: *Cato*, 129, 150
"Address from the Citizens of Augusta," 5, 6
Adelman, Jeremy, 37
Aeneas, 166
Aeolus, 169
African Americans. *See* Free blacks; Slaves
Africans, 55, 59, 167, 172, 200, 208, 210–11, 215, 273
Agriculture. *See* Farmers; South: agricultural economy
Alabama, 2, 5, 10, 263, 279
Alabama River, 279, 293
Albany Law Review, 322
Alcohol. *See* Whiskey
Alexander, 260
Alexandria, Va., 79, 204
Alibamon Indians, 30, 37
Allen, Edward, 227
American Geography (Morse), 60
American History Illustrated, 123
American Indians. *See* Indians
American Military Pocket Atlas (Sayer and Bennett), 52, 54
American Pocket Atlas (Carey), 61
American Revolution, 8, 9, 12, 24, 25, 26, 36, 58, 60, 70, 84, 86, 122, 123, 131, 132, 133, 148, 197, 198, 200–202, 204, 206–8, 212, 279–80, 293; Battle of Concord, 227, 234; Battle of Lexington, 227, 234; consumer boycott, 163–64; Continental Army, 133, 260, 265, 267–68, 315; Hessians, 267; history of, 155–57, 177; Ladies Association, 134; Loyalists, 14, 133, 167–68, 173–74, 177, 193n.36, 226, 233, 235, 236, 246, 280; memory of, 157; South Carolina and, 223–247; Tories and, 9, 148, 225; women and, 163–64. *See also* Whigs
The American Times (Odell), 173–76, 185–89
The American Universal Geography (Morse), 60
Amherst County, Va., 206
Anderson, Benedict, 65
Anderson, James, 203–4
André, John, 148
André (Dunlap), 150
Anglican Church, 168, 173, 237
Anti-Federalists, 8, 43, 62
Appalachian frontier. *See* Frontier
Appalachian Mountains, 46, 73, 262, 264, 272
Aptheker, Herbert, 224
Argyle (slave), 212–13
Arnold, Benedict, 148, 207
Aron, Stephen, 37
Atlantic coast (North America), 9, 46, 56, 272
Atlantic Ocean, 17, 55, 56, 246
Atlantic world, 72, 198, 265
Atlas of the United States (Scott), 61
Attakullakulla (Little Carpenter), 261, 264, 268–70, 274nn.4, 5
Augusta, Ga., 5, 6
Augusta County, Va., 214
Ayers, Edward, 44

Bab, Lady, 149
Backcountry. *See* Frontier; Virginia: backcountry
Bacon, Edmund: "A Hero Great and Good," 69
Bahamas, 210
Ball, Joseph, 125
Baltimore, Md., 201, 213
Barbados, 265
Barnard, Timothy, 286, 289–91, 298
Barnes, Abraham, 211
Bartram, William, 322; *Travels*, 261
Basset, Burwell, 202
Bear Creek, 31
Beckett (settler), 78–79
Belvoir, 72, 73, 127, 130, 131–32, 135, 139n.26
Bennett, John: *American Military Pocket Atlas*, 52, 54; "A General Map of the Southern British Colonies in America," 52
Bennett, William J., 144
Betty (slave), 201
Big Black River, 37
Big Warrior, 290
Billy (slave), 204
Blaeu, Willem, 46
Blathwayt Atlas (Blathwayt), 45
Blathwayt, William, 46; *Blathwayt Atlas*, 45
Blount, William, 27, 291
Blue Ridge Mountains. *See* Virginia: Blue Ridge Mountains
Board of Trade (England), 45
Bob (slave), 37
Bodsky, Isaak, 143
Bolingbroke, Henry St. John, Lord, 159
Boote, Captain, 295
Borderlands. *See* Frontier
Boson (slave), 211
Boston, Mass., 168, 171
Boudinot, Elias, 320
Boudinot, Hannah Stockton, 135
Boundaries: between Creek Indians and the United States, 284–91, 294; between Spain and the United States, 287; cultural, 23–38; ethnic, 23–38; geophysical, 64; political, 23–38, 64; racial, 226

Bowen, Emmanuel, 52; "A Map of the British and French Settlements in North America [Part Second] containing . . . ," 51; ". . . the British Plantations extending from Boston in New England to Georgia . . . ," 51
Braddock, Edward, 71, 145, 146, 160–61
Brady, Patricia, 125
Brahm, William De, 59
Brashears, Turner, 36
Brathwaite, Edward, 208
Breechy (slave), 211
Breen, T. H., 162–63
Brewton, Miles, 237
Britain, 32, 281; empire, 48, 50, 54, 56, 73, 160; maps, 45–59, 61; merchants in, 50. *See also* England; Land: British colonial; Loyalists
Brown, John P., 264
Brückner, Martin, 5–6
Bruslé (councilor in French New Orleans), 92; wife of, 92, 94, 102
Buell, Abel: "A New and Correct Map of the United States of North America," 60
Buffalo, 272
Buffon, Count, 49
Bull, William, 226, 230
Bulloch, William B., 296
Bulom Shore, 201
Burgoyne, John, 149; *The Maid of the Woods*, 149
Burke, Aedanus, 8
Burr, Aaron, 26
Burwell, Carter, 79–80
Byrd, William, II, 149

Cabell, William, 206
Caesar, Julius, 260
Caesar (slave), 203–4, 215
Callahan, North, 173–74
Cambridge, Mass., 171, 265–66
Camden County, Ga., 287–88
Campbell, Lord William, 9, 225, 228–31, 234–47
Canada, 96, 167–68, 317; Cape Breton, 147; New Brunswick, 173; Newfoundland, 48; Nova Scotia, 201

Cannon, Daniel, 238
Carey, Mathew: *American Pocket Atlas*, 61
Caribbean islands, 35, 45, 209. *See also* West Indies
Carlos III, King of Spain, 23, 26
Carlyle, Sarah Fairfax, 130
Carolina, 46, 48–49, 283. *See also* North Carolina; South Carolina
Carondelet, Hector Baron de, 29, 34, 35
"Carte de la Louisiane" (Delisle), 46
"Carte du Mexique et de la Floride" (Delisle), 46
Carter, Landon, 206
Carter, Robert, 206–7
Cartography, 43–65; Mercator projection, 48. *See also* Britain: maps; France: maps; Maps; South: maps
Cartouche, 54–56, 59; Fry-Jefferson, 57, 58
Carver, Jonathan: *Travels Through the Interior Parts of North-America*, 59–60
Catawba Indians, 10
Catholic Church, 28, 232; Ursuline, 97, 111n.30
Catin, Louis, 36
Cato (Addison), 129, 150
Cayton, Andrew, 145
Cellys, 127
Chantalou, Augustin, 87, 97–101, 103, 104, 105; wife of, 98, 101–4
Charles County, Md., 199
Charleston (Charlestown), S.C., 1, 9, 224–37, 246–47, 248–49n.14, 261, 266
Charlotte, N.C., 5
Chase, Benjamin, 202
Chattahoochee River, 279
Chattanooga, Tenn., 262
Cherokee-English War (1759–60), 266
Cherokee Indians (Ani-Yunwiya), 9, 31, 260–61, 263–64, 267, 270, 286, 291, 319, 321–22; and American Revolution, 267–69; Chota, 270; Chotte, 264; and disease, 266; Keowee, 266; land, 226, 261–63, 272, 292, 295; Middle Towns, 268; Overhill Towns, 264, 268–69; relations of, with United States, 313, 318; removal of, 261; suicide of, 266; Valley Towns, 268. *See also* Attakullakulla; Chickamauga Indians; Corn Tassel; Dragging Canoe; Oconostota; Old Tassel; the Raven; Tuskegetchee
Chickamauga Creek, 262–63, 269
Chickamauga Indians, 264, 269–72; Running Water Town, 273. *See also* Dragging Canoe
Chickasaw Bluffs, 34
Chickasaw Indians, 10, 27, 28–33, 35, 271, 286; language, 280; Long Town, 31; removal, 322. *See also* Piamingo
Chisholm, John, 291–92
Choctaw Indians, 10, 27, 28–37, 286, 316, 320–23; land, 293; language, 280; removal, 322; West Yazoo, 36. *See also* Franchimastabé; Taboca
Christian, William, 268
Church, Angelica Schuyler, 121, 129
Cincinnatus, Lucius Quintus, 151; Washington as, 13, 70, 151. *See also* Public Virtue; Society of Cincinnati
Civilization Plan (U.S. Indian policy), 280, 282, 286, 313–23
Civil War, 5, 157
Clark, Abraham, 272
Clark, Emily, 111n.30
Clarke, G.N.G., 55, 58
Class. *See* Social class
Clinton, William Jefferson, 144
Clothing, 138n.20; homespun, 86–87; imported, 86–98, 100–107, 113–14nn.52, 54–58, 118n.109; as social glue, 92
Cobb, Ty, 273
Cole, John, 37
Colerain, 297
Coles Point, 207
College of William and Mary, 134
Collet, John, 59
Colonial elites. *See* Elites
Colonists. *See* Settlers
Columbia (metaphor), 166, 169–70, 174
"Commemoration Ode" (Lowell), 259, 273
Compagnie des Indes, 89
Connecticut, 162
Constitutional Convention (1787), 124, 151, 261, 267, 270, 317
Constitution (U.S.), 1, 7, 8, 69, 124, 317, 321

Continental Army. *See* American Revolution
Cooper River, 225, 237
Coosa River, 279
Coram, John, 236–39, 241–43
Corn: as subsistence food, 77–79
Cornells, Alexander, 286
Cornells, Davy, 297
Corn Tassel, 270
Cornwallis, Lord, 201, 207
Corn whiskey. *See* Whiskey
Corvoisier et Richer, 90, 93–94, 97, 98; Le Lyon d'Argent, 90
Corvoisier (merchant), 90, 93, 94, 100, 103
Coslett, Charles Matthew, 238–41
Cosway, Maria, 121, 128
Crassus, 260
Creek Indians (Muskogees), 9, 10, 12, 27, 29, 30, 32, 35, 270, 271, 300–301n.1, 316, 320, 322; Chehaws, 291, 297; civil war, 300; Cowetas, 297; Cussetah, 297, 299; economic change, 281–82; elite, 281; farmers, 280; fur trade, 281; generational conflict, 289; headmen, 299; land, 282–83, 285–86, 289–97, 299–300; land cessions, 285–86, 288, 293, 297; language, 279–80, 283; Lower, 279, 291, 299; National Council, 286; political organization, 278–79, 286, 294; ranching, 281–83, 290; relations with Georgia, 279, 287–91, 295–98; relations with United States, 278, 284–89, 293, 298–300, 318; Red Sticks, 300; resistance to U.S. expansion, 286–300; settlement patterns, 282; Tensaw, 286; Tuckabatchee, 290, 298; Upper, 279, 286, 293, 299; Yuchis, 297–98. *See also* Big Warrior; Cornells, Alexander; Cornells, Davy; Efau Haujo; Fusihatchee Mico; McGillivray, Alexander; Sinnajijee; Tuskenehau Chapco; Tussekia Mico; Tustunnuggee Emaultau
Crèvecoeur, Hector St. John de: *Letters from an American Farmer*, 60
Croft, Peter, 234
Crosby, Alfred, 272
Culpeper County, Va., 214
Cumberland, Tenn., 297

Cumming, William, 46; *The Southeast in Early Maps*, 43
Cunliffe, Marcus: *George Washington: Man and Monument*, 144
Cupid (slave), 200
Curles, 207
Cusabo Indians, 320
Custis, Daniel Parke, 128, 133, 140n.41
Custis, Elizabeth, 141n.49, 202
Custis, Jacky, 123, 125
Custis, John IV, 133
Custis, John Parke, 207
Custis, Martha Dandridge. *See* Washington, Martha Dandridge Custis
Custis, Nelly, 125, 136n.2
Cyclops, 49

Dartmouth, Lord, 231, 241, 245–46
d'Auberville family, 96–97; Marie Louise Le Seneschal, 96; Céleste, 96
Davidson, John, 78–79
Davies, Samuel, 160–61, 169
Davis, James, 79
Davy (slave), 211, 213
Dealy, James, 232–33
Deane, Elizabeth, 162
Deane, Silas, 162
Dearborn, Henry, 285, 292, 294
Declaration of Independence, 259
Deference. *See* Social class
de la Chaise, Alexandrine (Mme. de Pradel), 87–96, 99, 100–102, 104–5, 111n.30
Delaware Indians, 271
Delaware River, 267
Delisle, Guillaume: "Carte de la Louisiane," 46; "Carte du Mexique et de la Floride," 46
Dewar (slave), 234
Dinsmoor, Silas, 293
Dinwiddie, Robert, 71–72, 74, 83, 145–46
Doghead, 49
Dogue Run Farm, 200, 203
Dominica, 208
Doughty, Major, 31
Douglass, Walter, 48
Dowd, Gregory: *A Spirited Resistance*, 264
Dragging Canoe (Tsi'yu-gunsi'ni), 13, 260–

73; death of, 264, 272–73; health of, 266; as military leader, 262, 267, 269–73; as negotiator, 271; son of, 264; as speaker, 270
Drayton, William Henry, 228–30, 232, 247, 249n.18
Drinker, Elizabeth, 134–35
Duane, James, 315
Dunlap, William: *André*, 150
Dunlap's Pennsylvania Packet, 161
Dunmore, Earl of (governor of Virginia). *See* Murray, John, Earl of Dunmore
Durant, Mrs., 294

Easley, Roderick, 296
East Florida, 26
Economics: accounting, 76–77, 81–82; cash economy, 76; competency, 73–75, 79, 82, 83; empire of goods, 73; European, 11, 162; exchange, 11, 73, 75–83, 105, 108n.6, 283–84; growth, 11, 12, 72–73, 82, 83; imports from Britain, 86, 97, 163–64; imports from France, 87–105, 112n.46, 113–14nn.52, 54–58, 115n.74; independence, 74–76, 162–64, 190–191n.20; interdependence of the states, 2, 7; regionalism, 12
Education: for women, 135
Edward III, King of England, 239
Efau Haujo, 288, 293–94, 297, 300
Elijah (slave), 213
Elites (Euro-American), 11, 89, 106, 156–58, 162–63, 166–68, 172–73, 176–77; as consumers, 87–97, 101–7
Elizabeth City County, Va., 127, 130
Elkridge Landing, Md., 201
Ellis, Joseph, 121
England, 11, 26, 30, 43, 50, 71, 87, 94, 125, 129, 130, 132, 155, 159, 162, 167–68, 171, 173, 176, 224, 226, 233, 236, 239, 267; Lancashire, 102; London, 51, 77, 135, 168, 170, 227, 246, 264; Parliament, 45; Restoration, 45. *See also* Britain
Enlightenment, 224, 314
Environment: natural, 48, 58, 59
"Epistle to General Washington" (Stockton), 181–83

Eskridge, George, 125–26
Essex Gazette, 227
Ethridge, Robbie, 12
Europe, 56, 76, 99, 101, 106; Renaissance, 49
Eustis, William, 296

Faden, William, 55–59; "The British Colonies in North America," 55; "A Map of South Carolina and Part of Georgia," 58; "A Map of the most Inhabited part of Virginia containing the whole Province of Maryland with part of Pensilvania, New Jersey, and North Carolina," 56; *The North American Atlas*, 55, 58
Fairfax, Ann, 72, 131, 132
Fairfax, Bryan, 132
Fairfax, Colonel William, 72, 75, 126–127, 130
Fairfax, George William, 127–28, 129–30, 132, 140n.32
Fairfax, Sarah "Sally" Cary, 14, 122, 127–33, 135, 139n.23
Fairfax, Thomas, Lord, 72, 73, 74, 77, 127, 132
Fairfax County, Va., 211
Fairfax Resolves (1774), 159–60
Fallen Timbers, Battle of, 263
"Farewell Address" (Washington), 2–3, 7, 42, 62, 64
Farmers, 8, 73, 77, 79, 81, 83
Fashion. *See* clothing
Fauquier County, Va., 214
Favre, Simon, 37
Favrot, Dame, 92
Fazende (councilor in French New Orleans), 92; wife of, 102
Federalists, 2, 7, 8, 14, 43, 60, 62
Federal Road, 286, 291
Fenn, Elizabeth, 265
Ferry Farm, 124
Fewtrell, John, 238, 240–41
Fielding, Henry, 57
Fitzpatrick, John C.: *The George Washington Scandals*, 134
Fleuriau (councilor in French New Orleans), 92; wife of, 102
Flexner, James Thomas, 122–23, 272

Fliegelman, Jay, 156
Flint River, 279, 293
Florence, Ala., 31
Florida, 4, 8, 9, 23, 24, 28, 30, 35. *See also* East Florida; West Florida
Folsom, Ebenezer, 36
Folsom, Elmore, 36
Folsom, Nathaniel, 36
Forbes, General John, 129–30
Fort Duquesne, 129–30
Fort Lee, 267
Fort Necessity, 70, 146
Fort Patrick Henry, 268–69
Fort San Fernando de las Barrancas, 34
Fort Washington, 267
France, 23, 35, 43, 51, 87, 89, 90, 92–105, 271; Brittany, 97; Burgundy, 88; colonial society, 11, 92; Limousin region, 89; Lyons, 90, 93; maps, 46; mercers, 90; Paris, 11, 88, 89, 90, 97, 98, 99, 101, 107, 121, 128, 135; Rochefort, 104; La Rochelle, 97, 98, 103, 104, 105; Versailles, 96–97. *See also* Louisiana; New Orleans
Franchimastabé, 32
Franklin, Benjamin, 128, 145, 156, 168, 177
Franklin, William, 173
Frederick County, Va., 199, 214
Fredericksburg, Va., 12, 79, 123, 124
Free blacks, 4, 9, 17, 36, 106–7, 202, 213, 227, 234, 238–41, 245. *See also* Jeremiah, Thomas; South Carolina; Wheatley, Phillis
Freeman, Douglas Southall, 71, 122
Freeman, Timothy, 295
French and Indian War. *See* Seven Years' War
French Broad River, 268
Frenches Paul (slave), 211, 215, 217n.11
French Revolution, 35
Frey, Sylvia, 224
Frontier, 2, 5, 6, 7, 8, 10, 26, 27, 36, 46, 72–74, 88, 149, 264, 315; southern, 282–300. *See also* Settlers; Virginia: backcountry
Frontiersmen. *See* Settlers
Fry, Joshua, 55, 56
Fugitive Slave Act (1793), 8
Fur traders. *See* Traders

Fusihatchee Mico, 298
Fyfe, Christopher, 201

Gadsden, Christopher, 163
Gambling, 50
Gardner, Newport, 168
Gay, Peter, 128
Gayoso de Lemos, Manuel, 32
Gazette of the United States, 152, 165
Gender relations: among Euro-Americans, 11, 16, 87–88, 102–3, 110–111n.30, 122, 209, 319, 322–23; among Indians, 282, 319–22; changes in, 313–14, 322; masculinity, 314, 316, 321–22; as power, 319
"A General Map of the Southern British Colonies in America" (Sayer and Bennett), 52
Gentleman's Magazine, 51, 71
Geographical Cards, 50
George III, King of England, 13, 71, 160, 162, 165, 228
Georgetown, 204
George Washington: Man and Monument (Cunliffe), 144
The George Washington Scandals (Fitzpatrick), 134
George Washington's Southern Tour, 1791 (Henderson), 2
Georgia, 1, 2, 5, 10, 17, 27, 29, 36, 59, 263, 267, 278–79, 285, 290, 295–300; legislature, 32
Georgics (Virgil), 147
Gerry, Elbridge, 161
Gibson, Josh, 273
Gooch, William, 80
Gordon, Thomas Knox, 231, 238, 241
Grasse, Admiral de, 271
Graves, Thomas, 200
Great Britain. *See* Britain
Great Smoky Mountains, 264
Greece, 49
Green, Charles, 131
Green, Rev. Charles, 211
Greene, Jack P., 24, 49, 74
Greene, Nathanael, 129
Greene, Samuel, 287–88
Greenland, N.H., 202

Gregory, William, 238, 241
Gulf of Mexico, 23; coast, 9, 24, 29, 30
Gulliver's Travels (Swift), 51
Gunston Hall, 207

Hadrian, 259
Hamilton, Alexander, 10
Hamilton, Elizabeth Schuyler, 135
Hampton, Va., 127, 212
Handley, Scipio, 247
Harley, J. B., 44
Harmar, Josiah, 263
Harry (slave), 211
Hart, Oliver, 235
Harvard University, 129, 259
Harvey, Thomas, 231
Hastings, Selina, countess of Huntingdon, 168, 316–18
Hattiesburg, Miss., 16
Hawkins, Benjamin, 279–83, 285–99
Hawkins, George Fraser, 199
Henderson, Archibald: *George Washington's Southern Tour, 1791*, 2
Henderson, Richard, 261–62
Henderson Purchase, 264
Henrico County, 207
Henry, Patrick, 8
Hercules (slave), 198, 203, 211
"A Hero Great and Good" (Bacon), 69
Hewatt, Alexander, 321
Hierarchy. *See* Social class
Higginbotham, Don, 14–15, 16
High Shoals, Ga., 296
Hill, James, 199
HMS *Savage*, 200
HMS *Scorpion*, 230–31
Hodge, David, 37
Hoffman, Ronald, 223
Hofstra, Warren, 11
Hogarth, William, 57
Hollingsworth, Abraham, 81
Holston River, 268
Honeyman, Robert, 207
Honor's Voice (Wilson), 122
Hopewell, 29, 321
Howard, Appy, 287–88
Howe, William, 148, 267–68

Hubart, Michael, 232–33
The Human Tradition in the American Revolution, 264
Hunting, 289
Hutchinson, Thomas, 246

Indians, 4, 9, 10, 15, 16, 25, 27–33, 35, 36, 37, 43, 48, 71, 72, 145, 146–47, 226, 232, 263–64, 313; removal of, 314; southern, 278–80, 295, 300, 318–21. *See also* Civilization Plan; Land: Indian; *names of individuals and groups*
Indian Trade and Intercourse Act (1790), 28
Innes, Alexander, 227, 229–31, 233, 242–44, 250n.32
Ireland, 45, 231
Irwin, Governor (of Georgia), 295–96
Italy, 76

Jack, Mr., 202
Jack (slave), 200, 213
Jackson, Andrew, 37, 261
Jackson, Robert, 126
Jacob (slave), 213
Jamaica, 206, 208, 209, 210
James, Benjamin, 32, 36
James River, 207
James (slave), 37
Jamey, Coachman (slave), 198–99, 214–15
Jay, James, 316
Jefferson, Martha Wayles, 134
Jefferson, Peter, 55, 56
Jefferson, Thomas, 8, 33–34, 83, 128–29, 151, 152, 259, 279–80, 283; as misogynist, 121–22; *Notes on the State of Virginia*, 60; as slave owner, 206–7. *See also* Republicans
Jefferys, Thomas, 55, 59
Jemmy (slave in South Carolina), 234, 236, 238, 241–43
Jemmy (slave in Virginia), 197, 211
Jeremiah, Thomas, 9, 225–26, 229, 238–40, 244–47, 249n.18; execution of, 225, 236, 238, 243–45; as slaveowner, 225; trial of, 225, 234–37, 242–43
Joe (slave), 213
Jordan, Winthrop, 121

Joseph (slave), 203
Judge, Oney, 15, 198, 201–3, 212–13
Jumonville, Va., 70

Kaplan, Sidney, 192n.31, 224
Kate (slave), 37
Kentucky, 5, 29, 262, 272
Keowee River, 29
Kerber, Linda, 134, 163, 319
Kerlerec, Governor (of French Louisiana), 89–90; wife of, 91, 99, 102
King (slave), 213
Kitchin, Thomas, 51
Knox, Henry, 27, 28, 263, 318
Knoxville, Tenn., 265
Kudzu, 5

Labrador, 52
Ladies Association. *See* American Revolution
Ladies' teas, 151–52
Lafayette, Marquis de, 270
Lancaster, Penn., 135
Lancaster County, Va., 214
Land: British colonial, 45, 46, 48, 51, 55; companies, 2, 32; French colonial, 46, 51; Indian, 4, 27–33, 272, 280, 285, 291, 293–97, 315–23; schemes, 2, 28; speculators, 291. *See also* Civilization Plan; *names of land companies*
Langer, Thomas, 226
Latrobe, Benjamin H., 133
Laughlin, King, 139n.26
Laurens, Henry, 224, 227–30, 233–37, 241–47
Lawson, John, 320
Lear, Tobias, 8
Lee, Arthur, 227, 231
Lee, Charles, 267
Lee, Richard Henry, 8
Leeper, Dr., 199
Legge, William, Earl of Dartmouth, 168, 227
Lenin, Vladimir, 143
"Letter of George Washington to Annis Boudinot Stockton," 178–79

Letters from an American Farmer (Crèvecoeur), 60
Lewis, Betty, 124
Likely, Tom, 151
Lincoln, Abraham, 122, 125, 131, 259
Liston, Lady Henrietta, 140n.38
Liston, Robert, 140n.38
Little Carpenter. *See* Attakullakulla
Little Miami River, 271
Little Tennessee River, 264
Locke, John, 45
Lockridge, Kenneth, 121
London Magazine, 51
London (slave), 37
Longe, Alexander, 319
Long Island, N.Y., 267, 268
Longmore, Paul, 159
Lookout Mountain, 273
Louisiana, 5, 11, 24, 26, 28, 29, 30, 31, 34, 35; French colonial, 87–97, 99–106, 108–9n.12, 115n.74; as plantation society, 88, 102, 104–7; Spanish colonial, 107; Superior Council, 92, 97; Upper, 88. *See also* New Orleans
Lowell, James Russell: "Commemoration Ode," 259, 273
Lowndes, Rawlins, 8
Loyalists. *See* American Revolution
Lyttelton, William Henry, 266

Machiavelli, 147
Madison, James, 152
Madison, Rev. James, 207
Madison, Sarah Tate, 134
Magna Charta, 241
The Maid of the Woods (Burgoyne), 149
Manhattan, N.Y., 267
Manifest Destiny, 24, 160, 166–67, 169
Manigault, Gabriel, 236
Maps: Bennett's, 52–54; Bowen's, 51–52; Buell's, 60; Delisle's, 46; Faden's, 55–59; Melish's, 62–65; Moll's, 46–51; Purcell's, 60; Sayer and Bennett's, 52. *See also* Cartography; South: maps
Marcus (slave), 204, 212
Marion, Francis, 224

Martin, Governor (of North Carolina), 247
Martin, Laughlin, 232–33
Maryland, 5, 36, 60, 199–201, 211
Maryland Gazette, 211
Masculinity. *See* Gender
Mason, George, 8, 207, 211
Mason-Dixon survey, 54, 64
Massachusetts, 160, 246
Mather, James, 30
McGillivray, Alexander, 26, 28, 30, 37, 279; death of, 279
McLaughlin, Jack, 121
Meekins, Christmas, 211
Melish, John: "A Map of the Southern Section of the United States," 62–65; *Military and Topographical Atlas of the United States*, 62–64
Memphis, Tenn., 34
Mercator, 49
Mercer, Richard, 81
Merchants. *See* Traders
Meschianza, 148
Mexico, 24
Michel (*ordonnateur* of French Louisiana), 89
Middleton, Arthur, 224
Midway, Ga., 6, 10
Military. *See* Virginia: militia; Virginia: Virginia Regiment; Washington, George: military commander
Military and Topographical Atlas of the United States (Melish), 62–64
Milledge, Governor (of Georgia), 299
Milledgeville, Ga., 296
Milligan, George, 231–32, 234–36, 239, 244
Milsford, Leonard, 211
Minor, Stephen, 32, 36, 37
Miró, Esteban, 28, 30; "Proclamation of Good Government," 107
Mississippi, 2, 5, 37, 322
Mississippi River, 1, 5, 9, 25, 26, 28, 29, 32, 34, 46
Mississippi State University, 263
Mississippi Territory, 5, 6, 9, 25, 37
Mississippi Valley, 25, 26, 33, 37, 94
Missouri, 4

Mobile, Ala., 29, 30, 37, 271, 281, 285
Mobile River, 30
Mohegan Indians, 170
Moll, Herman, 46, 51, 59; "Map of the Dominions of Great Britain in North America," 46–51; ". . . the North Parts of America claimed by France under the name of Louisiana," 51; *The World Described*, 46
Monplaisir, 91, 117n.102
Montgomery, Archibald, 266
Morden, Richard, 46
Morgan, Philip D., 9, 14, 15, 224, 225, 226–27
Morristown, N.J., 266
Morse, Jedidiah, 49, 60; *American Geography*, 60; *The American Universal Geography*, 60
Mount Vernon, 8, 123, 124, 127, 130, 131, 132, 133, 165, 166, 197–201, 203–4, 206–7, 211–12, 260–61, 273. *See also* Washington, George
Mount Vernon Ladies Association, 139n.26
Mount Vernon: Yesterday, Today, Tomorrow, 123
Mouzon, Henry, 59
Moxon, James, 46
Mulford, Carla, 14, 16
Murray, John, Earl of Dunmore, 170–72, 247; Dunmore's Proclamation (1775), 170–72
Muscle Shoals, Tenn., 291–92
My Tears Spoiled My Aim, and Other Reflections on Southern Culture (Reed), 4

Nadelhaft, Jerome J., 223–24
Nairne, Thomas, 320
Nance (slave), 37
Naniabe Island, 293
Nantahala Gorge, 261
Nashville, Tenn., 31, 37
Natchez, Miss., 26, 28, 30, 32, 37
Native Americans. *See* Indians; *names of individual groups*
Natt (slave), 214
Negro Act (1740), 235, 238–41, 246

Neptune (slave), 198, 200, 211, 216–17n.7
Nesbitt, Mr., 243
Nevis, 208
"A New and Correct Map of the United States of North America" (Buell), 60
Newburgh, N.Y., 271
New England, 56, 57, 168; people of, 60, 160
New Hampshire, 198, 202
New Jersey, 57, 168, 173, 267, 272
New Kent County, Va., 207, 211
New Orleans, 10, 11, 17, 37, 87, 285; French colonial, 87–94, 96–100, 102–4, 106, 111n.30; Spanish colonial, 106–7, 271
New Orleans Rebellion (1768), 106
Newport, R.I., 168
New Spain, 23. *See also* Spain
Newspapers, 33, 152, 205, 208, 211. *See also names of specific newspapers*
Newton, Isaac, 81
New York City, 124, 155, 165, 166, 201, 267
New York state, 46, 124, 173, 201, 208
Niagara Falls, 48
Nicholls, Michael L., 9, 14, 15
Nicias, 260
Nicoll, Thomas, 232
Noble, George, 199
Noble Captain, 75, 77, 83
Nogales fort, 32
Nomini Hall, 206
North, U.S., 8, 50, 64, 203, 215. *See also* Regionalism
North America, 35, 48, 51, 52, 55, 59, 159–61, 165, 166, 167, 170, 171, 176, 265
The North American Atlas (Faden), 55, 58
North Carolina, 5, 7, 8, 36, 37, 52, 57, 221n.27, 261, 267, 273, 279, 320. *See also* Carolina
Northwest Indian wars. *See* Ohio Valley Indian Confederacy
Notes on the State of Virginia (Jefferson), 60

O'Bluster, Sir Darby, 151
Occom, Samson, 170
Ocmulgee River, 285, 290, 293, 298, 299
Oconee River, 278, 285, 290–91, 293, 297

Oconostota, 261, 268
Odell, Jonathan, 14, 167–68, 173–76; *The American Times*, 173–76, 185–89
O'Fallon, James, 28
Ogeechee River, 285
Ogilby, John, 46
Ohio River, 27, 161, 263–64, 313
Ohio Valley, 145
Ohio Valley Indian Confederacy, 15, 31, 34, 263, 277n.41
Old Northwest, 263
Old Southwest, 25, 28, 36
Old Tassel, 268
Olwell, Robert, 224
Onuf, Peter, 7, 10, 44
Osborn, Sarah, 168
"Our Saviour and Our Guide," 69
Oxford English Dictionary, 54

Paine, Thomas: *Pennsylvania Magazine*, 171
Panton, Leslie & Company, 30, 32, 34, 35, 36
Panton, William, 32
The Papers of Nathanael Greene (Showman), 129
Paris. *See* France
Parmenter, John, 264–66
Parson Weems' Fable (Wood), 143
Pate, James, 263–64, 269
Paternalism, 12
Patriarchy. *See* Social class; Gender relations
Paul (slave), 201
Payne, Daniel, 201
Payne, Dolley, 152
Peale, Charles Willson, 143
Pendleton, Edmund, 207
Pennsylvania, 8, 36, 77, 83, 130, 131, 208, 261, 267, 283, 314; Revolutionary government, 134; Supreme Executive Council, 135
Pennsylvania Magazine (Paine), 171
Pensacola, Fla., 28, 29, 37, 271, 281, 285
Perdue, Theda, 14, 15, 16
Perier, Governor (of Louisiana), 95, 104–5
Peros (slave), 200
Perry, Hardy, 37
Person, Thomas, 8

Péry (councilor in French New Orleans), 92
Peter (slave), 37
Petty, William, 45
Philadelphia, Penn., 79, 124, 134, 155, 160, 171, 198, 200–203, 261, 263
Phillips, William, 207
Phillis (slave), 214
Piamingo, 31
Pickens, Andrew, 31, 224
Pinckney, Thomas, 26
Plantations Office (English Board of Trade), 45, 46
Pleasants, Robert, 207
Plutarch, 259–60, 273
Plymouth Rock, 57
Poetics of national memory, 14
Point Coupée, 89
Portsmouth, N.H., 201, 202
Potomac River, 27, 199, 200, 207, 273
Powell, Elizabeth Willing, 135
Pradel, Jean-Charles, Chevalier de, 11, 87–93, 97, 98, 99, 102–6, 113n.52; brother of, 104; daughters of, 96, 97, 102, 104, 105; son of, 97, 102, 104; wife of, 87–96, 99, 100–102, 104–5, 111n.30
Presbyterians, 160
Princeton, N.J., 165, 166
"Proclamation of Good Government" (Miró), 107
Proclamation of 1763, 262
Providence, R.I., 171
Ptolemy, 49
Public virtue, 11–14, 69–72, 75, 83–84, 143–53, 157–58, 162, 166, 176, 316, 320. *See also* Valor; Washington, George: public morality
Purcell, Joseph: "A Map of the States of Virginia, North Carolina, South Carolina, and Georgia," 60
Puritans, 57

Quacca, George, 213
Quakers, 134, 207, 261
Quamine, John, 168
Quarles, Benjamin, 224
Queen's Creek, Va., 213

Rachel (slave), 213
Racism, 314–15
Randolph, Edmund, 267, 270
Randolph, John, 267
Ransom, William, 211
The Raven, 268
Reed, A., 232
Reed, Esther DeBerdt, 134
Reed, John Shelton, 4–5, 12; *My Tears Spoiled My Aim, and Other Reflections on Southern Culture,* 4
Reed, Joseph, 171
Regionalism, 2–10, 17, 25, 27, 29, 42–46, 49–52, 54–65. *See also* South
Religion. *See* South: religious pluralism
Renaissance, 76
Republicans: Jeffersonian, 7, 133
Republican virtue. *See* Public virtue
Revolutionary War. *See* American Revolution
Rhode Island, 7, 160, 171
Richmond Academy, 69
River Farm, 198
Rivington, James, 173
Robinson, John, 74
Rogers, Edward, 79, 81
Rogers, Richard, 79, 81
Roman Catholic Church. *See* Catholic Church
Roman Empire, 259
Romans, Bernard, 300
Rome, 143, 147, 224
Rose (slave), 201
Routledge, John, 224
Royal Navy, 124, 125, 226
Rush, Benjamin, 155–56, 161, 169, 177
Rutledge, Ann, 131
Ryan, William R., 9

Salem, Mass., 227
Sambo (slave in South Carolina), 234, 242
Sambo (slave in Virginia), 217n.8
Sam (slave), 199, 211, 215
Saunt, Claudio, 264
Savage, Edward, 238, 241
Savannah, Ga., 5, 281

Sayer, Robert, 52; *American Military Pocket Atlas*, 52, 54; "A General Map of the Southern British Colonies in America," 52
Schuyler, Philip, 315
Schuylkill River, 261
Sciopod, 49
Scott, Joan Wallach, 319
Scott, Joseph: *Atlas of the United States*, 61
Seagrove, James, 279, 297
Sealy (slave), 213
Sectionalism. *See* Regionalism
Sellers, John, 46
Seminole Indians, 9–10, 287
Settlers, 35; Acadian, 35; American, 30, 35, 282–83, 287, 305n.24, 315, 318; British, 44, 48; Canary Island, 35; Dutch, 72; English, 35, 72, 283; European, 25; French, 35, 72, 90, 96, 283; frontier, 11, 71, 282–83; German, 35, 71, 72, 77, 80, 283; interactions with Indians, 284–85, 289–300; Irish, 72, 77, 80, 283; lifestyle of, 283–84; Scottish, 73, 80, 283; Spanish, 72, 283; Tennessee, 31. *See also* Frontier
Seven Years' War, 70, 125, 145–46, 148, 159, 161, 169, 174, 176
Shag, Will (aka Will Jones), 197–99, 211, 215
Sharp, Granville, 168
Shawnee Indians, 265, 271, 277n.41, 298; Chillicothe, 271. *See also* Tecumseh
Shays, Daniel, 83
Shearer, John, 79
Sheels, Christopher, 197, 204, 212
Shenandoah Valley. *See* Virginia: Shenandoah Valley
Shields, David, 13–14, 16
Showman, Richard: *The Papers of Nathanael Greene*, 129
Sierra Leone, 198, 201; Washington Hill, 201
Simon (slave), 217n.8
Simpson, James, 238, 241
Sinnajijee, 299
Slavery, 4, 59, 73, 105, 106, 107, 168; abolition, 8, 9, 15, 215; emancipation, 170–73
Slaves, 1, 9, 14, 15, 17, 25, 35, 56, 59, 73, 89, 106, 167, 170, 172, 227, 240; fugitive, 8, 15, 36–37, 197–215, 216n.2, 218n.14, 234, 239, 247; insurrection by, 225, 227, 229–36, 238–39, 249n.21, 252n.54; language of, 213, 215; owned by Washington, 8, 9, 15, 197–204, 207–12, 214–15, 218n.14; sales of, 37, 214. *See also names of individual slaves*; South Carolina; Virginia; Wheatley, Phillis
Smallpox, 265–66
Smith, Captain, 295
Smith, Josiah, 229
Smith, Mrs., 299
Smith, Page, 131–32
Smith, Rev. Robert, 237–38, 241, 243
Social class, 11–14, 55, 73, 87–97, 104–7, 109nn.14–16, 118n.109; 149, 227–28, 233, 319
Society of Cincinnati, 151. *See also* Cincinnatus
Sophia (slave), 203
Soto, Hernando de, 278
South, U.S.: agricultural economy, 4, 9, 56, 58, 59, 73, 75, 77–80, 159; antisouthern bias, 49–51, 59–60; boundaries, 6, 10, 44, 52; culture, 43, 57, 157–60, 162, 166, 176; diversity, 13, 17, 44, 87, 278, 283–300; Gulf, 27, 29, 32–36; history, 17; landscape, 75; maps, 6, 13, 43–46, 49–52, 54–60, 62, 64–65; military outposts, 295; religious pluralism, 73, 75; vernacular, 12; violence, 297. *See also* Regionalism; Slavery; Southern identity
South Carolina, 1, 5, 8, 9, 10, 54, 59, 61, 163, 267, 320; Council of Safety, 232–35, 241; Commons House of Assembly, 227, 239, 245; free blacks in, 224, 238–40; General Assembly, 228; General Committee, 227; history, 223; Negro Act (1740), 235, 238–41, 246; Provincial Congress, 227, 229, 235, 247; slaves in, 208–10, 213, 224, 226, 229–30, 236; tension in during the American Revolution, 226, 231–34, 236, 246–47. *See also* American Revolution; Carolina; Jeremiah, Thomas; *names of parishes and towns*

South Carolina Gazette, 225, 232
South Carolina Gazette and Country Journal, 229–30, 233
South Carolina Yazoo Company, 28
The Southeast in Early Maps (Cumming), 43
Southern identity, 44, 59, 60, 64, 65
Southern Indians. *See* Indians; *names of individual groups*
Soviet Union, 143
Spacks, Patricia Meyer, 151
Spain, 11, 17, 23, 25, 26, 28, 29, 30, 35, 36, 37, 106; Cartagena, 146; and Indians, 28–30, 32, 35, 36, 271; Madrid, 33, 34; military, 36; territory in U.S., 8, 17. *See also* New Spain
A Spirited Resistance (Dowd), 264
Squash, Deborah, 201
Stamp Act (1765), 227
St. Ange, 88; 109nn.15–16
Stapleton estate, 208
St. Christopher, 198
St. Clair, Arthur, 263
St. Croix, 208
St. Dominique, 35, 199; Port-au-Prince, 199
Steuben, Baron von, 270
St. Johns Berkeley Parish, S.C., 226
St. Louis, Mo., 271
St. Marys River, 297
Stockton, Annis, 14, 152, 164–67, 168, 171, 173, 176; "Epistle to General Washington," 181–83; "To the President of the United States," 179–81
Stono Rebellion (1739), 249n.21
Strabo, 49
Stuart, Dr., 204
Stuart, John, 261, 293
Sumter, Thomas, 8, 224
Swift, Jonathan: *Gulliver's Travels*, 51
Sycamore Shoals, 261, 267, 272–73

Taboca, 32, 36
Tallapoosa River, 279
Tanner, Obour, 168, 171
Taxation, 8
Tecumseh, 291

Te Deum festivity, 89–90
Tennant, Rev. William, 228
Tennessee, 2, 5, 29, 263, 272, 295, 300. *See also names of counties and towns*
Tennessee River, 31, 262–63, 273
Testar (merchant), 97, 99, 100, 101, 103; wife of, 98, 103
Texas, 4, 9
Theater: early American, 150, 152
"To His Excellency General Washington" (Wheatley), 183–85
Tombigbee River, 30, 32, 278, 293, 299
Tom (slave), 37, 198, 212
Tony (slave), 214
"To the President of the United States" (Stockton), 179–81
Traders, 37, 76–77, 81–82; American, 31, 32, 316; British, 30, 86, 280; children of, 35, 36, 281; European, 25; French, 99. *See also names of traders*
Trading posts, 31, 32; American, 35, 293, 316
Trajan, 259
Travels (Bartram), 261
Travels Through the Interior Parts of North-America (Carver), 59–60
Treaties: Colerain (1796), 279, 285, 287, 290; of conquest, 317; Fort Stanwix (1768), 262; Fort Wilkinson (1802), 285, 288, 290, 297; Greenville (1795), 263; Hard Labor (1768), 262; Holston (1791), 291–92, 318; Hopewell (with the Cherokees, 1785), 279; Hopewell (with the Choctaws, 1786), 29, 31, 33, 320–21; Lochaber (1770), 262; Natchez (1792), 32; New York (1790), 279, 285; Nogales (1793), 32; Paris (1783), 26, 280–81; Pensacola (1776), 293; San Lorenzo (1795), 26, 35, 287; Washington (1805), 285, 293
Trenton, N.J., 165
Trinidad, 208
Turnbull, John, 30, 32, 36
Turner, Nat, 275–76n.19
Tuskegetchee (the Long Fellow), 270
Tuskenehau Chapco, 297
Tussekia Mico, 299
Tustunnuggee Emaultau, 298

Union Farm, 203–4, 217n.11
United States, 25, 26, 27, 29, 30, 32, 36, 37, 281, 319; Attorney for District of Georgia, 296; citizens, 44, 314; Confederation period, 315; Congress, 62, 152, 272, 317; Continental Congress, 150, 160, 169, 224, 267, 269, 294; Copyright Law (1790), 62; expansion, 24; government, 8, 10; Indian policy, 15–16, 31, 33, 34–35, 280, 313–23; maps, 60–62; military, 294, 313–14; national character, 166–67, 176–77; state debts, 10; taxation, 8; Trade and Intercourse Act (1790), 301n.6; War Department, 292–93, 295. *See also* American Revolution; Civilization Plan; Declaration of Independence; Manifest Destiny
The United States of America (Wallis), 60
Universal Magazine, 51
University of Georgia, 264
University of Southern Mississippi, 16
U.S. Constitution. *See* Constitution (U.S.); Constitutional Convention (1787)
Usner, Daniel H., Jr., 5–6, 9, 105, 108nn.6, 12
USSR. *See* Soviet Union

Valley Forge, Penn., 134, 148, 150, 266
Valor, 145–49, 151, 152, 165–66
Vansant, Anna, 299
Vansant, Isaac, 299
Varenius, 49
Venezuela, 52
Vernon, Admiral, 146
Vickery, Amanda, 102, 116n.92, 117n.98
Vicksburg, Miss., 32
Villebeuvre, Jean de la, 32, 34, 36
Virgil: *Georgics*, 147
Virginia, 3, 5, 8, 9, 46, 48, 52, 57, 70, 159–61, 170, 270, 283; backcountry, 11, 74–79, 82, 83, 273; Blue Ridge Mountains 1, 71, 73, 75, 79, 214; Chesapeake, 72–74, 77, 211, 271; constitutional ratifying convention, 124, 267; eastern shore, 199; General Court, 199; gentry, 16, 125, 163, 205, 260–61; House of Burgesses, 71, 74, 125, 146; legislature, 123, 215; low country, 2; militia, 74, 268; northern neck, 72, 126, 127, 214; piedmont, 209, 214; ports, 79; Royal Council, 127; Shenandoah Valley, 10, 11, 73, 75, 79, 214; slaves in, 15, 197–215; social distinctions, 73; tidewater, 79–80, 209, 264; Virginia Regiment, 74–75. *See also names of counties and towns*
Virginia Gazette (Dixon and Hunter), 171–72
Virtue. *See* Public virtue; Valor

Walker, George, 236, 254n.82
Wallace, Anthony, 64
Wallis, John: "The United States of America," 60
Walpole, Sir Robert, 146
Walsh, Richard, 233
Ward, Joshua, 235
Ward, Samuel, Jr., 129
War of 1812, 62
War of Jenkins' Ear, 146
Warren, Mercy Otis, 135
Washington, Augustine, 125–26, 143, 145
Washington, Fanny Bassett, 133
Washington, George, 14, 44, 77, 79, 81, 82, 144, 156–57, 169, 224; author, 160; birth, 264; childhood, 265; clothing, 86, 97, 100–101, 107n.1–n.2, 112–13n.51; death, 16, 123, 204, 259, 273; diplomacy, 271; dislike of others, 71–72, 74–75, 83–84, 315–16; elite, 11, 71, 73, 87, 144–45, 149; family life, 121–27, 130–35; "Farewell Address," 2–3, 7, 42, 62, 64; fomenter of American Revolution, 173–76; health, 130, 265; hero, 1, 12–13, 69, 71, 157, 161, 165, 169; icon, 3–4, 13, 14, 16, 17, 70, 143–45, 152–53, 159–63, 168–73, 175–77, 260; inauguration, 86; landowner, 11, 12, 74, 83, 272, 315, 317; "Letter of George Washington to Annis Boudinot Stockton," 178–79; military leader, 3, 8, 12, 23, 70, 71, 74–75, 83, 87–88, 121, 125, 127, 130, 134, 135–36, 145–48, 150–52, 160–61, 165, 171, 174, 190n.12, 260, 265, 267, 269–71, 314; nationalism of, 2–3, 26–27, 42–45, 62, 64, 83, 157, 161–62, 164–66, 175–77, 314; northern tour, 7; patriarch, 143; physical appearance, 160; planter, 72–73, 125, 158–59, 197–200,

203, 205, 272; president, 1, 2, 4, 6, 8, 12, 24, 26, 27, 28, 31, 33, 42, 69, 83, 124, 135, 138n.20, 144, 151–52, 157, 164–65, 176–77, 202–3, 260–61, 263, 267, 272; public morality, 70–71, 150; relationships with women, 14–16, 121–35, 140n.38, 141nn.45, 49, 164; role in forming U.S. Indian policy, 15–16, 31, 279, 313–19, 321–23; slave owner, 1, 8, 15, 144, 159, 197–204, 207–12, 214–15; southerner, 2, 4, 12, southern tour, 1–2, 5, 6–7, 8, 10, 12; surveyor, 12, 74, 124, 145, 265, 272; view of history, 156; Virginian, 12, 72, 158–59, 260; wealth, 105. *See also* Cincinnatus; Mount Vernon; Public virtue; Slaves
Washington, Harvey (Henry), 198, 201
Washington, John, 272
Washington, John Augustine, 74
Washington, Lawrence, 72, 124, 127, 131, 145, 146, 265
Washington, Lund, 137n.9, 217n.9
Washington, Martha Dandridge Custis, 14, 15, 122, 124, 125, 127, 131, 132, 133–35, 140n.41, 141n.45, 151, 176; portrait of, 133; republican court of, 122, 135, 151–52; slaves belonging to, 197, 201–2, 204, 211; as widow, 133
Washington, Mary Ball, 14, 122–26, 137n.9; breast cancer of, 123; children of, 126; death of, 126
Watauga River, 261, 267, 272–73
Watson, Sir Brook, 168
Wayne, Anthony, 263
Weems, Parson, 143, 152, 265
Weld, Isaac, 73
Wentworth, General, 146
West Africa, 35
Western frontier. *See* Frontier
West Florida, 26, 29, 30, 31, 32

West Indies, 50, 96, 198. *See also* Caribbean islands
Westmoreland County, Va., 126, 264
Wheat: as subsistence food, 79
Wheatley, Phillis, 14, 167–73, 175–76, 191–92n.28; gains manumission, 168; in England, 168; patrons of, 171; "To His Excellency General Washington," 183–85
Wheatley, Susanna, 171
Whigs, 9, 175, 225, 227, 231–32, 238, 240, 246; "country party," 14, 159–60, 163, 166–67, 176
Whiskey, 8, 32; tax on, 83–84
Whiskey Rebellion, 314
Whitaker, Arthur, 26
White, James, 28
White, Sophie, 11
Whitefield, George, 168
Wilkinson, James, 26, 27, 28
Williamsburg, Va., 71, 134, 267
William (slave), 213
Wilson, Douglas L., 131; *Honor's Voice*, 122
Wilson, John, 213
Winchester, Va., 74, 75
Wofford's Settlement, Ga., 291–92, 295; multiracial, 292, 300
Wollaston, John, 133
Wood, Grant: *Parson Weems' Fable*, 143
Wood, Peter H., 13, 14, 224
Woods, Margaret, 37
The World Described (Moll), 46
Wyatt-Brown, Bertram, 158

Yamma, Bristol, 168
Yazoo River, 32
Yeocomico Church Cemetery, 126
York County, Va., 198, 199, 211
York River, 207
Yorktown, Va., 123, 198; battle at, 200
Young, Alfred F., 223

www.ingramcontent.com/pod-product-compliance
Lightning Source LLC
Chambersburg PA
CBHW022102150426
43195CB00008B/229